Restoring the Lost Constitution

Restoring the Lost Constitution

THE PRESUMPTION OF LIBERTY

Randy E. Barnett

PRINCETON UNIVERSITY PRESS

PRINCETON AND OXFORD

Library of Congress Cataloging-in-Publication Data

Barnett, Randy E.
Restoring the lost constitution : the presumption of liberty / Randy E. Barnett.
p. cm.
Includes bibliographical references and index.
ISBN 0-691-11585-0 (cloth : acid-free paper)
1. Constitutional history—United States. 2. Constitutional law—United
States. 3. Judicial review—United States. 4. United States. Supreme Court. I. Title.

KF4541.B313 2004
342.73'029—dc21   2003044205

British Library Cataloging-in-Publication Data is available

This book has been composed in Sabon

Printed on acid-free paper. ∞

www.pupress.princeton.edu

Printed in the United States of America

10   9   8   7   6   5   4   3   2

To James Madison and Lysander Spooner

Contents

Preface

GROWING UP, I was like most Americans in my reverence for the Constitution. Not until college was the first seed of doubt planted in the form of an essay by a nineteenth-century abolitionist and radical named Lysander Spooner. In his best-known work, *No Treason: The Constitution of No Authority* (1870), Spooner argued that the Constitution of the United States was illegitimate because it was not and could never have been consented to by the people on whom it is imposed. Although as an undergraduate I found Spooner's argument unanswerable (and I must admit so it remained until I was in my forties), the problem was largely theoretical. My mind may have doubted, but my faith remained.

Until I took Constitutional Law at Harvard Law School. The experience was completely disillusioning, but not because of the professor, Laurence Tribe, who was an engaging and open-minded teacher. No, what disillusioned me was reading the opinions of the U.S. Supreme Court. Throughout the semester, as we covered one constitutional clause after another, passages that sounded great to me were drained by the Court of their obviously power-constraining meanings. First was the Necessary and Proper Clause in *McCulloch v. Maryland* (1819), then the Commerce Clause (a bit) in *Gibbons v. Ogden* (1824), then the Privileges or Immunities Clause of the Fourteenth Amendment in *The Slaughter-House Cases* (1873), then the Commerce Clause (this time in earnest) in *Wickard v. Filburn* (1942), and the Ninth Amendment in *United Public Workers v. Mitchell* (1947).

Nor were these landmark decisions isolated cases. In countless other opinions, the Supreme Court justices affirmed they meant it when they said the Constitution did not mean what it apparently said. According to the Supreme Court, a majority in Congress could restrict the liberties of the people pretty much any way it wished unless a law violated an express prohibition of the Constitution—or some privileged but unenumerated right such as the right of privacy. Even an express right, such as the "right to keep and bear arms," could effectively be read out of the Constitution when the Supreme Court disapproved. Were this not enough, the most famous decision in which the Supreme Court had once tried holding the line, *Lochner v. New York* (1905), was taught along with other cases from the Progressive Era precisely as examples of how courts were *not* supposed to act. That *Lochner* is among the worst decisions the Supreme Court ever made was the received and unquestioned wisdom then, and largely remains so to this day on both the left and right of the political spectrum.

By the time I was finished with Constitutional Law, I was finished with the Constitution as well. The idea of protecting liberty by imposing written constraints on the government was an experiment that obviously had failed. When Spooner's argument on legitimacy was combined with the practice of the Supreme Court, there was nothing left to take seriously. When I became a law professor and needed to decide what to write about or teach, I chose contracts, where courts seemed to take both written law and writings in general more seriously. Constitutional law was last on my list and I avoided it successfully for many years.

Then Brian Brille, at the time a law student at Stanford Law School, invited me to speak at the Fifth Annual National Student Symposium of the Federalist Society to be held there in the winter of 1986. The Federalist Society had been founded, after I had graduated, by students at several law schools who had been disillusioned in their own way by their law school experience. Their means of fighting back was to form a student organization where they could meet and support each other. They would also invite dissenting speakers to their campuses to challenge the conventional wisdom of their professors and they would gather once a year to hear their champions debate the best of the opposition, the sort of intellectual discourse so sorely missing at their home schools.

The topic of the symposium was the First Amendment and I was asked to participate on a panel on "freedom of association." It was a distinguished group of speakers and, as a relatively unknown contracts professor, I sorely wanted to accept. Nevertheless, I declined. "Brian," I said, "I would really like to participate but you know what I think about the Constitution. I just do not do constitutional law" (or words to this effect). "Oh, come on," he replied. "You only need to talk for ten minutes. You can come up with ten minutes of something to say" (or words to that effect). Against my better judgment, I agreed.

As I painfully wrote my comments on freedom of association, I got to the part of the speech where I anticipated what I was sure would be the overwhelming sentiment of what I wrongly thought was a monolithically conservative group: the First Amendment specifies the right of freedom of speech, freedom of assembly and petition, and the free exercise of religion. It says nothing explicit about a freedom of association. "I know what you're thinking," I wrote, mimicking Dirty Harry, "what gives unelected lifetime appointed federal judges the power to protect a right not mentioned in the Constitution?" In my speech, my answer was to read the text of the Ninth Amendment: "The enumeration in the Constitution of certain rights shall not be construed to deny or disparage others retained by the People."

At the conference, I so expected a hostile reaction that I began my talk by nervously joking about having bought only a one-way ticket. As I read my speech the audience was respectfully quiet, which I came to learn is a Federalist Society tradition. Also listening intently was my fellow panelist, Judge Frank Easterbrook, sitting at my side on the dais. After hearing my Clint Eastwood–inspired challenge, Judge Easterbrook gestured toward me with both his palms up as if to say, "Well, punk, what's the answer?" intimating that no reasonable answer was possible. When I finished reading the words of the Ninth Amendment in reply, a roaring cheer came up from the students. I was startled to discover that, contrary to their detractors, the Federalist Society was indeed a robust coalition of both conservative and libertarian students with a diversity of views among them. Even many years later I would still be approached by lawyers who told me they had been at Stanford when I "debated" Frank Easterbrook on the Ninth Amendment.

I was energized by the experience; contracts professors simply do not get invited to speak to five hundred bright and, yes, cheering law students about contract law. But my views on the Constitution had not changed, so now what? Well, for one thing, like every other law professor and judge, I knew nothing about the Ninth Amendment besides what it said. I also knew that it had been dismissed by the Supreme Court and received its only furtive and brief serious attention in a concurring opinion by Justice Goldberg in *Griswold v. Connecticut* (1965). I knew as well that the Ninth Amendment was considered a constitutional joke, as in, "what are you going to argue, the Ninth Amendment?" Do I divert my valuable time away from serious concerns to learn about this disparaged, if not denied, constitutional injunction?

After some time passed, I shifted my research agenda in this unexpected direction. I distinctly recall my mental calculation: I was about to be granted tenure. The Ninth Amendment had not been repealed. Once safely tenured, I should be able to write about any part of the Constitution that was still there. Given its marginal status in respectable quarters, however, was it worth the effort? At the time, judicial conservatives like Professor Robert Bork and Ronald Reagan's attorney general, Edwin Meese, were getting a lot of attention for their claims that the Constitution should be interpreted according to the original intent of the framers, and also that constitutional rights should be limited to those that were listed and certainly should not include an unenumerated right of privacy. It seemed only a matter of time before respectable academics would pit one of these tenets against the other by pointing to the Ninth Amendment, which seemed to suggest that the original intent of the framers supported rather than undermined the protection of unenumerated rights. When they did, what if I were there already with a body of scholarship on the meaning of the Ninth Amendment?

Upon initial investigation, I discovered that so little had been written about the Ninth Amendment that I could read it *all* and almost instantly become an expert in the field. The first thing I learned is that the Ninth Amendment had been devised by the father of the Constitution, James Madison himself. This might work out after all. So I put in motion several projects: a law review article, an anthology of previously published Ninth Amendment scholarship, and a law review symposium of politically diverse scholars offering their opinions on its meaning.

In 1987, while all these were in press but before any appeared, Judge Robert Bork was nominated by President Reagan to the Supreme Court. Perhaps his most famous comment at his televised confirmation hearings was this response to a question by Senator Dennis DeConcini, who asked him about the meaning of the Ninth Amendment:

> I do not think you can use the ninth amendment unless you know something of what it means. For example, if you had an amendment that says "Congress shall make no" and then there is an ink blot and you cannot read the rest of it and that is the only copy you have, I do not think the court can make up what might be under the ink blot if you cannot read it.

This ink blot reference was like a red flag to constitutional scholars, and did not sit all that well with some conservative proponents of original intent. After all, the framers must have meant *something* by this amendment! But what?

Soon thereafter all my Ninth Amendment scholarship hit the fans and I was suddenly a "player" in a field I had dismissed just a year or so before. In the years since then, one article led to another as I discovered that the Ninth Amendment was inextricably linked to the other clauses the Supreme Court had redacted from the text: the Necessary and Proper Clause, the Commerce Clause, the Privileges or Immunities Clause, and the Tenth Amendment. They all had to go if Congress and state legislatures were going to be given the discretion to pass laws in the "public interest" unconstrained by any limits on their powers besides a few judicially favored rights.

Over these years, I developed a newfound respect for the Constitution, if not for the judges who had disregarded what they had sworn to preserve, protect, and defend. I also came to admire the genius of the founders, especially that of James Madison, and the importance of the contribution made by the Republicans in the Thirty-ninth Congress who substantially changed the constitutional structure by devising the Fourteenth Amendment.

Spending so much time reading about the origins of the Constitution and the Fourteenth Amendment raised a central question I had not yet confronted adequately: how exactly should this document be interpreted? Early on, I had been persuaded that adhering to the original intent of the framers was *not* the way to go. I accepted the argument that we were not bound by the intentions of long-dead men, especially in light of Spooner's argument that the Constitution could not possibly be founded on original consent. Still, most of my constitutional scholarship consisted of parsing the statements of these same dead men and the historical meaning of the words they enshrined in the Constitution's text. I was definitely suffering from cognitive dissonance.

The resolution came from a completely unexpected and unlikely source: Lysander Spooner. Teaching my constitutional theory seminar, I ran across a reference in a footnote to Spooner's essay *The Unconstitutionality of Slavery* (1847). I was intrigued. How could Spooner possibly have argued that slavery was unconstitutional prior to the enactment of the Thirteenth Amendment in light of the passages that everyone knows sanctioned it? Although I had admired Spooner since college, I had never read his other writings—indeed did not know what sort of writings even existed. Searching for this essay, I discovered it in a six-volume set of Spooner's works.

In his three-hundred-page monograph, Spooner responded to the Garrisonian argument that the Constitution was a "covenant with death and an agreement with hell" because it sanctioned slavery. As evidence for this contention, Garrison's legal colleague, Wendell Phillips, had seized upon the newly released, formerly secret records of the Constitutional Convention that clearly showed the framers' intentions to preserve slavery in those states where it was still practiced.

Spooner replied that we are not bound by the secret intentions of the framers but only by those intentions they put in writing. Each word must be interpreted the way a normal speaker of English would have read it when it was enacted. Moreover, where the words admitted of more than one meaning, we should not impute to the document an intention to do something manifestly unjust. Spooner argued that, in each of the places where the Constitution supposedly sanctioned slavery, the framers had spoken euphemistically, refusing to name the thing to which they were referring. If they could not bring themselves to enshrine slavery into the text explicitly, we were not bound to adhere to their unexpressed intentions but should instead give each of the terms they used their normal innocent meaning.

Whether or not Spooner was right in this assessment of the constitutionality of slavery, his argument opened for me an entirely new position: a defense of original meaning rather than original intent that could withstand the well-known critique of originalism. The final missing ingredient was an answer to Spooner's later charge that the Constitution was without authority because it lacked actual consent. My answer to Spooner's challenge is presented in part I of this book.

So this book is dedicated to James Madison and Lysander Spooner. To Madison, the moving force behind our written constitution, who devised the Ninth Amendment—the as-yet-unrepealed provision that initially restored my interest in the lost Constitution. To Lysander Spooner for forcing me to squarely confront the legitimacy of the Constitution and for inspiring a theory of interpretation that would, in part, answer that challenge. Without these two men, I would not have written this book. Although of the two, Madison would surely be more comfortable with the approach I defend here, I suspect that the younger Spooner would take to it as well, while the older Spooner would recognize his handiwork.

I also thank my good friend Tom Palmer of the Cato Institute for all his efforts on behalf of this project. Without the financial support of the Cato Institute and its donors, I would not have had the free time to engage in so substantial a venture. My thanks goes as well to the Earhart Foundation for its generosity, and to Boston University and my Dean, Ronald Cass, for providing me with the sabbatical leave during which the first draft of this manuscript was written, as well as generous summer research support.

There are many individuals who have given me helpful comments on portions of this work as it has developed over the years: Akhil Amar, Jack Beermann, Bob Bone, Robert Clinton, Jules Coleman, David Currie, Einer Elhauge, Richard Epstein, Suzanne Goldberg, Oona Hathaway, Richard Hyland, Susan Koniak, Gary Lawson, Gerry Leonard, David Lyons, Steve Marks, Michael Meurer, Richard McAdams, Frank Michelman, Oliver Moreteau, Dawn Nunziato, Glenn Reynolds, Michael Seidman, David Snyder, and Nancy Staudt. I also benefited greatly from insightful comments on the entire manuscript by Michael Zuckert and Keith Whittington. I am most grateful to Kate McFarland and Chris Newman for proofreading the entire manuscript. Finally, I extend a special thanks to my dear friend Larry Solum for all his encouragement and advice, and my sincerest apologies to anyone I have neglected to mention.

The argument presented in chapter 5 on originalism was first formulated for the Brendon Brown Lecture at Loyola of New Orleans School of Law and also given as a Distinguished Lecture at St. Thomas University School of Law. Pieces of this work have been presented at faculty workshops and I benefited greatly from the comments I received from participants there. These include law school workshops at Boston University, University of Chicago, University of Florida, George Mason University, Georgetown University, George Washington University, Harvard Law

School, Loyola Marymount University, Loyola University of New Orleans, Rutgers University–Camden, University of Houston, University of Notre Dame, Seton Hall University, Villanova University, New York University's Austrian Economics Workshop, and at conferences held by the American Public Philosophy Institute, Ashland University, University of Arkansas, and University of North Carolina–Greensboro. Portions of this work have been greatly revised from articles that appeared in the *Columbia Law Review*, *Constitutional Commentary*, *Notre Dame Law Review*, *University of Chicago Law Review*, *U.C.L.A Law Review*, *University of Pennsylvania Journal of Constitutional Law*, and *Loyola Law Review*.

Finally, I thank my wife, Beth, for letting me escape to my study to write, tolerating my frequent preoccupation with this project, my travels to speak at the aforementioned workshops and conferences, and for her overall encouragement and support. Without her I would be as lost as the original Constitution.

Restoring the Lost Constitution

Why Care What the Constitution Says?

> The powers of the legislature are defined, and limited; and
> that those limits may not be mistaken, or forgotten, the con-
> stitution is written. To what purpose are powers limited, and
> to what purpose is that limitation committed to writing, if
> these limits may, at any time, be passed by those intended to
> be restrained? The distinction, between a government with
> limited and unlimited powers, is abolished, if those limits do
> not confine the persons on whom they are imposed.[1]
>
> —JOHN MARSHALL (1803)

HAD JUDGES done their job, this book would not need to be written.
Since the adoption of the Constitution, courts have eliminated clause after
clause that interfered with the exercise of government power. This started
early with the Necessary and Proper Clause, continued through Reconstruction with the destruction of the Privileges or Immunities Clause, and
culminated in the post–New Deal Court that gutted the Commerce Clause
and the scheme of enumerated powers affirmed in the Tenth Amendment,
while greatly expanding the unwritten "police power" of the states. All
along, with sporadic exceptions, judges have ignored the Ninth Amendment. As a result of judicial decisions, these provisions of the Constitution
are now largely gone and, in their absence, the enacted Constitution has
been lost and even forgotten.

Without these missing clauses, the general scheme of the Constitution
has been radically altered, which is precisely why they all had to go. The
Constitution that was actually enacted and formally amended creates islands of government powers in a sea of liberty. The judicially redacted
constitution creates islands of liberty rights in a sea of governmental powers. Judicial redaction has created a substantially different constitution
from the one written on parchment that resides under glass in Washington. Though that Constitution is now lost, it has not been repealed, so it
could be found again.

All this has been done knowingly by judges and their academic enablers
who think they can improve upon the original Constitution and substitute

---

[1] *Marbury v. Madison*, 5 U.S. 137, 176 (1803).

for it one that is superior. This begs the question: Why care what the Constitution actually says, as opposed to what we might prefer it to say (or not say)? Whatever may be in their hearts, many constitutional scholars write as though we are not bound by the actual words of the Constitution because those words are obstacles to noble objectives. One way to slip these bonds is to imply that the original Constitution is illegitimate by repeating the refrain that we cannot be bound by the "dead hand of the past" or by constantly invoking the various sins of the framers. By delegitimizing the original Constitution, such rhetoric seeks to free us from its constraints. Yet it is both curious and significant that few come out and admit this. Why this avoidance? Why not frank confession?

Perhaps because those who practice and advocate judicial amendment of the Constitution seek the obedience of the faithful and, were their delegitimation entirely successful, why would anyone obey the commands of a mere judge, much less a law professor, a philosopher, or a political scientist? Why obey the commands of the man or woman in a black robe, apart from the fact that disobedience is likely to land you behind bars in an extremely treacherous environment?

To openly challenge the legitimacy of the Constitution—held sacred and regarded as authoritative by so much of the public—would be to admit that there is no "man behind the curtain." Instead, by subtly undercutting the legitimacy of the Constitution while at the same time preserving its much-revered form, a judge or even a clever constitutional scholar can become the man behind the curtain. Pay no attention to that figure in the black robe or to that bookish professor; the great and powerful Constitution has spoken!

This is a fraud on the public. Imply but do not say aloud that the Constitution is illegitimate so we need not follow what it actually says. Remake it—or "interpret" it—as one wills and then, because it is The Constitution we are expounding, the loyal but unsophisticated citizenry will follow. This strategy also allows one to adopt a stance of moral superiority toward past generations without having to assume the responsibility of proclaiming that the document they wrote and by which the government rules is of no authority.

Because it is constantly under siege, the Constitution's legitimacy cannot be taken for granted. Unless we openly confront the question of its legitimacy, we cannot respond to those who would replace it with something they think is better. We will never know whether we should obey it, improve upon it, or ignore it altogether. In this book, I begin by asking and answering the question that others shy away from: Why should anyone obey the commands issued by persons who claim to be authorized by the Constitution?

I explain why the most commonly held view of constitutional legitimacy—the "consent of the governed"—is wrong because it is a standard that no constitution can meet. Holding the Constitution to this unattainable ideal both undermines its legitimacy and allows others to substitute their own meaning for that of the text. This result is paradoxical because, notwithstanding the great expansion of suffrage, any new and improved "interpretation" of the Constitution will also fail to be legitimated by the "consent of the governed." And this fiction turns dangerous when factions purporting to speak for "the People" claim the power to restrict the liberties of all.

Equally untenable is the principal alternative to the "consent of the governed": the argument that the benefits received by citizens from a constitutional order and a duty of fair play obligate them, in return, to obey laws regardless of whether they consent to them. By dispensing with any need for obtaining even the fictional consent of the governed, this alternative turns out to be even more dangerous to liberty. We can do much better.

I contend that lawmaking by real unanimous consent is both possible and pervasive, although not in the sort of polity governed by present-day constitutions. Even in the absence of such consent, however, laws can still bind in conscience if the constitution that governs their making, application, and enforcement contains adequate procedures to assure that restrictions imposed on nonconsenting persons are just (or not unjust). Such a constitutional order can be legitimate even if it was not consented to by everyone; and a constitution that lacks adequate procedures to ensure the justice of valid laws is illegitimate even if it was consented to by a majority. Indeed, only by realizing that the "consent of the governed" is a fiction can one appreciate the imperative that lawmakers respect whatever may be the requirements of justice.

Although my thesis concerning legitimacy does depend on the claim that "justice" is independent of whatever may happen to be commanded by positive law, it does not depend on acceptance of any particular conception of justice. Regardless of what conception of justice one holds, constitutional legitimacy can be seen as a product of procedural assurances that legal commands are not unjust. Even those who reject the view of justice held by the founders, and which I have defended elsewhere,[2] can accept this conception of constitutional legitimacy provided they also

---

[2] See Randy E. Barnett, *The Structure of Liberty: Justice and the Rule of Law* (Oxford: Clarendon Press, 1998) (defending a liberal conception of justice based in certain individual natural rights that distinguish "liberty" from "license"). Although I am unable to re-create here all the arguments presented there on behalf of this conception of justice, I shall summarize them briefly in chapter 3. Readers need not, however, be convinced by my arguments for these liberty rights to be persuaded by the thesis of this book—provided they accept

accept the proposition that justice is independent of legality. That is, that laws are not just solely because they are validly enacted.

To assess the legitimacy of any given legal system, however—including the system governed by the Constitution of the United States—requires both this procedural conception of legitimacy and a theory of justice by which to assess the adequacy of lawmaking procedures it employs. In short, while readers need not agree with the founders' or my conception of justice based on "natural rights" to accept the procedural conception of constitutional legitimacy I shall advance, they must produce and defend a conception of justice before they can pass judgment on the legitimacy of the Constitution. So must I.

To that end I will explain the founders' view that "first come rights, and then comes the Constitution." The rights that precede the formation of government they called "natural rights." I contend that if a constitution contains adequate procedures to protect these natural rights, it can be legitimate even if it was not consented to by everyone; and one that lacks adequate procedures to protect natural rights is illegitimate even if it was consented to by a majority.

The natural rights to which they and I refer are the "liberty rights" that, given the nature of human beings and the world in which we live, make it possible for each person to pursue happiness while living in close proximity to others and for civil societies to achieve peace and prosperity. It is precisely because the consent of the governed is impossible on a national scale that a constitution must provide protection for the preexisting rights retained by the people if the laws it sanctions are to create a duty of obedience in a nonconsenting public.

With this analysis of constitutional legitimacy and natural rights, we will then be in a position to understand why the words of the Constitution should be interpreted according to their original meaning and, where this meaning is incomplete or vague, how the inevitable gaps in meaning ought to be filled. Although I do not believe we are bound by the dead hand of the past, I will explain how, by committing ourselves to a written constitution, we commit ourselves to adhere to the original meaning of the text and any later amendments. In addition, original meaning must be respected so that those who are to govern by laws have little or no hand in making the laws by which they govern. We will also see that, where the original meaning is incomplete or vague, the text must be "construed," as opposed to "interpreted," in a way that enhances its legitimacy without contradicting the meaning that does exist.

---

these rights for other reasons the reader finds more compelling. In this important respect, the analysis presented here is independent of that presented in *The Structure of Liberty*.

It will then be time to examine the original meaning of key provisions of the text that have been either distorted or excised entirely from the judges' Constitution and ignored: the Commerce and the Necessary and Proper Clauses in the original Constitution, the Ninth Amendment, and the Privileges or Immunities Clause of the Fourteenth Amendment. We will also need to examine the nature and scope of the so-called police power of states—a power that appears nowhere in the text of the Constitution and results from construction rather than interpretation.

Finally, I shall show how, when the meaning of these missing provisions is correctly understood, we can choose properly between two opposing constructions of the powers the Constitution delegates to government officials: Are all restrictions on the liberties of the people to be presumed constitutional unless an individual can convince a hierarchy of judges that the liberty is somehow "fundamental"? Or should we presume that any restriction on the rightful exercise of liberty is unconstitutional unless and until the government convinces a hierarchy of judges that such restrictions are both necessary and proper? The first of these is called "the presumption of constitutionality." While this construction has never been accepted in its entirety, the exceptions that have been created to it are revealing in the way they run afoul of the text. The second of these constructions may be called the Presumption of Liberty, which can provide a practical way to restore the lost Constitution.

It is an open question whether the U.S. Constitution—either as written or as actually applied—is in fact legitimate. Intellectual honesty requires us to acknowledge the possibility that no constitution lacking unanimous consent is capable of producing laws that bind in conscience. Therefore, while the theory of constitutional legitimacy, the conception of natural rights, the method of constitutional interpretation, the interpretations of key clauses, and the Presumption of Liberty I advance here all raise serious questions—is there any constitutional theory that does not?—readers should think long and hard before rejecting them. For the alternative may be to admit that, when judges pronounce constitutional law, there really is no one behind the curtain and their commands are utterly devoid of binding authority.

We need not, I submit, reach this conclusion. The lost Constitution has not, after all, been repealed. It remains before our eyes and its restoration within our grasp. Once it is remembered in its entirety, the case for a constitutional Presumption of Liberty becomes compelling. But to restore, we must first remember.

PART I

Constitutional Legitimacy

THE CONSTITUTION of the United States is a piece of parchment under glass in Washington, D.C. Why should we pay any attention to it? Why should we follow what it says when the best minds among us—or those who think themselves the best—are sure it is defective in important ways and that they can do better? After all, it was written long ago for a very different age. Its authors were remarkably able, prescient even, but they were not divine. They could err and they knew it. They would be the first to admit their imperfections even on the most pressing moral question of their own day. Were they alive today they would most certainly expect and want their creation modified to adapt to problems they could not have anticipated. So why, more than two hundred years later, do legislators or judges need to follow this particular document to the letter?

The most common answer to this question is that the Constitution of the United States is based on the "consent of the governed" or what is sometimes called "popular sovereignty." "We the People" established this Constitution, it is said, and the people are therefore bound to it until it is changed. The consent of "We the People" is what got the Constitution up and running, and the continued consent of the governed keeps it binding upon us. I reject this answer. Not only is it inaccurate, but even as an ideal this idea can prove dangerous in practice, and can nurture unwarranted criticism of the Constitution's legitimacy. Ironically, few ideas are more conducive to undermining the governing authority of the Constitution than that of "We the People."

In chapter 1, I explain why the consent of the governed cannot justify a duty to obey the laws. Though genuine consent, were it to exist, could give rise to a duty of obedience, the conditions necessary for the governed actually to consent to anything like the Constitution have never existed and could never exist. But despite the failure of the argument from consent, I maintain that laws passed pursuant to a legitimate constitutional authority can still bind us in conscience.

In chapter 2, I contend that a constitutional regime is legitimate only if it provides sufficient assurances that the laws it produces are "necessary and proper"—the standard for acts of Congress specified in the Constitution itself. Because both necessity and propriety are needed for a law to be justified, constitutional legitimacy requires legal procedures that ensure these *qualities go in before the name "law" goes on,* as well as procedures to ensure the just application of necessary and proper laws to individuals. In short, constitutional legitimacy is *procedural,* not consensual.

One vital aspect of a law's propriety is whether it violates the background or "natural" rights retained by the people. While the *consent* of "We the People" is a fiction, as I explain in chapter 1, this does not mean that the *rights* of the people are at all fictitious. On the contrary, in the absence of consent, laws bind in conscience only if there is reason to be confident that they do not violate the "liberty rights" of the people. In chapter 3, I show that the persons who drafted and adopted the Ninth and Fourteenth Amendments viewed natural rights as "liberty rights" and why they were correct to do so. A clearer picture of natural rights helps to illuminate why and when there is a duty to obey the law. Here, then, is a second irony: many are wedded to the fiction of "We the People" precisely because they reject the reality of natural rights and can see no alternative path to constitutional legitimacy. They are wrong on both counts.

CHAPTER ONE

The Fiction of "We the People": Is the Constitution Binding on Us?

> Government requires make-believe. Make believe that the king is divine, make believe that he can do no wrong or make believe that the voice of the people is the voice of God. Make believe that the people *have* a voice or make believe that the representatives of the people *are* the people. Make believe that governors are the servants of the people. Make believe that all men are equal or make believe that they are not.[1]
> —EDMUND S. MORGAN (1988)

THE CONSTITUTION begins, "We the People of the United States . . . do ordain and establish this Constitution for the United States of America." This was not idle rhetoric. These words were offered to claim legitimacy for the document that followed. The founders' claim of legitimacy was based not on the divine right of kings, but on the right of "We the People" to govern themselves. They declared that "We the People" had exercised their rights and manifested their consent to be ruled by the institutions "constituted" by this document. They made this declaration because they believed that the consent of "We the People" was necessary to establish a legitimate government and that, upon ratification, they would have gained this consent.[2]

I challenge the idea, sometimes referred to as "popular sovereignty," that the Constitution of the United States was or is legitimate because it was established by "We the People" or the "consent of the governed." I deny that the conditions needed to make this claim valid existed at the time the Constitution was adopted or ever could exist. Though "the People" can surely be bound by their consent, this consent must be real, not fictional—unanimous, not majoritarian. Anything less than unanimous consent simply cannot bind nonconsenting persons. Moreover, if taken too seriously, the fiction of "We the People" can prove dangerous in practice and can nurture unwarranted criticisms of the Constitution's legitimacy. To understand what constitutional legitimacy requires, we must first consider what it means to assert that a constitution is "binding."

[1] Edmund S. Morgan, *Inventing the People: The Rise of Popular Sovereignty in England and America* (New York: Norton, 1988), 13–14.

[2] For the historical origins and evolution of this belief see ibid.

Constitutional Legitimacy and the Duty to Obey the Law

Sometimes we speak as though the Constitution itself is (or is not) binding on the citizenry. Yet, with rare exception,[3] the Constitution does not purport to bind citizens; rather, it binds the government itself. As Rufus King, delegate from Massachusetts, stated to the Constitutional Convention: "In the establishment of Societies the Constitution was to the Legislature what the laws were to individuals."[4] Though the Constitution is law, it is law in a secondary, not a primary sense.[5] It purports to bind government officials, not private individuals.

The real question, then, is not whether the Constitution is binding on citizens, but whether citizens are bound by the commands or laws issued by officials acting in its name. Does the fact that a "law" is validly enacted according to the Constitution mean that it binds one in conscience? In other words, is one morally obligated to obey any law that is enacted according to constitutional procedures? Or is the only reason to obey a valid law the fear of punishment should one be caught in disobedience?

While some legal philosophers disagree (as we shall see in chapter 2), most citizens think that when a command is called a "law," it carries with it a moral duty of obedience, though this duty may not be absolute.[6] Certainly most lawmakers and government officials assert that citizens have a moral duty to obey properly enacted laws. When this is the common perception of "the law," and when the system that produces these legal commands lacks the requisite institutional quality—whatever it may be—to justify this favorable presumption, lawmakers in such a society will get a powerful benefit of the doubt—or "halo-effect"—to which they are not entitled. Therefore, if the term "law" is to carry the implication that there is a moral duty to obey, then the requisite binding quality must go in before the name "law" goes on.

A lawmaking system is legitimate, then, if it creates commands that citizens have a duty to obey. A constitution is legitimate if it creates this type of legal system. What quality must a constitution have to make it legitimate in this sense? Why do citizens have a duty to obey the commands of those who are designated by a constitution as lawmakers and

---

[3] The Thirteenth Amendment prohibits private persons, not just government, from enslaving another or holding them in involuntary servitude. See U.S. Const., Amend. XIII.

[4] James Madison, *Notes of Debates in the Federal Convention of 1787* (New York: Norton, 1987), 231 (statement of R. King).

[5] See H.L.A. Hart, *The Concept of Law* (Oxford: Oxford University Press, 1961), 77–96 (distinguishing "primary rules" that direct individuals from "secondary rules" that define how the primary rules are determined).

[6] This is what philosophers call a *prima facie* duty, meaning that one has a duty unless it can be shown that there is some reason why this duty does not adhere.

enforcers? All government officials and most constitutional scholars avoid explicitly addressing these questions.

If pressed for an answer, most people would probably rely on "the consent of the governed" or what is sometimes called "popular sovereignty."[7] Characteristic is the following statement by Michael McConnell: "The people's representatives have a right to govern, so long as they do not transgress limits on their authority that are fairly traceable to the constitutional precommitments of the people themselves. . . ."[8] Or, as George Washington said in his farewell address: "The basis of our political systems is the right of the people to make and to alter their constitutions of government. . . . The very idea of the power and the right of the people to establish government presupposes the duty of every individual to obey the established government."[9]

Although Bruce Ackerman emphatically denies that legislators govern in the name of the people,[10] throughout two massive works entitled *We the People*, he too apparently assumes that the people can bind themselves, though he never states this explicitly. Instead, he writes of "decisions by the People,"[11] "the constitutional judgement of We the People,"[12] the "will of We the People,"[13] "revision by the People,"[14] and the people's "right to change their mind."[15] In short, for liberals like Ackerman, no less than for conservatives like McConnell, "the People" are an entity capable of making decisions, reaching judgments, having a will, and changing "their mind."[16]

---

[7] For an explanation of the concept of "popular sovereignty," and an insightful but different critique, see Christopher W. Morris, "The Very Idea of Popular Sovereignty: 'We the People' Reconsidered," *Social Philosophy and Policy* 17, 1 (Winter 2000): 1–26.

[8] Michael W. McConnell, "The Importance of Humility in Judicial Review: A Comment on Ronald Dworkin's 'Moral Reading' of the Constitution," *Fordham Law Review* 65 (1997): 1291.

[9] "Washington's Farewell Address," in Henry Steele Commager, *Documents of American History*, 6th ed. (New York: Appleton-Century-Crofts, 1958), 172. This passage of Washington's speech was reputedly drafted by Alexander Hamilton. See Joseph Ellis, *Founding Brothers: The Revolutionary Generation* (New York: Alfred A. Knopf, 2001), 152.

[10] Bruce Ackerman, *We the People: Foundations* (Cambridge: Harvard University Press, Belknap Press, 1991), 184 ("No small group can ever be transubstantiated into the People by virtue of legal form").

[11] Ibid., 6.

[12] Ibid., 9.

[13] Ibid., 10.

[14] Ibid., 13.

[15] Ibid., 14.

[16] Ibid. The very phrase "their mind" signals that something is amiss beneath the surface. If "We the People" have a single mind, should Ackerman not speak of "*its* mind"? He would then have to tell us what exactly the "it" is—everyone? a majority?—and how a diverse multitude of millions of people can have a single mind. If, on the other hand, there is no

In the next section, I will show that "We the People" is a fiction. I will demonstrate that constitutional legitimacy has not been conferred by either the individual or the collective consent of "We the People." As we shall see, the idea of the "consent of the governed" is not one but a series of different commonly made arguments that we must distinguish and consider separately to see that none of them work. Though genuine consent, were it to exist, could give rise to a duty of obedience, the conditions necessary for "We the People" actually to consent to anything like the Constitution or amendments thereto have never existed and could never exist.[17] Only when this is understood will we be in a position to understand how the Constitution of the United States could be legitimated on grounds other than consent.

WHY "WE THE PEOPLE" IS A FICTION

Those who justify a duty to obey the law on the basis of the "consent of the governed" must explain exactly how and when "We the People"—you and me and everyone else—consented to obey the laws of the land. Some claim that by voting we consent to obey the resultant laws; others contend that residence or the failure to revolt or amend the Constitution implies consent. All of these theories of "tacit consent" collapse upon close examination. Let us consider each in turn.

Does Voting Constitute Consent to Obey the Law?

Because we do not live in a direct democracy in which every individual votes on every law, to some it seems obvious that we consent to obey the laws when we vote for the lawmakers who enact them. Just as a person empowers an agent to represent and bind him, when each of us votes for people to represent us in the legislature, have we not consented to obey the laws that they, our agents, vote for? Perhaps. But suppose the candi-

---

single mind, then should he not have said "their minds"? Yet this expression would weaken the desired imagery of a single deliberating, willing, and acting agent that—or is it "who"?—exercises judgment.

[17] Although Ackerman's preoccupation with the trope of "We the People" makes his work an obvious target of this critique, nowhere in his two pathbreaking books does he, to my knowledge, systematically defend the normative assumption that the "will of We the People" is actually binding on any particular person, or that constitutionally enacted laws are binding on the citizenry. Instead, he defends his "dualist" approach as the best description of the American constitutional tradition (about which he may well be correct). See, e.g., ibid., 13 ("My argument . . . focuses on the fact that our Constitution has never . . . explicitly entrenched existing higher law against subsequent revision by the People"). I discuss Ackerman's dualist theory of constitutionalism below.

date we voted for was defeated. In what way did we consent to be "represented" by his opponent, the person we voted against? Or suppose the person we voted to be our representative votes against a particular law. In what way have we consented to be bound by a law to which we and our representative were opposed?

"Well, consent doesn't work that way," comes the response. By choosing to vote, it is said, we have consented to the outcome of the election, whatever it may be. In a game, you consent to play by the rules even when you are losing. People often consent to a process of binding arbitration in which they know that they may win or lose. By the same token, when we participate in the electoral "game" or process, have we not committed ourselves to respect the outcome when our candidate loses?

But if consent is a message we communicate to others—"I consent to be bound by the outcome"—it is not clear that voting conveys such a message. Suppose some people vote, not because they consent to the outcome of an election, but "in self-defense"—that is, they vote because they hope to influence, however marginally, the result so that it is not as unfavorable to them as it might otherwise be. For example, some people might vote for the candidate who promises to support a tax cut, not because they consent to whatever the candidate might do in office, but solely because they hope to make a tax cut more likely and a tax increase less likely. The same holds true for persons who vote for candidates who support or oppose abortion rights. To infer from their having voted for such a candidate the message that these voters consent either to the outcome of the election or to the outcome of the lawmaking process, whatever it may be, is to misunderstand the meaning of their vote.

Yes, but by using a vote to try to influence the outcome, has not a person chosen to participate in the process, and does not this choice necessarily entail a consent to abide by the outcome? After all, should their candidate prevail, voters would expect those who supported the losing candidate to go along with the winning side. Unless losing voters go along with the winners, the system will fail to accomplish anyone's objectives. Although this may be so, it does not follow that individual voters, by voting, have consented to be bound themselves. They could still be voting simply to minimize the threat to their interests posed by the lawmaking process. Voting for this motive in no way implies consent to any outcome that may result. Therefore, the simple act of voting does not tell us whether the voter consents to the outcome of the election (and all that follows from that) or whether he or she is voting for different motives entirely.

While I do not agree that consent to the outcome follows from a vote cast in self-defense, suppose for the sake of argument that it does. What, then, do we say about the consent of those who abstain from voting altogether? They have not expressed any consent to the outcome of an election, win or lose, or the decisions of "representatives" whom they have voted neither for nor against. Surely, on the argument presented so far, they are not bound to obey the law by virtue of their consent.

"Not so fast," comes the reply. Provided that they were given the option of voting, those who have chosen not to participate in the election cannot complain. Consider the right of a criminal defendant to be represented in court by a lawyer. Should he waive his right to counsel and represent himself, or even stand mute, he cannot object if he is convicted—provided he was given the right to be represented. By the same token, so long as we are free to vote, if we fail to do so we cannot complain, however the election comes out. After all, we had the opportunity to influence the outcome and we freely chose not to employ it.

The analogy to the right to an attorney, however, is inapt. We do not find the defendant guilty because he consented to be so found. We find him guilty because we conclude that he *is* guilty. There is no reason to expect or require a defendant to consent to his prosecution. Though some defendants probably do, most probably do not. We do not know and we do not care because their consent does not matter. In contrast, the argument that we are bound to obey the laws because we have been given a right to vote *is* based on consent—the consent of the governed. It is not clear why, by giving someone the opportunity to consent, for example by voting, one may then infer consent from a refusal to vote.

This point becomes clearer when one realizes that, if consent is an expression of a willingness to go along with something, then this presupposes it is possible to express an *un*willingness to go along. Just as I can say, "I consent," there must also be a way to say, "I do not consent." I am not here talking about the likelihood of such a refusal or all the considerations that might leave one "little choice" but to consent. Rather, I am simply insisting that, just as the word "no" means the opposite of "yes," for consent to have any meaning, it must be possible to say, "I do not consent" instead of "I consent." But notice where the argument has taken us when consent to obey the laws is based on voting:

> If we vote *for* a candidate and she wins, we have consented to the laws she votes for, but we have also consented to the laws she has voted against.
> If we vote *against* the candidate and she wins, we have consented to the laws she votes for or against.
> And if we *do not vote at all*, we have consented to the outcome of the process, whatever it may be.

It is a queer sort of "consent" where there is no way to refuse one's consent. "Heads I win, tails you lose," is the way to describe a rigged contest.

"Heads" you consent, "tails" you consent, "didn't flip the coin," guess what? You consent as well. This is simply not consent.

Does Residency Imply Consent?

When confronted with this argument, some might respond that I have attacked a straw man. No one argues that consent is to be inferred from voting, or from having a right to vote. (I dispute this, by the way. In my experience, many people do argue in this manner—or at least they believe it—until the difficulties of the argument are brought to their attention.) Rather, the response continues, one consents to obey the laws of the land because one has chosen to live here.

Just as you are bound to obey your employer (within limits) because you consented to work at your job, you are bound to obey your landlord (within limits) because you consented to rent your apartment, and you are bound to obey the referee (within limits) when you consented to play basketball in a league, you are bound to obey the commands of the law-making system in place where you have chosen to live. You can always leave your job, find another apartment, or quit the basketball team, but as long as you remain, you have consented to live by the authority of others and are bound to do so. By the same token, though you can emigrate from the country if you wish, so long as you chose to remain, you have "tacitly" consented to obey the laws of the United States. Call this the "love it or leave it" version of consent.

While it is fair to say that one implicitly consents to obey one's employer, a sports official, or the usher in the movie theater, it is not at all clear that one has consented to obey the laws of the United States simply by virtue of one's failure to emigrate. Certainly no one has ever asked me for my consent, nor you for yours. Unlike immigrants who become citizens by taking an explicit oath, those born within the boundaries of the United States are not asked or required to take an oath promising to obey the laws.

Consider for a moment the implication of such a demand. Suppose one refused to take the oath. Would one then not be bound to obey the laws of the United States? Or would one then be expelled from the country? The latter prospect presupposes that the person who is demanding we take an oath is an "authority" who has the right to expel us if we refuse, but it is his authority that is at issue in the first place and that supposedly depends on our consent. All this is quite circular.

It is always hard to explain why a circular argument is circular (without sounding circular yourself), so consider this. Suppose I come to you and demand that you sign an oath to respect my commands and you refuse. Upon your refusal I claim a right to your house and order you to leave the country. You rightly say that this is absurd. I have no authority to demand that you take an oath, so you are free to ignore me. Your refusal to take the oath in no way obligates you to leave the country. You would be right. Because you have not consented to my authority, unless my authority is based on something other than your consent, I am in no position to demand that you either take an oath or leave the country.

Were the present government to demand we take an oath, it would be making exactly the same claim. If the reason for taking an oath is to give the lawmakers authority by our consent, then unless they first have authority, they cannot demand that we take an oath. But if they already have the authority to demand we take an oath, then the oath is unnecessary to establish that authority.[18]

That which is true for oaths is just as true for mere residence. It is equally unwarranted to base the authority of lawmakers on the "tacit" consent of everyone who chooses to live here and does not leave the country. For remaining in this country tacitly indicates consent only if you assume that the lawmakers have the initial authority to demand your obedience or your exit in the first place. But it is their authority that is supposed to be justified on the basis of your and my tacit consent. So the problem with inferring consent from a refusal to leave the country is that it presupposes that those who demand you leave already have authority over you. Your decision to stay, therefore, cannot be the source of their authority. And their authority, if it exists, does not rest on your consent.

Lea Brilmayer has dubbed this the "bootstrapping objection."[19] Brilmayer correctly identifies this as an objection to territorial jurisdictions that purport to be based on consent, not an objection to nonterritorial jurisdiction based on actual consent:

These bootstrapping objections to contractarian formation of a government do not necessarily arise when parties create governmental entities that lack territorial status. One might, for instance, agree with another individual that in the event of a dispute both will submit to binding arbitration. Although the arbitrator's authority is established by consent, its authority is not territorial. In such cases, only the actual participants are bound; the extent of authority is not defined territorially.[20]

[18] As the idea of popular sovereignty was first developing in England, one group—the Levellers—"proposed . . . an 'Agreement of the People' to be signed by every Englishman who agreed to transfer to his representative the powers specified therein. (What would happen to those who did not agree is unclear.)" Morgan, *Inventing the People*, 72. Though their proposal was never implemented, it illustrates what taking the consent of the governed literally would require.

[19] Lea Brilmayer, "Consent, Contract, and Territory," *Minnesota Law Review* 74 (1989): 10.

[20] Ibid., 16.

Thus, this objection will not apply to lawmaking jurisdictions based on actual unanimous consent described in chapter 2.

Besides its circularity, there is another reason to reject the "love it or leave it" conception of consent. As I have already noted, "I consent" is a message we communicate to others. Saying the words "I consent" is fairly unambiguous (so long as there is a way to refuse to consent). Depending on the context, there are few, if any, other meanings we can attach to these words. Simply remaining in the country, however, is highly ambiguous. It might mean you consent to be bound by the laws enacted by Congress; or it might mean you have a good job and could not find a better one in another country; or it might mean that you speak only English; or it might mean that you do not want to leave your loved ones behind. It is simply unwarranted to conclude from the mere act of remaining in the country of one's birth that one has consented to all or any of the laws thereof.

Before the Holocaust—and even after it began—many Jews remained in Germany when they had a chance to escape, but chose to stay for a variety of reasons. Whatever else we can say about their decision, we cannot conclude that, merely by their presence, they tacitly assented to the Nuremberg laws. I do not mean to put too much stress on this argument. There were many characteristics of the Third Reich that undermined its authority and that made it substantially different in this regard from the United States. My point is merely that, simply by remaining in their homeland at a time they were free to leave, German Jews cannot be said to have consented to whatever laws were enacted in that country. Neither have we. And to return to the first argument, the Nazis had no authority based on the consent of the Jews to put them to this choice.

Are We Bound by the Consent of the Founders?

Those who base the duty to obey the laws on popular sovereignty or the "consent of the governed" will not give up at this point. They will then point to the fact that the U.S. government predates the birth of everyone alive today. Because it was here first, it can demand that one consent to its authority or leave the country. Recall the quotation from Michael McConnell: "The people's representatives have a right to govern, so long as they do not transgress limits on their authority that are fairly traceable to the constitutional precommitments of the people themselves. . . ."[21]

The initial source of the authority of "the people's representatives" was not your or my consent, goes the argument, but the consent of "We the People" at the time the government was founded. It is that consent that got the government up and running legitimately, and it is that consent

---

[21] McConnell, "Importance of Humility," 1291.

that empowers it to demand that you "love it or leave it." If you are born in and grow up in someone else's house, for example, you must obey the rules of the home owner or move out. Your continued presence constitutes consent to the authority of the home owner.

Moreover, a popular sovereignty theorist might also make the somewhat different argument that the issue of the "consent of the governed" was never whether you or I consented to obey the laws by our vote or by remaining in the country. The real source of consent was the initial consent of "We the People" to the formation of a government, and from then on, so long as the people do not successfully revolt against the government, they can be said to have tacitly consented to it. It is the failure to overthrow the government, not the refusal to leave the country, that constitutes our consent to obey its commands.

Both arguments invoke the legitimate origin of the Constitution and rest that legitimacy on the consent of "We the People" of 1789. It is this consent that gives the Constitution its initial legitimacy and puts the onus on the citizenry afterward either to obey, leave the country, or successfully revolt. This shift in argument from our consent to the consent of "We the People" at the time of the founding now requires us to ask who exactly consented to the creation of this government and what gave them the power to bind themselves and their posterity. We shall immediately see the exact same problems here as we saw with voting, only once removed. Now we are talking about deficiencies in other people's consent, not ours.

The Constitution was not approved by a unanimous vote, nor even by a majority of all persons in the country at the time. It was approved by a majority of delegates to conventions in each state. These delegates were elected by a majority of those who voted for delegates. Were the delegates who voted against the Constitution (and those who voted for these delegates) bound by their consent? And what about the majority of inhabitants who were not permitted to vote for any delegate? Though voting requirements varied with local jurisdictions, in no place could women, children, indentured servants, or slaves vote. Moreover, it was not uncommon to have a property requirement that limited the voting rights of white males and free black males. How can a small minority of inhabitants presuming to call themselves "We the People" consensually bind anyone but themselves? And assuming they could somehow bind everyone then alive, how could they bind, by their consent, their posterity?[22]

One response to this, already suggested above, is that the refusal to revolt or overthrow the government is what constitutes an ongoing tacit consent to obey the lawful commands of the system the founders created.

---

[22] For what it is worth, in the Preamble to the Constitution, the framers did not purport to *bind* their posterity but rather to secure for it "the Blessings of Liberty."

But this is asking much too much of those who would refuse their consent. Does one really manifest a consent to obey the commands of someone much more powerful simply because one does not physically resist the threat of violence for noncompliance? True, physical resistance is evidence of a lack of consent, but if the cost of physical resistance is high enough, we cannot conclude that a passive nonresistance equals consent.

The same can be said to a lesser extent of the failure to emigrate. The cost of emigration, in terms of what one gives up by leaving, is too high to permit the inference from the failure to emigrate a consent to obey the laws of the land. Moreover, the failure of enough people to band together to overthrow a government tells us nothing about the consent of the individual to be bound by the commands of the government and therefore it tells us nothing about why laws are binding on the individual. To argue otherwise is to assert that the majority by *its* failure to revolt, can bind the minority to obey the laws.

To this the popular sovereignty theorist might respond that when the Constitution provides less costly mechanisms for change—such as an amendment process—it is the failure to amend the Constitution, rather than the failure to successfully revolt against the government, that manifests consent to obey all the laws. But this response is transparently inadequate. Whether a constitutional amendment requires a supermajority vote of both houses of Congress and approval by three-quarters of state legislatures, or a simple majority of the electorate, the failure to obtain an amendment through this process hardly indicates consent by anyone to the existing regime. A refusal to approve a change in the Constitution implies neither that those who supported the defeated amendment nor those who opposed it consented to the existing regime. In the end, we return to the problem of inferring the consent of the minority or of the individual from the consent of the majority. Consent simply does not work that way.

We are now in a position to appreciate the fundamental reason why none of the foregoing arguments based on consent succeeds: For consent to bind a person, there must be a way to say "no" as well as "yes" and that person himself or herself must have consented. Unless we are speaking of children, incompetents, or principals who have actually consented to be represented by an agent, no person can literally consent for another. This fact poses an insurmountable obstacle for all arguments that base the "consent of the governed" on anything less than unanimity. As Jeffrey Reiman has argued,

> there is nothing inherently legitimating about the electoral process. If anything, the electoral process is the problem, not the solution. . . . [T]he policies that emerge from the electoral process will be imposed on the dissenting minority against its wishes. And then, rather than answering the question of legitimacy, this will raise the question with respect to those dissenters. Why are the exer-

cises of power approved by the majority against the wishes of (and potentially prohibiting the desired actions of) the minority obligatory with respect to the minority? Why are such exercises of power not simply a matter of the majority tyrannizing the minority?[23]

Arguments on behalf of constitutional legitimacy based on majoritarian rather than unanimous consent attempt the moral equivalent of squaring a circle.

Why Acquiescence Does Not Equal Consent

The appeal of arguments based on tacit consent dies hard, however, and perhaps here is the reason: Can we not say that almost everyone in some sense "accepts" the current government of the United States as legitimate? Would not the number who reject its legitimacy be very small indeed? Were this not the case, would not the government be hopelessly unstable? If general acquiescence in the existing legal regime is an empirical fact, and one that is essential to its functioning existence, can the regime not also claim the tacit consent of the population and the legitimacy that flows from such consent?

This is the sort of "consent" that Edmund Morgan had in mind when he wrote, "all government rests on the consent, however obtained, of the governed."[24] The need to obtain this consent so that the many accede to be ruled by the few, he contended, fully justifies the use of such fictions as "We the People." "I can only hope that readers who persevere to the end of the book will recognize that the fictional qualities of popular sovereignty sustain rather than threaten the human values associated with it. . . . My purpose is not to debunk but to explore the wonder that . . . most of us submit willingly to be governed by the few of us."[25]

Those who base their notion of "consent" on general acquiescence, however, have confused a "rule of recognition"—a concept made famous

---

[23] Jeffrey Reiman, "The Constitution, Rights, and the Conditions of Legitimacy," in Alan S. Rosenbaum, ed., *Constitutionalism: The Philosophical Dimension* (New York: Greenwood Press, 1988), 134. As he elaborates: "These questions not only point up the error of taking electoral accountability as an independent source of legitimacy, they also suggest that it is mistaken to think of electoral accountability and constitutional provisions as alternative sources of legitimacy. Rather, the Constitution *with its provisions limiting the majority's ability to exercise power* is the answer to the question of why decisions voted by a majority are binding on the minority who disagree" (ibid.).

[24] Morgan, *Inventing the People*, 13.

[25] Ibid., 15. Perhaps Morgan does not believe that general acquiescence "however obtained" justifies the rule of the many by the few, but the general tenor of his book suggests otherwise. At any rate, this normative issue is not addressed in his otherwise magnificent intellectual history of the idea of popular sovereignty.

by H.L.A. Hart—with the conditions of constitutional legitimacy. A rule of recognition is the way the population can identify the existence of an operating legal regime.[26] But just as knowing that a particular command is "the law" does not tell us whether it is binding in conscience, knowing that a legal regime "exists" as a result of general acquiescence does not tell us whether there is a moral duty to obey its commands.

Of course, some form of general acquiescence is necessary for any constitution to be implemented and to maintain its continued existence as positive law. As Frederick Schauer has noted, this acquiescence distinguishes the Constitution of the United States from another document entitled "The Constitution of the United States" I might write and have my friends ratify.[27] Ratification by plebiscite or representative conventions can provide an effective rule of recognition to the population and can help to attain a general acquiescence to the constitutional regime, though these procedures are far from indispensable.

Mere acquiescence however acquired—which, as Morgan insisted, every existing government and scheme of positive law can claim—and consent cannot be the same thing. For what is at issue is not whether a legal system exists, but whether a particular existing constitutional regime is legitimate. Only if it is legitimate can an existing legal system issue commands to the citizenry that bind individuals in conscience. If acquiescence, which every functioning regime can claim, equaled the requisite consent, even the most oppressive regime could claim to be entitled to a duty of obedience on the basis of such "consent" so long as it manages to maintain its existence. Clearly this proves too much.

Therefore, though some degree of acquiescence may be necessary to establish a command as positive law, more than acquiescence is needed to create a moral duty to obey such a command. James Madison caught a glimpse of the moral problem when he observed in 1784 that the unratified Virginia "Constitution rests on acquiescence" only, which is a "dan-

---

[26] See Hart, *Concept of Law*, 92–93 (A rule of recognition is "a rule for conclusive identification of the primary rules of obligation"). Notice Hart's reference here to the "rules of obligation." Hart also contended that if the rule of recognition was satisfied, citizens would then not only be compelled or "obliged" to obey the law, they would also be under an "obligation" or moral duty to obey. This I reject for reasons I have given elsewhere. See Randy E. Barnett, *Structure of Liberty: Justice and the Rule of Law* (Oxford: Clarendon Press, 1998), 17–23. And this is conceded by those modern positivists who deny that the mere legality of a command entails a duty of obedience, as we shall see in the last section of this chapter.

[27] Frederick Schauer, "Precedent and the Necessary Externality of Constitutional Norms," *Harvard Journal of Law and Public Policy* 17 (1994): 52. ("[O]nly one of these 'Constitutions' would be *the* Constitution of the United States, because only one of these documents would have been accepted, socially and politically, by the people of the United States as their Constitution.")

gerous basis."[28] The consent of the individual, were it to exist, would do the trick—but one individual or generation cannot consent for another, and unanimous consent, all concede, cannot exist and has never existed.[29]

There is considerable irony in the assertion of "tacit" consent as the source of the duty to obey the laws. Many who assert this would never accept so attenuated a notion of consent to justify, say, the lease of a television or the waiver of liability for harm. In these contexts, they demand a pristine version of "informed" consent that rarely if ever exists. For everyday contracts they require "complete information" of everything one is consenting to (or giving up) and a diversity of sufficiently attractive alternative choices before concluding that consent justifies enforcement. Unless these conditions are met, they insist that such consent is "fictitious" or "coerced."[30] Yet we are asked to accept the proposition that merely by virtue of living in the town in which we were born, or by failing to leave the country, we have "consented" to obey nearly any command that is enacted by the reigning legal system. And the consent of a majority is supposed to bind not only themselves, but dissenters and future generations as well.

The problem of legitimacy considered here is whether the commands of an existing legal system bind the citizenry in conscience. If the issue of legitimacy is raised only when a functioning legal system exists—and no legal system can exist without some form of acquiescence—then acquiescence (and whatever is needed to obtain it) could be viewed as a necessary, but not sufficient, condition of legitimacy. By the same token, if the perception of legitimacy is necessary to obtain acquiescence, then whatever contributes to that perception could also be viewed as a necessary condition of legitimacy.

Nevertheless, incorporating acquiescence and the means by which it is obtained into the requirements of legitimacy in this way does not affect my basic thesis: in the absence of actual consent, to be legitimate, an existing legal system must provide assurances that the laws it imposes are both necessary and proper. However it is obtained, acquiescence is

[28] Notes for a Speech [June 14 or 21, 1784], William T. Hutchinson et al., eds., *The Papers of James Madison*, vol. 8 (Chicago: University of Chicago Press, 1962–91), 77. Madison believed that if "ratified by" the people, the Virginia constitution would be "more stable and secured agst. the doubts & imputations under which it now labors." Ibid.

[29] Though unanimous consent to something like the Constitution is impossible to obtain, I explain in chapter 2 why, contrary to popular assumption, unanimous consent to other effective governance structures is both quite possible and quite common.

[30] This view is almost too widespread to require citation, but see, e.g., Jean Braucher, "Contract versus Contractualism: The Regulatory Role of Contract Law," *Washington and Lee Law Review* 47 (1990): 697–739; Peter Linzer, "Is Consent the Essence of Contract?—Replying to Four Critics," *Annual Survey of American Law* (1988): 213.

insufficient to provide this assurance. Though acquiescence may be needed to establish a legal system as positive law, it is neither the same as, nor an adequate substitute for, actual consent.

PROBLEMATIC ALTERNATIVES TO "WE THE PEOPLE"

In the final analysis, the only way that a duty to obey the law can be based on consent is when consent is given. Anything less than unanimous consent cannot bind those who dissent. Those who acknowledge this take one of two positions. Some maintain that there is no prima facie or presumptive duty to obey the law just because it is the law. I shall return to this argument in chapter 2. Though conceptually defensible, as we shall see, this position is unacceptable in regimes where lawmakers are given the benefit of the doubt and it is widely thought that there exists a duty to obey enacted laws. Others abandon popular sovereignty by contending that lawmaking authority is based not on the "consent of the governed" after all, but on something else. (It is remarkable how fast people drop the argument based on consent when confronted with its difficulties.) What is this "something else"?

Fair Play: Does the Receipt of Benefits Obligate Us to Obey?

According to one such argument, laws are binding, not because of the consent of "We the People," but because people who receive the benefits of the legal system are bound to obey its demands. It is not consent, they say, but receipt of benefits that binds one. Sometimes called the "principle of fair play,"[31] this theory has been extensively discussed among philosophers, and I shall not try to summarize the nuances of the debate.[32]

---

[31] John Rawls's early theory of legal obligation based on the "duty of fair play," though superficially resembling a benefits received argument, actually depends "upon our having accepted and our intention to continue accepting the benefits of a *just* scheme of cooperation that the constitution defines." John Rawls, "Legal Obligation and the Duty of Fair Play," in Sydney Hook, ed., *Law and Philosophy* (New York: New York University Press, 1964), 10 (emphasis added). This therefore is not a pure benefits received argument. "[A]n essential condition of the obligation is the justice of the constitution and the general system of law being roughly in accordance with it. Thus the duty to obey . . . an unjust law depends on there being a just constitution" (ibid.). This makes the structure of Rawls's old theory very similar to that presented in chapter 2, though it adds an extra requirement of voluntary acceptance of benefits that I think is unnecessary to justify a prima facie duty to obey laws that are produced by procedures that assure their justice.

[32] See Williamson A. Edmunson, ed., *The Duty to Obey the Law: Selected Philosophical Readings* (Lanham, Md.: Rowman & Littlefield, 1999).

One powerful criticism of this position by Robert Nozick is that it, too, is ultimately based not merely on "receipt" of benefits but on some notion of consent.[33] If out of the blue I send you a valuable item, are you obliged to pay for it in the absence of consent? Are you even obliged to return it to me? Most answer no. Likewise, we are not obligated to pay for benefits that are thrust upon us by others.

Some may say that if you choose to use the item, then you have obligated yourself to pay for it. There may be some merit to this suggestion; using an item that you know has been sent to you with the expectation of repayment may indicate a consent to pay. (Even this does not mean, however, that you are obligated to return the item rather than discarding it.) It is still not clear that one is obligated to pay for all unsolicited benefits one receives from others. We may get great pleasure from wonderful architecture, or from seeing an attractive person walk by, without conceding for a moment that we could be charged for the genuine enjoyment we experience.

But I shall not pursue the matter further here, because the kinds of benefits supposedly received from a legal system—the benefit of social cooperation, for example—are benefits that one cannot refuse no matter how much one wants to. Unless one can somehow refuse a benefit that is thrust upon him or her, it is not at all clear that one is obligated to pay for it either in money or in obedience. For the same reason it is not at all clear why the "benefits" one receives from living in the particular legal system we have—benefits we cannot decline to "enjoy" even if we want to—obligate one to obey the commands of this system.

When we move beyond the benefits of a "scheme of cooperation" supposedly represented by the legal system to tangible benefits—such as roads, parks, or schools—we find that most are paid for by taxation: payments that certainly are not consented to in any meaningful way. Must everyone whose income is confiscated to pay for roads, parks, and schools (to some unknowable extent) decline to make use of these resources lest they be accused of voluntarily benefiting from them and, therefore, of owing not only a duty to obey the laws, but a moral duty to pay for them as well?

In an influential essay, John Simmons defends the "fair play" argument against Nozick's critique by denying it is based on mere "receipt" of benefits. A fairer reading, he contends, is that it is based instead on *acceptance* of benefits by *participants* in a particular system.

> [F]or an individual to be a real participant in a cooperative scheme, he must have either (1) pledged his support, or tacitly agreed to be governed by the

scheme's rules, or (2) played some active role in the scheme after its institution. It is not enough to be associated with the "schemers" in some vague way; one must go out and do things to become a participant or "insider" . . . .[34]

For Simmons, the problem with the argument, reformulated so as to avoid collapsing into the tacit consent position, is that "it will by no means be a standard case in which all beneficiaries of a cooperative scheme's workings have accepted the benefits they receive."[35]

Simmons contends that "benefits accepted," like unanimous consent, can potentially provide the basis for a duty to obey, but (also like unanimous consent) its conditions cannot ordinarily be obtained in modern political structures.

> While it is clear that at least most citizens of most states *receive* benefits from the workings of their legal and political institutions, how plausible is it to say that they have voluntarily *accepted* those benefits, in even the cases of the most democratic political societies now in existence? Not, I think, very plausible.[36]

Simmons describes "acceptance" as an attitude that requires certain attributes.

> Among other things, we must understand that the benefits flow from a cooperative scheme, rather than regarding them as "free" for the taking. And we must, for instance, think that the benefits we receive are worth the price we must pay to get them (with the burdens involved) or leaving them.[37]

Simmons then denies that most persons have the requisite beliefs and attitudes.

> Most citizens will, I think, fall into one of these two classes: those who have not "accepted" because they have not taken the benefits (with accompanying burdens) willingly, and those who have not "accepted" because they do not regard the benefits of government as the product of a cooperative scheme.[38]

For all of these reasons, the argument for a duty to obey the laws based on benefits either "received" or "accepted" has fared little better than the argument based on the tacit consent of the governed. But there is more. Someone defending a duty of obedience on the receipt of benefits might respond that both of these criticisms evade the basic point: benefits received provide an argument for obedience wholly apart from either con-

---

[34] A. John Simmons, "The Principle of Fair Play," in Edmundson, *Duty to Obey*, 124–25.

[35] Ibid., 132.

[36] Ibid., 136.

[37] Ibid., 137.

[38] Ibid.

sent or acceptance and, for this reason, it is inadequate to respond that tacit consent to obey or pay or acceptance of a benefit is lacking.

So let us take this argument at face value and assume that one really does owe a duty of obedience to anyone who takes it upon himself, and without either the consent or the acceptance of the recipient, to provide another with (vital?) benefits. Assume that one does owe a duty of obedience, regardless of one's consent, to anyone who provides one with (vital?) benefits. Could this not be offered as a justification for the legitimacy of chattel slavery? Could not a slaveholder claim, and often accurately, that he was indeed providing his slaves with vital benefits, including food, clothing, shelter, medical attention when needed, and protection from predation by outsiders?

Of course, one might quarrel with the accuracy of this claim, but on what grounds? That food, shelter, and the rest are not "benefits"? Hardly. That these benefits are not adequate? According to what scale of adequacy? Do citizens of severely impoverished countries have no duty to obey the law because the benefits provided by those governments are too niggardly? At what point do the benefits become great enough to generate a duty of obedience in the absence of consent? Is the problem with chattel slavery that masters do not pay the minimum wage?

To better appreciate why the nonconsensual receipt of benefits cannot be the source of a duty of obedience, imagine a generous master who provides all essentials and even a degree of choice or freedom to his vassals—or house slaves—that they are nevertheless unable to refuse. Are the slaves of sufficiently bounteous (defined however you wish) masters morally obligated to obey them? What is the problem with this entire line of argument? The obvious answer is that what is lacking is the consent of the slave. Were there consent to the relationship, then we would not (or should not) describe it as slavery at all—provided that the servant were free to exit the relationship.[39] But if consent is required to convert a morally impermissible slavery into a duty of obedience, then such consent cannot be fictitious. It must be real, and we have already seen how there is and can be no real consent to the sort of legal system established by the Constitution.

Though it is not hard to see why consent is needed to convert a slave relationship to one that is morally permissible, it is sometimes overlooked that this strongly implies the existence of human rights. For only if per-

[39] Indentured servitude coexisted with chattel slavery throughout its history in America. Such arrangements were voluntary, but still objectionable in my view because the servant was bound to service for a period of years and could not exit. For reasons why this, too, violates the inalienable rights of persons, see Barnett, *Structure of Liberty*, 77–82. Other classical liberals have defended such "voluntary slavery" arrangements as morally permissible. See, e.g., Nozick, *Anarchy, State and Utopia*, 331.

sons have a right to refuse their consent can we ever say they have consented. Such a right of refusal must, therefore, precede the creation of a
duty of obedience. If consent is the source of a duty to obey the law, then
first comes rights and only then comes law. As we shall see in chapter 2,
in the absence of consent, the preexistence of these rights has important
implications for any legal system that claims a duty of obedience.

Hypothetical Consent and the Importance of Rights

Some political theorists rely upon a notion of "hypothetical consent" or
that to which a rational person would consent.[40] To evaluate claims based
on "We the People," we need not get enmeshed in the intricacies of such
"rational choice" theories. It is sufficient to note that hypothetical consent
is not actual consent. Indeed, actual consent plays no role in such approaches. Rather, rational choice theories attempt to demonstrate the constraints to which people, under certain conditions, ought to consent regardless of whether they do consent or not.

In other words, though an analysis of "hypothetical consent" may well
provide an argument in favor of certain moral or political principles, such
an argument is not based on the real-world consent of anyone to anything.
This means, however, that hypothetical consent provides no consent-
based reason to ignore or evade the background rights of the people—
provided that (as I have shown elsewhere and will summarize in the next
chapter) people do have rights prior to the formation of a legal system.
Properly understood, arguments based upon hypothetical consent actually help us understand why lawmakers must respect the rights of the
people they purport to bind.

Lysander Spooner was perhaps the earliest constitutional theorist to
recognize that an argument based on hypothetical or presumptive consent
"exist[ing] only in theory"[41] is required to respect the rights of the individual because everyone cannot be presumed—in the absence of express or
actual consent—to have given up their rights. "Justice is evidently the only
principle that *everybody* can be presumed to agree to, in the formation of

---

[40] See, e.g., John Rawls, *A Theory of Justice* (Cambridge: Harvard University Press,
1971), 12 ("The choice which rational men would make in this hypothetical situation of
equal liberty . . . determines the principles of justice").

[41] Lysander Spooner, "The Unconstitutionality of Slavery," rev. ed. (1860), reprinted in
Charles Shively, ed., *The Collected Works of Lysander Spooner*, vol. 4 (Providence: M & S
Press, 1971), 153. ("Our constitutions purport to be established by 'the people,' and, *in
theory,* 'all the people' *consent* to such government as the constitutions authorize. But this
consent of 'the people' exists only in theory. It has no existence in fact.") See also ibid., 225
("The whole matter of the adoption of the constitution is mainly a matter of assumption
and theory, rather than of actual fact").

government."[42] In the absence of actual consent, a government that protects the rights of all "is the *only* government which it is practicable to
establish by the [theoretical] consent of all the governed; for an unjust
government must have victims, and the victims cannot be supposed to
give their consent."[43]

Thus, an argument based on hypothetical consent is inadequate to
justify overriding background rights. On the contrary, for a constitution
to be legitimate on the basis of hypothetical consent, it must be shown
that such a constitution is *consistent* with whatever may be the rights of
the individual.

CONCLUSION

If one accepts that "We the People" is a fiction, does this entail that
the constitutionality of a law tells us nothing about our duty to obey it?
I think not. In the next chapter, I shall consider an alternative conception of constitutional legitimacy that explains both how laws can bind
the citizenry in conscience in the absence of consent and why, because
consent is lacking, the lawmaking power of government must be constitutionally limited. Indeed, I shall argue that, in the absence of unanimous
consent, there is a duty to obey the law only when the legislature's powers
are limited.

The point of this chapter is to make plain why such an alternative conception of constitutional legitimacy is required. It is needed because (a)
consent to the sort of lawmaking processes established by the Constitution is nonexistent and impossible and (b) the dispensation of benefits by
lawmakers does not generate a duty to obey their commands in the absence of consent. If such a duty of obedience exists, it must be justified in
some other manner, and, in the absence of some alternative justification,
there is no duty to obey the commands of these lawmakers.

Let me now add an important caveat to the analysis just presented. I
am arguing only that a duty to obey the law cannot be grounded on the
consent of the governed when there has been anything less than unanimous consent and that, obviously, no government legal system can claim
this degree of consent. *I am not claiming that adoption of constitutions
(or laws) by popular vote or conventions is a bad idea.* It may well be that
such ratification processes are an excellent idea because they enhance
the likelihood that whatever *does* legitimate a constitution actually
exists. Moreover, such adoption procedures may secure the general acqui-

[42] Ibid., 143.
[43] Ibid.

escence that is a requirement of any functioning legal order, whether or not it is legitimate.

On the other hand, the need to obtain popular acceptance and ratification can come at a cost. Because the framers of the U.S. Constitution knew they could not obtain ratification in certain states were they to abolish slavery, they felt moved to compromise on this issue—a pragmatic decision for which they have long been criticized and which set the stage for the bloodiest war in American history. When it comes to slavery the founders get little credit for their effort to obtain the "consent of the governed" and rightly so when the issue is the unjust claim of some to enslave others.

In this chapter, I am not considering whether some procedures for adopting a constitution are better than others. I am only challenging the widely held assumption that, because of popular sovereignty or the consent of the governed, "We the People" are bound in conscience to obey any law that is enacted by constitutional means. Further, because unanimous consent is never required, in practice the "consent of the governed" is reduced to the consent of a majority of legislators who are elected by a majority of those who vote in an election. In short, "We the People" is a fiction. In the next chapter we shall see how this fiction became dangerous and how constitutional legitimacy can be achieved in the absence of the consent of the governed.

CHAPTER TWO

Constitutional Legitimacy without Consent: Protecting the Rights Retained by the People

> Wherever the real power in a Government lies, there is the danger of oppression. In our Governments the real power lies in the majority of the community, and the invasion of private rights is chiefly to be apprehended, not from acts of Government contrary to the sense of its constituents, but from acts in which the Government is the mere instrument of the major number of the Constituents.[1]
>
> —JAMES MADISON (1788)

SOME FICTIONS are harmless; some are even beneficial. As Edmund Morgan has shown, the fiction of popular sovereignty originated as an antidote to the fiction of the divine right of the king. If the king obtained his authority from God, the Commons gained its authority from the people. Paradoxically the fiction of the divine king was used to limit his power. First, it could be used to deny any intentions to the king that were unworthy of a perfect being. "[D]ivinity, when assumed by mortals (or imposed upon them) can prove more constricting than subjection. Indeed, the attribution of divinity to the king had probably always been motivated in some measure by the desire to limit him to actions becoming a god."[2] Second, the divinity of the king did not extend to anyone but himself, especially not to the ministers who ran afoul of the Commons. "The king was divine and unaccountable, but those he commissioned to act for him shared neither his divinity nor the unaccountability that went with it. To the Commons his agents were all subjects; and if they acted in the king's name, they must do so at their peril."[3]

In a like manner could the fiction of the legislature deriving its just powers from the people be used to constrain its power. True, the "immediate objective of the change in fictions was to magnify the power not of the people themselves, but of the people's representatives."[4] But a danger

---

[1] Letter from James Madison to Thomas Jefferson (October 17, 1788), in Madison, *Letters and Other Writings of James Madison*, vol. 1 (Philadelphia: J. B. Lippincott, 1867), 425.

[2] Morgan, *Inventing the People*, 21.

[3] Ibid., 33.

[4] Ibid., 58.

then emerged: "With the fictional people suddenly supreme, actual people, as embodied in local communities, found their traditional rights and liberties in jeopardy from a representative body that recognized only a fictional superior."[5] Without some constraint, "the sovereignty of the people would pose graver threats not only to the wishes but also to the rights and liberties of actual people, than the divine right of kings had ever done."[6]

The English responses to this threat were varied and took considerable time and struggle to develop.[7] Later in the United States, after an initial near-disastrous experimentation with legislative supremacy unchecked by a monarchy, the response took the form of constitutional constraints not only on the legislature but on the fictional people themselves. Those who drafted and adopted the Constitution realized better than some of their compatriots what we have largely forgotten: that the reality of rule by legislative majorities combined with the fiction of "We the People" can be a dangerous mixture. Understanding their effort to constrain the fiction they themselves accepted will help illuminate what it takes to achieve constitutional legitimacy in the absence of consent.

DEMOCRATIC MAJORITARIANISM AND THE PROBLEM OF FACTION

Despite their rhetorical commitment to "popular sovereignty," by the time the Constitution was written, its framers were pretty well convinced that pure majority rule or democracy was a bad idea. They had experienced state governments dominated by powerful one-house legislatures, weak governors, and a subservient judiciary—and they did not like what they saw. The result was what Madison called "the problem of faction." "By a faction," Madison wrote in *Federalist* 10, "I understand a number of citizens, *whether amounting to a majority or minority* of the whole, who are united and actuated by some common impulse of passion, or of interest, *adverse to the rights of other citizens*, or to the permanent and aggregate interests of the community."[8]

As the quotation that heads this chapter shows, Madison understood, perhaps better than some others of the period, that majorities were as great a danger to the rights retained by the people as a corrupt minority or individual despot. When power is given to majorities operating

[5] Ibid., 53.
[6] Ibid., 82.
[7] See ibid., 55–121.
[8] *Federalist* 10, in James Madison, Alexander Hamilton, and John Jay, *The Federalist*, ed. Clinton Rossiter (New York: Penguin Books, 1961), 78 (emphasis added).

through their representatives, the interest of majorities becomes a greater source of danger to minorities and to the general welfare under popular government than under other forms. So great a danger needs to be guarded against carefully.

This was no secret sentiment expressed to a confidant. Madison made a similar point to the Constitutional Convention in words that foretold the argument of *Federalist* 10: "In all cases where a majority are united by a common interest or passion, the rights of the minority are in danger."[9] He then continued:

> We have seen the mere distinction of colour made in the most enlightened period of time, a ground of the most oppressive dominion ever exercised by man over man. What has been the source of those unjust laws complained of among ourselves? Has it not been the real or supposed interest of the major number? Debtors have defrauded their creditors. The landed interest has borne hard on the mercantile interest. The Holders of one species of property have thrown disproportion of taxes on the holders of another species. The lesson we are to draw from the whole is that where a majority are united by a common sentiment, and have an opportunity, the rights of the minor party become insecure.[10]

And to the Virginia ratification convention he observed that "on a candid examination of history, we shall find that turbulence, violence, and abuse of power, by the majority trampling on the rights of the minority, have produced factions and commotions, which, in republics, have, more frequently than any other cause, produced despotism."[11]

Nor was Madison alone in his skepticism of majoritarianism. Reading the notes of the Constitutional Convention, one is struck by the care that the framers took to check and harness democratic processes, while not suppressing them altogether. As Elbridge Gerry, deputy from Massachusetts stated: "The evils we experience flow from the excess of democracy."[12] After listing a number of abuses, he admitted that he "had been too republican heretofore."[13] He "was still however republican, but had been taught by experience the danger of the levilling spirit."[14] Experience, he claimed, "had shewn that the State legislatures drawn immediately from the people did not always possess their confidence."[15]

---

[9] Madison, *Notes of Debates*, 76 (statement of Madison).

[10] Ibid., 77.

[11] Jonathan Elliot, *Debates on the Adoption of the Federal Constitution*, vol. 3 (Philadelphia: J. B. Lippincott, 1859), 87 (Friday, June 6, 1788).

[12] Madison, *Notes of Debates*, 39 (statement of E. Gerry).

[13] Ibid.

[14] Ibid.

[15] Ibid., 41.

Roger Sherman, of Connecticut—who later came to serve on the congressional committee that drafted the Bill of Rights—contended that the people "immediately should have as little to do as may be about the Government."[16] Virginian Edmond Randolph observed that "the general object was to provide a cure for the evils under which the U.S. laboured."[17] And that "in tracing these evils to their origin every man had found it in the turbulence and follies of democracy."[18] Gouverneur Morris, deputy from Pennsylvania, noted that "Every man of observation had seen in the democratic branches of the State Legislatures, precipitation—in Congress changeableness, in every department excesses against personal liberty private property & personal safety."[19] Even those who remained more amenable to democracy, like George Mason of Virginia, "admitted that we had been too democratic" in forming state governments though he "was afraid that we should incautiously run into the opposite extreme."[20]

When speaking skeptically of "democracy," these delegates were referring to a system of majoritarian decision making by annually elected representatives. Even those opposed to democratic processes asserted that "the People" must hold the ultimate check on the powers of government. But this check was best exercised indirectly and through, in Madison's words, "the policy of refining the popular appointments by successive filtrations"[21] (though this filtration principle should not be "pushed too far").[22] For this reason, Madison favored a popularly elected House so that "the people would [not] be lost sight of altogether; and the necessary sympathy between them and their rulers and officers, [would not be] too little felt."[23]

Given that the popularly elected House was designed to be the most democratic branch, the desire to cabin democratic majoritarianism was revealed most clearly during discussion of the manner by which the president and, especially, the Senate was to be chosen. Edmond Randolph put

[16] Ibid., 39 (statement of R. Sherman) (advocating that House members be chosen by state legislatures).

[17] Ibid., 42 (statement of E. Randolph).

[18] Ibid.

[19] Ibid., 233 (statement of G. Morris).

[20] Ibid., 39 (statement of G. Mason, advocating popular elections of representatives to the House). Later he amplified this: "Notwithstanding the oppressions & injustice experienced among us from democracy; the genius of the people is in favour of it, and the genius of the people must be consulted" (ibid., 64). In evaluating the degree to which his views were reflected in the finished product, it is useful to recall that Mason eventually ended up refusing to sign the Constitution and opposed its ratification in the Virginia ratification convention. But then again, so did Randolph and Gerry.

[21] Ibid., 40 (statement of J. Madison).

[22] Ibid.

[23] Ibid.

the matter succinctly: "The democratic licentiousness of the State Legislatures proved the necessity of a firm Senate. The object of this 2nd branch is to controul the democratic branch of the National Legislature."[24] In accord was Gouverneur Morris, who stated that the object of the Senate was "to check the precipitation, changeableness, and excesses"[25] of the House. "The use of the Senate," said Madison, "is to consist in its proceeding with more coolness, with more system, & with more wisdom, than the popular branch."[26] Hence, whereas representatives were to be elected by the people for two-year terms, senators were to be chosen by state legislatures, to sit for six years, and to be paid from the national treasury so as better to serve as "the impartial umpires & Guardians of justice and the general Good."[27]

How then can one square the founding generation's clear commitment to the fiction of popular sovereignty with their distrust of both majority and minority factions—a distrust so great that they wrote a new constitution to supersede the existing "republican" forms of government? After a century in which the ideology of democratic majoritarianism has taken firm hold, it is difficult to re-create the precise view of "popular sovereignty" that lay behind the original constitutional scheme, and I do not claim that the founding generation was of a single mind on this issue. To some degree, it was fundamental disagreement over what popular sovereignty required that separated "Federalist" supporters of the Constitution from their "Anti-Federalist" opponents.

Still, once one distinguishes between the government, the electorate, and the people, matters become clearer. The government was an institution charged with performing certain essential tasks that required the exercise of good judgment and that could be performed by no other part of civil society. The problem was how to empower a government that would exercise good judgment in performing these functions without enabling it also to violate the rights retained by the people. At first, the solution seemed obvious: Let the people rule as directly as possible through their representatives. After all, the people can be trusted not to violate their own rights.

Experience with "republican" state governments organized this way proved to the framers that this theory was wrong. They had underestimated the problem of faction in which a majority of the electorate—which is not to be identified with the people as a whole—could exercise their power to serve their own interests at the expense of the minority. Given

---

[24] Ibid., 110 (statement of E. Randolph, advocating seven-year terms for senators).
[25] Ibid., 233 (statement of G. Morris).
[26] Ibid., 83 (statement of J. Madison).
[27] Ibid., 199 (statement of J. Madison).

the identification of these republican governments with the people, however, those who now saw the deficiencies of democratic majoritarianism were in a difficult political position. How could they shift away from this "popular" form of government without engendering insurmountable opposition?

They did so by preserving the republican or democratic state governments while changing the form of the national government—and empowering the national government to intervene to prevent those abuses of individual rights by state governments about which both Northerners and Southerners concurred.[28] They did not completely abandon their republican theories but, with their theories modified by practice, adopted what they called a "mixed" form of government. Rather than attempt literal self-rule, they opted for a government that was capable of exercising an independent judgment that would then be "checked" in various ways by an electorate who represented the interests of the people. Eventually, the constitutions of state governments would themselves be revised to conform to the new mixed government model.

In the legislative branch, the electorate checked the enactment of laws by voting for members of the House. In the executive branch, the electorate checked the selection of the president by voting for members of the electoral college. In the judicial branch, the electorate checked the decision to punish an individual by serving on juries. All these popular external checks, combined with internal institutional "checks and balances," such as the presidential veto and judicial review, were supposed to allow an energetic government, but one of strictly limited powers, to exercise the judgment that could not be achieved by the people acting collectively. "In all very numerous assemblies, of whatever characters composed, passion never fails to wrest the sceptre from reason," wrote Madison. "Had every Athenian citizen been a Socrates, every Athenian assembly would still have been a mob."[29]

The danger of viewing legislatures as rulers rather than as checks on rulers had been warned of even as the English Parliament was asserting its authority against the king. Writing in 1651, Isaac Penington, Jr., observed: "The proper use of Parliaments is to be a *curb* to the extravagancy of Power, of the *highest standing Power*: But if they themselves become *the standing Power*, how can they be a fit curb for it?"[30] In America, after

---

[28] In their experiment with republican or democratic government at the *national* level, the post-Revolutionary French were not so fortunate. When democratic majoritarianism turned to factionalized oppression and then tyranny, they had no place "higher" to which to turn.

[29] *Federalist 55*, 342 (Madison).

[30] Isaac Penington, Jr., *The Fundamental Right, Safety and Liberty of the People* (London: Giles Calvert, 1657), 13. This is a reprint of the essay that originally appeared in 1651.

their experience with legislative supremacy at the state level, the conviction took hold that the "majority deserved not so much to rule as to be protected from misrule, not so much to legislate in pursuit of its interests as to be secured against statutes that would reflect the ambitions of the privileged class." Rakove continues:

> A full representation was necessary for two purposes: to prevent the adoption of measures, especially taxes, that would distribute the *burdens* of government unequally across society; and to instill in the people the confidence in government that would obviate the need to resort to coercion (that is, armed force) to enforce the laws.[31]

In sum, after their initial experimentation in "republican" or democratic rule, the founders devised a new scheme in which an electorate of "the People" by voting in elections would exercise, not a lawmaking power, but the power to check the lawmakers. "We the People" would not rule directly, but an electorate reflecting the rights and interests of the people would have effective power to check those who would issue commands to the people.[32] By the same token, state governments would have the power to check federal legislation through Senators chosen by state legislatures. Their novel—even ingenious—scheme of multiple checks and balances was positioned somewhere between rule by a "democratic" majority and rule by an "aristocratic" minority.

Of course, the tragedy of the founding was the framers' inability to end the most egregious violation of individual rights then extant, human slavery—what Madison referred to above during the Constitutional Convention as "the most oppressive dominion ever exercised by man over man."[33] It was clear to the Constitutional Convention, and to all who sought to improve the form of government, that the union of the thirteen states would be unobtainable should they push forward to impose abolition on slaveholding states. Indeed, even after compromising with the slave states by permitting their continued autonomy on this issue, the framers' Constitution met with stiff opposition from those Anti-Federalists who did not share the Federalists' fear of majority faction, or who

[31] Jack N. Rakove, *Original Meanings: Politics and Ideas in the Making of the Constitution* (New York: Vintage 1997), 233. Rakove's discussion of "the Mirror of Representation" makes clear that the framers of the Constitution were rejecting, or at least mitigating, the competing principle of republican or popular rule that had arisen in the states in the wake of the Revolution. See ibid., 203–43.

[32] Notice that while it is a fiction to speak of *rule by* "the people" as a whole, it is no fiction to speak of imposing rules on the people.

[33] Max Farrand, *The Records of the Federal Convention of 1787*, vol. 1 (New Haven: Yale University Press, 1966), 135.

perhaps feared the tyranny of an aristocratic minority even more. These voices were powerful and nearly succeeded in defeating the Constitution.

In the intervening two hundred years, we have moved away from the conception of "popular sovereignty" in which the people, through the electorate, effectively check the exercise of government power, and toward a fiction of "popular sovereignty" in which a "democratic" majority rules. Many people no longer conceive of Congress as an institution charged with performing certain vital tasks, a group of select men and women who are the "servants" of—and checked by—the people. Instead they picture Congress as *We the People itself.* Under the prevailing theory of "popular sovereignty," the legislature is thought of as the people personified, entitled to exercise all the powers of a sovereign people.

Some use such slogans as "we are the government" or "the government is us." This view of government gives legislators an enormous power to do what they will, provided only that they muster the requisite number of votes. For if "we are the government," then anything the government does is consented to by the people and "we" can consent to anything. This shift has also allowed majority and minority factions of the electorate to gain control and wield the power of the legislative branch at the expense of the public good or the aggregate rights of their fellow citizens.

The fiction of popular sovereignty was beneficial insofar as it limited or checked the power of legislatures and prevented them from violating the rights retained by the people (which I shall discuss at greater length in chapter 3). The fiction of popular sovereignty becomes dangerous when legislatures are conceived of as a surrogate for "We the People" themselves. Because "the People" can "consent" to alienate any particular liberty or right—though not their more abstract inalienable rights—legislatures, as the people's surrogate, can restrict almost any liberty and justify it in the name of "popular consent." In short, if legislatures literally "represent" the people, then anything the legislature "consents" to is consented to by the people as well. This means the fiction of popular sovereignty allows a legislature to justifiably do anything it wills.

In this manner, by falsely assuming the presence of consent, the fiction of popular sovereignty has dangerously eroded the rights and liberties of the people, each and every one of them. In the next section, I shall consider an alternative conception of constitutional legitimacy that explains both how laws can bind the citizenry in conscience in the absence of consent and why, because actual consent is lacking, the lawmaking power of government must be limited. Indeed, I argue that, in the absence of unanimous consent, there is a duty to obey the law only when the legislature's powers are limited.

Constitutional Legitimacy in the Absence of Consent

Advocates of popular sovereignty ultimately concede the absence of real consent to obey the laws made pursuant to the Constitution, but argue that because majoritarian consent is the closest we can come to real consent, it is sufficient to legitimate governance. If, however, it can be shown that lawmaking based on unanimous consent is both possible and practical, then necessity could no longer be used to justify majoritarian consent. With unanimous consent no longer a hopeless ideal, it also becomes easier to see why, in the absence of unanimous consent, legitimacy requires that limits or constraints be imposed on majoritarian governance.

The argument in chapter 1 assumes, uncontroversially, that a duty of obedience could be grounded on consent if everyone consents to be so bound. This condition fails to be met in our constitutional system because the polity is too big ever to unanimously consent to anything. But suppose that the relevant lawmaking unit were much much smaller than the United States, indeed smaller than any state and even most cities. Would unanimous consent be possible then? I think it would. Let me now sketch how unanimous consent is practical in a legal system I have described elsewhere at greater length.[34]

More Consent, Less Freedom

My parents live in a large private residential community known as Leisure World. When they bought their home, they expressly agreed to a highly democratic governance structure. Leisure World is typical in this regard, although governance arrangements vary among different residential communities. As with most other communities, the structure of Leisure World empowers the governing boards to authorize numerous restrictions on behavior within the community. For example, houses can neither be expanded without a permit nor rented for long periods of time. No one under fifty-five years of age is allowed to purchase a home in this community.

I could go on and on listing the freedom-constraining regulations that exist in Leisure World. Have my parents consented to obey these rules? Yes, but not in the sense that they have consented to each and every rule as it is enacted. Rather, they expressly consented to the existing rules of Leisure World when they purchased their home and they also expressly agreed to the governance structure by which the rules would be adminis-

---

[34] See Barnett, *Structure of Liberty*, chapters 12–14 (discussing the nature of polycentric constitutional order).

tered and changed. They agreed to be bound by the outcome of this structure every bit as much as contracting parties agree to be bound by the outcome of private arbitration when such a clause is in their contract.

In Leisure World, then, there is actual unanimous consent to be bound by its rule-making process. Why cannot we say the same thing about other lawmaking authorities? One obvious reason is that our consent is never solicited. Would such a solicitation now be appropriate? Could the town I live in require my consent to the outcome of our municipal lawmaking process before it allows me to reside there? Could the state I live in require such consent before permitting me to move there? Not without encountering the vicious circle of authority or "bootstrapping" problem described in chapter 1.

Unlike the town and state I live in, Leisure World originally purchased and owned all the land on which it is built and sold parcels on condition that the purchaser accept its governance structure. Because of its original ownership, it could rightfully condition the sale of its property on obedience to the governance structure of Leisure World. There is a world of difference between obtaining land rightfully and conditioning its sale on consent to a lawmaking process, and imposing a lawmaking process on a nonconsenting rights holder. It is the difference between real consent and no consent.[35]

But initial ownership and initial consent are not the only morally relevant differences between communities like Leisure World and polities governed by federal, state, and municipal lawmakers. Leisure World and thousands of communities just like it are also distinguished by the low cost of exit that makes this initial consent meaningful. As Frank Knight emphasized, "effective freedom depends upon an alternative open to the non-conforming individual of leaving the group without suffering loss or damage. In fact, freedom is chiefly a matter of 'competition' between groups for members. . . ."[36]

Though Leisure World is fairly large—larger than many small towns— it is a relatively small part of a larger metropolitan area. If you do not like the rule-making system of Leisure World, you can buy a house across the street where the rules and rule-making procedures may be different

---

[35] Though I am not unaware of the serious philosophical issues raised by this paragraph, it would be unduly distracting to parse and pursue them at this point. For example, how do physical resources come justly to be privately owned in the first place, and what conditions can justly be placed on their alienation? However they are resolved, the difference remains: justifying the control over property exercised by persons who obtain title by the consent of previous rightful owners, or by first possession, is a substantially different matter from justifying the claims of some to rule territory belonging to others. For further discussion on the rightful acquisition of property, see Barnett, *Structure of Liberty*, 69–71, 153–54.

[36] Frank H. Knight, *Freedom and Reform* (Indianapolis: Liberty Press, 1982), 416.

and more to your liking. The cost of exit is quite low. By "cost of exit" I refer not only to the financial costs of moving to location A or B, but to the other sacrifices you make by that choice.[37] If you want to live in and enjoy a particular area, if you do not want to abandon your friends, social network, local customs and cuisine, or job, but you dislike the rules or rule-making process in Leisure World, you can buy a home across the street, or up the road a bit. This applies when you make your initial decision of where to live as well as when you continue to remain within the jurisdiction. And it also applies to nongeographic legal jurisdictions.

The jurisdiction of lawmakers over individuals need not be allocated geographically.[38] We can join and consent to the jurisdiction of myriad organizations, each with its own rules and regulations, that stretch around the world and comprise millions of persons. From employers, to professional associations, to health-care organizations, to book clubs, to file-sharing networks on the Internet—each group enjoys the unanimous consent of its members to obey its rules. With nongeographically based jurisdictions the cost of exit is low because members do not have to leave home to join or resign their membership. Members can consent to all sorts of limitations on their freedom. The exact composition of each person's duty to adhere to the various lawmaking powers of others is likely to be as unique as the individual.

It was Lon Fuller who famously contended that these sorts of rule-making activities are as entitled as geographically based legal systems to be called "lawmaking":

> If law is considered as "the enterprise of subjecting human conduct to the governance of rules," then this enterprise is being conducted, not on two or three fronts, but on thousands. Engaged in this enterprise are those who draft and administer rules governing the internal affairs of clubs, churches, schools, labor unions, trade associations, agricultural fairs, and a hundred and one other forms of human association. . . . [T]here are in this country alone "systems of law" numbering in the hundreds of thousands.[39]

What Fuller does not mention is that these myriad legal systems have the moral imprimatur of unanimous consent that large geographically based legal systems necessarily lack.

[37] See Randy E. Barnett, "The Sound of Silence: Default Rules and Contractual Consent," *University of Virginia Law Review* 78 (1992): 821, 902–5 (defending the claim that consent even to immutable rules can be actual when the cost of exit is sufficiently low).

[38] This possibility is greatly elaborated in Barnett, *Structure of Liberty*, chaps. 12–14 (describing a "polycentric" constitutional order).

[39] See Lon L. Fuller, *The Morality of Law*, rev. ed. (New Haven: Yale University Press, 1969), 124–25.

When jurisdiction is based on consent, rather than territory, there is no limit to how large such unanimous consent institutions can become. But when territory defines jurisdiction, size matters. The larger the land area, the higher the cost of exit and thus the less meaningful is "tacit" consent to the jurisdiction of the lawmaking process. Most modern cities are probably too large, but even if they are small enough, states are certainly too large to command meaningful unanimous consent. If these lawmaking authorities are to command a duty of obedience, it must be on some grounds other than the consent of the governed. Of course, when territorially based lawmaking authorities first purchase the land over which they claim jurisdiction, as in the case of Leisure World, we can say that consent by subsequent purchasers or lessors to the jurisdiction of the original owner is both consensual and unanimous.

To be clear, simply lowering the cost of exit is no substitute for the initial title by which a rightful owner can condition continued presence on acceptance of a lawmaking procedure. Even with this initial title, however, were consent-based territories to grow to the size of current jurisdictions, it becomes less clear that consent can be inferred from the unwillingness of persons born therein to incur the cost of exit. To maintain their authority, such consent-based regimes might have to subsidize the exit of those who do not consent. In the real world, however, the need to raise the funds to make initial purchases of land (without the benefit of the power of eminent domain) will naturally limit the size of such jurisdictional claims and keep the cost of exit within reason.

Contrary to conventional wisdom, then, unanimous consent to obey the law is quite possible, but only if the cost of exit is sufficiently small, either because jurisdiction is not territorially based or because the territory is not too large. Where such unanimous consent exists, legal regulations can cover virtually any subject provided they do not infringe upon inalienable rights or upon the rights of third parties. This is true because persons may consent to alienate or waive many of their rights. The difference between a prizefight and battery, between making love and rape, is consent.

Thus, under conditions of unanimous consent, then, *liberty is not inconsistent with both heavy regulation and even the prohibition of otherwise rightful conduct.* Ironically, with a governance structure based on unanimous consent, there may be far *less* freedom of action than in its absence.[40] To the extent that such communitarian constraints on freedom are desirable, this is the context in which they are permissible.

---

[40] It is precisely because persons may consent to alienate many of their rights that the concept of popular sovereignty is so dangerous; for it empowers a majority of the people— or even more dangerously a majority of a mere handful of elected representatives—to consent for everyone.

Less Consent, More Freedom

Only when lawmaking authority is imposed over a relatively large geographic territory does unanimous consent become impractical. Can such jurisdiction ever be legitimate in the absence of consent and, if so, under what conditions? The answer begins with understanding why consent legitimates lawmaking. Consent legitimates lawmaking only on the assumption that "[i]ndividuals have rights and there are things no person or group can do to them (without violating their rights)."[41] Nor is this merely an assumption. In the next chapter, I summarize the reasons why the existence of individual rights is an appropriate conclusion from the nature of human beings and the world in which we live.

Moreover, we shall see that this conclusion was accepted by the framers of the U.S. Constitution as well as by those who wrote the Fourteenth Amendment. Historically, the rights that people had independent of government were called "inherent" or "natural rights" and I shall explain the meaning of these terms. Today, they are often referred to as "human rights" or "background rights."

One need not accept any particular formulation of background rights, however, to accept the conception of constitutional legitimacy advanced here. For present purposes, it is necessary to note only that for consent to legitimize a lawmaking process, we must presuppose that consent matters—that people have a right to consent and, by necessary implication, they also have a right to withhold their consent. Otherwise consent would not be required and could not impart legitimacy.

For consent to matter in the first instance, we must assume (and there is good reason to conclude) that "first come rights, and then comes law" or "first come rights, then comes government." And this proposition, once accepted, helps explain how lawmaking can be legitimate in the absence of consent. For a law is *just*, and therefore binding in conscience, if its restrictions are (1) *necessary* to protect the rights of others and (2) *proper* insofar as they do not violate the preexisting rights of the persons on whom they are imposed.

The second of these requirements dispenses with the need to obtain the consent of the person on whom a law is imposed. After all, if a law has not violated a person's rights (whatever these rights may be), then that person need not consent to it. The first requirement supplies the element of obligation. If a law is necessary to protect the rights of others (again, whatever these rights may be), then it is as obligatory for the person on whom it is imposed as protecting that person's rights is obligatory on the

---

[41] Nozick, *Anarchy, State and Utopia*, ix.

legal system itself.[42] Persons have an obligation to obey such a law just as they have an obligation to respect the rights of others. While the protection of rights is not the only function performed by a government, it is the only function that—on this account of legitimacy—justifies restricting personal freedom in the absence of the actual consent of the individual. To be proper, other functions must be performed in other ways.

We have, then, reached an ironic conclusion: With unanimous consent, there can be many more legitimate restrictions on freedom than when consent is absent. Because people may consent to almost anything, they have the liberty to consent to laws that greatly restrict their freedom. In the absence of actual consent, however, their liberty remains intact and must not be infringed.

In sum, though actual consent can justify restrictions on freedom, without actual consent, liberty must be strictly protected. Therefore, when we move outside a community constituted by unanimous consent, every freedom-restricting law must be scrutinized to see if it is necessary to protect the rights of others without improperly violating the rights of those whose freedom is being restricted. In the absence of actual consent, a *legitimate* lawmaking process is one that provides adequate assurances that the laws it validates are *just* in this respect. If a lawmaking process provides these assurances, then it is "legitimate" and the commands it issues are entitled to a benefit of the doubt. They are binding in conscience unless shown to be unjust.

CLARIFICATIONS AND CAVEATS

This theory of constitutional legitimacy is susceptible to being misunderstood in several ways. To avoid this, I should emphasize precisely what I am claiming as well as the limits of this claim.

Beyond Respecting and Protecting Rights

At this juncture, I am only offering a justification for a duty of obedience in the absence of consent, a justification that extends only to laws that are both necessary to protect the rights of others and proper insofar as they do not violate the rights of the persons whose freedom they restrict. I do not claim that this argument on behalf of this limited duty of obedi-

---

[42] This is true as well when government is regulating or restricting the use of its own property. In such cases the rights it is protecting are its own, though it might be wise to put restrictions on how government may use or restrict use upon its own property.

ence also provides an affirmative argument against any other source of nonconsensual legitimacy that might broaden a moral duty of obedience.

In other words, *this* particular justification for a nonconsensual duty of obedience extends only so far and no farther. Readers who want more than this from lawmaking might wish to consider the protection of rights a baseline by which to assess legitimacy. That is, a legitimate legal system is one that provides assurances that its liberty-restricting commands are necessary to protect the rights of others and do not improperly violate the rights of those on whom they are imposed. Whether a legal system that does more (or less) than this is also legitimate is an open question that requires additional analysis and justification.

Although my argument does not rule out other potential justifications of nonconsensual duties of obedience, those who claim that a person's freedom may be restricted for ends other than the protection of rights must justify this further extension of power. In chapter 1, we saw the weaknesses of arguments based on tacit consent and benefits received. Elsewhere I have explored the surprising weaknesses of arguments based on retributive and distributive justice.[43]

Even without additional justification, however, the theory of constitutional legitimacy advanced here does not rule out more ambitious impositions of duties on persons than the protection of rights. On this account, there are not one but two sources of binding laws: laws that are produced by unanimous consent regimes, and laws that are produced by regimes whose legitimacy rests solely on their procedural assurances that the rights of the nonconsenting persons on whom they are imposed have been protected. Whatever additional types of laws and regulations beyond the protection of rights are thought desirable can usually be obtained within unanimous consent communities that, as we have seen, are both possible and pervasive.

Like Leisure World, academic and religious communities, for example, impose a wide variety of additional duties on their members. Those who insist that geographical nonconsent-based lawmaking is necessary because unanimous consent to lawmaking is impossible are simply in error. That which already exists is clearly possible. And those who contend that these unanimous consent communities are somehow inadequate must justify, not merely assert, their claim. In so doing, they must be careful to show why the same deficiencies do not apply as well to nonconsensual territorially based legal systems—especially in a world where a diversity of such systems compete with one another and no one legal system can ensure the "right outcome" in all the others.

---

[43] See Barnett, *Structure of Liberty*, 308–21.

Still, depending on the view of rights we adopt, even unanimous consent regimes may be subject to some limit to the duties they can legitimately impose. If there are some rights that cannot be waived or transferred even by the consent of the right-holder, then even unanimous consent regimes, to be legitimate, must offer procedural assurances that these inalienable rights have been protected. Inalienable rights are those that can be reclaimed, even after they are waived by a right-holder.[44] For example, though one can consent to fight in a ring or to have sexual relations with another person, the inalienable nature of the right to one's own person entails that one can always change one's mind and refuse to continue. On this account of inalienable rights, the most important procedural feature that even unanimous consent regimes must respect would be the preservation of a perpetual right to exit the regime.

This last point also highlights the relationship between the theory of legitimacy defended here and the theory of justice upon which the legitimacy of any particular legal system depends. Such a right of exit is not a feature of the concept of constitutional legitimacy defended here. Rather, it is procedure that would protect against the violation of certain inalienable rights. One can accept the procedural conception of legitimacy advanced here without concurring on a particular theory of justice, but determining which procedures are needed to ensure that laws promulgated by a particular legal system are not unjust will depend on the conception of justice one holds.

The Meaning of "Necessary and Proper"

I have borrowed the standard of "necessary and proper" from the Constitution itself. Article I grants Congress the power to "make all laws which shall be necessary and proper for carrying into execution" the other powers that are vested by the Constitution in the national government. I am not claiming that the original meaning of this clause is identical to the meaning I contend is the prerequisite of constitutional legitimacy. I will discuss the original meaning of this clause at length in chapter 6. Two differences are immediately apparent.

The Necessary and Proper Clause requires that laws be necessary to the execution of any power delegated to the national government by the Constitution, not just the power to protect the rights of others. In this respect, the clause is broader or more permissive. Part of the reason for this is that the government is charged with performing many functions the performance of which does not require the restriction of personal freedom.

[44] See, generally, Terrence McConnell, *Inalienable Rights* (New York: Oxford University Press, 2000), 3–44.

On the other hand, under the Constitution propriety includes not only the protection of individual rights but also an adherence to principles of federalism and separation of powers. In this respect, the clause is narrower or less permissive. A law that violates principles of federalism may be improper even though it does not infringe upon the rights of individuals.

The Meaning of "Legitimacy"

"Legitimacy" is often used to refer to whether a particular legal regime is accepted by the public or some substantial portion thereof. While popular acceptance may be essential to establishing a constitution as positive law, I am concerned here with whether this perception is warranted and a constitution or legal regime *ought* to be accepted. The concept of legitimacy I am describing is therefore normative, not descriptive.

By "legitimacy," I am not referring to whether a particular law is "valid" because it was enacted according to the accepted legal process. For example, the Constitution specifies that to be valid a law must be enacted by majorities of both houses of Congress and signed by the president. Nor do I equate the legitimacy of a law with its propriety or "justice"—though these two concepts are closely related—or with the perception that a particular law is proper or just. Rather, the concept of legitimacy employed here refers to whether a validly enacted law merits the benefit of the doubt and a prima facie duty of obedience.

According to my usage, a valid law could be illegitimate and a legitimate law could be unjust. A law may be "valid" because it was produced in accordance with all procedures required by a particular lawmaking system, but be "illegitimate" because these procedures were inadequate to provide assurances that a law is just. Such a law would not be binding in conscience. A law might be "legitimate" because it was produced according to procedures that assure that it is just, and yet be "unjust" because in this case the procedures (which can never be perfect) have failed. Such a law would be binding in conscience unless its injustice is somehow established.

In the absence of actual consent, a legitimate lawmaking process is one that provides adequate assurances that the laws it validates are just. If a lawmaking process provides these assurances, then it is "legitimate" and the commands it issues are entitled to a benefit of the doubt. They are binding in conscience unless shown to be unjust. To evaluate the legitimacy of any given constitution requires reference to a particular conception of justice. By the same token, to apply this conception of legitimacy to a given legal system requires a particular conception of legal validity to identify the positive laws that the system is actually imposing on nonconsenting citizens. But the conception of legitimacy is itself independent of any particular conceptions of either justice or validity one adopts.

The Meaning of "Law"

Some "positivist" philosophers of law rightly deny that the commands issued by the duly constituted authority necessarily create a duty of obedience. For example, according to Joseph Raz, "there is no obligation to obey the law. . . . [T]here is not even a prima facie obligation to obey it. . . . [T]here is no obligation to obey the law even in a good society whose legal system is just."[45] The claim is not that laws should be disobeyed, but that it is the rightness or justice of the law, rather than its legality, that creates a duty to conform to legal commands. The fact that such commands are legal or valid adds nothing to their obligatoriness. As Robin West has written: "If we wish to make our laws just, we must first see that many of our laws are unjust, and if we are to understand that simple truth, we must understand that the *legality* of those norms implies nothing about their justice."[46]

There is much to recommend this argument. If many laws are unjust, it is also true that the legality *simpliciter* of those norms tells us nothing about their justice. And, if this is true, then it follows that the mere fact that an edict is legal tells us nothing about whether there is a moral duty to obey its dictates. Yet, even if this claim is true as a conceptual matter—as it might well be—it is misleading, for it neglects the empirical fact that people almost uniformly believe that because a norm is legal, it creates at least a prima facie duty of obedience. After all, most people do not think every citizen ought to obey only those laws that he or she concludes are just. Perhaps this is why almost everyone goes with the legal flow and condemns lawbreakers for breaking the law without ever scrutinizing the justice of the law that was violated.

When this is the common perception of "the law," it cannot be the case that "the legality of those norms implies nothing about their justice." Or perhaps more accurately, regardless of how philosophers may use the term "law," we cannot be satisfied with so value-neutral a process of legality in a society in which "law" is such a value-laden term. Without lawmaking procedures that ensure the justice of enacted laws, lawmakers in a society that believes legal norms to be binding in conscience will get a powerful benefit of the doubt—"halo-effect"—to which they are not entitled. Unless we demand a lawmaking process in which the legality of a norm *does* imply something about its justice, we will have failed to achieve the objective of having a system of law creation, dissemination, and enforce-

[45] See e.g., Joseph Raz, *The Authority of Law: Essays on Law and Morality* (Oxford: Clarendon Press, 1979), 233.

[46] Robin West, "Natural Law Ambiguities," *Connecticut Law Review* 25 (1992): 831.

ment that creates a prima facie moral duty of obedience in the citizenry—where, in short, the widespread perception of legitimacy is warranted.

We can reach this same conclusion from a somewhat different direction by distinguishing between "producers" and "consumers" of legal commands. In our (and I would contend every) legal culture, those who produce laws implicitly claim that citizens have a duty to obey lawful commands. By the same token, in most cultures, law-consumers accept this claim of the law-producers. To the extent that this claim is both made and accepted, there is an implied warranty of merchantability that accompanies every lawful command. Just as the grocer selling sausages implicitly warrants that the sausages are wholesome and fit for human consumption,[47] the purveyors of lawful commands implicitly warrant that their commands are not unjust and, by virtue of their necessity and propriety, these commands create in the citizen a duty of obedience.

This implied warranty of merchantability could be disclaimed, for example, by an explicit statement that there is no moral obligation to obey a particular enactment. The fact that this disclaimer is never issued, however, conveys to the public the intent to warrant the merchantability of lawful commands. It may be true, as Otto von Bismarck is reported to have said, that it is better not to know how either sausages or laws are made. If, however, we are to eat the one and obey the other, then *someone* had better inquire as to the adequacy of the respective production processes. If each consumer has a moral duty to obey lawful commands without questioning each and every one (as people generally believe and as lawmakers want them to believe), then those who produce the laws and who implicitly warrant their merchantability have a corresponding duty to put adequate quality-control mechanisms in place to ensure the wholesomeness of the commands they purvey.

Therefore, although a "valid" law may be "unjust," as the positivists insist, the theory of legitimacy I am proposing here links the process that determines legal validity to the requirements of justice. Although a constitutional process by which legal validity is determined need not (as a conceptual matter) take justice into account, to be legitimate a lawmaking process ought (as a normative matter) to do so.[48] The problem of legiti-

---

[47] See UCC § 2–314(1) (Philadelphia: American Law Institute, 1990): "Unless excluded or modified . . . , a warranty that the goods shall be merchantable is implied in a contract for their sale if the seller is a merchant with respect to goods of that kind. Under this section the serving for value of food or drink to be consumed either on the premises or elsewhere is a sale."

[48] To the extent the issue is thought to be conceptual as opposed to normative, the traditional natural law–positivist debate is sterile. Even Aquinas was quite capable of distinguishing as a conceptual matter between those human laws that were just and those that were unjust when he declared that ". . . Laws framed by man are either just or unjust." Thomas

macy, therefore, is to establish why anyone should care what a constitutionally valid law may command. My answer is that we should care and, consequently, may owe a prima facie duty to obey a law, only if the processes used to enact laws provide good reasons to think that a law restricting freedom is necessary to protect the rights of others without improperly infringing the rights of those whose liberty is being restricted.

This part of my analysis can be summarized as follows: If lawmakers claim that people have a prima facie moral duty to obey legal commands, and if it is desirable that people accord laws the benefit of the doubt (albeit within limits), then the system that produces these legal commands must have the requisite institutional quality to justify this favorable presumption. To promulgate enactments without taking steps to ensure their necessity and propriety, and to call these enactments "laws" knowing that orders so labeled enjoy a benefit of the doubt, is to promise one thing while delivering another. Therefore, if the term "lawful" or "law" is to carry the implication that there is a moral duty to obey, then the requisite binding *quality must go in before the name "law" goes on.*

As we have already seen, this quality depends upon the presence or absence of consent. When consent is present, a lawful command can restrict almost any freedom except an inalienable right or the freedom to respect the rights of others. When consent is lacking, however, a law must be both necessary to the protection of the rights of others and proper insofar as it does not violate the rights of those upon whom it is imposed if it is to bind in conscience. And a legitimate lawmaking process provides an assurance that both these requirements have been met.

This makes legitimacy a matter of degree rather than an all-or-nothing-at-all characteristic. Above whatever threshold makes a law more likely than not to be just, the more effectively procedures ensure that valid laws are just, the greater the presumption to be accorded those laws that are enacted. The more confidence we have in enacted laws, the more skeptical we can be about a claim that a particular law is unjust.

By acknowledging that, above a threshold, constitutional legitimacy is a matter of degree, the theory I am proposing does not always provide a clean answer to the question of whether a particular lawmaking process, taken as a whole, is sufficient to provide enacted legislation with the benefit of the doubt. But it does confront the question that others neglect and

---

Aquinas, *Summa Theologica*, trans. Fathers of the English Dominican Province, *Great Books of the Western World*, vol. 20 (Chicago: Encyclopedia Britannica, 1952), 233. Rather, for Aquinas and other natural law thinkers, the issue of lawfulness is not conceptual, as it is for modern positivists, but normative. Only just laws "have the power of binding in conscience . . ." (ibid.). It is this issue of "binding in conscience" that informs his endorsement of Augustine's statement that " 'that which is not just seems to be no law at all;' therefore the *force* of a law depends on the extent of its justice" (ibid., 227; emphasis added).

answers it by positing something real, not fictitious, we should be looking for: procedures that assure that enacted legislation does not violate the rights retained by the people. And it also allows us to conclude that some constitutions are more legitimate than others.

CONCLUSION

As I have tried to make clear, you need not agree with the framers' or my account of justice or natural rights to accept the theory of constitutional legitimacy advanced in this chapter. We can agree that, when consent is lacking, a constitution is legitimate only when it provides sufficient procedures to assure that the laws enacted pursuant to its procedures are just.[49] At the same time, we can disagree about what it is that makes a law just and, for that matter, what procedures are sufficient for assuring that laws are likely to be just in the relevant sense. This is no different from theorists who agree that the "consent of the governed" legitimates a constitution but disagree about what constitutes such consent and whether it exists in a particular case.

My claim to this point is only that (a) anything short of actual consent, without something more, cannot bind a nonconsenting party; (b) the U.S. Constitution is legitimated neither by actual consent of the governed nor by receipt of benefits; and (c) in the absence of actual unanimous consent, to be legitimate a constitution must provide sufficient procedural assurances that, whatever makes a law just and therefore binding in conscience, this quality has gone in before the name law goes on a particular command. However, to apply this conception of legitimacy to the U.S. Constitution does require a conception of justice against which the effectiveness of the lawmaking procedures it establishes can be assessed. I now turn my attention to the theory held by those who wrote and ratified the Constitution and which, as we shall see, they incorporated therein.

---

[49] Compare Rawls, *A Theory of Justice*, 353 ("[I]n the constitutional convention the aim of the parties is to find among the just constitutions . . . the one most likely to lead to just and effective legislation in view of the general facts about the society in question. The constitution is regarded as a just but imperfect procedure framed as far as circumstances permit to insure a just outcome").

CHAPTER THREE

Natural Rights as Liberty Rights: Retained Rights, Privileges, or Immunities

> [I]t would not only be useless, but dangerous, to enumerate a number of rights which are not intended to be given up; because it would be implying, in the strongest manner, that every right not included in the exception might be impaired by the government without usurpation; and it would be impossible to enumerate every one. Let any one make what collection or enumeration of rights he pleases, I will immediately mention twenty or thirty more rights not contained in it.[1]
>
> —JAMES IREDELL (1788)

WE HAVE SEEN how the argument from popular sovereignty or consent of the governed fails to legitimate legal commands in the absence of unanimous consent. These commands would nevertheless carry with them a duty of obedience, even without consent, if there is a procedural assurance that they do not violate the rights of the persons on whom they are imposed and that their requirements are necessary to protect the rights of others. But what are these rights?

In this chapter, I shall consider the conception of rights held by the people who wrote and adopted the original Constitution and also by those who wrote and adopted the Fourteenth Amendment. The relevance of this information to my overall thesis is as follows: If (a) the framers held certain views of rights, (b) their conception of rights was correct, and (c) they incorporated effective procedural protections of these rights into the Constitution, then the laws that are produced by this constitutional process will be binding in conscience.[2]

The first step in this analysis is to determine the founding generation's views of rights. We shall see that they viewed natural rights as liberty rights—a concept of rights that, paradoxically, is both limited and limitless—and that they incorporated this view of rights into the text of the

---

[1] Elliot, *Debates*, 167 (James Iredell, North Carolina ratifying convention, Tuesday, July 29, 1788).

[2] Under the analysis of the previous chapter, it is open to someone to contend that the Constitution is legitimate because it provides effective procedural protections of rights other than those to which the founders adhered, but that is not the thesis I shall develop.

Constitution. I have defended these rights elsewhere and shall briefly summarize my arguments at the end of this chapter. The final issue—the procedural protections of these rights that are incorporated into the constitutional scheme—will occupy most of the rest of this book and will encompass issues of interpretive methodology, judicial review, and the proper interpretation and construction of particular substantive provisions of the text.

THE HISTORICAL UNDERSTANDING OF NATURAL RIGHTS

The founding generation universally believed that enactments should not violate the inherent or "natural" rights of those to whom they are directed. This is not to say that universal agreement existed about the precise content of these rights, though I believe there was considerable consensus about such rights in the abstract. Nor did everyone agree about the remedy that was appropriate for their violation. Still, the basic concept of natural rights was clear: Natural or inherent rights were the rights persons have independent of those they are granted by government and by which the justice or propriety of governmental commands are to be judged. To understand how the recognition of natural rights enhances legitimacy, we must be more specific about the sort of rights they are. As we shall see, they are the rights that define liberty, as opposed to license.

The Rights Retained by the People

The founding generation's commitment to natural rights is expressed in the Constitution itself. The Ninth Amendment to the Constitution reads: "The enumeration in the constitution of certain rights shall not be construed to deny or disparage *others retained* by the people."[3] When explaining to the House the nature of the various rights contained in the amendments he proposed be made to the Constitution, James Madison stated that "[i]n [some] instances, they specify rights which are *retained* when particular powers are given up to be exercised by the Legislature."[4] Madison's notes for this part of his speech read: "Contents of Bill of Rhts. . . . 3. Natural rights retained as speach."[5] In other words, for Madi-

---

[3] U.S. Const., Amend. IX (emphasis added).

[4] Joseph Gales and William Seaton, eds., *The Debates and Proceedings in the Congress of the United States*, vol. 1 (Washington, D.C.: Gales and Seaton, 1834) [hereinafter *Annals*], 454 (statement of Rep. Madison) (emphasis added).

[5] "Madison's Notes for Amendments Speech 1789," in Randy E. Barnett, ed., *The Rights Retained by the People: The History and Meaning of the Ninth Amendment* (Fairfax, Va.: George Mason University Press, 1989), 64. The next type of rights mentioned both in his

son even some of the rights enumerated in the Bill of Rights, such as the freedom of speech, were natural "retained" rights.

Additional evidence that the term "retained" rights referred to natural rights can be found in the deliberations of the select committee that the House of Representatives appointed to draft amendments to the Constitution and on which Madison served. A draft bill of rights authored by fellow select committee member Representative Roger Sherman was found in the 1980s among Madison's papers. Sherman's second amendment read as follows:

> The people have certain *natural rights* which are *retained* by them when they enter into Society, Such are the rights of Conscience in matters of religion; of acquiring property, and of pursuing happiness & Safety; of Speaking, writing and publishing their Sentiments with decency and freedom; of peaceably assembling to consult their common good, and of applying to Government by petition or remonstrance for redress of grievances. Of these rights therefore they Shall not be deprived by the Government of the united States.[6]

Along the same lines, Madison proposed to Congress that the following be added as a prefix to the Constitution: "The Government is instituted and ought to be exercised for the benefit of the people; which consists of the enjoyment of life and liberty, with the right of acquiring and using property, and generally pursuing and obtaining happiness and safety."[7]

Indeed, the evidence both that the founding generation were committed to natural rights, and that this commitment is reflected in the words of the Ninth Amendment, is so overwhelming that few deny it. Instead, the argument is made that the only natural rights that may be protected by courts are those that were specifically enumerated in the Constitution. The issue of judicial review based on unenumerated rights is one to which I shall return more than once in the course of this book. For the moment, however, I wish to examine why the framers did not include a complete list of natural rights in the Constitution. The simple reason is that they thought it would be impossible do so. Understanding why will help to illuminate the nature of the rights "retained by the people."

When opponents to the proposed constitution objected that it lacked a bill of rights, defenders argued vociferously that any effort to enumerate rights would be dangerous because the rights of the people were literally

---

speech as delivered and in his notes is "positive rights, which may result from the nature of the compact. Trial by jury cannot be considered as a natural right, but a right resulting from a social compact which regulates the action of the community, but is as essential to secure the liberty of the people as any one of the pre-existent rights of nature" (*Annals*, 1:454).

[6] "Roger Sherman's Draft of the Bill of Rights," in Barnett, *Rights Retained*, 351 (emphasis added).

[7] *Annals*, 1:451.

boundless. James Wilson, a member of the Constitutional Convention and the first professor of law at the University of Pennsylvania, was an ardent adherent of natural rights. In his lectures on jurisprudence delivered between 1790 and 1792, he explicitly rejected the views of both Edmund Burke and William Blackstone and contended instead that "Government, in my humble opinion, should be formed to secure and to enlarge the exercise of the natural rights of its members; and every government, which has not this in view, as its principal object, is not a government of the legitimate kind."[8] Nor for Wilson were these mere "theoretical" or "philosophical" rights with no real bite:

> I go farther; and now proceed to show, that in peculiar instances, in which those rights can receive neither protection nor reparation from civil government, they are, notwithstanding its institution, entitled still to that defence, and to those methods of recovery, which are justified and demanded in a state of nature. The defence of one's self, justly called the primary law of nature, is not, nor can it be abrogated by any regulation of municipal law.[9]

Nevertheless, when defending the Constitution against those who complained about the absence of a bill of rights, Wilson explained, "there are very few who understand the whole of these rights."[10] None of the classical natural rights theorists, he said, claim to provide "a complete enumeration of rights appertaining to the people as men and as citizens. . . . Enumerate all the rights of men! I am sure, sir, that no gentleman in the late Convention would have attempted such a thing."[11] And before the Pennsylvania ratification convention, Wilson observed:

> In all societies, there are many powers and rights, which cannot be particularly enumerated. A bill of rights annexed to a constitution is an enumeration of the powers reserved. If we attempt an enumeration, everything that is not enumerated is presumed to be given. The consequence is, that an imperfect enumeration would throw all implied power into the scale of the government; and the rights of the people would be rendered incomplete.[12]

---

[8] James Wilson, "Of the Natural Rights of Individuals," in *The Works of James Wilson*, vol. 2, ed. J. D. Andrews (Chicago: Callaghan and Company, 1896), 307.

[9] Ibid., 335 (citations omitted). Wilson's lectures also undermine the claim that by the time of the Constitution, Americans had lost their Lockean and revolutionary ardor for natural rights in favor of a more conservative Blackstonian positivism that favored legislative supremacy.

[10] Elliot, *Debates*, 454 (remarks of James Wilson).

[11] Ibid.

[12] Merrill Jensen, ed., *The Documentary History of the Ratification of the Constitution*, vol. 2 (Stevens Point, Wis.: Worzalla Publishing, 1976), 388 (statement of James Wilson to the Pennsylvania ratifying convention, November 28, 1787).

The same argument was made by Charles Pinckney in the South Carolina House of Representatives:

> [W]e had no bill of rights inserted in our Constitution: for, as we might perhaps have omitted the enumeration of some of our rights, it might hereafter be said we had delegated to the general government a power to take away such of our rights as we had not enumerated.[13]

Recall as well the colorful close of the quotation that heads this chapter, from future Supreme Court Justice James Iredell to the North Carolina ratification convention: "Let any one make what collection or enumeration of rights he pleases, I will immediately mention twenty or thirty more rights not contained in it."[14]

To today's ears, this statement is startling. No matter how long a list of rights anyone might write, Iredell claimed he could add twenty or thirty more. What conception of rights could possibly lead someone of Iredell's stature to make such a claim in so visible a forum? What conception of rights would lead a natural rights theorist like Wilson to deny that anyone in the Constitutional Convention would have presumed to enumerate all the rights retained by the people? And how could people with so expansive a view of rights, and who viewed them as so vitally important, have eventually adopted so short a list as those contained in the Constitution and the Bill of Rights?

One clue is to be found in the examples of natural "retained" rights provided by Roger Sherman in his proposed second amendment: "Such are the rights of Conscience in matters of religion; of acquiring property, and of pursuing happiness & Safety; of Speaking, writing and publishing their Sentiments with decency and freedom; of peaceably assembling to consult their common good, and of applying to Government by petition or remonstrance for redress of grievances." Each of the rights on Sherman's list—which was not intended to be exhaustive ("such are")—are liberties or freedoms to believe or act in certain ways. They are not positive claims on government or on others.

The claim that natural rights are unenumerable and dangerous to enumerate makes complete sense if the term "inherent rights" or "natural rights" is used as a kind of synonym for "liberties" or Liberty (as distinct from license). That the term "natural rights" was synonymous with "liberties" is also exemplified in the official letter to Congress by the members of the Constitutional Convention who wrote that "[i]ndividuals entering into society must give up a share of *liberty* to preserve the rest. . . . It is

---

[13] Elliot, *Debates*, 4:316 (Friday, January 18, 1788).
[14] Ibid., 167 (James Iredell, North Carolina ratifying convention, Tuesday, July 29, 1788).

at all times difficult to draw with precision the line between those *rights* which must be surrendered, and those which may be reserved."[15] Other direct evidence of the interchangeability of (natural) rights and liberties could be produced.[16]

According to this conception, natural rights define a private domain within which persons may do as they please, provided their conduct does not encroach upon the rightful domain of others. As long as their actions remain within this rightful domain, other persons—including persons calling themselves government officials—should not interfere without a compelling justification. Because people have a right to do whatever they please within the boundaries defined by natural rights, this means that the rights retained by the people are limited only by their imagination and could never be completely specified or enumerated.

This conception of rights as open-ended liberties is illustrated by an exchange that occurred during the debate in the House of Representatives over the wording of what eventually became part of the First Amendment. At one juncture in the debate, Representative Theodore Sedgwick criticized the select committee's inclusion of the right of assembly on the grounds that "it is a self-evident, unalienable right which the people possess; it is certainly a thing that never would be called in question; it is derogatory to the dignity of the House to descend to such minutia. . . ."[17] Representative Egbert Benson replied to Sedgwick that "The committee who framed this report proceeded on the principle that these rights belonged to the people; they conceived them to be inherent; and all they meant to provide against was their being infringed by the Government."[18]

Sedgwick's response to Benson is revealing of the conception of natural rights held generally at the time:

> [I]f the committee were governed by that general principle, they might have gone into a very lengthy enumeration of rights; they might have declared that a man should have a right to wear his hat if he pleased; that he might get up when he pleased, and go to bed when he thought proper. . . .[19]

---

[15] Madison, *Notes of Debates*, 627 (emphasis added) (letter of Constitutional Convention to Congress). I shall return to this quotation and its reference to "surrendered" rights in the second section of this chapter.

[16] See, e.g., Elliot, *Debates*, 2:201–2 (Speech of Oliver Wolcott to the Connecticut ratifying convention, Friday, January 18, 1788, discussing whether the proposed Constitution "secures the *liberties* of the people, or whether its tendency be unfavorable to the *rights* of a free people"). Ibid., 311 ("What is government itself but a restraint upon the *natural rights* of the people? What constitution was ever devised that did not operate as a restraint on their *original liberties?*").

[17] *Annals*, 1:759 (statement of Rep. Sedgwick).

[18] Ibid. (statement of Rep. Benson).

[19] Ibid., 759–60 (statement of Rep. Sedgwick).

Notice that Sedgwick was not denying that one did indeed have a natural right to wear one's hat or go to bed when one pleased. To the contrary, he equated these "inherent" rights with the right of assembly, which he characterized as "self-evident" and "unalienable."[20]

Indeed, Representative John Page's reply to Sedgwick both made this equation of liberty rights explicit and showed that there was no disagreement that "inherent" or natural rights was a reference to an open-ended liberty. "[L]et me observe to him," said Page,

> that such rights have been opposed, and a man has been obliged to pull off his hat when he appeared before the face of authority; people have also been prevented from assembling together on their lawful occasions, therefore it is well to guard against such stretches of authority, by inserting the privilege in the declaration of rights.[21]

Sedgwick's point was that the Constitution should not be cluttered with a potentially endless list of trifling rights[22] that "would never be called in[to] question"[23] and were not "intended to be infringed."[24] Sedgwick's argument implicitly assumes that the "self-evident, unalienable," and inherent liberty rights retained by the people are unnumerable because the human imagination is limitless. All the actions one might take with what is rightfully his or hers can never be specified or reduced to a list. It includes the right to wear a hat, to get up when one pleases and go to bed when one thinks proper, to scratch one's nose when it itches (and even when it doesn't), to eat steak when one has a taste for it, or take a sip of Diet Mountain Dew when one is thirsty. Make any list of liberty rights you care to and one can always add twenty or thirty more.

The problem, therefore, with any explicit protection of these liberties is that the liberty of the people can never be completely enumerated or listed. An enumeration of rights is likely to be taken as evidence that the people surrendered up to the general government any liberty that is not on the list. With the inevitable danger created by any limited enumeration of unlimited rights specifically in mind, James Madison devised what became the Ninth Amendment. As he explained to the House when introducing his proposed amendments:

> It has been objected also against a bill of rights, that, by enumerating particular exceptions to the grant of power, it would disparage those rights which were

---

[20] Ibid., 759 (statement of Rep. Sedgwick).

[21] Ibid., 760 (statement of Rep. Page).

[22] For a discussion of the founding generation's view of "trivial rights," see Philip A. Hamburger, "Trivial Rights," *Notre Dame Law Review* 70 (1994): 1.

[23] *Annals*, 1:759 (statement of Rep. Sedgwick).

[24] Ibid., 760 (statement of Rep. Sedgwick).

not placed in that enumeration; and it might follow, by implication, that those rights which were not singled out, were intended to be assigned into the hands of the General Government, and were consequently insecure. This is one of the most plausible arguments I have ever heard urged against the admission of a bill of rights into this system; but I conceive, that it may be guarded against.[25]

That Madison and Sherman spoke of "retained" rights and that this word is used in the Constitution also supports the view that natural rights are liberty rights. For these are rights that people possess *before* they form a government and therefore *retain*; they are not the "positive" rights created by government. To be clear, I am not claiming that all constitutional rights are liberty rights. On the contrary, there are unquestionably positive rights created by the Constitution, and by other laws, and enforceable duties to respect these rights that government owes its citizens. I am claiming only that the natural "rights . . . retained by the people" to which the Ninth Amendment refers are liberty rights.

This was not the last time Madison would have opportunity to discuss the Ninth Amendment on the floor of the House, but we shall wait to examine his next reference to it until chapter 9 when we consider how the Ninth Amendment can best be put into practice to protect the liberty rights to which it refers.

The Privileges or Immunities of Citizens

This conception of natural rights as liberty rights was not abandoned after the founding period. It was held, perhaps even to a greater degree, by the framers of the Fourteenth Amendment. Recall John Page's reference to "privilege" in his discussion of the right of peaceable assembly that became part of the First Amendment. The terms "rights," "liberties," "privileges," and "immunities" were often used interchangeably or in a cluster. This terminology is reflected in what is known as the Privileges or Immunities Clause of the Fourteenth Amendment, adopted in the wake of the Civil War: "No state shall make or enforce any law which shall abridge the privileges or immunities of citizens of the United States."

The Fourteenth Amendment was enacted to ensure the constitutionality of the Civil Rights Bill of 1866 and to prevent future Congresses from reneging on its guarantees.[26] The bill provided federal protections against infringement by state governments of the rights "to make and enforce contracts, to sue, be parties, and give evidence, to inherit, pur-

[25] Ibid., 456 (statement of Rep. Madison).
[26] See Michael Kent Curtis, *No State Shall Abridge: The Fourteenth Amendment and the Bill of Rights* (Durham, N.C.: Duke University Press, 1986), 71–91.

chase, lease, sell, hold, and convey real and personal property, and to full and equal benefit of all laws and proceedings for the security of person and property."[27]

As Michael Kent Curtis has shown, "privileges or immunities" was a common way of referring to "civil rights," which included the legally protected rights one received in return for surrendering to the government the natural right, or "executive power," to enforce one's own rights.

> Both in his prototype and in his final version of the Fourteenth Amendment, [Senator John A.] Bingham used the words *privileges* and *immunities* as a short-hand description of fundamental or constitutional rights. Use of the words in this way had a long and distinguished heritage. Blackstone's *Commentaries on the Laws of England*, published in the colonies on the eve of the Revolution, had divided the rights and liberties of Englishmen into those "immunities" that were *the residuum of natural liberties and those "privileges" that society had provided in lieu of natural rights.*[28]

If the framers of the Fourteenth Amendment meant to protect natural rights—or even civil rights—why did they use the term "privileges or immunities" instead? The short answer is that they did so because, while "privileges or immunities" includes natural rights, it is a broader term that includes additional rights.

To appreciate this, we must begin by considering what was then a controversial interpretation of Article IV, Section 2 of the original Constitution: "The Citizens of each State shall be entitled to all Privileges and Immunities of Citizens in the several States." From the earliest days of the United States some argued that this provision referred to the fundamental or natural rights that belonged to every citizen of the United States. That this was truly the original meaning of the Privileges and Immunities Clause in Article IV has been contested.[29] It is not seriously disputed, however, that some time after ratification it came to be widely insisted by some judges, scholars, and opponents of slavery that Article IV was indeed a reference to natural rights. Nor is it disputed that, whenever it first developed, the members of the Thirty-ninth Congress meant to import this

[27] Act of April 9, 1866, 14 Stat. 27.

[28] See Curtis, *No State Shall Abridge*, 64 (emphasis added).

[29] Compare Chester Antieau, "Paul's Perverted Privileges or the True Meaning of the Privileges and Immunities Clause of Article Four," *William and Mary Law Review* 9 (1967): 5 (contending that the clause referred to natural rights), with David S. Bogen, "The Privileges and Immunities Clause of Article IV," *Case Western Reserve Law Review* 37 (1987): 796 (arguing that the clause was "not a reference to natural law, but was solely concerned with creating a national citizenship"). In accord with Antieau is Michael Conant, "Antimonopoly Tradition under the Ninth and Fourteenth Amendments: Slaughter-House Cases Re-Examined," *Emory Law Journal* 31 (1982): 785.

meaning into the text of the Constitution by using the language of "privileges" and "immunities" in the Fourteenth Amendment.[30]

The antebellum argument that privileges and immunities included natural rights was made famously in 1823 by Justice Bushrod Washington, while sitting as a circuit court trial judge in the case of *Corfield v. Coryell.* Because this language was so often repeated by those seeking to find federal protection of fundamental rights, especially by members of the Thirty-ninth Congress, I present it in full:

> The inquiry is, what are the privileges and immunities of citizens in the several states? We feel no hesitation in confining these expressions to those privileges and immunities which are, in their nature, fundamental; which belong, of right, to the citizens of all free governments; and which have, at all times, been enjoyed by the citizens of the several states which compose this Union, from the time of their becoming free, independent, and sovereign. What these fundamental principles are, it would perhaps be more tedious than difficult to enumerate. They may, however, be all comprehended under the following general heads: Protection by the government; the enjoyment of life and liberty, with the right to acquire and possess property of every kind, and to pursue and obtain happiness and safety; subject nevertheless to such restraints as the government may justly prescribe for the general good of the whole. The right of a citizen of one state to pass through, or to reside in any other state, for purposes of trade, agriculture, professional pursuits, or otherwise; to claim the benefit of the writ of habeas corpus; to institute and maintain actions of any kind in the courts of the state; to take, hold and dispose of property, either real or personal; and an exemption from higher taxes or impositions than are paid by the other citizens of the state; may be mentioned as some of the particular privileges and immunities of citizens, which are clearly embraced by the general description of privileges deemed to be fundamental: to which may be added, the elective franchise, as regulated and established by the laws or constitution of the state in which it is to be exercised. These, and many others which might be mentioned, are, strictly speaking, privileges and immunities, and the enjoyment of them by the citizens of each state, in every other state, was manifestly calculated (to use the expressions of the preamble of the corresponding provision in the old articles

---

[30] This is conceded even by those who deny the original meaning of "privileges and immunities" in Article IV was a reference to natural rights. See Bogen, "The Privileges and Immunities Clause," 843: "This array of arguments [that the clause referred to natural rights] proved persuasive to a generation confronted with the moral breakdown of society represented by slavery. Slavery was constitutional, but contrary to fundamental principles of natural law. The symbolic honor and integrity of the Constitution could be saved by identifying it with fundamental rights. This the framers of the Fourteenth Amendment attempted to do in the privileges and immunities clause of that amendment."

of confederation) "the better to secure and perpetuate mutual friendship and intercourse among the people of the different states of the Union."[31]

While this passage includes reference to what were considered natural or inherent liberty rights, "privileges or immunities" here unquestionably refers also to such positive civil rights as the "protection of government" that one receives in exchange for surrendering one's power of enforcement. As employed by Justice Washington, it is a broader term that also includes other fundamental rights created by state and federal constitutions, such as "the elective franchise, as regulated and established by the laws or constitution of the state in which it is to be exercised."[32]

Chester Antieau observed that "it would be almost impossible to overestimate the importance of the above quotation upon American law."[33] Of greatest relevance, *Corfield* was repeatedly cited by some members of the Thirty-ninth Congress as constitutional justification for their passing the Civil Rights Act of 1866, which provided in Section 1 that

> [S]uch citizens, of every race and color, without regard to any previous condition of slavery . . . shall have the same right, in every State and Territory in the United States, to make and enforce contracts, to sue, be parties, and give evidence, to inherit, purchase, lease, sell, hold, and convey real and personal property, and to full and equal benefit of all laws and proceedings for the security of person and property, as is enjoyed by white citizens. . . .[34]

Most, if not all, of the rights on this list are unenumerated liberty rights of the sort accepted at the founding. That the statute sought to protect blacks by holding states to the protection afforded the rights of whites in no way undermines the fact that most of the "privileges or immunities" protected by this statute were natural liberty rights.

Senator Lyman Trumbell, a former justice of the Illinois Supreme Court, was the principal draftsman of both the Thirteenth Amendment prohibiting involuntary servitude and the Civil Rights Act of 1866. As chairman of the Senate Judiciary Committee, he took the floor of the Senate to argue that Congress had the authority to pass the Civil Rights Act under, among other provisions, the Privileges and Immunities Clause of Article IV: "What rights are secured to the citizens of each State under that provision? Such fundamental rights as belong to every free person."[35]

[31] 6 F. Cas. 546, at 551–52.

[32] Whether the right to vote was among the privileges or immunities protected by the Fourteenth Amendment later became a matter of some controversy. But there is little doubt that the right to a jury trial, though not a natural right, was considered a privilege or immunity of citizenship by the authors of the Fourteenth Amendment.

[33] Antieau, "Paul's Perverted Privileges," 12.

[34] Act of April 9, 1866, 14 Stat. 27.

[35] *Congressional Globe*, 39th Cong., 1st sess., 474.

To establish this interpretation, he cited several judicial opinions and then offered, in its entirety, the quotation from Washington's opinion in *Corfield* that appears above.[36]

In another speech advocating the override of President Johnson's veto of the Civil Rights Act, Trumbell posed the question, ". . . what rights do citizens of the United States have?" He answered, "They are those inherent, fundamental rights which belong to free citizens or free men in all countries, such as the rights enumerated in this bill, and they belong to them in all the States of the Union."[37] As examples of "natural rights" and "inalienable rights" he offered these: "The right of personal security, the right of personal liberty, and the right to acquire and enjoy property."[38]

Along the same lines was the speech by Representative James F. Wilson of Iowa, who was coauthor of the Thirteenth Amendment, manager of the Civil Rights Bill in the House, and chairman of the House Judiciary Committee. Wilson argued that "civil rights are the natural rights of man; and these are the rights which this bill proposes to protect every citizen in the enjoyment of throughout the entire dominion of the Republic."[39] After elaborating at length on these rights, he concluded, "Before our Constitution was formed, the great fundamental rights which I have mentioned, belonged to every person who became a member of our great national family. No one surrendered a jot or tittle of these rights by consenting to the formation of the Government."[40] Without "the power . . . to secure these rights which existed anterior to the ordination of the Constitution," the government would be "a failure in its most important office."[41]

After the Civil Rights Bill was vetoed by President Johnson on the grounds that it exceeded the constitutional powers of Congress, Representative William Lawrence, Republican of Ohio and a former state court judge, rose to advocate overriding that veto. After a lengthy examination of the authorities on behalf of the proposition that "[l]egislative powers exist in our system to protect, not to destroy, the inalienable rights of men,"[42] he concluded that

It has never been deemed necessary to enact in any constitution or law that citizens should have the right to life or liberty or the right to acquire

[36] Ibid., 475.
[37] Ibid., 1757.
[38] Ibid.
[39] Ibid., 1117.
[40] Ibid., 1119.
[41] Ibid.
[42] Ibid., 1832–33.

property. These rights are recognized by the Constitution as existing anterior to and independently of all laws and all constitutions. Without further authority I may assume that there are certain absolute rights which pertain to every citizen, which are inherent, and of which a State cannot constitutionally deprive him.[43]

Lawrence also cited with approval Justice Washington's opinion in *Corfield*, while elaborating that though the "Constitution does not define what these privileges and immunities" in Article IV are, they "are of two kinds, to wit, those which I have shown to be inherent in every citizen of the United States, and such others as may be conferred by local law and pertain only to the citizen of the State."[44] This statement by Representative Lawrence confirms that "privileges or immunities" was a reference both to inherent or natural rights and to various rights or privileges created by the positive law of particular governments.

Even more important to understanding the original meaning of the term "privileges or immunities" were the explanations later offered by members of Congress when discussing the Fourteenth Amendment. After reading the same quotation from Justice Washington's opinion in *Corfield*, Senator Jacob Howard, Republican and former attorney general of Michigan, stated: "Such is the character of the privileges and immunities spoken of in the second section of the fourth article of the Constitution."[45] He then continued: "To these privileges and immunities, whatever they may be—for they are not and cannot be fully defined in their entire extent and precise nature—to these should be added the personal rights guaranteed and secured by the first eight amendments of the Constitution."[46]

After listing these rights,[47] Howard noted the fact that courts had rejected the abolitionist argument that the Privileges and Immunities Clause of Article IV protected the rights of citizens from infringement by state governments.

[I]t is a fact well worthy of attention that the course of decision of our courts and the present settled doctrine is, that all these immunities, privileges, rights, thus guaranteed by the Constitution or recognized by it, are secured to the citizens solely as a citizen of the United States and as a party in their courts. They do not operate in the slightest degree as a restraint or prohibition upon State legislation. States are not affected by them. . . .[48]

[43] Ibid., 1833.
[44] Ibid., 1836.
[45] Ibid., 2765
[46] Ibid.
[47] Including the "personal" right "to keep and bear arms." Ibid.
[48] Ibid.

Thus the need for the Privileges or Immunities Clause of the Fourteenth Amendment:

> Now, sir, there is no power given in the Constitution to enforce and to carry out any of these guarantees . . . but they stand simply as a bill of rights in the Constitution, without power on the part of Congress to give them full effect; while at the same time the States are not restrained from violating the principles embraced in them except by their own local constitutions, which may be altered from year to year. *The great object of the first section of this amendment is, therefore, to restrain the power of the States and compel them at all times to respect these great fundamental guarantees.*[49]

The same sentiment was expressed by Congressman Frederick Wood-bridge, Republican of Vermont. The "object of the proposed amendment," he said, was to give "the power to Congress to enact those laws which will give to a citizen of the United States *the natural rights which necessarily pertain to citizenship*," or, in other words, "those privileges and immunities which are guaranteed to him under the Constitution of the United States."[50] That this represented a substantial change in the relationship between state and federal governments is difficult to overemphasize.

I have seen little in the historical record to suggest exactly how the rights "retained by the people" referred to in the Ninth Amendment compared with the "privileges or immunities" protected by the Fourteenth. The natural implication is that because both phrases originally referred to background, natural, or inherent rights, both provisions refer to the same set of unenumerable rights though they differ on the jurisdiction created for the protection of these rights. Just as the Fourteenth Amendment extended protection of the enumerated rights of the first eight amendments to violations by state governments, so too did it extend federal protection of the preexisting unenumerated rights "retained by the people." The quotations from Justice Washington and others suggest that "privileges or immunities" is a broader term including both natural or inherent rights as well as those particular "positive" procedural rights created by the Bill of Rights.

This was the view held by Ohio Senator John Sherman, a Republican member of the Thirty-ninth Congress and future secretary of state who, some years after the ratification of the Fourteenth Amendment, pointed to the Ninth Amendment as evidencing the existence of "other rights beyond those recognized"[51] in the Bill of Rights. Speaking to the Senate in 1872

---

[49] Ibid., 1265–66 (emphasis added).
[50] Ibid., 1088 (emphasis added).
[51] *Congressional Globe*, 42d Cong., 2d sess., Appendix, 26.

in support of a civil rights bill to guarantee blacks and other citizens equal access to public accommodations—rights nowhere mentioned in the Constitution—Sherman contended:

> [T]he ordinary rights of citizenship, which no law has ever attempted to define exactly, the privileges, immunities, and rights, (because I do not distinguish between them, and cannot do it,) of citizens of the United States, such as are recognized by the common law, such as are ingrafted in the great charters of England, some of them in the constitutions of different States, and some of them in the Declaration of Independence, our fathers did not attempt to enumerate. They expressly said in the ninth amendment that they would not attempt to enumerate these rights; they were innumerable, depending upon the laws and the courts as from time to time administered.[52]

Sherman conceded that "[t]here may be sometimes great dispute and doubt as to what is the right, immunity, or privilege conferred upon a citizen of the United States."[53] Nevertheless, the task of identifying that right must fall "from time to time [to] the judicial tribunals."[54] To determine these rights, immunities, or privileges, judges

> will look first at the Constitution of the United States as the primary fountain of authority. If that does not define the right they will look for the unenumerated powers to the Declaration of American Independence, to every scrap of American history, to the history of England, to the common law of England, the old decisions of Lords Mansfield and Holt, and so on back to the earliest recorded decisions of the common law. There they will find the fountain and reservoir of the rights of American as well as English citizens.[55]

If the founding generation that adopted the Ninth Amendment and the generation that adopted the Fourteenth Amendment were correct about

---

[52] Ibid., 844.

[53] Ibid.

[54] Ibid.

[55] Ibid. Senator Allen Thurman, an Ohio Democrat and former member of the Ohio Supreme Court, agreed with Sherman that the retained rights referred to in the Ninth Amendment are held by the people "against the Government of the United States by as good a title as they hold them against the world. They belong to them as people or as individuals. They have never surrendered them to any Government, and they do not hold them by the grace of any government whatsoever; they hold them because they were and are their inherent natural rights which have never been surrendered" (ibid., Appendix, 26). Nevertheless, Thurman also contended that these are not rights the people hold "as citizens of the United States, but so to speak, in despite of the United States" (ibid.). Thurmond was also concerned with the indefiniteness of identifying such extratextual rights. "Where are we to find a definition of them?" he asked. "The Senator from Massachusetts finds the definition in the Declaration of Independence; another Senator finds it in something else; and so on to the end of the chapter; and we have nothing certain, nothing definite, nothing upon which any man can rely" (ibid.).

natural rights, then constitutional legitimacy requires a lawmaking process that provides an assurance that the rights retained by the people, or the privileges and immunities of citizens, will not be disparaged, denied, or abridged. Whether such a process includes the direct protection of unenumerated rights by judges, however, is a separate question that we shall consider later in this book.

"SURRENDERING" ONE'S NATURAL RIGHTS

There are those, of course, who admit the founding generation's widespread commitment to natural rights, while diminishing its importance to matters involving the Constitution. They point to statements saying that people give up some of their natural rights when they enter into society and form a government. They also point to laws that restricted freedom as evidence that natural rights were not thought to impose any legal or enforceable constraints on government. Sometimes it is claimed that the professed commitment to natural rights was rhetoric to justify a revolution, but when it came to governance, this rhetoric was muted or abandoned entirely.

There is no question that the founders sometimes spoke of surrendering one's natural rights. They also enacted laws that some, then and now, might think violated natural rights. If, however, we approach these statements and practices with the same sympathy for natural rights that was felt by the founding generation and the framers of the Fourteenth Amendment, we may find that they are reconcilable with a strong commitment to the rights retained by the people.

Surrendering Only a Portion of Our Natural Rights

Let us begin with statements saying that one gives up one's natural rights when one enters into society or when one forms a government. Such statements were surely common. "What is government itself but a restraint upon the natural rights of the people?" rhetorically asked a member of the New York ratification convention. "What constitution was ever devised that did not operate as a restraint on their original liberties?"[56] Robert Barnwell asserted to the South Carolina ratification convention that in "the compacts which unite men into society, it always is necessary to give up a part of our natural rights to secure the remainder."[57]

---

[56] Elliot, *Debates*, 2:311 (New York convention, Wednesday, June 25). Notice, too, that this statement also equates "natural rights" with liberty.

[57] Ibid., 4:295 (South Carolina convention, Thursday, January 17, 1788).

Sometimes these statements may even mean what they appear to say. Then, as now, there is not complete unanimity on any issue if we move beyond abstractions and generalities. But for every statement to this effect there are many more that refer to the natural rights still possessed by the people. This is significant because, when these statements were made, popular governments existed and no one was thought to be in a state of nature.[58]

Typical is the statement by the ratification convention of Virginia that formally accompanied its ratification of the Constitution—a statement also copied and adopted by the ratification conventions of North Carolina and Rhode Island: "That there are certain natural rights, of which men, when they form a social compact, cannot deprive or divest their posterity; among which are the enjoyment of life and liberty, with the means of acquiring, possessing, and protecting property, and pursuing and obtaining happiness and safety."[59] To make sense of natural rights we should not use the aforementioned sorts of statements to discredit statements like these. Rather, we should appeal to a conception of natural rights that reconciles them both; and there is more than one way to reconcile them.

First, most references to giving up one's natural rights when entering into society say, as does Barnwell's, that one surrenders only "a *part* of our natural rights"[60] while retaining others. Only those rights whose alienation is necessary to form a government are yielded. Typical of this idea is the official letter to Congress by the members of the Constitutional Convention (which I cited earlier to illustrate how the word "rights" was synonymous with the word "liberty"):

It is obviously impractical in the federal government of these States to secure all rights of independent sovereignty to each, and yet provide for the interest and safety of all—Individuals entering into society *must give up a share of lib-*

---

[58] For the founding generation, the "state of nature" described the relationship between two or more persons who lack an established, common legal authority. See John Locke, *Two Treatises of Government* (1690), ed. Peter Laslett (Cambridge, Mass.: Mentor, 1963), 370 ("[W]here-ever any two Men are, who have no standing Rule, and common Judge to Appeal to on Earth for the determination of Controversies of Right betwixt them, there they are still *in the state of Nature*, and under all the inconveniences of it"). Therefore, because they were subject to no common law and subject to no common magistrate, princes or heads of state might still be considered in a state of nature with respect to each other. Furthermore, Locke contended that absolute monarchs "however intitled, *Czar*, or *Grand Signior*, or how you please, is as much *in the state of Nature*, with all under his Dominion, as he is with the rest of mankind" (ibid.).

[59] Elliot, *Debates*, 3:657 (Friday, June 27, 1788). Notice how the draft bill of rights by Roger Sherman mirrors this statement except for the use by Sherman of the word "retained," which links this sort of statement to the rights "retained by the people" in the Ninth Amendment.

[60] Elliot, *Debates*, 4:295 (emphasis added).

erty to preserve the rest. The magnitude of the sacrifice must depend as well on situation and circumstance, as on the object to be obtained. It is at all times difficult to draw with precision the line between *those rights which must be surrendered, and those which may be reserved.*[61]

So, for example, taxation by anyone except the government is theft and a violation of one's natural rights. When one forms a government with powers of taxation, one might be seen as giving up one's natural right to the possession and use of property to the degree that some taxation is necessary to pay for government. The same would be true of the power of eminent domain. Your neighbor cannot condemn your land for private use, but the government can take it for public use (provided just compensation is made). One way to handle the problem of government's possessing powers that ordinary citizens lack is to say that, when government is formed, certain rights are "surrendered up."

What supposedly follows from statements about surrendering natural rights is that, despite the fact they are devised to constrain governments, natural rights no longer appear to operate as an effective constraint on government. This conclusion is unwarranted. At the time of the founding, almost no one claimed or believed that one surrenders *all* one's natural rights up to government, but only those that were necessary. One cannot infer, then, from the fact that some natural rights were surrendered up, that other rights still retained by the people can be denied or disparaged with impunity.

Rather, the rights that are retained remain the measure of whether government is acting properly or improperly in the exercise of its delegated powers. As Madison explained to the Constitutional Convention, though the national government was formed to accomplish a variety of objects or ends, first among them was "the necessity of providing more effectually for the security of private rights, and the steady dispensation of Justice. Interferences with these were evils which had more perhaps than any thing else, produced this convention."[62]

Exchanging Natural for Civil Rights

Moreover, as was made clearer in the discussions of natural rights in the Thirty-ninth Congress, to the extent one surrendered one's natural rights, one received "civil rights" in return. The most important power surrendered to government is what Locke and others called "the executive power" and what is sometimes called the "police power." This is the

---

[61] Madison, *Notes of Debates*, 627 (emphasis added) (letter of Constitutional Convention to Congress).

[62] Madison, *Notes of Debates*, 76 (statement of J. Madison).

power to enforce or "police" one's rights when they have been violated by others. Indeed, John Locke argued that it was the "inconvenience" of exercising the executive power in the state of nature that justified the creation of an "impartial magistrate"—that is, government.

The particular problem with individuals retaining the executive power is that they are then the judges in their own cases.

> I easily grant, that *Civil Government* is the proper Remedy for the Inconveniences of the State of Nature, which must certainly be Great, where Men may be Judges in their own Case, since 'tis easily to be imagined, that he who was so unjust as to do his Brother an Injury, will scarce be so just as to condemn himself for it.[63]

When "surrendering" one's executive power to government, however, one receives in return a "civil" right to have one's retained rights protected by the police power now in the hands of the civil government. This civil right to "the protection of the laws" is the root of the Equal Protection Clause of the Fourteenth Amendment that mandates that no state shall "deny to any person within its jurisdiction the equal protection of the laws."[64]

Thus, in return for the surrendered natural right of enforcement, government assumes a positive obligation to protect the unsurrendered rights retained by the people. Those retained rights remain a measure of the propriety of government enforcement, since it is for their protection that the executive power is surrendered in the first instance. As Locke explained:

> The Supream Power cannot take from any Man any part of his Property without his own consent. For the preservation of Property being the end of Government, and that for which Men enter into Society, it necessarily supposes and requires, that the People should *have Property*, without which they must be suppos'd to lose that, by entring into Society, which was the end for which they entered into it, too gross an absurdity for any Man to own. . . . Hence it is a mistake to think, that the Supreme or *Legislative power* of any Commonwealth, can do what it will, and dispose of the Estates of the *Subject arbitrarily*, or take any part of them at pleasure.[65]

But even this account of exchanging natural for civil rights underestimates the role played by natural rights in civil society.

---

[63] Locke, *Two Treatises*, 316–17.

[64] See Steven J. Heyman, "The First Duty of Government: Protection, Liberty and the Fourteenth Amendment," *Duke Law Journal* 41 (1991): 507.

[65] Locke, *Two Treatises*, 406–7.

The Agency Theory of Government

To understand better how delegated governmental powers can be squared with retained rights, those seeking historical context must also take into account the law governing agency relationships or what is still sometimes referred to as the law of "master and servant."[66] The founders were accomplished private lawyers, familiar with eighteenth-century agency law and, not coincidentally, they also often professed their belief in the "agency theory" of government. The idea that government officials are the agents or servants and the people are the principals or masters, however quaint it may seem to political sophisticates today, was widely held. Benjamin Franklin articulated this popular view to the Constitutional Convention: "In free Governments the rulers are the servants, and the people their superiors & sovereigns."[67]

By definition, a principal "surrenders" certain powers to her agent. If I designate you my agent to sell my car, you now are in possession of the power to sell, which formerly only I had possessed. It is even possible that I delegate my exclusive power to sell the car to you and that, by the terms of our agreement, I no longer may rightfully sell the car to a third party. Think of authors who routinely give an exclusive license to a publisher to publish an article or book, which the author may then not republish on his or her own.

Yet, just because certain powers (or rights) are delegated does not entail that the agent is now the master. For, according to agency law, the agent is to exercise those powers only (a) "on behalf of" and (b) "subject to the control of" the master or principal.[68] Of course, the principal does not literally control the behavior of the agent—there would be no advantage to entering into a principal-agent relationship were that the case. Instead, the agent must yield to the control of the principal when the principal exerts it. And even when operating on his own, the agent must always exercise the powers delegated to him "on behalf" of the interests of the principal and can be held responsible for any breach of this fiduciary duty.

It would be more accurate and much neater if we were to speak not of rights delegated to government but only of powers. Unfortunately, lan-

---

[66] The rhetoric of "master/servant" is today limited to doctrines governing employer-employee relationships and primarily when employers are liable for the tortious acts of their employees, as opposed to when agents may bind their principals to contracts. See Harold Gill Reuschlein and William A. Gregory, *The Law of Agency and Partnership*, 2d ed. (St. Paul, Minn.: West, 1990), 102 ("[A] servant is one who works physically for another, subject to the control of that other who is called a master").

[67] Madison, *Notes of Debates*, 371 (statement of B. Franklin).

[68] For a general overview of agency law, see Randy E. Barnett, "Squaring Undisclosed Agency Law with Contract Theory," *California Law Review* 75 (1987): 1969.

guage then, as now, is not always used with precision. Though it must be admitted that statements can be found that speak of alienated "rights" when "powers" would have been the better term, one thing is remarkable: The framers of the Constitution were rigorously consistent in referring to the "powers" of government and the "rights" of the people. The Constitution refers to powers—and only powers—being delegated to government, whereas rights are retained by the people (and powers reserved to them as well). The best theory of this usage is that only powers, not rights, are delegated to government and that all rights are retained by the people as a measure of the propriety of the exercise of governmental power.

Regulating the Exercise of Inalienable Rights

Then there is the matter of "inalienable" rights, that is, rights that cannot be surrendered. How can this concept be squared with statements about surrendering natural rights and the enactment of freedom-constraining laws? One way to understand this is to think of inalienable rights as somehow more fundamental or important than trivial or trifling natural rights, and then posit that, while the latter can be surrendered and restricted, the former cannot. However, this formulation is misleading.

Instead, it is better to say that inalienable rights are more abstract than other specific natural rights or liberties. These inalienable rights can be classified as the rights of several property, freedom of contract, self-defense, first possession, and restitution. Together, these abstract natural rights define a boundary or jurisdictional space within which people should be free to make their own choices.

The specific choices people make within this jurisdictional space are the more particular natural rights or liberties. For example, the abstract and inalienable right to the possession, use, and enjoyment of several property includes the particular right to read a book in one's own house or to go to bed when one wishes, though such specific "trivial" rights are impossible to list and may themselves be alienated. Moreover, my inalienable property rights to the exclusive use and enjoyment of my body do not prevent me from waiving this right by consenting to get in the ring with Muhammad Ali. As was noted in chapter 2, I can exercise my inalienable natural right to freedom of contract and agree to live in a residential community like Leisure World that restricts how I may alter the external appearance of my house and may even restrict ownership to people over a certain age.

It is common to see statements to the effect that one's right to do something is subject to the "laws of the land." For example, while Locke argued that one completely surrendered the executive power to enforce one's rights by punishing one's attacker or extracting reparations from him, he contended that one "gives up" the natural right of self-preservation "to be *regulated* by Laws made by the Society, so far forth as the preservation of himself, and the rest of that Society shall require."[69] Likewise, in *Corfield*, Justice Washington says that "the right to acquire and possess property of every kind, and to pursue and obtain happiness and safety" is "subject nevertheless to such restraints as the government may justly prescribe for the general good of the whole."

Such statements raise the issue of the reasonable regulation of one's natural rights, a subject to which we shall return later in this book. One ought not, however, look to regulations that exist at the time of the founding as evidence of the limits of or nonexistence of natural rights. This would be to employ the modern and euphemistic meaning of "to regulate" as "to prohibit." In contrast, "to regulate" literally means "to make regular." As will be shown in chapter 10, this was (with some exceptions) the general sense in which the term was used in the Constitution. According to this usage, an inalienable right could be retained and its exercise still be regulated by the law of the land.

Assume that there is a natural and inalienable right to possess, use, and dispose of several property. Someone wants to transfer her property rights in a tract of land to her son after her death so she executes a document called a "will." How this document will be interpreted and enforced in a court of law requires the articulation of certain rules or laws governing what constitutes a valid will. Requirements of formality, for example, may be devised specifying the need for two or more witnesses to a signature. Such rules or laws regularize will making. The power to regulate will making in this sense does not, however, include the power to rewrite wills to contradict the demonstrable intent of the testator, nor the power to prohibit the making of wills altogether, nor the power to confiscate a percentage of the decedent's property in estate "taxes."

That the reasonable regulation of natural rights is essential to their efficacious exercise and enforcement in civil society does not entail that these rights are surrendered completely to the government. On the contrary, these rights remain the object and measure of any regulations. That is, the protection and facilitation of everyone's retained rights in civil society is the purpose of any "police" regulation by law, and this object or end is the measure of whether a particular regulation is or is not reasonable.

By this account, some natural rights can be surrendered to government in order to better secure those that are retained. As was said by Samuel Nasson, at the Massachusetts ratification convention: "When I give up any of my natural rights, it is for the security of the rest."[70] But it is better to adopt the terminology of the Constitution itself and speak of (limited)

[69] Locke, *Two Treatises*, 398 (emphasis added).
[70] Elliot, *Debates*, 2:134 (Massachusetts convention, Friday, February 1, 1788).

powers being delegated by the people—or principals or masters—to their servants or agents in government. The rights that are retained provide the measure of how these powers should be exercised. The "police power" to enforce or regulate a retained right is not the power to confiscate, prohibit, infringe, or abridge its exercise.

Locke made a similar point when he claimed that whatever liberty or powers are given up when one enters society are given up

> only with an intention in every one the better to preserve himself and his Liberty and Property; (For no rational Creature can be supposed to change his condition with the intention to be worse) the power of the Society, or *Legislative* constituted by them, *can never be suppos'd to extend farther than the common good*; but is obliged to secure every ones Property by providing against [the] . . . defects . . . that made the State of Nature so unsafe and uneasie.[71]

It is also worth noting that Locke distinguished the two powers that were given up, either entirely (the executive power) or to be regulated by law (the power of self-preservation), from a third species of natural rights that he does not claim a person surrenders either upon entering civil society or upon forming a government. This third species is "the liberty he has of innocent Delights."[72] We might also call this the right to the pursuit of happiness. Provided that such pursuits do not unjustly interfere with the rights of others, the civil authority has no role in the prohibition or even the regulation of "innocent Delights."

Few who caution us against taking the founders' expressed commitment to natural rights out of context address the views of those who wrote the Fourteenth Amendment. Even if their commitment to natural rights was more "liberal" and less "republican" than that of the founders, it is they—not the founders—who wrote the Fourteenth Amendment. When we consider the protections of "privileges or immunities" provided by the Fourteenth Amendment, it is their conception—not the founders'—that represents the original meaning of that phrase.

Finally, basing constitutional legitimacy on natural rights does not automatically mean that judges should use the concept of natural rights to decide actual cases or controversies. The argument to this point is only that, to be legitimate, a constitution must offer the assurance that the lawful commands it issues to the citizenry have the qualities that make law binding in conscience. Perhaps direct discussion of natural rights by judges would enhance legitimacy; perhaps natural rights would best be protected if judges ignored them altogether. This is a matter I shall con-

---

[71] Locke, *Two Treatises*, 398.

[72] Ibid., 397 ("For in the State of Nature, to omit the liberty he has of innocent Delights, a Man has two Powers").

sider at greater length in part III. I raise the issue now only to note that it would not be inconsistent with the conception of legitimacy presented here to maintain that unenumerated natural rights are best protected by mechanisms other than direct judicial enforcement.

In light of this, it would not be surprising to learn that the founding generation held a diversity of views on judicial review. Whether or not this was the case, however, the issue of constitutional legitimacy for us today is whether the Constitution, as amended, defines lawmaking procedures that, if followed, are capable of producing lawful commands that bind in conscience. This issue is not addressed by a historical analysis of whether the founding generation thought that natural rights were or were not to be directly protected by the judiciary.

Rather, the question of legitimacy facing us has two components: First, whether the system of lawmaking they devised and enacted—as amended —has the qualities necessary to impart the benefit of the doubt on lawful commands. Second, assuming that the system they enacted is legitimate, whether the lawmaking system in existence today adheres to that which was enacted. These are questions to be addressed later in this book.

NATURAL RIGHTS AND POPULAR SOVEREIGNTY

In the previous section, I identified a conception of natural rights that squares the founders' well-known commitment to these rights with the ideas of surrendered powers and reasonable regulation by the laws of the land, rendering otherwise disparate statements concerning natural rights and government powers coherent and explicable. It would seem more difficult to square the founders' belief in retained natural rights with their universal belief in popular sovereignty or the consent of the governed. Understanding how each person can possess natural and inalienable rights and yet consent to surrender a portion of these rights to a central authority is not the problem. As previously noted, a rights holder may consent to alienate some of his or her rights while retaining the remainder, or may be thought to retain all his or her fundamental rights consensually delegating certain powers to agents. The problem is understanding how the founders could have considered the consent of the majority to bind the minority; or how the consent of one generation can bind that of another; or how the consent of men can bind women.

In this regard, I think the founders were wrong, but for the right reasons. They saw that people had natural rights that could be alienated only by their consent. Because they believed that (a) it was necessary to form some type of government, (b) any government would necessarily require the surrender of some rights or powers, and (c) only consent would justify such a transfer, they further believed (d) there must be a type of consent that would to do the job. Majority consent was accepted then—as it still is—as the only way to get from point (a) to point (d). Because they held to this assumption of necessity, they no more would have questioned the "consent" that is sufficient to legitimate a government than most people would today. All that distinguishes between them and today's popular thought is that they believed that an enlightened "electorate" need not be everyone, whereas today there is a belief in (nearly) universal suffrage.

Still, both the founders and most today may be wrong in two different ways. First, it may be possible to organize a legal system in such a manner that everyone does consent in a real way to its operation. This is the suggestion I made briefly in chapter 2, and that I have pursued elsewhere in greater detail.[73] If such a system is feasible, the governmental legal system with which we are familiar might be both unnecessary and improper—or at least less legitimate than this polycentric alternative.

Second, as I also argued in chapter 2, there may be a way to legitimate to some degree even a governmental legal system without the consent of the governed. A legal system that provides assurances that it does not violate the background rights retained by the people—that the "quality goes in before the name law goes on"—is legitimate despite the fact that it did not originate in consent. If either of these possibilities is justified, then an argument based on the supposed necessity of recognizing majority will or "popular sovereignty" as real consent is less compelling than the founding generation appreciated or is appreciated by most today.

On the other hand, the initial ratification of a constitution by a majority of elected delegates to conventions or by a popular referendum may contribute to, though not establish, the legitimacy—as I am using the term—of a resultant constitution. Such an adoption process may make it more difficult to put in place a lawmaking system that is illegitimate, not because it lacks the "consent of the governed," but because it is procedurally inadequate. Presumably, those people who vote for a lawmaking system would not do so if it did not provide the requisite assurances that the laws that would be imposed upon them would be just.

Of course, it is not at all clear that this adoption process would provide equal confidence that laws imposed upon persons and groups who were never asked for their consent are also just. Nevertheless, it may be that if the procedural protections afforded by the original constitution are later extended to those who did not consent, such a lawmaking process might become as legitimate for them as it is for those who originally did consent. Why might this be?

[73] See Barnett, *Structure of Liberty*, 257–97 (discussing the merits of a "polycentric constitutional order").

While the consent of some does not of itself provide a lawmaking process that is legitimate for everyone, a ratification process that requires the "consent" of a large group of ratifiers might serve to induce a deliberative process that would help assure that *as to them* the resulting system has the procedural features that are the source of legitimacy. When these protective procedures are then extended to others who were not a part of the initial "consenting" group, they may nevertheless provide procedural legitimacy to enactments imposed on those who did not originally consent. To be clear, it is the nature of the lawmaking and enforcement procedures, not the partial consent that brought them into existence, that would make laws binding in conscience on those who never consented—though without the initial partial consent, these procedures might never have been devised and enacted. In this way, even partial consent can contribute indirectly to the establishment of a legitimate legal system.

The existence of that initial partial consent, however, is neither sufficient nor necessary to provide whatever legitimacy a legal system may have. (Consider, for example, Japan's constitution, which was written by U.S. Army lawyers and adopted by a captive parliament.) For all its advantages, however, the requirement of popular ratification is not an unmixed blessing. Recall that it was the need to win majorities of Southern delegates in their state ratification conventions that prevented the Constitutional Convention from doing more to prohibit the manifest injustice of slavery. The Fourteenth Amendment would never have received approval from the requisite number of states, had the Thirty-ninth Congress not used the Union Army to "reconstruct" the governments of the Southern states and made their ratification of the Fourteenth Amendment a condition of seating their representatives in Congress.[74]

In the end, if their commitment to natural rights led them to devise and enact a scheme of lawmaking that would impart legitimacy on validly enacted laws, it does not matter that the founding generation and those who enacted the Fourteenth Amendment may have been wrong about popular sovereignty.

But Were They Right about Natural Rights?

Just as we do not have to accept the founding generation's view of popular sovereignty, we do not have to accept their belief in natural or inherent rights. We are free to ask whether or not these beliefs were correct. Though the rhetoric of "natural rights" has largely been lost, most people

---

[74] See Bruce Ackerman, *We the People: Transformations* (Cambridge: Harvard University Press, Belknap Press, 1998), 110–11.

still believe that "first come rights, then comes government." That is, they reject the theory that the rights of the people are merely a grant or dispensation of government. Most share the founders' view, implicitly at least, that people have rights and they form governments to better protect these rights. Witness the popular support for "human rights" that governments everywhere, it is contended, may not transgress.

The widespread acceptance of "first come rights, then comes government" was displayed during the controversial confirmation hearing of Robert Bork. During his testimony Judge Bork was grilled by Senate Judiciary Committee chairman Joseph Biden about the meaning of the Ninth Amendment. After first asserting that he would be "delighted" to use the Ninth Amendment, "if anybody shows me historical evidence about what [the framers] meant,"[75] he then offered the following widely discussed analogy:

> I do not think you can use the ninth amendment unless you know something of what it means. For example, if you had an amendment that says "Congress shall make no" and then there is an ink blot and you cannot read the rest of it and that is the only copy you have, I do not think the court can make up what might be under the ink blot if you cannot read it.[76]

Popular reaction to this argument was not favorable. That this was the wrong answer is illustrated by the testimony of every Supreme Court nominee who was asked about the Ninth Amendment after Bork. No one again tried to argue that the meaning of this express provision of the Constitution is unknowable or unimportant.

When you move from a general claim that "first come rights, then comes government" to a discussion of what these rights may be, there is also a general consensus that they include the rights of person and property that enjoin murder, rape, robbery, and theft—acts that are universally prohibited. Nor does anyone claim that government officials should be able to murder, rape, or steal. This consensus quickly breaks down, however, as the list of "human rights" is expanded. The lack of consensus is aggravated by the open-ended nature of the term "rights" itself. Philosophers often define rights as "justified claims" and anything might be the subject of such a claim. One could claim a right to a million dollars, a right to an organ transplant, a right to unfettered views of the sunset, or a right to affordable access to opera. No wonder a basic commitment that "first come rights, then comes government" yields no consensus on the content

---

[75] *Nomination of Robert H. Bork to Be Associate Justice of the Supreme Court of the United States: Hearings before the Senate Comm. on the Judiciary*, 100th Cong., 1st sess., 1987, 249 (testimony of Robert Bork, September 16, 1987).

[76] Ibid.

of all these rights. Failure to agree upon the complete set of rights, however, should not conceal the fact that there is surely a consensus as to some.

We saw earlier how the classical conception of natural rights or liberties, as understood by the founders, could not be limited to a specific list and was, in this respect, unbounded. Paradoxically, this approach also provides a minimalist conception of background rights about which a general consensus probably exists. Whatever else people may believe they have a right to, most all people believe that they have the right to make their own choices and act as they please with what belongs to them; that they can do as they will with what is theirs provided their actions do not harm others.[77] There is good reason for this belief.[78]

Natural Rights Solve Pervasive Social Problems

People living in every society confront certain pervasive obstacles to the pursuit of happiness. These problems can be categorized as problems of knowledge, interest, and power.[79] The first problem of knowledge is enabling people to act on the basis of what they know about their particular circumstances while somehow taking into account all the personal and local knowledge of others of which they are hopelessly ignorant. The problems of interest include the "partiality problem." The partiality problem is to allow all persons to pursue their own interests while somehow taking into account the interests of those who are remote to them.

The way these problems are solved is the recognition and protection of a bounded freedom to make choices and act upon them. This bounded freedom is called Liberty (as opposed to an unbounded freedom called "license"). The recognition of "liberty rights" of this kind provides the inescapable means by which these and other social problems are solved.

According to this account, natural rights are the set of concepts that define the moral space within which persons must be free to make their own choices and live their own lives if they are to pursue happiness while living in society with others. They are rights insofar as they entail claims on other persons—including those who call themselves "government officials"—that ought to be enforceable. They are natural insofar as their

[77] Unfortunately, not everyone who believes this is crazy about *other* people's doing what *they* will with what is *theirs*, however.

[78] Though I do not base any of my arguments for rights on the existence of a consensus on their behalf, anyone who does contend that consensus is crucial should consider this implication: the only consensus about particular rights that can plausibly be claimed to exist is for the core liberty rights that the founders thought were natural. Where consensus breaks down is on whether to add rights to this core. This is not to claim, of course, a consensus that such liberty rights may never be regulated.

[79] The arguments that follow are taken from my much more extensive treatment of the basis and nature of natural rights in Barnett, *Structure of Liberty*.

necessity depends upon the nature of persons and the social and physical world in which persons reside. In sum, as Madison stated in his speech to the House, "the pre-existent rights of nature" are "essential to secure the liberty of the people."[80]

A respect for these rights is as essential to enabling diverse persons to pursue happiness while living in society with others as a respect for fundamental principles of engineering is essential to building a bridge to span a chasm. This type of justification for rights was offered by Elizur Goodrich in a sermon delivered to the governor and legislature of Connecticut on the eve of the Constitutional Convention. His account is worth quoting at length:

> The principles of society are the laws, which Almighty God has established in the moral world, and made necessary to be observed by mankind; in order to promote their true happiness, in their transactions and intercourse. These laws may be considered as principles, in respect of their fixedness and operation; and as maxims, since by the knowledge of them, we discover those rules of conduct, which direct mankind to the highest perfection, and supreme happiness of their nature. *They are as fixed and unchangeable as the laws which operate in the natural world.*
>
> Human art *in order to produce certain effects*, must conform to the principles and laws, which the Almighty Creator has established in the natural world. He who neglects the cultivation of his field, and the proper time of sowing, may not expect a harvest. He, who would assist mankind in raising weights, and overcoming obstacles, depends on certain rules, derived from the knowledge of mechanical principles applied to the construction of machines, in order to give the most useful effect to the smallest force: And every builder should well understand the best position of firmness and strength, when he is about to erect an edifice. For he, who attempts these things, on other principles, than those of nature, attempts to make a new world; and his aim will prove absurd and his labour lost. No more can mankind be conducted to happiness; or civil societies united, and enjoy peace and prosperity, without observing the moral principles and connections, which the Almighty Creator has established for the government of the moral world.
>
> Moral connections and causes in different circumstances produce harmony and discord, peace or war, happiness or woe among mankind, with the same certainty, as physical cases produce their effect. To institute these causes and connexions belongs not to men, to nations or to human laws, but to build upon them. It is no more in the power of the greatest earthly potentate to hinder their operation, than it is to govern the flowing and ebbing of the ocean.[81]

---

[80] *Annals*, 1:454.

[81] Elizur Goodrich, "The Principles of Civil Union and Happiness Considered and Recommended" (delivered May 10, 1787), in Ellis Sandoz, ed., *Political Sermons of the Ameri-*

Notice that Goodrich was not analogizing the "principles of society" to the natural laws one finds in the hard sciences like physics or chemistry. Instead, he analogized them to what we might call the "normative disciplines"[82] of agriculture, engineering, and architecture. Unlike the natural sciences, each of these disciplines seeks to guide human conduct by providing certain principles of action. In normative disciplines, the justification of these principles takes the following form: Given the nature of the world, if you want to accomplish certain ends, then you had best respect certain means. Goodrich's argument on behalf of certain "principles of society" takes the same form.

The argument in defense of natural rights is that, given the nature of human beings and the world in which we live, if you want a society in which people can pursue happiness, and in which civil society can enjoy peace and prosperity, then you had best respect certain rights. In particular you need to protect the bounded freedom of individuals to make their own choices based on their personal and local knowledge in pursuit of their own interest. The proper boundaries of freedom are provided by the rights of several property, freedom of contract, first possession, self-defense, and restitution. These are the fundamental—and, in the abstract, inalienable—natural rights that all societies must recognize to some degree or they will cease to be functioning societies. The term for properly bounded freedom is Liberty.

Natural rights must be distinguished from "natural law" ethics (or what some refer to as natural right).[83] Natural law ethics or "natural right" is a method of assessing the propriety of individual conduct. This method is used to stipulate, for example, that persons should live their

---

can Founding: 1730–1805 (Indianapolis, Ind.: Liberty Press, 1991), 914–15 (emphasis added). Lest this quotation reinforce a modern misconception about traditional natural rights theory, note that although Goodrich identifies God as the original source of the laws that govern in the moral world, so too does he identify God as the source of the laws that govern agriculture and engineering. With both types of principles and laws, once established by a divine power they become part of the world in which we find ourselves and are discoverable by human reason. Thus, today one can no more disparage natural rights because eighteenth-century thinkers attributed their origin to a divine power than one can disparage the laws of physics because eighteenth-century scientists believed that such laws were also established by God. Whatever the source of these moral laws, Goodrich's argument is that they must be respected if individuals are to pursue happiness and civil society to achieve peace and prosperity. This view of moral laws assumes, of course, that happiness, peace, and prosperity are appropriate ends. Should anyone question this assumption, additional arguments will need to be presented.

[82] The term is George Smith's.

[83] See, e.g., Michael McConnell, "A Moral Realist Defense of Constitutional Democracy," *Chicago-Kent Law Review* 64 (1988): 89 (consistently referring to natural right as opposed to natural rights). Few of the founding generation used the term "natural right," referring almost always to "natural rights."

lives in certain ways and not in others.[84] The concept of natural rights, in contrast, while sharing a common intellectual ancestry and methodology with natural law, addresses a quite different problem. Natural rights do not specify what the good life is for each person nor how each person should act, but what moral "space" or "jurisdiction" each person requires in order to pursue the good life in society with others.

In short, natural law ethics tells people how to exercise the Liberty or bounded freedom defined by natural rights. Whereas natural law ethics assesses the propriety of individual conduct, natural rights assesses the propriety or justice of restrictions imposed on individual conduct.[85] Of course, the same conduct—murder, for example—might be thought to violate natural law because it is "bad" (persons should not kill others except in self-defense), and violate natural rights because it is unjust (persons have a right not to be killed except in self-defense). The reasons why actions are bad, however, are not always the same as why they are unjust.

Moreover, it has long been recognized that many actions that are bad are not unjust, in the sense that they violate the rights of others. For example, natural law theorist Thomas Aquinas, writing centuries before natural rights developed as a separate subject of study, argued:

> Now human law is framed for a number of human beings, the majority of whom are not perfect in virtue. Therefore human laws do not forbid all vices, from which the virtuous abstain, but only the more grievous vices, from which it is possible for the majority to abstain, and *chiefly those that are to the hurt of others, without the prohibition of which human society could not be maintained*; thus human law prohibits murder, theft and the like.[86]

On rare occasion, it may not be bad to act unjustly—as for example when, in an emergency, one wrongfully takes property that belongs to another to save one's life. The goodness of such an act does not necessarily negate its wrongfulness.[87]

Contrary to the claims of critics of classical liberalism, then, natural rights are not conceived of as "presocial";[88] nor do they assume "atomis-

---

[84] See, e.g., Henry B. Veatch, *For an Ontology of Morals: A Critique of Contemporary Ethical Theory* (Evanston, Ill.: Northwestern University Press, 1971).

[85] I do not claim that everyone, or even most people, use all these terms in precisely this way. I claim only that the subject of natural law ethics is distinguishable from that of natural rights and that this terminology best describes the difference between them. Moreover, running these two modes of thought together leads to serious confusion.

[86] Aquinas, *Summa Theologica*, 232 (emphasis added).

[87] See Barnett, *Structure of Liberty*, 170–72.

[88] These rights are, however, conceived of analytically as pregovernmental. Perhaps the charge that liberals conceive of rights as presocial is persistent because some critics of liberalism are so committed to statism that they equate government with society.

tic" individuals. Rather, natural rights are those rights that are needed precisely to protect individuals and associations from the power of others—including the power of the stronger, of groups, and of the State—when and only when persons are deeply enmeshed in a social context. Such rights would be entirely unnecessary if individuals were not in society with each other, or if the actions of some persons did not adversely affect the welfare of others.

Further, when the difference between natural rights and natural law ethics is understood, it becomes plain that a constitutional commitment to protecting natural rights does not entail any general mandate to legislate morality. In this regard, it is confusing and unhelpful that many legal academics use the terms "natural law" and "natural rights" interchangeably.[89] Rather than imposing moral duties on persons to live their lives in certain ways, natural rights protect persons from the State and from each other.

For this reason, the constitutional protection of these rights may include both a "negative" duty of government to refrain from infringing these rights and a "positive" duty upon government to protect the rights of its citizens from infringement by others.[90] Both of these duties are reflected in the thesis presented in chapter 2: to bind in conscience a law must be necessary to protect the rights of others without improperly violating the rights of those upon whom it is imposed. Of course, to claim that a constitution imposes positive duties on government is not to concede that it imposes positive duties on the citizenry. In the main, as discussed in chapter 1, the Constitution "constitutes" the government of the United States and regulates its powers; it does not purport to regulate the rights of the people.

Natural Rights and the Duty to Obey the Law

When this conception of natural rights is understood, it is easier to see why constitutional legitimacy requires that they not be violated. At the same time lawmakers claim that the subjects of their laws have a moral duty of obedience, they also invariably claim that their laws advance the general welfare or the common good. Indeed, if pressed, many would make the latter claim in defense of the former—that is, people have a duty to obey the law because adherence to such laws does advance the general

[89] See Randy E. Barnett, "A Law Professor's Guide to Natural Law and Natural Rights," *Harvard Journal of Law and Public Policy* 20 (1997): 655.

[90] See Heyman, "The First Duty of Government," 510 ("[T]he classical conception of liberty was not merely negative, but had a crucial positive dimension—the protection of individual rights under law").

welfare. Yet if the arguments on behalf of these natural liberty rights that I have summarized here are correct, then laws that violate these rights do not advance the general welfare or common good. Indeed, they harm it, and by so doing undermine the justification for claiming a duty of obedience. Thus human laws that violate natural rights are not obligatory; only those human laws that respect natural rights can be obligatory.

This suggests yet another reason why legal rights should not violate natural rights. In chapter 1, I considered and questioned the claim that the authority of lawmakers can be grounded on the "consent of the governed" to the lawmaking regime. To the contrary, the obligation of lawmakers to respect natural rights rests, at least in part, on the "consent of the governors" to respect these rights. For do not lawmakers explicitly or implicitly claim that their laws promote the common good and are not unjust? By doing so are they not consenting to adhere to principles of justice that, if violated, would thwart the common good?

For example, the Preamble to the U.S. Constitution explicitly claims its purpose to "establish Justice, ensure domestic tranquility, . . . promote the general Welfare, and secure the blessings of Liberty to ourselves and our posterity. . . ."[91] Do not lawmakers in the United States who take an oath to uphold the Constitution explicitly obligate themselves to pass laws that actually do establish justice, do ensure peace, do promote the general welfare, and do secure liberty? Are not laws that fail to accomplish these ends both unnecessary and improper? If a proper respect for certain natural rights is necessary to accomplish the ends for which government was established, then these background rights must be respected by lawmakers if for no other reason than because those who claim authority to make laws have promised or consented to do so.

Conclusion

Just as you need not agree with my conception of justice to accept the view of constitutional legitimacy I advance here, you need not accept my particular defense of natural liberty rights retained by the people to accept these rights themselves. So long as you find persuasive some justification of these rights, you should view the Constitution as legitimate if it provides adequate procedural assurances that enacted laws properly respect the rights of those on whom they are imposed and are necessary to protect

[91] U.S. Const., Preamble.

the rights of others. We now turn our attention to some of these procedural assurances. In particular, we need to examine the manner by which the text of the Constitution should be interpreted and construed and whether, properly interpreted, the scheme established by the Constitution permits the judiciary to assess the necessity and propriety of laws enacted by Congress.

PART II

Constitutional Method

IN LIGHT of this conception of constitutional legitimacy, what is the proper method of interpreting the Constitution? Does the fact that legitimacy is based on the existence of procedures that protect natural rights mean that the text of the Constitution should be disregarded when it appears to conflict with natural rights? In chapter 4, I argue that the Constitution must be interpreted according to its original meaning. This may surprise some readers, because "originalism" is often seen as following from popular sovereignty and I have rejected popular sovereignty as the source of constitutional legitimacy. It may surprise others who think a commitment to natural rights should trump the original meaning of the text. I shall argue, however, that originalism is entailed by a commitment to a written constitution, which is a vital means of subjecting lawmakers to limits on their lawmaking powers.

Written constitutions are valuable to the extent they preserve or "lock in" an initially legitimate lawmaking scheme, and such "lock in" is not achieved if the meaning of the writing can be changed without formal amendment. While this rationale justifies interpreting the Constitution according to the original meaning of its words, it does not justify going beyond that meaning in an effort to recapture the original intent of its framers. Thus I defend what is sometimes called a "moderate" theory of originalism. Both the specific characteristics of original meaning originalism and the normative rationale I provide obviate the well-known criticisms of originalism based on an original intent and grounded in notions of popular sovereignty.

Originalist interpretation, properly understood and justified, has its limits. The failure to recognize these limits makes originalism more vulnerable to criticism than need be. In chapter 5, I explain how interpretation, originalist or otherwise, does not always produce unambiguous rules of law that can be applied to cases. For this reason, it becomes necessary to "construe" the Constitution in ways that effectuate its purposes but that do not contradict its original meaning. Constitutional "constructions" (as distinct from interpretations) that are consistent with original meaning should be chosen to enhance the legitimacy of the laws that are going to be imposed on the people without their consent. Finally, in chapter 6 I apply these concepts of interpretation and construction to the contentious issue of judicial review and examine the originalist evidence that overwhelmingly supports the judicial power to nullify unconstitutional laws.

CHAPTER FOUR

Constitutional Interpretation: An Originalism for Nonoriginalists

> They who are to govern by *Laws* should have little or no
> hand in making the *Laws* they are to govern by.[1]
> —ISAAC PENINGTON, JR. (1651)

IN THE PREVIOUS CHAPTER, I argued that the phrase "others retained by the people" in the Ninth Amendment was originally a reference to "inherent" or "natural" rights, that the term "natural rights" originally referred to what we would today call "liberty rights," and that "privileges or immunities" included both liberty rights and rights created by positive law. Should we interpret these words by looking to what they meant at the time they were enacted? We had best answer this question now since many other provisions of the Constitution will require interpretation throughout the course of this book. For example, what does the phrase "necessary and proper" mean? What does it mean to regulate "commerce" among the states?

In this chapter, I argue that the words of the Constitution should be interpreted according to the meaning they had at the time they were enacted. This method of interpretation is known generally as "originalism," and it has been the subject of extensive criticisms over the past twenty years. The version of originalism I shall defend will be based on "original meaning" as distinct from "original intent." I will explain how original meaning originalism avoids the prominent objections leveled at originalism. I will, however, part company from most originalists who justify originalism as an extension of popular sovereignty. Relying on this rationale has left originalism vulnerable to valid criticism. I shall show, instead, that originalism is warranted because it is the best method to preserve or "lock in" a constitution that is initially legitimate because of what is says.

ORIGINALISM IS DEAD—LONG LIVE ORIGINALISM

The received wisdom among law professors is that originalism in any form is dead, having been defeated in intellectual combat sometime in the

---

[1] Penington, *Fundamental Right*, 3.

1980s. According to this story, Edwin Meese[2] and Robert Bork[3] proposed that the Constitution be interpreted according to the original intentions of its framers. Their view was trounced by many academic critics, perhaps most notably by Paul Brest in his widely cited article, "The Misconceived Quest for Original Understanding"[4] and by H. Jefferson Powell in his article, "The Original Understanding of Original Intent."[5] Taken together, these (and other) articles represent a two-pronged attack on originalism that was perceived at the time as devastating: as a method of constitutional interpretation, originalism was both unworkable and itself contrary to the original intentions of the founders.[6] These criticisms are so familiar and widely accepted[7] that I need only list them here.

According to Brest, originalism was unworkable because it was practically impossible to ascertain and then aggregate the "intention votes" of a multitude of framers, much less to carry them forward to apply to a current controversy. "The act of translation required . . . involves the counterfactual and imaginary act of projecting the adopters' concepts and attitudes into a future they probably could not have envisioned. When the interpreter engages in this sort of projection, she is in a fantasy world more of her own than of the adopters' making."[8]

Powell, in turn, decisively showed that, to quote from the abstract preceding the article, "the modern resort to the 'intent of the framers' can gain no support from the assertion that such was the framers' expectation, for the framers themselves did not believe such an interpretive strategy to be appropriate."[9] This seemingly reduced originalists to a contradictory

---

[2] See Edwin Meese III, "Before the American Bar Association" (July 9, 1985), in *The Great Debate: Interpreting Our Written Constitution* (Washington, D.C.: The Federalist Society, 1986), 9; see also Meese, "A Return to Constitutional Interpretation from Judicial Law-Making," *New York Law School Law Review* 40 (1996): 925–33.

[3] Robert H. Bork, "Neutral Principles and Some First Amendment Problems," *Indiana Law Review* 47 (1971): 1.

[4] Paul Brest, "The Misconceived Quest for Original Understanding," *Boston University Law Review* (1980): 204. As of March 23, 2003, this article had been cited in 637 articles. Westlaw search in Journals and Law Reviews database: [brest /s ("misconceived quest")].

[5] H. Jefferson Powell, "The Original Understanding of Original Intent," *Harvard Law Review* 98 (1985): 885. As of March 23, 2003, this article had been cited 452 times. Westlaw search in Journals and Law Reviews database: [powell /s ("original understanding of original intent")].

[6] A useful collection of articles representing the arguments made on both sides of this issue in the 1970s and 1980s is Jack N. Rakove, ed., *Interpreting the Constitution: The Debate over Original Intent* (Boston: Northeastern University Press, 1990).

[7] See, e.g., Daniel A. Farber and Suzanna Sherry, *Desperately Seeking Certainty: The Misguided Quest for Constitutional Foundations* (Chicago: University of Chicago Press, 2002), 10–28.

[8] Brest, "Misconceived Quest for Original Understanding," 221.

[9] Powell, "Original Understanding of Original Intent," 885.

position: we should violate the original intentions of the framers by relying on their original intent.

Even those who get beyond the Brest and Powell criticisms still encounter two additional and seemingly insurmountable obstacles to originalism. If constitutions are based on popular sovereignty or consent, the framers and ratifiers of the U.S. Constitution represented only white males, not the people, and therefore could not legitimately bind those who were not parties. And even were the Constitution somehow binding when adopted, it was adopted by long-dead men who cannot rule us from the grave.

Moreover, a generation that countenanced slaveholders has not the moral legitimacy to rule us from the grave or from anywhere else. Because their intentions were racist and sexist, we are far from bound by them; we ought loudly to denounce and reject them. According to this view, not only was the Constitution not a product of consent, it was a product of original sin.

If ever a theory had a stake driven through its heart, it seems to be originalism. But despite the onslaught of criticism, the effort to discern the original meaning of constitutional terms continues unabated. Indeed, by some accounts it may be the dominant method actually used by constitutional scholars—even by those who disclaim originalism. As Jack Rakove observed after listing those constitutional scholars who have offered originalist arguments, "[b]ut in truth, the turn to originalism seems so general that citation is almost beside the point."[10] And this movement toward originalism has cut across ideological lines. "In recent years, the originalist premise has also been manifested in the emerging strain of broad originalism in liberal and progressive constitutional theory."[11]

Though it is possible to characterize this intellectual movement as a shift, not to originalism, but to "textualism," this distinction is hard to maintain. Once the importance of text or "writtenness" is conceded, some version of originalism becomes much harder to resist. For, as I will show, the reasons why text is important are the same reasons that support some modest version of originalism and shift the burden of persuasion to anyone proposing to replace reliance on the text by some other method of interpretation. The modest nature of the originalism I defend, and the reasons I offer to justify it, should appeal even to many who consider themselves, as I once did, nonoriginalists. Indeed, many may be closet originalists without even knowing it.

[10] Jack N. Rakove, "Fidelity through History (or to It)," *Fordham Law Review* 65 (1997): 1592 n. 14 (listing Bruce Ackerman, Akhil Amar, Chris Eisgruber, Daniel Farber, Martin Flaherty, Michael Klarman, Michael McConnell, Mark Killenbeck, Larry Kramer, Henry Monoghan, and William Treanor).

[11] James E. Fleming, "Fidelity to Our Imperfect Constitution," *Fordham Law Review* 65 (1997): 1344.

Viewing originalism as following from a commitment to a written text also helps explain why the shift to originalism has occurred, if indeed it has. It takes a theory to beat a theory and, after a decade of trying, the opponents of originalism have never converged on an appealing and practical alternative. The inability of the most brilliant and creative legal minds to present a plausible method of interpretation that engenders enough confidence to warrant overriding the text has helped make some version of originalism much more attractive.

Perhaps most important of all, however, is that originalism has itself changed—from original intention to original meaning. No longer do originalists claim to be seeking the subjective intentions of the framers. Now both Robert Bork and Antonin Scalia, no less than Ronald Dworkin and Bruce Ackerman, seek the original meaning of the text. As stated by Robert Bork:

> Though I have written of the understanding of the ratifiers of the Constitution, since they enacted it and made it law, that is actually a shorthand formulation, because what the ratifiers understood themselves to be enacting must be taken to be what the public of that time would have understood the words to mean. It is important to be clear about this. The search is not for a subjective intention. If someone found a letter from George Washington to Martha telling her that what he meant by the power to lay taxes was not what other people meant, that would not change our reading of the Constitution in the slightest. Nor would the subjective intentions of all the members of a ratifying convention alter anything. When lawmakers use words, the law that results is what those words ordinarily mean.[12]

By the same token Justice Scalia has written:

> We look for a sort of "objectified" intent—the intent that a reasonable person would gather from the text of the law, placed alongside the remainder of the *corpus juris.* . . . Government by unexpressed intent is . . . tyrannical. It is the *law* that governs, not the intent of the lawgiver.[13]

Whereas "original intent" originalism seeks the intentions or will of the lawmakers or ratifiers, "original meaning" originalism seeks the public or objective meaning that a reasonable listener would place on the words used in the constitutional provision at the time of its enactment. As Edmund Randolph, who served as a delegate to the Constitutional Convention and later as first attorney general, replied to those who would rely

---

[12] Robert H. Bork, *The Tempting of America: The Political Seduction of the Law* (New York: Free Press, 1990), 144.

[13] Antonin Scalia, *A Matter of Interpretation: Federal Courts and the Law* (Princeton: Princeton University Press, 1997), 17.

on the deliberations of the Convention: "But ought not the constitution to be decided on by the import of its own expressions? What may not be the consequence if an almost unknown history should govern the construction?"[14]

This shift to original public meaning obviates some, but not all, of the most telling practical objections to originalism and can be very disappointing for critics of originalism—and especially for historians—when they read original meaning analysis. They expect to see a richly detailed legislative history only to find references to dictionaries, common contemporary meanings, an analysis of how particular words and phrases are used elsewhere in the document[15] or in other foundational documents and cases,[16] and logical inferences from the structure and general purposes of the text. Nowadays, those presenting evidence of the true "subjective" intentions of the framers are often nonoriginalists seeking to rebut a particular "objective" original meaning offered by an originalist.

Moreover, while some originalists still search for how the relevant generation of ratifiers expected or intended their textual handiwork would be applied to specific cases, original meaning originalists need not concern themselves with this, except as circumstantial evidence of what the more technical words and phrases in the text might have meant to a reasonable listener. This aspect of original meaning originalism is captured by Ronald Dworkin's useful distinction between "semantic originalism" and "expectations originalism." "This is the crucial distinction between what some officials intended to say in enacting the language they used, and what they intended—or expected or hoped—would be the consequence of their saying it."[17] For example, when a statute is interpreted, there is a difference "between the question of what a legislature intended to say in the laws it enacted, which judges applying those laws must answer, and the question of what the various legislators as individuals expected or hoped the consequences of those laws would be, which is a very different matter."[18]

Similarly, when the Bill of Rights is interpreted, " 'semantic' originalism . . . insists that the rights-granting clauses be read to say what those who

---

[14] Edmund Randolph, "Attorney General's Opinion" (February 12, 1791), in M. St. Clair Clarke and D. A. Hall, eds., *Legislative and Documentary History of the Bank of the United States* (1832; reprint, New York: Augustus M. Kelley Publishers, 1967), 90.

[15] For an elaborate description of just this last aspect of interpretation, see Akhil Reed Amar, "Intratextualism," *Harvard Law Review* 112 (1999): 747.

[16] What Amar calls "intertextual" analysis. Ibid., 799–800.

[17] Ronald Dworkin, "Comment," in Scalia, *Matter of Interpretation*, 116.

[18] Ibid., 118. Expectations originalism sounds much like the "strict intentionalism" criticized by Brest: "Strict intentionalism requires the interpreter to determine how the adopters would have applied a provision to a given situation, and to apply it accordingly." Brest, "Misconceived Quest for Original Understanding," 222.

made them intended to say"; whereas " 'expectation' originalism . . . holds that these clauses should be understood to have the consequences that those who made them expected them to have."[19] Dworkin concludes:

> [I]f we read the abstract clauses of the Bill of Rights [and other rights-granting clauses such as the Fourteenth Amendment] as they were written—if we read them to say what their authors intended them to say rather than to deliver the consequences they expected them to have—then judges must treat these clauses as enacting abstract moral principles and must therefore exercise moral judgment in deciding what they *really* require. That does not mean ignoring precedent or textual or historical inquiry or morphing the Constitution. It means, on the contrary, enforcing it in accordance with its text, in the only way that this can be done.[20]

Though he himself rejects the semantic originalist position,[21] Dworkin's distinction helps to clarify the movement from original intentions originalism to original meaning originalism. It is not only a movement from subjective to objective meaning. Depending on the textual provision being interpreted—for some at least—it is also a movement, to employ another Dworkinian distinction, from relatively specific rule-like commands to more abstract principle-like injunctions, the approximate meaning of which we must still look to the past to discover.

REVISITING BREST AND POWELL

Perhaps the shift to original meaning originalism should not have come as a surprise. For when one rereads Brest and Powell with the distinction

---

[19] Dworkin, "Comment," 119. It may be, however, that seemingly abstract provisions had a narrower original meaning.

[20] Ibid., 126.

[21] See Ronald Dworkin, "The Arduous Virtue of Fidelity: Originalism, Scalia, Tribe, and Nerve," *Fordham Law Review* 65 (1997): 1258 n. 18 ("I did not mean, in my brief remarks, to abandon . . . my long-standing opposition to any form of originalism . . ."). He explains further: "But I want to insist on two things. First, that semantic originalism is the only form of originalism that can be defended. . . . Second, that the semantic question—what did those who wrote the Constitution mean to say in it, while not dispositive, must nonetheless figure in an overall interpretive argument. It may be that historical practice has overridden semantic intent, and since any interpretation must be sensitive to history, that fact might justify an overall interpretive conclusion different from what semantic originalism would suggest." Letter by Ronald Dworkin to author, May 17, 1999. Many nonoriginalist scholars share Dworkin's view that original meaning is an important *part* of constitutional interpretation. Considering their sometimes vehement objections to originalism, however, the question arises as to why they think it plays any role at all. Though Dworkin attempts to answer this, others typically do not. Moreover, anyone who concedes a role for original meaning as part of a proper constitutional analysis cannot object at the same time that it is impossible.

between "original intent" and "original meaning" in mind, one finds that both critiques left considerable room for originalism to survive and flourish. True, Brest berated strict textualism along with strict intentionalism, though his criticisms here are more limited and less persuasive.[22] But he left the door open, however reluctantly, to what he terms "moderate intentionalism"—in a passage that also reflects the closeness between textualism and originalism.

> A moderate textualist takes account of the open-textured quality of language and reads the language of provisions in their social and linguistic context. A moderate intentionalist applies a provision consistent with the adopters' intent at a relatively high level of generality, consistent with what is sometimes called the "purpose of the provision." Where the strict intentionalist tries to determine the adopters' actual subjective purposes, the moderate intentionalist attempts to understand what the adopters' purposes might plausibly have been, an aim far more readily achieved than a precise understanding of the adopters' intentions.[23]

If this method is not subject to the same practical objections Brest leveled at strict or original intention originalism, what is wrong with moderate originalism? Indeed, Brest concedes that "[m]oderate originalism is a perfectly sensible strategy of constitutional decisionmaking."[24] His principal remaining objection is that moderate originalism "ha[s] contributed little to the development of many doctrines . . . accept[ed] as legitimate."[25] This is not the same sort of practical objection to originalism for which he is so often (and justifiably) cited. Instead, Brest rejects moderate originalism, not because it is incoherent or impossible to achieve, but because it will not support many modern constitutional doctrines that Brest thinks are essential to the Constitution's efficacy and legitimacy.

---

[22] He argues that one still needs to determine the "social context," which "refers to a shared understanding of the purposes the provisions might plausibly serve." Brest, "Misconceived Quest for Original Understanding," 206. "We understand the range of possible meanings of provisions only because we know that some interpretations respond to the kinds of concerns that the adopters' society might have while others do not" (ibid., 207). And this, he argues, "calls for a historical inquiry quite similar to the intentionalist interpreter's" (ibid., 209). After that, however, he primarily considers only the practical obstacles to determining and aggregating historical intentions. When he discusses textualism, his principal objection is our inability to situate ourselves adequately enough in the past to be accurate (ibid., 219). However, the well-known and widely accepted reply to this is that we can be accurate enough for practical purposes, or "close enough for government work." See e.g., Ronald A. Cass, "Trade Subsidy Law: Can a Foolish Inconsistency Be Good Enough for Government Work?" *Law and Policy in International Business* 21 (1990): 609 (discussing interpretation of legislation).

[23] Brest, "Misconceived Quest for Original Understanding," 223.

[24] Ibid., 231.

[25] Ibid.

This is the reason that many scholars oppose originalism. Not because it cannot be done, but because the original meaning of the text *can* be ascertained and they find this meaning to be inadequate or objectionable. They reject the meaning of the Constitution as enacted and wish to substitute another meaning that they contend is superior. I shall say more about this shortly but it is worth noting that this particular objection is inconsistent with claims made by Brest and others that the text is "wholly open-ended."[26] Were that the case, they could get everything they want out of its original meaning.

If our goal is to discover what the Constitution (rather than our own opinion) specifies or requires, we first need to know how a constitution ought to be interpreted. Only once we apply a normatively justified method of interpretation to a particular text to determine what it says, can we then decide if its meaning is or is not desirable. Assessing the merits of what the Constitution says is not the same thing as determining its meaning. In other words, *what* the constitution says is one thing; whether we *approve* of what it says is a separate question. Interpretation answers only the first of these two issues. For this reason, choosing a method of interpretation because it justifies currently accepted outcomes puts the evaluative cart before the interpretive horse.

True, we may and probably should ignore or disregard a constitution that is not good enough in what it says to merit respect and adherence. But, as I shall make clear in the next section, this requires the critic to candidly admit what he or she is up to. They cannot have it both ways: claim to be interpreting "the Constitution," while at the same time substituting for what it says something they think is morally superior. For, as we shall see, the fact the Constitution was put in writing is what mandates that its meaning must remain the same until it is properly changed—or candidly rejected—and the very actors whose behavior it is supposed to constrain cannot on their own change it to something they prefer without defeating the purpose of putting its guarantees and restrictions in writing in the first place.

A reexamination of Powell's now-classic historical treatment of originalism is also revealing. While he persuasively argues that the founding generation itself abjured from original intention originalism, generally overlooked or forgotten is that he persuasively establishes the founders' commitment to original meaning originalism:

> When a consensus eventually emerged on a proper theory of constitutional interpretation, it indeed centered on "original intent." But at the time, that term referred to the "intentions" of the sovereign parties to the constitutional

compact, as evidenced in the Constitution's language and discerned through structural methods of interpretation; it did not refer to the personal intentions of the framers or anyone else.[27]

This method of constitutional interpretation is closely akin to the methods of contractual interpretation whence it came. "One construed a contract's 'intent' not by embarking on a historical inquiry into what the parties actually wished to accomplish, but by applying legal norms to the contract's terms—that is, by construing the contract in accordance with the common understanding of its terms, and in light of the nature and the character of the contracting parties."[28] In other words, the objective or publicly accessible meaning of the terms is sought.

Powell examines James Madison's theory of constitutional interpretation, which "rested primarily on the distinction he drew between the public meaning or intent of a state paper, a law, or a constitution, and the personal opinions of the individuals who had written or adopted it."[29] Powell cites Madison's response to an alleged misuse of one of his presidential veto messages by his successor Andrew Jackson. Madison wrote:

> On the subject of the discrepancy between the construction put by the Message of the President [Jackson] on the veto of 1817 and the intention of its author, the President will of course consult his own view of the case. For myself, I am aware that the document must speak for itself, and that that intention cannot be substituted for [the intention derived through] the established rules of interpretation.[30]

"Madison was quite insistent," writes Powell, "that a distinction must be drawn between the 'true meaning' of the Constitution and 'whatever might have been the opinions entertained in forming the Constitution.'"[31] Contrary, then, to how it is commonly used, the historical evidence presented in Professor Powell's pathbreaking article supports, rather than undermines, an adherence to original meaning originalism. It also supports the view that an objective or "true meaning" must be ascertained independent of our approval or disapproval of that meaning.

As has been pointed out by others, however, Powell's evidence that the founders opposed reliance on original intent is actually evidence that they opposed reliance on the original intentions of the framers of the Constitu-

[27] Powell, "Original Understanding of Original Intent," 948.
[28] Ibid., 931 (footnotes omitted).
[29] Ibid., 935.
[30] Letter from James Madison to Martin Van Buren (July 5, 1830) as it appears in Powell, "Original Understanding of Original Intent," 936 (bracketed words added by Powell).
[31] Powell, "Original Understanding of Original Intent," 938 (quoting letter from James Madison to C. E. Haynes, February 25, 1831).

tion, as opposed to the understanding of the ratifiers and the people.[32] As Powell notes, interest in the intentions of the framers began to develop in the 1820s.[33]

The rejection of reliance upon the framers' intent resulted in part from the objection that the Constitutional Convention usurped its original authority to propose changes to the Articles of Confederation, rather than a complete replacement. Federalists responded that the Convention could only propose a new constitution, which would be a dead letter until ratified by the people through their state conventions. The later antipathy to interpretation based on the original intent of the framers was a logical extension of this earlier argument that it was the ratifiers who enacted the Constitution, not its framers.

Powell's sources show support for interpreting the Constitution according to the understanding of the ratifying conventions and of the general public. As Madison wrote:

> As a guide in expounding and applying the provisions of the Constitution, the debates and incidental decisions of the Convention can have no authoritative character. However desirable it be that they should be preserved as a gratification to the laudable curiosity felt by every people to trace the origin and progress of their political Institutions, and as a source, parhaps [sic] of some lights on the Science of Govt. the legitimate meaning of the Instrument must be derived from the text itself; or if a key is to be sought elsewhere, it must be not in the opinions or intentions of the Body which planned and proposed the Constitution, but in the sense attached to it by the people in their respective State Conventions, where it recd. all the authority which it possesses.[34]

Madison was here asserting not the complete irrelevance of the records of the Convention, but only denying their authoritative character. The public meaning of the words of the Constitution, as understood by the ratifying conventions and the general public, could be gleaned from a number of sources, including the records of the Convention, but where

---

[32] This deficiency in Powell's account was pointed out early, forcefully, and independently by two different scholars. See Robert N. Clinton, "Original Understanding, Legal Realism, and the Interpretation of 'This Constitution,' " *Iowa Law Review* 72 (1987): 1177; Charles A. Lofgren, "The Original Understanding of Original Intent?" *Constitutional Commentary* 5 (1989): 77.

[33] See Powell, "Original Understanding of Original Intent," 945 ("With the growing availability of original materials revealing the actions and opinions of the individual actors who played roles in the Constitution's framing and adoption, popular and legal interest in that episode of history markedly increased").

[34] Letter from James Madison to Thomas Ritchie (September 15, 1821), quoted in Farrand, *Records*, 3:447–48.

those intentions differed from the public understanding, it was the public meaning that should prevail.[35]

Moreover, Powell underplays the commitment of Madison and others to an originalist objective meaning rather than to a public meaning that evolves over time.[36] As Madison wrote:

> I entirely concur in the propriety of resorting to the sense in which the Constitution was accepted and ratified by the nation. In that sense alone it is the legitimate Constitution. And if that be not the guide in expounding it, there can be no security for a consistent and stable, more than for a faithful, exercise of its powers. If the meaning of the text be sought in the changeable meaning of the words composing it, it is evident that the shape and attributes of the Government must partake of the changes to which the words and phrases of all living languages are constantly subject. What a metamorphosis would be produced in the code of law if all its ancient phraseology were to be taken in its modern sense. And that the language of our Constitution is already undergoing interpretations unknown to its founders will I believe appear to all unbiased Enquirers into the history of its origin and adoption.[37]

Madison's commitment to original meaning originalism was qualified, not contradicted, by his belief that ambiguities in meaning will be resolved by later legislative practice and judicial decisions. In *Federalist* 37, he wrote: "All new laws, though penned with the greatest technical skill, and passed on the fullest and most mature deliberation, are considered as more or less obscure and equivocal, until their meaning be liquidated and ascertained by a series of particular discussions and adjudications."[38] These apparently conflicting positions reflect the much-neglected distinction between "interpretation" based on original meaning and "construction." As I explain in chapter 5, interpretation determines the meaning of

---

[35] For a discussion of how the issue of "objective" original meaning versus "subjective" original intent played out in the debate between Lysander Spooner and Wendell Phillips in the 1840s over the constitutionality of slavery, see Randy E. Barnett, "Was Slavery Unconstitutional before the Thirteenth Amendment? Lysander Spooner's Theory of Interpretation," *Pacific Law Journal* 28 (1997): 977.

[36] See Clinton, "Original Understanding," 1186–1220; Lofgren, "Original Understanding of Original Intent?" 113 ("[T]he original understanding of original intent most emphatically does not rule out a resort to the understandings and expectations of the ratifiers in 1787–88, or to the range of materials that may illuminate their views").

[37] Letter from Madison to Henry Lee (June 25, 1824), reprinted in G. Hunt, ed., *The Writings of James Madison*, vol. 9 (New York: Knickerbocker Press, 1910), 191–92.

[38] *Federalist* 37, 229 (Madison). In chapter 7, we shall see how Madison, as president, signed the bill establishing the national bank, despite his earlier contention that a national bank was unconstitutional, in part because of "the obligations derived from a course of precedents amounting to the requisite evidence of national judgment and intention." Letter from James Madison to Mr. Ingersoll (June 25, 1831), in *Letters*, 4:186.

words. Constitutional construction fills the inevitable gaps created by the vagueness of these words when applied to particular circumstances. Vagueness must exist before construction is warranted, however, and any construction must not contradict whatever original meaning has been discerned by interpretation.

For reasons that will become clearer by the end of this chapter, I do not think we are bound by James Madison's opinions concerning constitutional interpretation. And as a politician, some say Madison was not always consistent in his interpretive methodology.[39] Nevertheless, in the balance of this chapter, we shall see why Madison's view that only an originalist method of interpretation would provide security for a consistent, stable, and faithful exercise of the Constitution's powers remains today a powerful reason to adhere to the original meaning of the text.

"WRITTENNESS" AND THE RELEVANCE OF ORIGINAL MEANING

Why should we interpret the Constitution according to its original meaning? To answer this question, I will be relying in part on insights revealed by contract law theory. To avoid confusion, then, let me emphasize that I do not view the Constitution as a contract in a literal sense. A contract requires the unanimous consent of all its parties and the Constitution, for reasons emphasized in chapter 1, must lack this requisite consent. Nevertheless, the Constitution of the United States is a written document and it is its writtenness that makes relevant contract law theory pertaining to those contracts that are also in writing.[40]

In short, I shall argue that the impetus behind original meaning is the same as that which lies behind the statute of frauds, the parol evidence rule, and the objective theory of contractual interpretation. All these doctrines have been attacked by law professors as backward and formalist, yet all remain with us today. Such is the power of written texts. My thesis is that the movement to textualism in constitutional law is motivated by the same sorts of considerations that lead to textualism in contracts. Original meaning follows naturally, though perhaps not inevitably, from the commitment to a written text.

[39] See Joseph M. Lynch, *Negotiating the Constitution: The Earliest Debates over Original Intent* (Ithaca: Cornell University Press, 1999) (detailing shifts in interpretive method by Madison—and others—over the course of his congressional career). At least some of these alleged shifts, I think, are actually misunderstandings of Madison's substantive and methodological stances.

[40] For a discussion on the centrality of writtenness in our constitutional tradition, see Steven G. Calabresi, "The Tradition of the Written Constitution: A Comment on Professor Lessig's Theory of Translation," *Fordham Law Review* 65 (1997): 1445–47.

The Functions of Writings

Though not all contracts must be in writing, in 1677 the English Parliament enacted the first statute of frauds—entitled an "Act for the Prevention of Frauds and Perjuries"—requiring that agreements of a certain magnitude be in writing to be enforceable. Over three hundred years later, there are statutes of frauds in every state of the union. Why? As Lon Fuller taught us some fifty years ago, the functions of formality are evidentiary, cautionary, and channeling.[41] To these three functions Professors Calamari and Perillo have added a fourth: the clarifying function. Here is their description of all four:

> Formalities serve important functions in many legal systems. . . . Important among these is the *evidentiary function*. Compliance with formalities provides reliable evidence that a given transaction took place. A *cautionary function* is also served. . . . Before performing the required ritual the promisor had ample opportunity to reflect and deliberate on the wisdom of his act. . . . A third function is an earmarking or *channeling function*. The populace is made aware that the use of a given device will attain a desired result. When the device is used, the judicial task of determining the parties' intentions is facilitated. A fourth function is *clarification*. When the parties reduce their transaction to writing . . . they are more likely to work out details not contained in their oral agreement. In addition, form requirements can work to serve regulatory and fiscal ends, to educate the parties as to the full extent of their obligations, to provide public notice of the transaction, and also to help management efficiency in an organizational setting.[42]

This is also a concise summary of why, from Magna Carta onward, there has always been an interest in getting political commitments in writing. Though they differ in significant ways, putting a constitution in writing performs many of the same functions as a written contract.

Like a written contract, a written constitution provides good evidence of what terms were actually enacted when later they might be disputed. The fact that the original constitution and subsequent amendments were in writing induced deliberation and caution in those considering whether to formally adopt the new text. Depending on one's views of why they failed to be ratified, the flag-burning amendment and the equal rights amendment both potentially illustrate the value of deliberation and caution.

[41] See Lon L. Fuller, "Consideration and Form," *Columbia Law Review* 41 (1941): 799.
[42] John Calamari and Joseph Perillo, *Contracts*, 3d ed. (St. Paul, Minn.: West, 1987) (emphases added).

Formal methods of adding written amendments permit people seeking to modify the Constitution to channel their actions accordingly and peacefully, knowing that if they satisfy the requisite procedures, their actions will have a legally binding effect and the authoritative text will be changed. Finally, the act of hammering out the terms of the Constitution and later amendments in writing causes people to clarify their meaning and intentions in a way that a vague general agreement to informally expressed rules or principles could never do. In the early years of the United States, the virtues of putting political guaranties in writing were widely understood. As St. George Tucker explained:

> The advantages of a written constitution, considered as the original contract of society must immediately strike every reflecting mind; power, when undefined, soon becomes unlimited; and the disquisition of social rights where there is no text to resort to, for their explanation, is a task, equally above ordinary capacities, and incompatible with the ordinary pursuits, of the body of the people.[43]

While the functions of formality help explain the appeal of a written constitution, the impetus for an original meaning method of interpretation is also suggested by the parol evidence rule, which rejects extrinsic evidence that contradicts the meaning of a contract at the time of its formation. When a writing can be contradicted by testimony of a differing understanding, the purposes for which the agreement was put in writing in the first place is undercut. In other words, for all its difficulties, something like a parol evidence rule is needed to preserve the original meaning of the writing and thereby enable it to fulfill its evidentiary, cautionary, channeling, and clarification functions. If we let writings be contradicted by extrinsic evidence, then they lose their ability to perform these functions, and little or no purpose would be served by the original writing.

A focus on the parol evidence rule and its value in preserving the function of a writing is helpful in other respects. First, as Tom Grey noted, the parol evidence rule bars the use of extrinsic evidence to supplement, as opposed to contradict, a writing only if the writing is "completely integrated." That is, unless a writing is the final and *exclusive* written expression of the parties' agreement, it may be supplemented in ways that do not contradict its terms.[44] Contradicting the explicit provisions of a writing undermines its ability to satisfy the functions of formality in a way that

---

[43] St. George Tucker, appendix to *Blackstone's Commentaries: With Notes of Reference to the Constitution and Laws of the Federal Government of the United States and of the Commonwealth of Virginia*, by William Blackstone, vol. 1 (Philadelphia: William Young Birch and Abraham Small, 1803), 154–55.

[44] See Thomas C. Grey, "The Uses of an Unwritten Constitution," *Chicago-Kent Law Review* 645 (1988): 223–29.

supplementing it when it is incomplete or when it explicitly authorizes supplementation does not.

Whether the Constitution can be supplemented, as opposed to contradicted or changed, depends on what it says and what it fails to say. Grey argues that the Ninth Amendment explicitly authorizes supplementation. I leave this important issue to one side because it bears only indirectly on choosing the appropriate method of interpretation to tell us, among other things, what the Ninth Amendment really means. After all, we cannot know if the Ninth Amendment authorizes supplementation until we know how to interpret its words.

This brings us to the question of how the words of a writing are to be interpreted. In contract law, the objective approach looks to the publicly accessible meaning that a reasonable person would attach to the words in context. The reasons for this are important. Because people cannot read each other's minds, they must rely on appearances when making their decision of whether to enter or to refrain from entering into a contractual relationship. Thus, in contract law, though we are concerned about the intentions of the parties, we are concerned about only those intentions the parties have succeeded in manifesting to each other, and not with any uncommunicated subjective intentions. We rely on the public or objective meaning of the contractual terms because this is the meaning to which the parties have committed themselves. This, not any unexpressed intentions, is the meaning they wish to be preserved or "locked in" in case of future disputes. The same is true of constitutions.

The Importance of "Lock In"

The Constitution is a law designed to restrict the lawmakers. Although the Constitution itself may have multiple purposes and functions, its "writtenness" has many fewer. Though it is entirely possible to have an unwritten constitution, written constitutions are in writing for a reason. Primarily, constitutions are put in writing to better constrain the political actors it empowers to accomplish various ends. In particular, it is put in writing so these actors cannot themselves make the laws by which they make law. Putting a constitution in writing helps accomplish the objective of early English constitutionalists who, like Isaac Penington, maintained that "[t]hey who are to govern by *Laws* should have little or no hand in making the Laws they are to govern by."[45]

Under the fiction of popular sovereignty this separation is absolutely critical for, in its absence, the legislators, like the king before them, are supreme and cease to be the servants of the people. As Penington ex-

[45] Penington, *Fundamental Right*, 3.

plained, "if Parliaments succeed in the place of the *supream-administering-power*, there will be as much need of somewhat else to stand between the people and them, as there was of them to stand between the people and the *Kingly Power*."[46]

In America, this was the primary reason why elected state conventions, rather than elected state legislatures, were asked to ratify the Constitution. What matters most about ratifying conventions is that they are not the legislature who will be bound by that which is ratified. It is not so much the wisdom of the conventions as their independent existence that serves to negate the power in the legislature to change what was ratified into something else.

Though the representative character of ratification conventions may be as fictional as that of the legislature, then, the functional separation of lawmaking and constituent powers is very real indeed and can be understood in wholly practical terms. Unless rulers are constrained by law, they are dangerous to the not-at-all-fictional rights of the people. Lawmakers must be constrained somehow, and the device of another body both granting and limiting their powers in a writing that legislatures had no power themselves to change was a crucial innovation. This point was explained by William Rawle:

> It is not necessary that a constitution should be in writing; but the superior advantages of one reduced to writing over those which rest on traditionary information, or which are to be collected from the acts and proceedings of the government itself are great and manifest. A dependence on the latter is indeed destructive of one main object of a constitution, which is to check and restrain governors. If the people can only refer to the acts and proceedings of the government to ascertain their own rights, it is obvious, that as every such act may introduce a new principle, there can be no stability in the government. The order of things is inverted; what ought to be the inferior, is placed above that which should be the superior, and the legislature is enabled to alter the constitution at its pleasure.[47]

In this way, the act of putting written constraints on lawmakers had—and still has—enormous value apart from the wisdom of what a constitution says. Constitutional scholars neglect this value when they advocate methods of interpretation whose purpose is to improve upon the content of a written constitution, thereby undermining the function of its writtenness. How can a meaning be preserved or "locked in" and governors

---

[46] Ibid., 13.

[47] William Rawle, *A View of the Constitution*, 2d ed. (Philadelphia: Philip H. Nicklin, 1829), 15–16.

checked and restrained if the written words mean only what legislatures or judges want them to mean today?

Requiring that judges and legislators respect an independent original meaning of the Constitution until it is properly changed does not require that they discern the original intentions of those who wrote or ratified the document. The public meaning of their words is independent of what particular individuals may have intended when they wrote and enacted them. As Lysander Spooner understood:

> We must admit that the constitution, *of itself, independently of the actual intentions of the people*, expresses some certain fixed, definite, and legal intentions; else the people themselves would express no intention by agreeing to it. The instrument would, in fact, contain nothing that the people *could* agree to. Agreeing to an instrument that had no meaning *of its own*, would only be agreeing to nothing.[48]

In other words, "if the intentions could be assumed independently of the words, the words would be of no use, and the laws of course would not be written."[49]

The seeming paradox of determining "intentions" without relying on evidence of particular subjective intent is routinely resolved by the fact that the English language contains words with generally accepted meanings that are ascertainable independent of any of our subjective opinions about their meaning. The most common way of doing this is by resorting to dictionaries and this is a useful starting point, but one must also take into account the context in which a word or phrase appears. This contextual understanding includes how these words are used elsewhere in the document and the general purposes for these clauses that can be ascertained from the document itself and from circumstances surrounding its formation.[50]

Interpretation, then, is to be distinguished from either contradicting or supplementing the meaning of a writing. Given that the meanings of words can change or evolve, in searching for the "generally accepted" or reasonable meaning within a particular community of discourse, at what point in time do we look for the meaning? Here is where textualism meets and melds with originalism. With a constitution, as with a contract, we look to the meaning established at the time of formation and for the same reason: If either a constitution or a contract is reduced to writing and executed, where it speaks it establishes or "locks in" a rule of law from

---

[48] Spooner, "Unconstitutionality of Slavery," 222.

[49] Ibid., 220.

[50] None of these interpretive inquiries, by the way, violates the parol evidence rule. Properly understood, the parol evidence rule does not bar resort to extrinsic evidence to determine meaning of the writing. See E. Alan Farnsworth, " 'Meaning' in the Law of Contracts," *Yale Law Journal* 76 (1967): 951–65.

that moment forward. Adopting any meaning contrary to the original meaning would be to contradict or change the meaning of the text and thereby to undermine the value of writtenness itself. Writtenness ceases to perform its function if meaning can be changed in the absence of an equally written modification or amendment.

For this reason virtually all written contracts require modifications to be in writing.[51] The need for written modification or amendment is driven by the same desideratum of formality that recommends a written constitution in the first place.[52] Meaning must remain the same unless it is changed, and changes require the same degree of writtenness and formality as the original writing. A commitment to textualism, therefore, begets a commitment to original meaning unless this meaning is altered by a written amendment.

By this route, we have arrived at the original meaning position in just the way that Powell showed the founders did: by analogy to contract law. True, contracts to which all parties consent differ in principle from constitutions that must lack unanimous consent. Contract law recognizes that a subjective agreement between the parties can trump the objective meaning either to show a mistake in integration, or to show that the parties attached an idiosyncratic meaning to a particular term. Even if the Constitution is a kind of contract, however, there are simply too many parties ever to find unanimous agreement to an idiosyncratic meaning.[53]

But this difference only magnifies the importance of writtenness and the need to protect a constitution from unwritten modifications. While we can easily imagine, and it is not uncommon for, all parties to a contract

---

[51] The issue of "waiver" of clauses requiring express modification, while not exactly beyond the scope of this chapter, would take us too far afield into the realm of contract law. Suffice it to say that waivers must be consented to by all the parties, and such unanimous consent is unobtainable in this constitutional context for the same reason it is unavailable at the formation stage.

[52] The fact that amendments ought to be in writing does not necessarily entail that the methods of ratification of written amendments be limited to those specified in the original writing. The functional desirability of ratifying written amendments by unwritten procedures is separate from the importance that amendments, however ratified, themselves be in writing. Of course, if the amendment procedures specified in the writing are reasonably interpreted as exclusive, then it defeats the function of writtenness to supplement them with other procedures.

[53] As he viewed the Constitution as a contract, this argument figured in Spooner's analysis of the unconstitutionality of slavery. Because the framers of the Constitution used euphemisms for the terms "slavery" or "slave," "[i]f there were a single honest man in the nation, who assented, in good faith, to the honest and legal meaning of the constitution, it would be unjust and unlawful towards him to change the meaning of the instrument so as to sanction slavery, even though every other man in the nation should testify that, in agreeing to the constitution, he intended that slavery be sanctioned." Spooner, "Unconstitutionality of Slavery," 123.

to want to change the terms of their agreement,[54] because there is no original consent to a constitution, there can be no subjective consent to its change. Later acquiescence to a change in meaning can no more be taken as unanimous consent to this change than can acquiescence at the time of the founding be taken as initial consent.

Unlike a contract that can be changed by the parties, in the constitutional sphere, writtenness ceases to perform its function of constraining political actors if meaning can be changed by these actors in the absence of an equally written modification or amendment whose ratification is outside their power. At the national level, whether the power of ratification lies in the hands of state legislatures or state conventions matters less than that it does not lie in the hands of Congress. I shall argue in part III that any judicial doctrine, such as the presumption of constitutionality, that effectively leaves to Congress the power to determine the limits on its powers is objectionable for this reason and should be rejected unless mandated by the text itself.

Putting a constitution in writing can be viewed as just another structural feature of our constitutional order along with separation of powers and federalism. It can no more be changed legitimately by those who are its servants than they can legitimately reject these other structural features. While the writtenness of the Constitution can obstruct the ability of Congress or the courts to make improvements to the constitutional scheme, so too can separation of powers and federalism.

I ask those readers who may not like structural obstacles to what they consider right results to consider their opinion of placing a burden of proof beyond a reasonable doubt on criminal prosecutors. Does not this barrier also obstruct juries from reaching the right result in particular cases? Do not guilty and dangerous murderers and sex offenders go free because proof of their guilt beyond a reasonable doubt is lacking? Yet we adhere to this structural restriction on right outcomes because of the benefits it brings to the rights of the innocent accused. The same is true of writtenness. Overriding writtenness to reach results that some deem superior places the rights of everyone at peril. Originalism as a method of interpretation is crucial to the structural protection provided by writtenness.

[54] See E. Allan Farnsworth, *Contracts*, 3d ed. (New York: Aspen Publishers, 1999), sec. 7.9, 461: "In the rare cases of a common meaning shared by both parties, the subjectivists have had the better of the argument. Though it is generally safe to say that a party's 'secret intention' will not carry the day, this is not a safe assertion if it happens that both parties shared the same 'secret intention.' " See also Melvin Aron Eisenberg, "The Responsive Model of Contract Law," *Stanford Law Review* 36 (1984): 1107 ("The rule that a mutually held subjective interpretation is determinative even if it is objectively unreasonable is well-supported by authority." Ibid., 1125).

Although I have claimed that the writtenness of a constitution entails a commitment to an original meaning that cannot be contradicted by later meanings or intentions, I have not claimed that the U.S. Constitution is a completely integrated writing. The original meaning of the terms of the Constitution as amended—such as the Ninth Amendment or the Privileges or Immunities Clause—might well authorize supplementation of its express terms in ways that do not contradict their original meaning.

To determine whether this is true, however, we must examine the original meanings of these open-textured provisions. About this originalists may differ among themselves.[55] If both the Ninth Amendment and the Privileges or Immunity Clause of the Fourteenth refer to natural rights not contained in the text, as was shown in chapter 3, then this requires we look outside the four corners of the Constitution to determine the content of these rights, privileges, or immunities. Any such inquiry would respect, rather than violate, the original meaning of the text.

There remains, of course, the difficult and important problem of producing a synthetic meaning of the Constitution from provisions enacted at different times by different generations. This problem has received close attention from Bruce Ackerman and I generally approve of his approach to the issue of synthesis.[56] I do not agree, however, that judicial changes to constitutional law—such as those adopted by the Supreme Court in the wake of the New Deal—are binding amendments of the Constitution itself that must be synthesized with its written provisions. The issue is not, as he believes, simply about whether the method of ratifying these changes conforms to the procedures detailed in Article V.[57] The analysis presented here reveals another issue he overlooks: whether the so-called New Deal amendments were put in a definitive and identifiable writing along with the rest of the Constitution.

[55] For an originalist who contests the view that the Ninth Amendment authorizes textual supplementation, see Thomas B. McAffee, "Prolegomena to a Meaningful Debate of the 'Unwritten Constitution' Thesis," *University of Cincinnati Law Review* 61 (1992): 107. It is more difficult to characterize the positions of those originalists who take issue with Michael Curtis's view of the Privileges or Immunities Clause, but a useful compendium is contained in Bret Boyce, "Originalism and the Fourteenth Amendment," *Wake Forest Law Review* 33 (1998): 909 (discussing the views of, among others, Raoul Berger, John Harrison, Earl Maltz, and William Nelson).

[56] See Ackerman, *Transformations*, 131–62 (providing syntheses of the founding with the Reconstruction and alleged New Deal amendments to the Constitution).

[57] See Bruce Ackerman, "A Generation of Betrayal," *Fordham Law Review* 65 (1997): 1519 ("The question, in short, is whether the reception debate will be structured by a formalist understanding that the only constitutional achievements the present generation is bound to notice are those monumentalized through the process of Article Five").

As Ackerman acknowledges, President Roosevelt decided to refrain from seeking a written amendment.[58] In Roosevelt's own words: "There are many types of amendment proposed. Each one is radically different from the other. There is no substantial group within the Congress or outside it who are agreed on any single amendment."[59] This decision doomed the changes implemented by his appointed justices to less than constitutional status. The effort required to settle on a single written formulation produces the virtues of formality—deliberation, caution, and clarity—wholly apart from the formality by which that formulation is ratified. Because changes made to constitutional law in the absence of a written amendment lack these virtues, they are not entitled to the same respect as written amendments. Though judges may not change the Constitution, they are free to change their own constitutional doctrines, especially where those doctrines themselves violate the terms of the written Constitution.

ORIGINAL MEANING AND CONSTITUTIONAL LEGITIMACY

Though practical considerations are sufficient to justify respecting the original meaning of the Constitution, considerations of legitimacy justify originalism as well. Constitutional legitimacy requires assurance that only proper laws are enacted, applied, and enforced. A written constitution is a crucial structural feature that helps provide such assurance. This assurance would not be forthcoming, however, if the political actors who must respect these limits, including judges, are free to disregard them. In short, it contributes to constitutional legitimacy for the original meaning of written limits on the powers of lawmakers to remain the same until they are properly amended.

To be clear, the substance of what the Constitution says is one thing, its writtenness is another. If the substance of a constitution's original meaning falls short of what it takes to establish a legitimate lawmaking process, then that constitution is not binding and can be ignored despite the fact it is in writing. Interpretation is one thing; assessing the merits of the meaning so discerned is quite another.

Serious confusion results from conflating a commitment to a written constitution with the merits of what a particular constitution may say. Judges and legislators cannot change what the Constitution says without destroying their commitment to the written Constitution. But we

[58] See Ackerman, *We the People*, 320–32 (discussing proposed amendments and Roosevelt's decision to reject that means of constitutional change).

[59] Samuel Rosenman, ed., "The Public Papers of and Addresses of Franklin D. Roosevelt" (1937), 132, as it appears in Ackerman, *We the People*, 326.

are bound by laws passed pursuant to the written Constitution only if what it says establishes lawmaking procedures that are good enough to impart the benefit of the doubt on the laws that emerge from the constitutional process.

Of course, to determine the existence of a prima facie duty to obey a law, we must look beyond what the Constitution says to see how it has in fact been interpreted and construed over the years since its adoption and amendment. Suppose the original meaning of these provisions was "good enough" to establish a lawmaking process that imparts legitimacy upon the commands issued by government officials acting in its name. This would still not impart legitimacy on legal commands if the procedures and constraints mandated by the original meaning are ignored by judges and other officials. This is especially so if these procedures and constraints were changed to something that is not "good enough" from the standpoint of legitimacy.[60] If so many deviations have been made from the original meaning that the lawmaking processes no longer have the same legitimacy-providing integrity, then the binding nature of its products may be more dubious.

Some may argue that the original scheme as formally ratified was not "good enough" to create laws that bind in conscience or, even if it once was, it would be no longer in today's world. Only because the system we now have differs in important respects from the original meaning of the written Constitution does this lawmaking process provide the assurances that legitimacy requires. This appears to be Paul Brest's position when he rejects moderate originalism on the ground that it cannot justify those aspects of current constitutional doctrine that he and others today deem important.[61]

Whatever its merits, were this claim to be made explicitly, it would improve the quality of the discourse concerning the appropriate method of constitutional interpretation and the value of originalism. For those who make this claim would have to admit that they have deviated from the original meaning of the Constitution as formally ratified and then

[60] There are two closely related but distinguishable threats to legitimacy posed by unwritten changes: The first is that deviations from the original meaning of a written constitution will undermine the legitimacy of a lawmaking process, one of whose components is the commitment to a written constitution. The second is the substitution of inferior lawmaking processes for the superior ones stipulated in the written constitution. Even if the second of these has not occurred—perhaps because the deviation represents an *improvement* in the lawmaking process—this means for accomplishing it still undermines legitimacy in the first of these two ways.

[61] See Brest, "Misconceived Quest for Original Understanding," 231. See also Jack Balkin, "Agreements with Hell, and Other Objects of Our Faith," *Fordham Law Review* 65 (1997): 1703 (discussing the implications of "constitutional evil" for a duty of fidelity to a constitution).

identify their criteria of legitimacy and how the resultant system can produce laws that are binding in conscience on the individual. They would also have to explain how the values provided by a written constitution can be preserved when the writing can be contradicted without formal amendment by legislatures or judges who object to its provisions. Moreover, those who would deviate from the written Constitution in this manner would have to explain why we bother to keep it around, except perhaps as a soporific for the masses.

To repeat, if the original meaning of the Constitution is not "good enough," then originalism is not warranted because the Constitution is itself defective and illegitimate. This represents a rejection of the Constitution, not a rejection of originalism per se. Whatever is put in its place is not the Constitution, however much an improvement it may be. Nor is this a purely hypothetical situation.

It may well be that the original Constitution was not legitimate, at least with respect to slaves (and perhaps in other respects as well). In which case, slaves would have had no duty to obey a command because it was constitutional, nor would others have had a moral duty to obey laws protecting slavery, such as the fugitive slave acts. The more difficult question, much debated among abolitionists at the time, is whether a judge—having consented by oath to be bound by the Constitution—had a duty to enforce laws that are consistent with the original meaning of the Constitution.[62] Once again, to claim that they are not bound is to reject the Constitution, not originalism.

Before the Constitution can be rejected, however, two things must occur. First, one must determine what its words mean to see if they come up short. These words were put in writing so they would remain the same until properly changed in writing. Therefore the meaning to be evaluated is that which was established at the time of enactment or amendment. Ascertaining the original meaning of the text is, then, a prerequisite for rejecting it as inadequate.

Second, it must be shown and admitted that the written Constitution has failed because its substance is inadequate to provide the assurances that legitimacy requires and, therefore, we are not governing by its terms any longer. In its place will be a provision that a court finds superior to that contained in the text. Any actor who tries to substitute another provision from that contained in the Constitution without rejecting the text is trying to have his cake and eat it too.

---

[62] See Robert Cover, *Justice Accused: Antislavery and the Judicial Process* (New Haven: Yale University Press, 1975). The debate over judicial duties was somewhat muddied by the claim that judges had a duty to interpret the Constitution according to the original *intent* of its framers, even where that intent had not clearly been expressed in the written Constitu-

Short of making the claim of illegitimacy, however, we are bound to respect the original meaning of a text, not by the dead hand of the past, but because we today—right here, right now—profess our commitment to this written Constitution, and original meaning interpretation follows inexorably from this commitment. Though a judge or scholar can jettison that original meaning by disclaiming his or her commitment to this particular written Constitution on the ground that what is says is not good enough, this is a rhetorical choice both courts and scholars have been generally unwilling to make.

Judges very much want the general public—especially those who disagree with the judge's decision—to believe that it is not the judge but "the Constitution" that commands both a particular legal result and the obedience of the public to the ruling of the court. Judges do not want to be in the position of saying, "Do this because I say so"; they want to say, "I do this and you must obey because the Constitution says so." If a judge were openly to disregard the written Constitution by unilaterally changing its meaning in favor of a "better" result, would the general public submit as readily? Would they be bound in conscience to submit at all? Because the risk of disobedience and illegitimacy is too great, judges continue to pledge their fealty to the written Constitution. Though constitutional scholars and activists may be more daring than judges, even they are generally reluctant to abandon the rhetoric of adherence to the written Constitution. Even they want to argue that it is the Constitution, not them, that mandates a particular result. Otherwise, what exactly is the expertise of a "constitutional scholar"? For this reason, if no other, originalism refuses to die.

Some may find it odd or unexpected to see originalism linked with natural rights. They associate natural rights with the argument that an unjust law is not binding and can be trumped by considerations of justice. If originalism is grounded on considerations of legitimacy based on natural rights, rather than on popular sovereignty or consent, does this not entail that we can override the original meaning of a constitutional provision whenever we conclude that this meaning conflicts with justice?

Any such objection would confuse the status of a statute with that of a constitution. Whereas ordinary legislation potentially can be overridden by considerations of justice (if a constitution so permits), a constitutional provision cannot. If as a matter of positive law, the original meaning and proper construction of a written constitution permit judges to protect natural rights by finding statutes unconstitutional—as I will contend the Constitution does—it does not follow that judges are authorized to disre-

---

tion. The debate over just this question between abolitionists Lysander Spooner and Wendell Phillips is described in Barnett, "Was Slavery Unconstitutional?"

gard the original meaning of a legitimate written constitution when they think this meaning violates the background rights retained by the people. Allowing this would undercut the writtenness that is necessary to lock in an initially legitimate system.[63]

In short, to decide whether a particular written constitution creates a legitimate process of lawmaking requires, first, an interpretation of its meaning and, second, an evaluation of whether the process created by that meaning is "good enough" to impart legitimacy on validly made laws. Step two of this assessment does not entail any duty or power to disregard the meaning determined in step one. To the contrary, it takes that meaning as given as a matter of positive law and evaluates it.

HANDLING THE OBJECTIONS TO ORIGINALISM

How does this version of originalism—based on original meaning and justified on grounds of constitutional legitimacy rather than popular sovereignty—meet the criticisms that have been leveled at theories based on original intent? As was already discussed, the same historical evidence offered by Powell in opposition to original intent supports original meaning based on "the public meaning or intent of a state paper."[64] And this public meaning is "evidenced in the Constitution's language and discerned through structural methods of interpretation; it did not refer to the personal intentions of the framers or anyone else,"[65] including those who "adopted it."[66]

If the reasons I am offering for why original meaning should be the starting point of constitutional interpretation are correct, however, it ultimately does not matter if this was the method intended or practiced by the founders. There are independent normative reasons for adopting it anyhow. Nevertheless, the fact that the founding generation settled on this method (before it was eventually abandoned) undercuts any suggestion that we are disregarding their original intent to adhere to original meaning. Further, though some say the founders tended to shift their methods of interpretation to serve partisan concerns, it is also clear that

[63] In a fundamentally illegitimate system, judges, like other citizens, might have different duties. Lacking a duty of obedience, they might have a right of resistance. So the duty of judges to adhere to the original meaning of a particular constitution depends on whether the lawmaking processes established by that constitution are good enough to establish its legitimacy. If they are, then originalist interpretation is warranted; if they are not, then the constitution itself is not binding and all bets are off.

[64] Powell, "Original Understanding of Original Intent," 935.

[65] Ibid., 948.

[66] Ibid., 935.

those who had original meaning (as opposed to original intent) on their side were not shy to assert it, and were rarely condemned for doing so.[67] Perhaps most importantly, the fact that this method of interpretation was endorsed by the same persons who devised the Constitution should give us confidence that it makes some sense.

What of the objection against originalism made by Brest and others that it is simply too hard to discern the intentions of the framers? We have already seen how, while rejecting a strict originalism as impractical, Brest conceded the efficacy of a more moderate originalism. Yet even his criticisms of strict original intent originalism have been answered with some persuasiveness by Richard Kay, whose arguments apply with even greater force to the issue of original public meaning.

When making the binary decisions of whether a particular act of government is within or without its powers, or has or has not violated a background right, Kay contends, we need only "decide which of the two possible answers in that case is *more likely* correct."[68] Picking one of two alternatives, though sometimes difficult, is far from impossible.

> It is true that we can never know the original intentions with certainty, but then we can never know any speaker's or writer's intent with certainty. Nevertheless, it is almost always possible to examine the constitutional text and other evidence of intent associated with it and make a reasonable, good faith judgment about which result is more likely consistent with that intent. Of course confidence in these judgments will be different in different situations, but one answer will almost always appear better than the other. Indeed, one of the two possible responses may be obviously incorrect because, while it is theoretically possible that the lawmakers held such an intention, the available historical evidence will be overwhelmingly against it.[69]

What is true of original intentions is true a fortiori of the easier-to-discern original meaning.[70]

Moreover, compelling analyses of the original meaning of even the most controversial provisions of the Constitution have been developed, from those where the evidence of original meaning is overwhelming—the

---

[67] See Lynch, *Negotiating the Constitution.*

[68] Richard S. Kay, "Adherence to the Original Intentions in Constitutional Adjudication: Three Objections and Responses," *Northwestern University Law Review* 82 (1988): 244. Though Kay defends an original intention version of originalism based on popular sovereignty which is not the version that I am defending here, some of his arguments on behalf of original intent originalism apply to original meaning originalism as well.

[69] Ibid. (footnotes omitted).

[70] See also Keith E. Whittington, *Constitutional Interpretation: Textual Meaning, Original Intent, and Judicial Review* (Lawrence: University Press of Kansas, 1999) (discussing the problem of summing intentions).

Second Amendment, for example[71]—or closer but still persuasive as it is with the Ninth Amendment[72] and the Privileges or Immunities Clause.[73] Indeed, the past fifteen years has yielded a boom tide of originalist scholarship that has established the original meanings of several clauses that had been shrouded in mystery primarily for want of serious inquiry.[74] Like any other form of legal argument, a commitment to original meaning requires only that we respect the meaning supported by the most persuasive evidence.

That original meaning originalism is possible is also evidenced by the respect we have seen that it receives from such scholars as Bruce Ackerman, Akhil Amar, Ronald Dworkin, and—when speaking of moderate originalism—even Paul Brest himself. Though not all originalists themselves, these and other thoughtful scholars do not dismiss original meaning originalism as impractical. Even those who, like Joseph Lynch, criticize the framers for inconstancy to their professed originalism have little difficulty discerning when they have deviated from original meaning.

For me, however, these were never the most persuasive arguments against originalism. I was always moved more by the "dead hand" objection. Why are we bound by the intentions, expectations, or original meanings of long-dead ancestors—in my case and most others, someone else's ancestors at that? Then and now, why are those who were excluded from the ratification process—because of race, gender, age, or the fact they had yet to be born or immigrate into this country—bound to the commands of the founders as expressed in the original Constitution or to the commands of those who later amended it?[75]

In one sense, the simple answer to these questions is that we are not. As I explained in chapter 1, with rare exceptions the Constitution binds government officials and does not purport to bind citizens. It is easier to see how each government official, including each judge, who takes an oath to preserve, protect, and defend the Constitution is consensually bound to its provisions in a way nonconsenting citizens are not. What would that oath signify if the Constitution had no meaning independent

---

[71] See Randy E. Barnett and Don B. Kates, "Under Fire: The New Consensus on the Second Amendment," *Emory Law Journal* 45 (1996): 1210 (summarizing this evidence and providing citations to the literature).

[72] See Randy E. Barnett, "James Madison's Ninth Amendment," in *The Rights Retained by the People*, vol. 1; Randy E. Barnett, "Implementing the Ninth Amendment," in *The Rights Retained by the People*, vol. 2.

[73] See Michael Kent Curtis, *No State Shall Abridge: The Fourteenth Amendment and the Bill of Rights* (Durham, N.C.: Duke University Press, 1986).

[74] Yet another reason for concluding that originalism is alive and well.

[75] See Dorothy E. Roberts, "The Meaning of Blacks' Fidelity to the Constitution," *Fordham Law Review* 65 (1997): 1761 (discussing whether black Americans have any duty of fidelity to the Constitution).

of that which these same government officials may give to it in their unfettered discretion?[76]

Regardless of whether government officials have consented to be bound by the Constitution, I have shown why the paramount issue of constitutional legitimacy is whether the commands, not of the Constitution itself, but of government officials rendered pursuant to constitutional authority, are binding in conscience on us. The answer to this question will depend on the quality of the lawmaking and enforcement processes that the Constitution establishes. One of these qualities is adherence to a written constitution by those who speak and act in its name, a commitment belied by unwritten changes to the meaning of the Constitution.

Finally, because the binding nature of laws made pursuant to constitutional processes governed by the original meaning of the Constitution is not based on popular sovereignty or consent, it is not undercut, except indirectly, by the fact that women, slaves, children, resident aliens, convicts, or all of us now living were excluded from the ratification process and therefore did not consent to be governed by the Constitution. Though my ancestors arrived in the late eighteenth and early twentieth centuries, I am still bound in conscience by the laws produced pursuant to the Constitution if there is reason to be confident that the manner by which these laws were produced and enforced effectively ensures their necessity and guards against their injustice; that there is reason to believe that such laws are not merely a product of faction and they do not violate my rights or the rights of others.

If the lawmaking and law enforcement process described in the Constitution are "good enough" to merit such a benefit of the doubt, I am at least presumptively bound independent of how this lawmaking process might have come about.[77] But this also means that, if those processes are good enough, then they need to be protected by an originalist interpretation of the document that established them. This is a version and justification of originalism that I think even most nonoriginalists ought to accept.

CONCLUSION

The relationship between a written constitution and legitimacy, then, is twofold. First, constitutional legitimacy depends on what the writing

[76] Spooner, "Unconstitutionality of Slavery," 222.

[77] Nevertheless, as was mentioned above, the fact that it was designed by some very smart, sophisticated, and generally well-motivated persons and was subject to the ratification of representatives of a large segment of the population provides some reason for confidence—though not enough to establish its legitimacy standing alone.

says. Are its provisions sufficient to create a lawmaking process that produces necessary and proper commands that bind in conscience even those who did not consent to it? For the laws that result from a constitutional process to be legitimately imposed on those who have not consented, we must be persuaded that the lawmaking procedures implemented by such a constitution give assurances that lawmaking and law enforcement will not violate the background rights retained by the people—whether or not they consented to its implementation.

Second, assuming that the lawmaking process initially established by a written constitution is legitimate, the fact that a constitution says the right things in writing helps assure that these provisions will be respected over time—an assurance that an unwritten constitution or a written constitution that can be freely modified by legislative practice or judicial opinion cannot provide. Only if lawmakers cannot change the scope of their own powers can the rights of the people be in any way assured. In this way, constitutional legitimacy based on natural rights, rather than popular sovereignty or consent, can ground a commitment to originalism.

CHAPTER FIVE

Constitutional Construction: Supplementing Original Meaning

> Ordinary language simply has not got the "hardness," the logical hardness, to cut axioms in it. . . . If you begin to draw inferences [common speech] soon begins to go "soft" and fluffs up somewhere. You may just as well carve cameos on a cheese *soufflé*.[1]
>
> —FRIEDRICH WAISMANN (1959)

VAGUENESS AND THE LIMITS OF INTERPRETATION

Although both constitutional legitimacy and the commitment to a written constitution necessitate reliance upon the original meaning of the text, originalist interpretation has its limits—limits that inhere in the use of language to guide conduct. As the framers were well aware, language can be vague and this is no less true of the language found in the Constitution. For example, during a colloquy in the Constitutional Convention over whether states were precluded from laying certain duties on shipping, Madison said this depended on the extent of the power "to regulate commerce." "These terms are vague," he conceded, "but seem to exclude this power of the States."[2]

Depending on the context any word can be vague, but some words are more vague than others. Indeed, terms and phrases are often chosen by legal drafters precisely because they are less rather than more precise than other available formulations. Drafters who, perhaps for political reasons, wish to avoid appearing to endorse a controversial result in a particular situation may use a phrase whose meaning is sufficiently "fuzzy at the edges" that it is unclear whether or not it would reach that result. More often, a vague term is chosen because drafters realize that the resolution of a future problem will depend on specific factual circumstances that cannot be specified in advance and therefore must be decided by others. Though they cannot determine the outcome of these future disputes with a precise rule, the drafters may still wish to guide or limit the discretion

---

[1] Friedrich Waismann, "How I See Philosophy," in A. J. Ayre, ed., *Logical Positivism* (New York: Free Press, 1959), 345.

[2] Madison, *Notes of Debates*, 644 (statement of J. Madison).

of these future decision makers and attempt this by deliberately using vague, though not vacuous, language.

Terms that are vague must be distinguished from those that are ambiguous. A word is ambiguous if it has more than one meaning and it is unclear which meaning is intended.[3] Does the right to keep and bear "arms," for example, refer to weapons or to human limbs? By consulting extrinsic historical evidence, we find that, given the context, "weapons" was the objective meaning of "arms" in the Second Amendment at the time of its enactment. Interpreting "arms" to mean "limbs" would be factually erroneous. Discovering—as a historical matter—which meaning was conveyed by the use of the term "arms" is an act of interpretation.

In contrast, vagueness is the problem of applying a term to a marginal object. Such weapons as guns and knives are clearly included in the term "arms." How about long heavy flashlights of the sort carried by the police? How about a starter's pistol that fires only blanks? Whether a particular term includes or does not include a particular object can, but need not, be a historical question. How general or abstract was the usage of a particular word in context?

The term "arms" appears on its face to apply to any weapon, but perhaps there is evidence that it was understood by reasonable listeners as referring only to weapons in use at the time; or that it referred only to those weapons that could be "borne" or carried by a single person; or that it referred only to weapons that, if used as intended, would not create an unreasonable risk of harm to innocent third parties. Convincing evidence of a more narrow historical usage would establish an original meaning that would displace a more general "plain" meaning.

Interpreting the objective meaning of the Constitution requires a historical inquiry into, not only the choice of meanings embraced by ambiguous terms, but also what constitutional scholars call the "level of generality" or degree of abstraction conveyed by the framers' vague words or phrases. In Michael McConnell's words, "A genuine commitment to the semantic intentions of the Framers requires the interpreter to seek the level of generality at which the particular language was understood by its Framers."[4] As Keith Whittington has argued: "The level of generality at which terms were defined is not an a priori theoretical question but a contextualized historical one. In some instances, the founders may have used terms quite expan-

---

[3] See Farnsworth, " 'Meaning' in the Law of Contracts," 953–56 (explaining the concept of vagueness and distinguishing it from ambiguity).

[4] McConnell, "Importance of Humility," 1280. But compare Ronald Dworkin, "Reflections on Fidelity," *Fordham Law Review* 65 (1997): 1808 ("[T]here is no such thing as the level of generality at which someone's moral opinions are most accurately reported, though there *is* such a thing as the most accurate report of the level of generality at which a person spoke on a particular occasion").

sively, and at other times seemingly broad terms were conceptualized at a relatively narrow level."[5] In short, part of finding original meaning is determining the level of generality with which a particular term was used.

Even when a historical inquiry can establish that the original meaning of a particular term was broader or narrower than its plain meaning today, this original meaning may not by itself tell us whether it includes a particular object that lies outside its core meaning but still possibly within its margins. For example, is thermal imaging of a house to detect the heat produced by marijuana cultivation a "search" referred to in the Fourth Amendment?[6] There can be no purely historical answer to this question in this example because the object to which the term is being applied did not exist at the time of the framing. To ask whether the founders would have considered thermal imaging to be included in the meaning of "search" is a counterfactual, not a factual, inquiry.

The more general or vague the term (determined historically), the more likely it is that uncertain applications will arise outside its core meaning. When this occurs, "interpretation," strictly speaking, will have run out and the meaning of the text must be *determined* rather than found. After a level of generality is established historically, whether an object falls within or outside the ambit of a vague term is a matter of "construction" rather than of interpretation. We could try to avoid such determinations or constructions by limiting the judicial application of constitutional terms to their core meanings, but such a limitation would itself be a choice or construction and not the result of any interpretation.

Because every word has a core meaning, even vague terms are not usually wholly indeterminate.[7] But when the application of a constitutional provision depends on whether a particular object falls within the marginal meaning of a vague term, such a provision may be underdeterminate.[8] Any lack of determinacy that results from using vague terms is one of the prices we (or the framers) pay for a writing that uses general concepts and abstract principles in place of specific rules; it is also one of the well-known virtues of this particular writing. Because its language is

---

[5] Whittington, *Constitutional Interpretation*, 187. This claim is more elaborately explained in the context of Ronald Dworkin's characterization of originalism in Keith E. Whittington, "Dworkin's 'Originalism': The Role of Intentions in Constitutional Interpretation," *Review of Politics* 62 (2000): 197.

[6] See *Kyllo v. United States*, No. 99–8508 (2001) in which Justice Scalia found that it was a search.

[7] See Lawrence B. Solum, "On the Indeterminacy Crisis: Critiquing Critical Dogma," *University of Chicago Law Review* 54 (1987): 473: "The law is *indeterminate* with respect to a given case if and only if the set of materials is identical with the set of all imaginable results."

[8] See ibid. "The law is *underdeterminate* with respect to a given case if and only if the set of results in the case that can be squared with the legal materials is a nonidentical subset of the set of all imaginable results."

deliberately vague in places, the Constitution can be applied to far more situations and changed circumstances than had every provision been expressed with rule-like precision.

For better or worse, then, the U.S. Constitution requires more than originalist interpretation to be applied to cases and controversies. Owing to the vagueness of language and the limits of historical inquiry, originalist interpretation may not result in a unique rule of law to be applied to a particular case or controversy. When interpretation has provided all the guidance it can but more guidance is needed, constitutional interpretation must be supplemented by constitutional construction—within the bounds established by original meaning. In this manner, construction fills the unavoidable gaps in constitutional meaning when interpretation has reached it limits. It is to that "gap-filling" method I now turn.

CONSTITUTIONAL CONSTRUCTION

While the original meaning of the text might be demonstrably inconsistent with a multitude of possible outcomes, it may still not provide enough guidance to identify a single rule of law to apply to a particular case at hand. Indeed, it frequently will not. When this occurs, it becomes necessary to adopt a construction of the text that is consistent with its original meaning but not deducible from it. Keith Whittington distinguishes between interpretation and construction as follows:

> Constitutional interpretation is essentially legalistic, but constitutional construction is essentially political. Its precondition is that parts of the constitutional text have no discoverable meaning. Although the clauses and structures that make up the text cannot be simply empty of meaning, for they are clearly recognizable as language, the meaning that they do convey may be so broad and underdetermined as to be incapable of faithful reduction to legal rules. . . . Regardless of the extent of judicial interpretation of certain aspects of the Constitution, there will remain an impenetrable sphere of meaning that cannot be simply discovered. The judiciary may be able to delimit textual meaning, hedging in the possibilities, but after all judgments have been rendered specifying discoverable meaning, major indeterminacies may remain. The specification of a single governing meaning from these possibilities requires an act of creativity beyond interpretation. . . . This additional step is the construction of meaning.[9]

---

[9] Whittington, *Constitutional Interpretation*, 7. See also Keith E. Whittington, *Constitutional Construction: Divided Powers and Constitutional Meaning* (Cambridge: Harvard University Press, 1999), 1–19.

He then offers a long list of constitutional constructions adopted either by courts in their opinions or by the other branches of government in legislation or executive orders to fill the gaps in the original meaning of the text and help "transform constitutional theory into constitutional practice."[10]

Whittington groups constructions into seven categories: (1) organic structures—e.g., specification of size of Supreme Court; (2) delegation and distribution of political powers—e.g., judicial refusal to issue advisory opinions; (3) individual and collective rights—e.g., no right to secession; (4) structures of political participation/citizenship—e.g., specification of a single date for national elections; (5) jurisdiction—e.g., state annexation through treaty; (6) domestic government role—e.g., national bankruptcy law; and (7) international posture—e.g., entrance into NATO.[11] Each of these doctrines fleshes out how the government is "constituted" in ways that are not specified in the written Constitution, but which require some specification nevertheless.

Though the process of constitutional construction fills the gaps within original meaning, I do not share Whittington's characterization of the process of construction as "political." This term implies that construction is necessarily and always political or that it involves a completely open-ended choice unguided by constitutional principle. That is not, I think, even Whittington's conception of constitutional construction. Rather, there is often a gap between abstract or general principles of the kind found in the Constitution and the rules of law that are needed to put these principles into action. This does not mean, however, that the choice of rules is unguided by these abstract or general principles.

The need for construction brought on by generality arises also with abstract principles of justice based on natural rights. With natural rights, this gap arises because these rights are based on general features of human life. That is, we abstract from the particulars of a complex reality to identify general lessons that apply to different situations. These abstract rights still need to be applied to actual controversies in a factually complex world. While abstract rights or principles may remain constant over time and circumstances, their application to particular situations by means of legal rules will of necessity vary with the situation. Moreover, there is often more than one way to satisfy the requirements of these general principles. For this reason, some degree of "construction" or determination of a particular legal rule, not inconsistent with the require-

---

[10] Whittington, *Constitutional Construction*, 8.

[11] For the entire list of Whittington's examples, see ibid., 12. Note that in several instances he lists constructions that oppose each other, e.g., "federal incorporation of banks" and "no federal incorporation of banks." Ibid.

ments of justice, is needed so that people can have knowledge of what justice requires of them.[12]

The same problem of applying general principles to factually complex cases arises with the Constitution. When the abstract terms of the Constitution do not directly resolve a particular dispute, some construction (as opposed to interpretation) of constitutional meaning is needed. As Whittington observes, constructions operate "where the text is so broad or so underdetermined as to be incapable of faithful but exhaustive reduction to legal rules."[13]

Of course, some provisions of the Constitution are rule-like enough to be applied directly to most cases without need of intermediate doctrine. The most oft-cited example of this is the provision limiting the presidency to persons who are at least thirty-five years old. In contrast, other provisions, like the Equal Protection and Due Process Clauses, are abstract and general and some choice must be made among possible ways of putting them into effect. Still other provisions, such as the Ninth Amendment and the Privileges or Immunities Clause, explicitly refer to standards or principles that lie outside the text and therefore authorize supplementation of the text by other materials. With the latter two categories of text, some construction is required.

Because originalist scholars have typically been preoccupied either with defending originalism against criticism by nonoriginalists or doing originalist analysis of particular clauses, few have addressed the limits of originalism and the need for nonoriginalist constitutional construction. Among those who have is Robert N. Clinton, who expands upon Michael Perry's distinction between "extraconstitutional" and "contraconstitutional" interpretation.

Extraconstitutional interpretation "adds normative principles or powers to the document that were neither envisioned by its adopters *nor contrary to their intentions*, as demonstrated by the language and structure of the document as originally understood or by affirmative historical proofs of the original meaning of that language."[14] Contraconstitutional interpretation, in contrast, "refers to ahistorical interpretations that are inconsistent with the constitutional language as originally understood or with affirmative historical demonstrations of the original meaning of that language."[15]

Clinton contends that, when the original meaning of the Constitution is exhausted, "extraconstitutional interpretation generally constitutes a legitimate interpretive methodology, facilitating the flexible enforcement

[12] See Barnett, *Structure of Liberty* (discussing second-order problem of knowledge).
[13] Whittington, *Constitutional Construction*, 5.
[14] Clinton, "Original Understanding," 1264–65.
[15] Ibid., 1265.

and growth of the document."[16] In contrast, "contraconstitutional interpretation is illegitimate because it tends to undermine public confidence in
constitutional governance and the instrumentalist value of constitutional
stability."[17] In other words, allowing extraconstitutional but not contraconstitutional construction is consistent with the reasons we adhere to a
written constitution. "If a written constitution is to be treated seriously
for its value in fostering constitutional stability, a *construction* that is
inconsistent with the text as originally understood surely cannot be accepted." That the value of writtenness extends beyond constitutional stability only bolsters Clinton's claim.[18]

While there is every reason to call interpretations or constructions that
contradict the original meaning "contraconstitutional" and some reason
to call constructions that supplement its meaning "extraconstitutional,"
I nevertheless think the latter term is unfortunate and misleading. Like
Whittington's use of "political," it suggests that such constructions are
themselves completely unconstrained by the determinable original meaning of the text, and that any construction that does not contradict the
original meaning is equally acceptable.

As Clinton himself recognizes, however, constitutional construction
should be constrained, though it cannot be entirely determined, by interpretation based on original meaning. "While the failure of historical inquiry to demonstrate a single correct original meaning of the Constitution
on a particular interpretive question justifies the invocation of nonoriginalist interpretive strategies, it does not automatically negate the significance of the explored originalist history to the nonoriginalist interpretive
inquiry."[19] Rather, the original meaning of the text can limit the range of
acceptable choices made on nonoriginalist grounds:

> [I]n some cases, depending on the reason for the failure of the originalist quest,
> the originalist history might limit the interpretive choices generated by the non-
> originalist methodologies. In some instances interpretive choices that are plausi-
> ble from a nonoriginalist perspective may prove to be inconsistent with a *range*
> of historically derived potential interpretations of the Constitution.[20]

Because constitutional constructions are neither *wholly* "political" nor
wholly "extraconstitutional," I would avoid these terms. The choice
among possible constructions, while not dictated by original interpretation, can be and often is limited by them. In this way, constitutional con-

---

[16] Ibid.
[17] Ibid.
[18] Ibid. (emphasis added).
[19] Ibid., 1275.
[20] Ibid.

structions, though not deducible immediately from the text, still may properly be connected to or constrained by it.

The text provides what Frederick Schauer has helpfully called a "frame" that excludes many potential constructions. "The language of a [constitutional] clause, whether seemingly general or seemingly specific, establishes a boundary, or a frame, albeit a frame with fuzzy edges. Even though the language itself does not tell us what goes on within the frame, it does tell us when we have gone outside it."[21] Therefore, although by definition constructions are not *in* the Constitution, they can be *of* the Constitution.[22]

CONSTITUTIONAL CONSTRUCTION AND LEGITIMACY

Though both Whittington and Clinton are originalists who see the limits of originalist interpretation and the need for construction, neither says much about how to choose among the constructions that are consistent with the original meaning of the text. Most who engage in constitutional construction strive to take into account constitutional principles that underlie the text. The most important of these are the structural principles of separation of powers and federalism. Much construction seeks to stay true to the meaning and implications of these widely held constitutional principles. For example, Thomas Jefferson maintained that

> When an instrument admits two constructions, the one safe, the other dangerous, the one precise, the other indefinite, I prefer that which is safe & precise. I had rather ask an enlargement of power from the nation, where it is found necessary, than to assume it by a construction that would make our powers boundless.[23]

The discussion of constitutional legitimacy in part I suggests another important but generally overlooked criterion for determining constitutional constructions. Because lawmakers acting pursuant to their constitutional powers govern those who did not consent, to be legitimate the law-

---

[21] See Frederick Schauer, "Easy Cases," *Southern California Law Review* 58 (1985): 430 (footnotes omitted).

[22] None of the subtleties explored by either Whittington or Clinton are addressed by Farber and Sherry in their criticism of originalism. See Farber and Sherry, *Desperately Seeking Certainty*, 10–28. Nor do they respond to an earlier formulation of the argument for original meaning originalism presented in chapter 4, though it is cited by them for the claim that "it takes a theory to beat a theory." See ibid., 171 n. 5. Though they reject this proposition (ibid., 6), Farber and Sherry seem not to realize that their "pragmatic alternative to grand theory" is just another theory, however "grand," that must be shown to be normatively and practically superior to the alternatives, which is precisely what they attempt to do.

[23] Letter to Wilson Carey Nicholas (September 7, 1803), in Merrill D. Peterson, ed., *Thomas Jefferson: Writings* (New York: Library of America, 1984), 1140.

making processes must provide assurances that both the enumerated and unenumerated rights of those who are governed will not be violated. To enhance legitimacy, therefore, vague terms should be given the meaning that is most respectful of the rights of all who are affected, and rules of construction most respectful of these rights should be adopted to put general constitutional provisions into legal effect.

This relationship between natural rights and positive law was asserted early and forcefully by Justice Samuel Chase in the case of *Calder v. Bull* (1798):

> There are certain vital principles in our free republican governments, which will determine and overrule an apparent and flagrant abuse of legislative power; as to authorize manifest injustice by positive law; or to take away that security for personal liberty, or private property, for the protection whereof the government was established. An act of the legislature (for I cannot call it a law), contrary to the great first principles of the social compact, cannot be considered a rightful exercise of legislative authority.[24]

Seven years later, a rule of construction—though statutory, not constitutional—that reflects this position was provided by Chief Justice Marshall, who wrote: "Where rights are infringed, where fundamental principles are overthrown, where the general system of laws is departed from, the legislative intention must be expressed with *irresistible clearness* to induce a court of justice to suppose a design to effect such objects."[25]

One can call this making the Constitution "the best it can be," as Ronald Dworkin might, but this method of construction—as distinct from interpretation—is appropriate only when terms are genuinely vague, when the original level of generality can be satisfied by more than one rule of law, or when the Constitution authorizes supplementation. In none of these situations should the process of construction be used to change the original meaning of the Constitution without adhering to the formalities governing amendments that are needed to preserve its integrity as a written constitution.

Robert Clinton offers a helpful flowchart to illustrate how construction works alongside originalist interpretation, presented here in modified

---

[24] *Calder v. Bull*, 3 U.S. 386, 388 (1798).

[25] *United States v. Fisher*, 6 U.S. [2 Cranch] 358, 390 (1805) (emphasis added). Though Marshall uses the term "intention," Powell makes clear that the founding generation took an "objective" approach to determining such intentions. See Powell, "Original Understanding of Original Intent." For a discussion of how Lysander Spooner used this as a canon of *constitutional* construction sufficiently powerful to call the constitutionality of slavery into question, see Barnett, "Was Slavery Unconstitutional?"

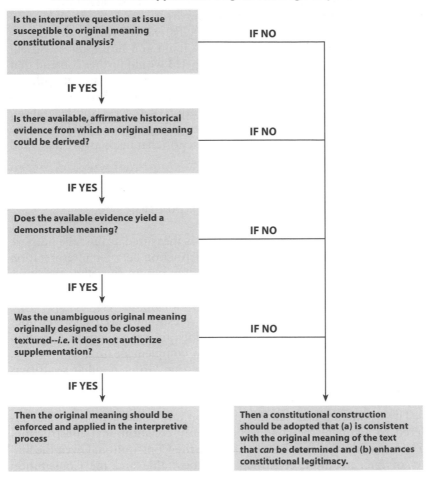

How Construction Supplements Original Meaning Interpretation

Is the interpretive question at issue susceptible to original meaning constitutional analysis?

IF NO

IF YES

Is there available, affirmative historical evidence from which an original meaning could be derived?

IF NO

IF YES

Does the available evidence yield a demonstrable meaning?

IF NO

IF YES

Was the unambiguous original meaning originally designed to be closed textured--*i.e.* it does not authorize supplementation?

IF NO

IF YES

Then the original meaning should be enforced and applied in the interpretive process

Then a constitutional construction should be adopted that (a) is consistent with the original meaning of the text that *can* be determined and (b) enhances constitutional legitimacy.

form to reflect the approach and terminology I advocate in this chapter.[26] Notice that as you move down the left-hand column, original meaning operates increasingly to constrain the process of constitutional construction. By the account presented here, the process of constitutional interpretation and construction has two steps: (step 1) Determine original meaning. If that meaning describes a rule specific enough to be applied to a

[26] Among the alterations I have made, I use the term "constitutional construction" in the lower right-hand box in place of Clinton's phrase "nonoriginalist, extraconstitutional interpretation legitimate to the extent not inconsistent with the historical evidence." See Clinton "Original Understanding," 1267.

case at hand, then it gets applied. If the original meaning is too vague to provide a resolution of the case or controversy at issue, then (step 2) Choose a construction that yields a specific enough rule or doctrine to reach a unique resolution of the case at hand and future cases without violating the meaning ascertained in step 1. I would further contend that when construction is needed, adopt one that (a) is consistent with the original meaning of the terms at issue and yet (b) furthers the constitutional principles of, for example, separation of powers and federalism, and enhances the legitimacy of the lawmaking process. That is, where original meaning allows, adopt a construction that helps assure that valid legal commands are binding in conscience.

SEPARATING INTERPRETATION FROM CONSTRUCTION

The value of any conceptual distinction is measured against the purpose it serves. One purpose of drawing the distinction between interpretation and construction is to highlight the binding nature as well as the limits of original meaning. The fact that original meaning may sometimes be vague or nonexistent does not deprive it of all import. The fact that original meaning does not answer every legal question we need answered does not mean it can be overridden where it does answer a question. Constitutional construction may be necessary to complement original meaning, but it does not trump it. As Jefferson wrote, "[o]ur peculiar security is in the possession of a written Constitution. Let us not make it a blank paper by construction."[27]

The distinction between interpretation and construction was also offered to highlight the contingency of any constitutional construction. There is nothing illicit about construing the Constitution. Given the limits of interpretation, construction is inevitable and the Constitution would not long survive without it. Unlike interpretation based on original meaning, however, constitutional constructions are open to challenge and reform. A commitment to a written constitution does not entail a commitment to every construction that may be placed upon it. Overriding the original meaning of the Constitution is one thing; overriding a meaning that has been largely or wholly constructed by courts or by Congress is another.

By distinguishing between interpretation and construction of the Constitution, I did not mean to suggest that these two activities are always separate. To the contrary, construction often flows so imperceptibly from interpretation it is sometimes hard to distinguish between the two. With

[27] Letter to Wilson Carey Nicholas, in *Jefferson: Writings*, 1140.

the doctrine of judicial review, for example, we shall see in the next chapter that it is sometimes difficult to tell exactly where the interpretation of the "judicial power" ends and constructions of the sort provided by Hamilton and Marshall begin.

Nevertheless, there are some doctrines that are almost pure interpretations and others that are wholly constructions. The example of the former already mentioned is the requirement that the president be at least thirty-five years old. An example of the latter is the "political question doctrine," which characterizes some parts of the Constitution as unsuitable for judicial interpretation and enforcement and leaves the implementation of these clauses solely to the political branches. "Political questions are controversies that the U.S. Supreme Court has historically regarded as nonjusticiable and inappropriate for judicial resolution."[28] Though there is no such doctrine anywhere to be found in the text of the Constitution, even where the Supreme Court has jurisdiction over cases involving such questions, "it has often chosen not to decide them, preferring instead to allow them to be resolved by the 'political' branches of government."[29]

The political question doctrine has been applied, for example, to the Guarantee Clause of Article IV that reads:

> The United States shall guarantee to every State in this Union a Republican Form of Government, and shall protect each of them against Invasion; and on Application of the Legislature, or of the Executive (when the Legislature cannot be convened), against domestic Violence.

Nowhere in this provision does it say that courts may not use it to decide cases and controversies. Indeed, its language suggests otherwise. It does not say "*Congress* shall guarantee to every State . . ." but "The *United States*"—a term that, when referring to the government of the United States, would seem to suggest all or any department thereof. Despite this, after an early effort to interpret and apply this provision,[30] the Supreme Court has considered it to be a political question and left the matter of honoring the guarantee of a "Republican Form of Government" to Congress alone.

Perhaps by reading the provision as if it said "Congress" rather than "the United States," this construction of the Guarantee Clause violates the "frame" provided by the original meaning of the text. Regardless of whether it is appropriately applied to the Guarantee Clause, however, the political question doctrine is an example of a pure construction that is

---

[28] Joel B. Grossman, "Political Questions," in Kermit Hall, ed., *The Oxford Companion to the Supreme Court* (New York: Oxford University Press, 1992), 651.

[29] Ibid.

[30] *Luther v. Borden*, 48 U.S. 1 (1849).

not itself a product of constitutional interpretation. Another example of a pure construction will be the point of departure for the balance of this book. It is called "the presumption of constitutionality." In part III we will consider the merits of this construction as well as its opposite: the Presumption of Liberty. First, however, we turn to the power of judicial review, which some have claimed is an unwarranted construction placed on the text. We shall see, instead, that a power to nullify statutes is authorized by the original meaning of the "judicial power."

CHAPTER SIX

Judicial Review: The Meaning of the Judicial Power

> This Constitution defines the extent of the powers of the general government. If the general legislature should at any time overleap their limits, the judicial department is a constitutional check. If the United States go beyond their powers, if they make a law which the Constitution does not authorize, it is void; and the *judicial power*, the national judges, who, to secure their impartiality, are to be made independent, will declare it to be void. On the other hand, if the states go beyond their limits, if they make a law which is a usurpation upon the general government, the law is void; and upright, independent judges will declare it to be so.[1]
> —OLIVER ELSWORTH (1788)

MOST PEOPLE TODAY assume that judges are authorized by the Constitution to declare statutes unconstitutional. Yet the Constitution does not seem to grant this power expressly. Article III says: "The judicial Power of the United States, shall be vested in one Supreme Court, and in such Courts as Congress may from time to time ordain and establish." In sharp contrast with the presidential veto power,[2] nowhere in the Constitution does it say explicitly that the "Supreme Court, and such inferior courts as may be established by Congress, shall have power to nullify a Law enacted by Congress and signed by the President if the Law is unconstitutional."

The absence of a clearly expressed grant of power has moved some critics of judicial review to question its legitimacy. One of these, Charles Hyneman, argued that the Constitution "expressly endows the president with powers to restrain Congress and the judiciary," and it "expressly endows Congress . . . with powers enabling it to check the president and the judiciary."[3] Nevertheless, "it contains no provision which asserts that

---

[1] Elliot, *Debates*, 2:196 (speech of Oliver Elsworth to the Connecticut ratification convention, January 7, 1788) (emphasis added).

[2] See U.S. Const., Art. I, § 7 ("Every Bill . . . shall, before it becomes a Law, be presented to the President of the United States; If he approve he shall sign it, but if not he shall return it, with his Objections to that House in which it shall have originated . . .").

[3] Charles S. Hyneman, *The Supreme Court on Trial* (New York: Atherton Press, 1963), 125.

the Supreme Court or any other court may exercise a specific power which would restrain the president or Congress in the exercise of their powers."[4] Hyneman contended that the most reasonable inference to draw from the "silence about a restraining power" for the judiciary is that the courts "should not exercise significant restraint on the other two"[5] departments.

Was Hyneman right? While this position has negligible support today among legal academics, there has developed a veritable cottage industry in defenses of judicial review. My purpose is not to rehearse all these defenses here. Few of these elaborate analyses would have been necessary, however, if the Constitution contained words whose plain meaning made it irresistibly clear that courts may declare acts of Congress unconstitutional. The absence of this plain language provides an opening for Hyneman to dismiss such "inferences" as depending "too much on imagination, too little on the plain meaning of plain words."[6] And it leads others to rest the justification for judicial review on highly contestable nonoriginalist interpretive techniques.

The overwhelming majority of courts and scholars are right, I submit, to accept the legitimacy of judicial review on originalist grounds, and Hyneman and other dissenters are wrong to reject it. Hyneman claims that the power of judicial review rests on questionable "inferences" from the "plain meaning of the plain words" of the text. This would merely make judicial review a construction that could still be acceptable to an originalist if it does not contradict what the Constitution says. As we saw in the previous chapter, just because a doctrine rests on construction is not, standing alone, sufficient reason to reject it.

Still, the power of judicial review would be on far stronger footing if it rests on interpretation rather than construction. Hyneman does not consider evidence that the original meaning of the "judicial power" found in Article III was more specific than what today is its plain meaning and at the founding it included a power of judicial nullification. If this is established by the weight of the evidence, then some power of judicial review would be justified by an originalist interpretation even if it is not within today's "plain meaning" of the text.

The "Judicial Power" Included the Power of Nullification

Far more evidence exists to suggest that the original public meaning of the term "judicial power" included the power to nullify unconstitutional

---

[4] Ibid.
[5] Ibid.
[6] Ibid., 124.

legislation than even many constitutional scholars realize. Several members of the Constitutional Convention explicitly assumed this power to reside in the judiciary—even before they settled on the particular wording of the various clauses. Roger Sherman (Connecticut) argued that a congressional power to negative state laws was "unnecessary, as the Courts of the States would not consider as valid any law contravening the Authority of the Union. . . ."[7] Madison (Virginia) favored such a negative because states "will accomplish their injurious objects before they can be . . . set aside by the National Tribunals."[8] He then cited the example of Rhode Island, where "the Judges who refused to execute an unconstitutional law were displaced, and others substituted, by the Legislature. . . ."[9] Gouverneur Morris (Pennsylvania) argued that the legislative negative was unnecessary because "A law that ought to be negatived will be set aside in the Judiciary department."[10] No one disputed the power of the judiciary to set aside unconstitutional laws passed by states.

Nor did anyone question that federal judges would have the same power to set aside unconstitutional legislation from Congress. During a debate concerning whether judges should be included with the executive in a council empowered to revise laws, the comments of several delegates revealed their assumption that federal judges had the inherent power to hold federal laws unconstitutional. Luther Martin (Maryland) stated that "as to the Constitutionality of laws, that point will come before the Judges in their proper official character. In this character they have a negative on the laws."[11] George Mason (Virginia) observed that "in their expository capacity of Judges they would have one negative. . . . They could declare an unconstitutional law void."[12] While he favored the idea of the council, James Wilson (Pennsylvania) conceded that there "was weight in this observation" that "the Judges, as expositors of the Laws would have an opportunity of defending their constitutional rights."[13]

Much is made by critics of judicial review of the Convention's rejection of the proposed council of revision, inferring from this refusal an intention that the judiciary defer to legislative will. They rarely mention, however, that the most discussed and influential reason for rejecting the council of revision proposal was the existence of a judicial negative on unconstitutional legislation. So powerful is this and other evidence that it strongly

[7] Madison, *Notes of Debates*, 304 (statement of R. Sherman).
[8] Ibid. (statement of J. Madison).
[9] Ibid., 305.
[10] Ibid. (statement of G. Morris).
[11] Ibid., 340 (statement of L. Martin).
[12] Ibid., 341 (statement of G. Mason).
[13] Ibid., 336–37 (statement of J. Wilson).

supports the conclusion that judicial nullification was included within the original public meaning of the "judicial power."

The assumption that judges possess the inherent power to nullify unconstitutional laws crops up in a variety of other contexts during the Convention. For example, Gouverneur Morris favored ratification of the Constitution by the people in convention because legislative ratification of the new Constitution was prohibited by the terms of the Articles of Confederation. "Legislative alterations not conformable to the federal compact, would clearly not be valid. The Judges would consider them as null & void."[14] James Madison argued that a difference between a league or confederation among states and a Constitution was precisely its status as binding law on judges. "A law violating a treaty ratified by a pre-existing law, might be respected by the Judges as a law, though an unwise or perfidious one. A law violating a constitution established by the people themselves, would be considered by the Judges as null & void."[15] Hugh Williamson (North Carolina) argued that an express prohibition on ex post facto laws by states "may do good here, because the Judges can take hold of it."[16]

Throughout the duration of the Convention no one disputed the existence of a judicial power to nullify unconstitutional laws. Still, the fact that judicial nullification was taken as given by all members of the Constitutional Convention does not mean everyone liked this power. John Mercer (Maryland) "disapproved of the Doctrine that the Judges as expositors of the Constitution should have authority to declare a law void."[17] Instead he "thought laws ought to be well and cautiously made, and then to be uncontroulable."[18] But Mercer's was a lone voice. Even John Dickenson (Delaware) who "was strongly impressed with the remark of Mr. Mercer as to the power of the Judges to set aside the law,"[19] said he "was at the same time at a loss to know what expedient to substitute."[20] Gouverneur Morris took issue with Mercer more sharply, stating that he could not agree that the judiciary "should be bound to say that a direct violation of the Constitution was law. A control over the legislature might have its inconveniences. But view the danger on the other side."[21]

The principal criticism of judicial nullification was not its existence but its weakness. Some framers were not sanguine about the ability of courts to stand up for constitutional principle when necessary. James Wilson

---

[14] Ibid., 351 (statement of G. Morris).
[15] Ibid., 352–53 (statement of J. Madison).
[16] Ibid., 511 (statement of H. Williamson).
[17] Ibid., 462 (statement of J. Mercer).
[18] Ibid.
[19] Ibid., 463 (statement of J. Dickenson).
[20] Ibid.
[21] Ibid. (statement of G. Morris).

thought that Congress should have the power to nullify state laws because "[t]he firmness of Judges is not itself sufficient."[22] Moreover, he argued—in words that assume a judicial power to declare "improper" laws unconstitutional (a point to which I return in chapter 7 when discussing the Necessary and Proper Clause)—that it "would be better to prevent the passage of an improper law, than to declare it void when passed."[23] Despite this concern, a congressional negative on state laws along with the council of revision was rejected by the Convention, leaving the other structural constraints, including the doctrine of judicial nullification, to keep state and national governments from exceeding their proper powers.

Although I argued earlier that we are not bound by the original intentions of the framers, their expressions of intention are evidence of the original meaning of the "judicial power." Drafters typically strive to choose words whose public meaning reflects their intentions. This evidence of framers' intent should also quiet the concerns of those originalists who do care about that intent. More pointedly, originalists who oppose judicial review must abandon original intent originalism because the evidence of such intent is overwhelming. They would also have to disregard the evidence that suggests that the original public meaning of "judicial power" at the time of ratification included judicial review. For the fact that judges were to be empowered to nullify unconstitutional legislation was no secret intention held only by delegates to the Constitutional Convention in Philadelphia.

The state ratification debates are replete with assertions of the power of judicial nullification. Supporters of the Constitution offered it as a means of limiting the powers of government. Speaking to the Pennsylvania convention, James Wilson stated: "If a law should be made inconsistent with those powers vested by this instrument in Congress, the judges, as a consequence of their independence, and the particular powers of government being defined, will declare such law to be null and void; for the power of the Constitution predominates. Any thing, therefore, that shall be enacted by Congress contrary thereto, will not have the force of law."[24] To the objection that judges would "be impeached, because they decide an act null and void, that was made in defiance of the Constitution," Wilson replied: "What House of Representatives would dare to impeach, or Senate to commit, judges for the performance of their duty?"

In the Virginia convention, future chief justice John Marshall openly stated the principle of nullification he would later enunciate (and then

[22] Ibid., 518 (statement of J. Wilson).
[23] Ibid.
[24] James Wilson, December 4, 1788, before Pennsylvania ratification convention, in Elliot, *Debates*, 2:489.

expand upon) in *Marbury v. Madison*. If the government of the United States "were to make a law not warranted by any of the powers enumerated," said Marshall, "it would be considered by the judges as an infringement of the Constitution which they are to guard. They would not consider such a law as coming under their jurisdiction. They would declare it void."[25]

This chapter began by quoting Oliver Elsworth's ringing endorsement in the Connecticut convention of the judicial power to nullify unconstitutional acts of both Congress and state legislatures.[26] The power of the federal judiciary to strike down unconstitutional state laws was also asserted in the North Carolina convention by William Davie, who stated that "Every member will agree that the positive regulations ought to be carried into execution, and that the negative restrictions ought not to [be] disregarded or violated. Without a judiciary, the injunctions of the Constitution may be disobeyed, and the positive regulations neglected or contravened."[27] He then argued that should states impose duties on imported goods, "the Constitution might be violated with impunity, if there were no power in the general government to correct and counteract such laws. This great object can only be safely and completely obtained by the instrumentality of the federal judiciary."[28]

Even opponents of the Constitution conceded the existence of judicial nullification, though some again questioned its efficacy. In his statement to the legislature of Maryland, Luther Martin said: "Whether, therefore, any laws or *regulations* of the Congress, any acts of *its President or other officers*, are contrary to, or not warranted by, the Constitution, rests only with the judges, who are appointed by Congress, to determine; by whose determinations every state must *be bound*."[29] In the Virginia ratification convention, Patrick Henry made a similar charge in a manner that suggests he included judicial nullification within the meaning of the word "judiciary":

> The honorable gentleman did our judiciary honor in saying that they had firmness to counteract the legislature in some cases. Yes, sir, our judges opposed the acts of the legislature. We have this landmark to guide us. They had fortitude to declare that they were *the judiciary*, and would oppose unconstitutional acts. Are you sure that your federal judiciary will act thus? Is that judiciary as well constructed, and as independent of the other branches, as our state judiciary? Where are your landmarks in this government? I will be bold to say you cannot

[25] John Marshall, June 20, 1788, in the Virginia convention, in ibid., 3:553.
[26] Ibid., 2:196 (Oliver Elsworth of State of Connecticut, January 7, 1788).
[27] Ibid., 4:156 (July 29, 1788).
[28] Ibid., 157.
[29] Ibid., 1:380 (statement of Luther Martin, January 27, 1788).

find any in it. I take it as the highest encomium on this country, that the acts of the legislature, if unconstitutional, are liable to be opposed by the judiciary.[30]

Also in Virginia, William Grayson, another opponent of the Constitution, observed that "If the Congress cannot make a law against the Constitution, I apprehend they cannot make a law to abridge it. The judges are to defend it."[31]

Nor was this conception of judicial power short-lived. Two years after ratification of the Constitution, Representative James Madison delivered his speech to the first session of the House explaining his proposed amendments to the Constitution. In it he asserted the importance of judicial nullification:

> If they are incorporated into the constitution, independent tribunals of justice will consider themselves in a peculiar manner the guardians of those rights; they will be an impenetrable bulwark against every assumption of power in the legislative or executive; they will be naturally led to resist every encroachment upon rights expressly stipulated for in the constitution by the declaration of rights.[32]

No one in Congress rose to object to this assertion of "judicial power."

Similarly instructive is the understanding of Thomas Jefferson. Because Jefferson was in France during the drafting and ratification of the Constitution, some originalists disparage any reliance upon his views. Yet the very fact that Jefferson did not participate in writing or debating the meaning of the Constitution makes his reading of the text relevant to an assessment of its original public meaning. Added to this is the fact that Jefferson was less of a partisan at this time. While he generally supported the Constitution, Jefferson had serious reservations about several of its features—particularly the absence of a bill of rights and rotation in office (what we call today "term limits"). As he put it, "I am neither federalist nor antifederalist; . . . I am of neither party, nor yet a trimmer between parties."[33]

Of special interest are statements in two letters written closely in time to James Madison. In the first, a well-known exchange, Jefferson attempts to persuade Madison of the value of a bill of rights, which Madison had previously disparaged in a letter to Jefferson as mere "parchment barri-

---

[30] Ibid., 3:324–25 (Patrick Henry to Virginia ratification convention, Thursday, June 12, 1788) (emphasis added).

[31] Ibid., 567 (Mr. Grayson in Virginia convention, June 21, 1788).

[32] *Annals*, 1:457 (statement of Rep. Madison).

[33] Letter to Francis Hopkinson (March 13, 1789), in Julian P. Boyd et al., eds., *The Papers of Thomas Jefferson*, vol. 14 (Princeton: Princeton University Press, 1950), 651.

ers."[34] Madison contended that "experience proves the inefficacy of a bill of rights on those occasions when its controul is most needed."[35] In Jefferson's reply he invoked the importance of judicial nullification:

> In the arguments in favor of a declaration of rights, you omit one which has great weight with me, the legal check which it puts into the hands of the judiciary. This is a body, which if rendered independent, and kept strictly to their own department merits great confidence for their learning and integrity.[36]

Jefferson's affirmation of a judicial power to nullify unconstitutional laws is of special significance in light of an earlier objection to the Constitution he had made in a letter to Madison: "I like the negative given to the Executive with a third of either house, though I should have liked it better had the Judiciary been associated for that purpose, or invested with a similar and separate power."[37] A judicial "negative," which the Constitution omitted, like the presidential veto to which Jefferson referred, could be exercised for any reason, not just on the ground that a law was unconstitutional. From Jefferson's later exchange with Madison asserting the existence of judicial review, we can discern that the omission of judicial negative or veto on legislation in the Constitution did not undermine Jefferson's view that the judicial power included a power to nullify unconstitutional laws.

Finally, Madison's early skepticism of the merits of judicial review confirms, rather than undermines, the conclusion that the original meaning of the "judicial power" included the power of nullification. In his *Observations on the "Draught of a Constitution for Virginia,"* written within days of his "parchment barriers" letter to Jefferson, Madison proposed that vetoed or nullified bills repassed by specified supermajorities in either or both houses should become law over the objection of either the executive or the judiciary. "It sd. not be allowed the Judges or the Ex to pronounce a law thus enacted, unconstitul. & invalid."[38] Nevertheless, he acknowledges that in the Constitution then pending ratification, only the executive veto may be overridden by a supermajority of both houses. As a result,

> In the State Constitutions & indeed in the Fedl. one also, no provision is made for case of a disagreement in expounding them; and as the Courts are generally

---

[34] James Madison to Thomas Jefferson (October 17, 1788), in *Papers of James Madison*, vol. 11 (Chicago: University of Chicago Press, 1961), 297 ("Repeated violations of these parchment barriers have been committed by overbearing majorities in every State").

[35] Ibid.

[36] Letter to James Madison (March 15, 1789), in *Jefferson Papers* 14:659.

[37] Letter to James Madison (December 20, 1787), in ibid., 12:440.

[38] James Madison, "Observations on the 'Draught of a Constitution for Virginia,' " (ca. October 15, 1788), in *Madison Papers*, 11:293.

the last in making their decision, it results to them, by refusing or not refusing to execute a law to stamp it with its final character. This makes the Judiciary Dept paramount in fact to the Legislature, which was never intended, and can never be proper.[39]

I disagree with Madison here. Being last does not make the judiciary in any sense "paramount" but merely equal to the other branches. After all, Congress may refuse to enact a law because it deems it to be unconstitutional and, because it is first, the bill never reaches the courts who may disagree. This does not render Congress paramount to the courts. By the same token, if the president vetoes a bill and his veto is sustained, the courts do not get to reverse that decision and uphold the bill as constitutional. Instead, in our system, absent a legislative supermajoritarian override of a presidential veto, all three branches must concur before it is found constitutional. Any one branch may scuttle a law because it alone deems it unconstitutional. Of course, as we have seen, by the time he introduced his proposed amendments in the first Congress, Madison came to be persuaded by Jefferson (and presumably others) to change his mind on the propriety of judicial nullification and he strongly asserted the need for such a power.

Moreover, by bemoaning this feature of the Constitution as written, Madison assumes, rather than denies, that the "judicial power" includes the power of nullification. Observing so influential a supporter of the Constitution taking issue with its propriety here, rather than denying that "judicial power" includes the power of nullification, is particularly potent evidence of its original meaning.

That Madison's objection confirms the original meaning of the "judicial power" is also a vindication of the practicality of original meaning originalism and shows its advantages over original intent. While Madison's intent may have changed or conflicted with that of other framers, the meaning of the term "judicial power" in the Constitution remained constant and readily discoverable by historical evidence. This example illustrates how original meaning can be discerned from the contemporaneous statements of those who oppose no less than those who support a particular provision.

I have presented so many different statements asserting the existence of the power of judicial nullification because there are those today who question whether the doctrine was widely held by the founding generation. Like Charles Hyneman, they suggest that it was invented in 1803 by John Marshall in *Marbury v. Madison*. Given the weight of the historical evidence (which Hyneman, for example, does not discuss), their argument

---

[39] Ibid.

ultimately rests on the fact that the power of nullification is not explicit in the Constitution. Rarely do they examine the original meaning of "judicial power," however, choosing to rely instead on the "plain meaning" that term has today.

A power of judicial nullification is warranted not only by interpretation of the term "judicial power" but also by construing other provisions. According to Article III, Section 2: "The judicial Power shall extend to all Cases, in Law and Equity, arising under this Constitution and Laws of the United States. . . . [and] to Controversies to which the United States shall be a party." Second, the Supremacy Clause of Article VI provides that "This Constitution, and the Laws of the United States which shall be made in Pursuance thereof; and all Treaties made, or which shall be made, under the Authority of the United States, shall be the supreme Law of the Land; and the Judges in every State shall be bound thereby, any Thing in the Constitution or Laws of any State to the Contrary notwithstanding."

These provisions support the following construction: Courts are empowered under Article III to decide "all cases . . . arising under this Constitution and Laws of the United States." When deciding such a case, a court is required to apply the laws that are applicable to the case at hand. In cases where both the Constitution and a statute apply and the latter is in conflict with the former, the court must decide which is a superior authority. The Supremacy Clause suggests that the Constitution should take precedence over a statute. (I say "suggests," because the Supremacy Clause speaks of the superiority of the Constitution only to state laws and constitutions, not to acts of Congress.) Therefore, when the court finds that a statute is in conflict with the Constitution, it is bound to obey the Constitution and disregard the statute.

This was the construction provided by Alexander Hamilton in *Federalist* 78:

> The interpretation of the laws is the proper and peculiar province of the courts. A constitution is, in fact, and must be regarded by the judges as, a fundamental law. It therefore belongs to them to ascertain its meaning as well as the meaning of any particular act proceeding from the legislative body. If there should happen to be an irreconcilable variance between the two, that which has the superior obligation and validity ought, of course, to be preferred; or, in other words, the Constitution ought to be preferred to the statute, the intention of the people to the intention of their agents.[40]

Why is the Constitution "superior" to an act of Congress? "There is no position which depends on clearer principles than that every act of a delegated authority, contrary to the tenor of the commission under which it

---

[40] *Federalist* 78, 467 (Hamilton).

is exercised, is void. No legislative act, therefore, contrary to the Constitution, can be valid."[41] Moreover, Hamilton argued: "To deny this would be to affirm that the deputy is greater than his principal; that the servant is above his master; that the representatives of the people are superior to the people themselves; that men acting by virtue of powers may do not only what their powers do not authorize, but what they forbid."[42] Hamilton also rejected the idea that this construction makes the judicial branch "superior" to Congress.

> Nor does this conclusion by any means suppose a superiority of the judicial to the legislative power. It only supposes that the power of the people is superior to both, and that where the will of the legislature, declared in its statutes, stands in opposition to that of the people, declared in the Constitution, the judges ought to be governed by the latter rather than the former. They ought to regulate their decisions by the fundamental laws rather than by those which are not fundamental.[43]

Hamilton's argument is undoubtedly a constitutional construction rather than a straightforward interpretation of the "judicial power." This becomes even clearer when he bases his analysis on the premise that "The complete independence of the courts of justice is peculiarly essential in a limited Constitution. By a limited Constitution, I understand one which contains certain specified exceptions to the legislative authority; such, for instance, as that it shall pass no bills of attainder, no ex post facto laws, and the like."[44] If the legislature is to be limited in this manner, who besides the courts can police this limitation?

> Limitations of this kind can be preserved in practice no other way than through the medium of courts of justice, whose duty it must be to declare all acts contrary to the manifest tenor of the Constitution void. Without this, all the reservations of particular rights or privileges would amount to nothing.[45]

Notice that nothing in this rationale for judicial review would empower the judiciary to permit Congress to exceed the limits on its powers by changing via "interpretation" the written Constitution. To the contrary, this whole justification for judicial review assumes that the Constitution provides written limitations that Congress is to follow and judges to enforce. In short, this construction permitting judicial nullification provides still more support for originalist interpretation.

[41] Ibid.
[42] Ibid.
[43] Ibid., 467–68.
[44] Ibid., 466.
[45] Ibid.

Is Hamilton's argument for judicial review undermined because it is a "mere" construction rather than a straightforward interpretation of the text? Hardly. First, it is entirely consistent with evidence of the original meaning of the "judicial power." Second, the contrary position—that the Constitution's silence is to be taken as support for congressional supremacy—is also a construction. Indeed, Hamilton himself appreciated this:

> If it be said that the legislative body are themselves the constitutional judges of their own powers and that the construction they put upon them is conclusive upon the other departments it may be answered that this cannot be the natural presumption where it is not to be collected from any particular provisions in the Constitution. It is not otherwise to be supposed that the Constitution could intend to enable the representatives of the people to substitute their *will* to that of their constituents. It is far more rational to suppose that the courts were designed to be an intermediate body between the people and the legislature in order, among other things, to keep the latter within the limits assigned to their authority.[46]

In this passage, Hamilton shows that the opposing view is itself one of construction, but a construction inferior to the one he advocates. Where the text of the Constitution is silent ("where it is not to be collected from any particular provisions in the Constitution") and therefore not subject to straightforward interpretation, we ought not adopt a construction ("this cannot be the natural presumption") that Congress is to be "the constitutional judges of their own powers and that the construction they put upon them is conclusive upon the other departments." Rather, in light of the purposes for which the Constitution was adopted and the limitation of power it imposes upon Congress, "[i]t is far more rational to suppose that the courts were designed to be an intermediate body between the people and the legislature in order, among other things, to keep the latter within the limits assigned to their authority."[47]

However, this last formulation that courts were designed "to keep [the legislature] within the limits assigned to their authority" is vague. Because Hamilton does not add "by nullifying the enforcement of unconstitutional statutes that come before them," his formulation could also be taken to justify a broader power to order or compel other branches of the government to keep them "within the limits assigned to their authority." To claim this power for the judiciary would be to move beyond judicial nullification to something that could be called judicial supremacy. Hamilton, of course, said no such thing and, in context, it is not clear that such meaning could fairly be attached to his words. Yet in 1803, this power was claimed for the courts in the landmark case of *Marbury v. Madison*.

---

[46] Ibid., 467.
[47] Ibid.

JUDICIAL SUPREMACY IS A CONSTRUCTION

We speak today of the power of "judicial review," not judicial nullification. The modern power of judicial review is not limited to refusing to enforce an unconstitutional law being applied to an individual—a power that is warranted by the original meaning of the "judicial power." Modern judicial review also includes a power to command or order other branches of the government to follow the judiciary's interpretation of the Constitution—a power that is sometimes called "judicial supremacy." Although I am not entirely satisfied with this term,[48] I shall use it to distinguish between a conception of judicial review limited to judicial nullification and one that extends as well to the power to command or direct other branches and levels of government to conform to the judiciary's view of what the Constitution requires.

The distinction between judicial nullification and judicial supremacy can be hard to grasp because nullification seems like a subset of supremacy. A power of nullification gives the judiciary the last word on whether a statute is "law" that is binding on the individual and this seems like "supremacy," but the appearance is misleading. The explicit division of the government into three departments, commonly said to be "coequal" (though this term also does not appear in the text), suggests that the judicial branch must reach its own decision on what the Constitution requires in cases of conflict between the Constitution and an act of Congress when deciding which to enforce. A power of nullification is not one of supremacy, but one of judicial equality. Were it absent, the legislative and executive branches alone would decide on the constitutionality of their laws. Judges would have to merely take their orders. This would render the judiciary inferior to the other branches rather than their equal.

The confusion of judicial nullification with judicial supremacy arises if one ignores the proposition that judicial negation is not legislation.[49] If Congress refuses to enact a statute, perhaps because in its opinion it would be unconstitutional, it does not matter if a court would uphold it as constitutional. Courts cannot mandate the passage of a statute. On the issue of which statutes to enact—the legislative power—the legislature is "supreme." Only if the Congress enacts a measure because enough of its members believe it to be constitutional (or do not care) and the president signs the bill believing it is constitutional (or does not care) may the Court have the opportunity to express its opinion on its constitutionality. A

---

[48] "Supremacy" strikes me as needlessly pejorative. I would prefer a term to describe this power that does not prejudge the outcome of an inquiry into its propriety.

[49] I thank Leonard Liggio for providing this helpful formulation.

court's power to negate unconstitutional legislation renders it equal, not superior, to the other branches.

Just as a power to negate legislation does not imply a power to enact it, neither does it imply a judicial power to mandate that the executive branch exercise its powers in a particular mode. True, judicial nullification would extend to refusing to hold a person liable for disobeying an unconstitutional command of the executive branch. Nullification, however, does not include the further power to order or "mandate" that someone act in a particular manner or to desist from acting in a manner a court finds to be unconstitutional. Whether or not this additional power can be justified on the basis of interpretation or construction is a separate question. While historical evidence strongly supports the conclusion that the original meaning of "judicial power" included the power to nullify, there is little if any evidence to support a claim that the original meaning of "judicial power" also included a power to command other branches.

Nor was such a power exercised by the Supreme Court in *Marbury v. Madison*.[50] This famous case grew out of legislation enacted by a lame-duck Congress dominated by Federalists to create numerous judicial positions that could be filled with Federalists by outgoing President Adams before the newly elected Republican Thomas Jefferson could assume the presidency. In a bizarre twist by today's lights, all these "midnight commissions" had been sealed by John Marshall himself—who was not only chief justice, but also the outgoing secretary of state—and delivered by his brother James. In the haste to seal and deliver the commissions, Marbury's was left behind. At the instruction of incoming President Jefferson, James Madison, the incoming secretary of state, refused to deliver it.

Marbury then brought suit in the Supreme Court to issue a writ of mandamus to compel the secretary of state "either to deliver the commission, or a copy of it from the record."[51] The Court rejected this request because the Judiciary Act that authorized the Court to grant writs of mandamus on government officials exceeded the powers of Congress and was unconstitutional.[52] By avoiding the issue of whether a judicial command of this kind to the executive branch would exceed the judicial power, Marshall needed only to justify in his opinion the judicial power to nullify the Judiciary Act as beyond the powers of Congress to enact. Although this conclusion could have been well-supported by evidence of the original meaning of the "judicial power," Marshall's opinion in *Marbury* is entirely an exercise in constitutional construction.

[50] 5 U.S. 137 (1803).

[51] 5 U.S. at 173.

[52] The ruling was based on the distinction between "original" and "appellate" jurisdiction explicit in Article III rather than on any inherent constitutional limitation on the judiciary. The Court found that the act improperly allowed for such relief in cases initiated in

Marshall begins by recourse to "certain principles, supposed to have been long and well established."[53] Among these is the principle that the Constitution is "superior law . . . unchangeable by ordinary means."[54] Although the text says the Constitution is superior to state constitutions and statutes, it does not say it is superior to acts of Congress. Nor does it say that it cannot be changed by ordinary means, though this can be implied by the extraordinary mechanisms of amendment it provides in Article V. Marshall notes that "all those who have framed written constitutions contemplate them as forming the fundamental and paramount law of the nation."[55] He concludes from all this that a "legislative act contrary to the constitution is not law."[56]

Marshall then claims that it is "emphatically the province and duty of the judicial department to say what the law is. Those who apply the rule to particular cases, must of necessity expound and interpret that rule."[57] Like Hamilton, Marshall notes that "[i]f two laws conflict with each other, the courts must decide on the operation of each."[58] In such a case, "the court must determine which of these conflicting rules governs the case. That is of the very essence of judicial duty."[59] Like Hamilton, he finds the answer in the superior authority of the Constitution. "If, then, the courts are to regard the constitution, and the constitution is superior to any ordinary act of the legislature, the constitution, and not such ordinary act, must govern the case to which they both apply."[60]

Marshall emphasizes that to hold otherwise would be to thwart the idea of a written constitution and would violate the first principles of this particular system of government:

> This doctrine would subvert the very foundation of all written constitutions. It would declare that an act which, according to the principles and theory of our government, is entirely void, is yet in practice, completely obligatory. It would declare, that if the legislature shall do what is expressly forbidden, such act, notwithstanding the express prohibition, is in reality effectual. It would be giving to the legislature a practical and real omnipotence, with the same breath which professes to restrict their powers within narrow limits. It is prescribing limits, and declaring that those limits may be passed at pleasure.[61]

---

the Supreme Court instead of only those cases that the Court heard on appeal from a suit commenced in a lower court.

[53] 5 U.S. at 176.
[54] Ibid., 177.
[55] Ibid.
[56] Ibid.
[57] Ibid.
[58] Ibid.
[59] Ibid., 178.
[60] Ibid.
[61] Ibid.

Most modern admirers of Marshall and of *Marbury* fail to realize how the "principles and theory of our government" he advances for the power of judicial nullification also argue strongly for originalist interpretation. For only if the Constitution has a meaning independent of the judiciary, and that must remain the same until properly changed, does the existence of the "superior" law that is the written Constitution justify judges' nullifying the "ordinary" authority of a statute.

Not until the end of his opinion does Marshall reinforce his analysis with "additional arguments" furnished by inferences drawn from "the peculiar expressions of the constitution of the United States."[62] With respect to the "judicial power," Marshall argues that it "is extended to all cases arising under the constitution."[63] He asks: "Could it be the intention of those who gave this power, to say that, in using it, the constitution should not be looked into? That a case arising under the constitution should be decided without examining the instrument under which it arises?"[64]

Marshall then lists various explicit prohibitions and restrictions in the Constitution and concludes, "From these, and many other selections which might be made, it is apparent, that the framers of the constitution contemplated that instrument, as a rule for the government of *courts*, as well as of the legislature."[65] In this way, "the particular phraseology of the constitution of the United States confirms and strengthens the principle, supposed to be essential to all written constitutions, that a law repugnant to the constitution is void; and that *courts*, as well as other departments, are bound by that instrument."[66]

Notice that none of Marshall's arguments presented to this point support a judicial power to command another coequal branch of government. Indeed, he explicitly denies that the court may issue a writ of mandamus to the president himself, confining his attention only to whether the secretary of state can be compelled to perform a merely "ministerial act." He concludes that

> where the heads of departments are the political or confidential agents of the executive, merely to execute the will of the President, or rather they act in cases in which the executive possesses a constitutional or legal discretion, nothing can be more perfectly clear than that their acts are only politically examinable. But where a specific duty is assigned by law, and individual rights depend upon the performance of that duty, it seems equally clear that the individual who considers himself injured, has a right to resort to the laws of his country for a remedy.[67]

[62] Ibid.
[63] Ibid., 178.
[64] Ibid., 179.
[65] Ibid., 179–80.
[66] Ibid., 180 (emphasis added).
[67] Ibid., 166.

Later in the opinion Marshall denies that a court may "enquire how the executive, or executive officers, perform duties in which they have discretion. Questions, in their nature political, or which are, by the constitution and laws, submitted to the executive, can never be made in this court."[68]

Because I do not wish to question whether courts may compel executive branch officials to perform acts required by law, I shall not rehearse here all the arguments made by Chief Justice Marshall on behalf of such a judicial power. My point is simply that, unlike the case of judicial nullification, there is little or no evidence that such a power can be justified by the original meaning of the "judicial power," and Marshall offered no such evidence. Because it held that the power was improperly granted to the Court by Congress, any suggestion in *Marbury* that a court has power to mandate behavior is dicta.

Marshall's opinion that courts may sometimes have such a power is a construction, rather than an interpretation, of the Constitution, as is the contrary position favored, for example, by President Jefferson. Jefferson was of the opinion that federal courts "cannot issue a mandamus to the President or legislature, or to any of their officers."[69] Although the writ existed at common law, "the constitution [controls] the common law in this particular."[70] Because he was speaking of judicial supremacy, not judicial nullification, Jefferson was not contradicting his earlier endorsement of judicial review as some have charged.[71]

Regardless of who was right about judicial supremacy, the narrower power of judicial nullification gives rise to an important issue of constitutional construction. When exercising this power to decide whether an enactment exceeds the powers of Congress under the Constitution, how much deference do the courts owe a judgment by Congress or by a state that it was acting constitutionally? Is Congress entitled to a benefit of the doubt when it claims the existence of a power? Or does the benefit of the doubt go to the citizen who claims that the restriction on his or her liberty was beyond the proper power of the legislature that enacted it? This is the question to be addressed in part III.

---

[68] Ibid., 170.

[69] Letter of Thomas Jefferson to Spencer Roane (September 6, 1819), in Paul Leicester Ford, ed., *The Writings of Thomas Jefferson*, vol. 10 (New York: Putnam's, 1892–99), 140.

[70] Ibid.

[71] Jefferson has been accused of changing his position on judicial review when Federalist judges obstructed his political agenda. A more nuanced account is provided by David Mayer, who shows that while Jefferson never wavered in his support for judicial nullification, his objection was to affirmative judicial interference with the "Revolution of 1800." See David N. Mayer, *The Constitutional Thought of Thomas Jefferson* (Charlottesville: University Press of Virginia, 1994), 257–94.

PART III

Constitutional Limits

IF COURTS have the power to nullify unconstitutional laws, as argued in chapter 6, how much deference do judges owe to Congress in making this assessment? The Supreme Court has adopted a doctrine called "the presumption of constitutionality" by which acts of Congress are presumed constitutional unless shown to be in error. An early statement of this approach was offered by Justice Bushrod Washington—the same justice who endorsed the use of first principles in assessing the constitutionality of a statute: "It is but a decent respect due to the wisdom, the integrity, and the patriotism of the legislative body, by which any law is passed, to presume in favour of its validity, until its violation of the constitution is proved beyond all reasonable doubt."[1]

One of the most deferential versions of this presumption was offered by another justice willing to consider first principles, Justice Clarence Thomas, in the case of *F.C.C. v. Beach Communications, Inc.*,[2] in which he wrote:

> On rational-basis review, a classification in a statute . . . comes to us bearing a strong presumption of validity, and those attacking the rationality of the legislative classification have the burden "to negative every conceivable basis which might support it". . . . Moreover, because we never require a legislature to articulate its reasons for enacting a statute, it is entirely irrelevant for constitutional purposes whether the conceived reason for the challenged distinction actually motivated the legislature.[3]

In other words, a statutory distinction is presumed constitutional if there is a conceivable basis for having made it regardless of whether this basis was relied upon by the legislature. This formulation of the presumption was too deferential for Justice Stevens, who replied: "In my view, this formulation sweeps too broadly, for it is difficult to imagine a legislative classification that could *not* be supported by a 'reasonably conceivable state of facts.' Judicial review under the 'conceivable set of facts' test is tantamount to no review at all."[4]

As we shall see in the next two chapters, the commitment to the presumption of constitutionality has waxed and waned over the centuries, and is not without important—and revealing—exceptions. At this point, however, I want only to note that the presumption of constitutionality, in any form, is a construction rather than an interpretation of the text of the Constitution. Nowhere in the Constitution is it said, or even implied, that

---

[1] *Ogden v. Saunders*, 25 U.S (12 Wheat.) 213, 270 (1827).
[2] 508 U.S. 307 (1993).
[3] Ibid., 314–15. (case citations omitted).
[4] Ibid., 323 fn 3 (Justice Stevens, concurring).

the judiciary must defer to or presume the correctness of the judgment of the legislative branch that a statute it enacts is constitutional.

That a doctrine such as the presumption of constitutionality results from construction rather than interpretation is hardly fatal, though it requires us to ask how it squares with the original meaning of the Constitution's text. To answer this, we must consider its application to acts of Congress separately from how it applies to state legislation. To assess the merits of applying the presumption of constitutionality to federal laws, we must consider the original meaning of the provision of the Constitution that gives Congress the power

> To make all Laws which shall be necessary and proper for carrying into Execution the foregoing Powers, and all other Powers vested by this Constitution in the Government of the United States, or in any Department or Officer thereof.

This we shall do in chapter 7. In chapter 8, we turn our attention to the appropriateness of deferring to state legislatures by considering the original meaning of the clause in the Constitution that commands that

> No State shall make or enforce any law which shall abridge the privileges or immunities of citizens of the United States.

Finally, in chapter 9 we shall see that the presumption of constitutionality runs afoul of the constitutional mandate of the Ninth Amendment that

> The enumeration in the Constitution, of certain rights, shall not be construed to deny or disparage others retained by the people.

The original meaning of these nearly lost clauses argues strongly against a presumption of constitutionality and in favor of the contrary construction I describe in chapter 10: the Presumption of Liberty.

CHAPTER SEVEN

Judicial Review of Federal Laws: The Meaning of the Necessary and Proper Clause

> Whatever meaning this clause may have, none can be admitted, that would give an unlimited discretion to Congress.[1]
> —JAMES MADISON

AFTER THE PREAMBLE, the very first sentence of the Constitution reads: "All legislative Powers *herein granted* shall be vested in a Congress of the United States. . . ."[2] Therefore, evaluating whether a federal law is constitutional must begin with whether Congress has acted within the powers it is granted in the Constitution. Here is the entire list (save one) that appears in Article I, Section 8:

> The Congress shall have Power To lay and collect Taxes, Duties, Imposts and Excises, to pay the Debts and provide for the common Defence and general Welfare of the United States; but all Duties, Imposts and Excises shall be uniform throughout the United States;
>
> To borrow Money on the credit of the United States;
>
> To regulate Commerce with foreign Nations, and among the several States, and with the Indian Tribes;
>
> To establish an uniform Rule of Naturalization, and uniform Laws on the subject of Bankruptcies throughout the United States;
>
> To coin Money, regulate the Value thereof, and of foreign Coin, and fix the Standard of Weights and Measures;
>
> To provide for the Punishment of counterfeiting the Securities and current Coin of the United States;
>
> To establish Post Offices and post Roads;
>
> To promote the Progress of Science and useful Arts, by securing for limited Times to Authors and Inventors the exclusive Right to their respective Writings and Discoveries;
>
> To constitute Tribunals inferior to the supreme Court;

---

[1] *Annals*, 2:1898.
[2] U.S. Const., Art. I, § 1 (emphasis added).

To define and punish Piracies and Felonies committed on the high Seas, and Offences against the Law of Nations;

To declare War, grant Letters of Marque and Reprisal, and make Rules concerning Captures on Land and Water;

To raise and support Armies, but no Appropriation of Money to that Use shall be for a longer Term than two Years;

To provide and maintain a Navy;

To make Rules for the Government and Regulation of the land and naval Forces;

To provide for calling forth the Militia to execute the Laws of the Union, suppress Insurrections and repel Invasions;

To provide for organizing, arming, and disciplining, the Militia, and for governing such Part of them as may be employed in the Service of the United States, reserving to the States respectively, the Appointment of the Officers, and the Authority of training the Militia according to the discipline prescribed by Congress;

To exercise exclusive Legislation in all Cases whatsoever, over such District (not exceeding ten Miles square) as may, by Cession of particular States, and the Acceptance of Congress, become the Seat of the Government of the United States, and to exercise like Authority over all Places purchased by the Consent of the Legislature of the State in which the Same shall be, for the Erection of Forts, Magazines, Arsenals, dock-Yards, and other needful Buildings. . . .[3]

While at first glance this list looks lengthy enough to justify almost any exercise of power, early on Congress bumped up against its limits and has been bumping against them ever since. When the establishment of a national bank was proposed to the first Congress, it became necessary to consider whether Congress had such a power. The problem is obvious. Nowhere on that long list of powers does it say that Congress has the power to establish a national bank. Armies, yes. Navies, yes. Post offices and post roads, yes. Banks, nothing. Moreover, the establishment of a national bank involved issuing a charter of incorporation. Nowhere on the list is Congress delegated a power to do this either.

Because the aforementioned list of powers included neither the power to establish a bank nor the power to issue charters of incorporation, defenders primarily relied on the last power listed in Article I, Section 8, which gave Congress the power "To make all Laws which shall be necessary and proper for carrying into Execution the foregoing Powers, and all other Powers vested by this Constitution in the Government of the United States, or in any Department or Officer thereof." This provision—derisively called "the Sweeping Clause" by opponents of the Constitution—

---

[3] Ibid., Art. I, § 8.

has since come to be known as the Necessary and Proper Clause. Its existence gives rise to the following question: when considering a law's necessity or propriety, how much deference do courts owe Congress?

The Origin of the Necessary and Proper Clause

The Necessary and Proper Clause was added to the Constitution by the Committee on Detail without any previous discussion by the Constitutional Convention. Nor was it the subject of any debate from its initial proposal to the Convention's final adoption of the Constitution.[4] One thing we do know about its legislative history is the wording of a clause that was earlier proposed by Gunning Bedford and rejected by the Committee: that Congress shall have power "to legislate in all cases for the general interests of the Union, and also in those to which the States are separately incompetent, or in which the harmony of the U. States may be interrupted by the exercise of individual Legislation."[5] In other words, the Convention had before it an almost completely open-ended grant of power to Congress and rejected it, without discussion, in favor of the enumeration of particular powers and the ancillary Necessary and Proper Clause.

The likely reason why the Necessary and Proper Clause received no attention by the Convention became clear during the debates in the ratification conventions, as did its public meaning. There, opponents of the Constitution pointed to this power as evidence that the national government had unlimited and undefined powers. In the New York convention, for example, John Williams contended that it "is perhaps utterly impossible fully to define this power."[6] For this reason, "[w]hatever they judge necessary for the proper administration of the powers lodged in them, they may execute without any check or impediment."[7]

Federalist supporters of the Constitution repeatedly denied the charge that all discretion over the scope of its powers effectively resided in Congress. They insisted that the Necessary and Proper Clause was not an additional freestanding grant of power, but merely made explicit what was already implicit in the grant of each enumerated power. As explained by George Nicholas to the Virginia convention, "the Constitution had enumerated all the powers which the general government should have, but

---

[4] The only time it was considered was when Madison and Charles Pinckney proposed that it be modified by the insertion of the phrase "and establish all offices" because it appeared to them that this power might be questioned. Their proposal was rejected without discussion by a vote of 9–2. Madison, *Notes of Debates*, 489.

[5] Ibid., 303.

[6] Elliot, *Debates*, 2:331.

[7] Ibid., 338.

did not say how they were to be exercised. It therefore, in this clause, tells how they shall be exercised."[8] Like other Federalists, Nicholas denied that this clause gave "any new power" to Congress. "Suppose," he reasoned,

> it had been inserted, at the end of every power, that they should have power to make laws to carry that power into execution; would this have increased their powers? If, therefore, it could not have increased their powers, if placed at the end of each power, it cannot increase them at the end of all.[9]

In short, "this clause only enables them to carry into execution the powers given to them, but gives them no additional power."[10] Madison added his voice to the chorus: "the sweeping clause . . . only extended to the enumerated powers. Should Congress attempt to extend it to any power not enumerated, it would not be warranted by the clause."[11]

Also in Virginia, Edmund Pendleton, president of the convention, insisted that this clause did not go "a single step beyond the delegated powers."[12] If Congress were "about to pass a law in consequence of this clause, they must pursue some of the delegated powers, but can by no means depart from them, or arrogate any new powers; for the plain language of the clause is, to give them power to pass laws in order to give effect to the delegated powers."[13] The same point was made in the North Carolina convention: "This clause specifies that they shall make laws to carry into execution *all the powers vested* by this Constitution; consequently, they can make no laws to execute any other power. This clause gives no new power, but declares that those already given are to be executed by proper laws."[14] In Pennsylvania, James Wilson explained that this clause "is saying no more than that the powers we have already particularly given, shall be effectually carried into execution."[15] And Thomas M'Kean insisted that "it gives to Congress no further powers than those already enumerated."[16]

Here, then, is the likely explanation for the lack of debate surrounding the clause at the Philadelphia convention: If the power to make law was already thought implicit in the enumerated powers scheme, then it is not surprising that the clause would provoke no discussion at the Convention. Joseph Lynch offers a different explanation for the silence of the Convention. He suggests that the wording of the clause was made deliberately

[8] Ibid., 3:245.
[9] Ibid., 245–46.
[10] Ibid., 246.
[11] Ibid., 455.
[12] Ibid., 441.
[13] Ibid.
[14] Ibid., 4:141 (statement of William Maclaine).
[15] Ibid., 2:468.
[16] Ibid., 537.

ambiguous so that both sides could later argue for their favored interpretation. Nationalists from the Northern and Atlantic states could argue that the clause was equivalent to the rejected Bedford proposal, while the Southern and rural Federalists could argue that Congress was limited to enacting laws that were incidental to the enumerated powers. The silent reception of the clause by all sides, he claims, reflected their unwillingness to tamper with the compromise represented by this ambiguity. According to Lynch: "The ambiguity of the language that the committee proposed and the convention approved enabled both sides not only to approve its inclusion in the Constitution but also to argue afterwards that their construction was in accord with the framers' intent."[17]

Although the circumstantial evidence he offers on behalf of this theory is intriguing, it generally relates to the subjective original intent of the framers, not the original meaning the clause would have had to a reasonable person at the time of founding. As was seen in chapter 4, according to original meaning originalism, secret intentions are not binding. The issue is what interpretation best reflects the publicly accessible meaning of the clause.

Moreover, any ambiguity in the wording was clarified by the Federalists' public insistence during the ratification that the clause authorized only the enactment of laws that were incidental to the enumerated powers, and that this power would have been inherent in the enumerated powers had there been no Necessary and Proper Clause at the end of the list. In the conventions we know of no disagreement as to the meaning of the clause expressed by supporters of the Constitution. All denied it was the equivalent of the Bedford proposal. Professor Lynch concedes as much when he observes:

> Whatever private understandings the framers may have had among themselves—that proponents of a strong national government would be free to argue, for instance, that the Necessary and Proper Clause included an undefined bevy of congressional and presidential powers . . . —the supporters of the Constitution had for the most part publicly disavowed such understanding both in the *Federalist* and in the state conventions in their campaign to secure ratification.[18]

Such public utterances during ratification clarify what the original public meaning of a term was, and it is to that public meaning I now turn.

---

[17] See Lynch, *Negotiating the Constitution*, 25. I think Professor Lynch is correct to use the term "ambiguity" rather than "vagueness" for, as we shall see, at issue here is which of two possible meanings of "necessity" was the meaning conveyed by the term "necessary."

[18] Ibid., 112.

THE MEANING OF "NECESSARY"

Despite the uniform denials by the Constitution's advocates that the Necessary and Proper Clause expanded the powers of the national government, a national bank was proposed to the Federalist-dominated first Congress by Secretary of the Treasury Alexander Hamilton. There ensued the most hotly contested constitutional conflict of the early years of the Constitution.[19] Official opinions on the subject were issued by Attorney General Edmund Randolph, Secretary of State Thomas Jefferson, and Hamilton. Of these Randolph and Jefferson argued against its constitutionality, with Hamilton arguing in favor. Among the leaders of those in the House who contended that the bank was unconstitutional was James Madison. The ambiguity of the term "necessary" was quickly revealed by this controversy, requiring us to decide which meaning was the original one.

"Necessary" Means Really Necessary: Madison, Jefferson, and Randolph

The opening salvo on the constitutionality of the proposed bank was fired by James Madison, who was serving as a member of the first Congress, when on February 2, 1791, he delivered a lengthy speech on the merits of the bank bill. His speech began with "a general review of the advantages and disadvantages of banks,"[20] but in making these remarks, "he had reserved to himself the right to deny the authority of Congress to pass it."[21]

Before addressing the constitutionality of the bill, he first provided a list of principles that should guide constitutional interpretation and construction:

> An interpretation that destroys the very characteristic of the Government cannot be just.
>
> Where a meaning is clear, the consequences, whatever they may be, are to be admitted—where doubtful, it is fairly triable by its consequences.
>
> In controverted cases, the meaning of the parties to the instrument, if to be collected by reasonable evidence, is a proper guide.
>
> Contemporary and concurrent expositions are a reasonable evidence of the meaning of the parties.
>
> In admitting or rejecting a constructive authority, not only the degree of its incidentality to an express authority is to be regarded, but the degree of its

---

[19] The Alien and Sedition Acts were not enacted until 1798.

[20] *Annals*, 2:1894.

[21] Ibid., 1896.

importance also; since on this will depend the probability or improbability of its being left to construction.[22]

Notice that Madison is implicitly distinguishing here between an explicit power (which is a matter of interpretation "where a meaning is clear") and one that is only implicit (and "left to construction"). Given that the power to establish a bank or issue charters of incorporation was not explicitly granted, and viewing the Constitution in light of these principles, Madison was led to conclude that "it was not possible to discover in it the power to incorporate a Bank."[23]

Madison thought this conclusion was compelled both by general principles of congressional power and by the specific powers being invoked on behalf of the bank. On general principle:

> All power . . . had its limits; those of the general government were ceded from the mass of general power inherent in the people, and were consequently confined within the bound fixed by their act of cession. The constitution was this act; and to warrant Congress in exercising the power, the grant of it should be pointed out in the instrument.[24]

In Madison's view "this . . . had not been done" and he "presumed it could not be done."[25] When it came to constitutional construction, "such construction was only admissible as carefully preserved entire the idea on which the constitution is founded."[26]

Supporters of the bank had argued that it was justified as incidental to the power "To lay and collect Taxes, Duties, Imposts and Excises, to pay the Debts and provide for the common Defence and general Welfare of the United States" and the power "to borrow money on the credit of the United States." Madison noted that no argument could be based on the terms "provide for the common Defence and general Welfare of the United States" because these terms pertained only to the purposes for exercise of the Taxing Power and these "general purposes themselves were limited and explained by the particular enumeration subjoined."[27]

---

[22] Ibid., 1896.

[23] Ibid.

[24] Linda Grant De Pauw et al., *Documentary History of the First Federal Congress*, vol. 14 (Baltimore: Johns Hopkins University Press, 1995), 379. This passage is found in an article in the *General Advertiser*, February 7, 1791. It does not appear in the lengthier and otherwise more detailed report of Madison's speech included in the *Annals of Congress*, which was originally published in the *Gazette of the United States*, February 23, 1791.

[25] Ibid.

[26] Ibid.

[27] *Annals*, 2:1896.

In other words, according to Madison, Congress could use taxes to provide for the common defense and general welfare only when exercising the other powers that were enumerated in Article I. The Taxing Power could not be used to pursue any end that might be said to be conducive to the common defense or the general welfare. Why not? "To understand these terms in any sense, that would justify the power in question, would give to Congress an unlimited power; would render nugatory the enumeration of particular powers; would supersede all the powers reserved to the State Governments."[28]

Madison noted that the terms "common defence" and "general welfare" had been "copied from the articles of Confederation" and asked rhetorically whether it had "ever been pretended that they were to be understood otherwise than as here explained?"[29] Nor could the bill be justified as a direct exercise of the Borrowing Power. "It does not borrow a shilling."[30] If anything, it created the power to lend, not borrow.

Madison then turned his attention to the Necessary and Proper Clause. In a crucial passage of his speech he stated:

> Whatever meaning this clause may have, none can be admitted, that would give an unlimited discretion to Congress.
>
> Its meaning must, according to the natural and obvious force of the terms and the context, be limited to means necessary to the end, and incident to the nature of the specified powers.
>
> The clause is in fact merely declaratory of what would have resulted by unavoidable implication, as the appropriate, and, as it were, technical means of executing those powers. In this sense it had been explained by the friends of the Constitution, and ratified by State Governments.
>
> *The essential characteristic of the Government, as composed of limited and enumerated powers, would be destroyed*, if, instead of direct and incidental means, any means could be used, which, in the language of the preamble to the bill, "might be conceived to be conducive to the successful conducting of the finances, or might be conceived to tend to give facility to the obtaining of loans."[31]

[28] Ibid., 1896–97.

[29] Ibid., 1897. The Articles of Confederation, Article VIII, had provided that "All charges of war, and all other expenses that shall be incurred for the common defence or general welfare, and allowed by the United States in Congress assembled, shall be defrayed out of a common treasury," and, in Article IX, that "The United States in Congress assembled shall never . . . ascertain the sums and expenses necessary for the defence and welfare of the United States . . . unless by the votes of a majority of the United States in Congress assembled." In both instances, the terms "common defence" and "general welfare" qualified the spending power of Congress. It was not a freestanding power of its own.

[30] Ibid.

[31] *Annals*, 2:1898 (emphasis added).

Distinguishing between interpretation and construction, Madison noted "the diffuse and ductile interpretation of these words and the boundless latitude of construction given them by the friends of the bank."[32] He contended "that by their construction" of the Necessary and Proper Clause, "every possible power might be exercised. The government would then be paramount in all possible cases . . . and every limitation effectively swept away."[33] For this reason, "[t]he doctrine of implication, he warned the friends to this system, was a dangerous one."[34]

Madison thought that trying to justify the constitutionality of a national bank as necessary for carrying into execution an enumerated power required too great a stretch:

> Mark the reasoning on which the validity of the bill depends! To borrow money is made the end, and the accumulation of capitals implied as the means. The accumulation of capitals is then the end, and a Bank implied as the means. The Bank is then the end, and a charter of incorporation, a monopoly, capital punishments, &c., implied as the means.
>
> If implications, thus remote and thus multiplied, can be linked together, a chain may be formed that will reach every object of legislation, every object within the whole compass of political economy.[35]

Nine years later, in discussing another claim of power by Congress, Jefferson as president would compare this style of argument to the child's game "this is the house that jack built."[36]

Madison gave several examples of enumerated powers that were not left to implication, though if a latitudinarian interpretation of the Necessary and Proper Clause were correct, they surely could have been:

> Congress have power "to regulate the value of money;" yet it is expressly added, not left to be implied, that counterfeiters may be punished.
>
> They have the power "to declare war," to which armies are more incident than incorporated banks to borrowing; yet the power "to raise and support

---

[32] *Documentary History of the First Congress*, 14:380.

[33] Ibid.

[34] Ibid.

[35] *Annals*, 2:1899.

[36] In criticizing a House bill incorporating a company for the Roosevelt copper mines in New Jersey, President Jefferson observed that it was being justified under the Sweeping Clause, and supported by the following pedigree of necessities. "Congress are authorized to defend the nation. Ships are necessary for defence; copper is necessary for ships; mines necessary for copper; a company necessary to work mines; and who can doubt this reasoning who has ever played at 'This is the House that Jack Built'? Under such a process of filiation of necessities the sweeping clause makes clean work." Letter from Thomas Jefferson to Edward Livingston (April 30, 1800), reprinted in P. Ford, ed., *The Works of Thomas Jefferson*, vol. 9 (New York: Knickerbocker Press, 1905), 132–33.

armies" is expressly added; and to this again, the express power "to make rules and regulations for the government of armies;" a like remark is applicable to the powers as to the navy.

The regulation and calling out of the militia are more appertinent to war than the proposed Bank to borrowing; yet the former is not left to construction.

The very power to borrow money is a less remote implication from the power of war, than an incorporated monpoly [*sic*] Bank from the power of borrowing; yet, the power to borrow is not left to implication.[37]

Madison did not mean to exaggerate the significance of these sorts of drafting decisions: "It is not pretended that every insertion or omission in the Constitution is the effect of systematic attention. This is not the character of any human work, particularly the work of a body of men."[38] Yet he thought that these examples "with others that might be added, sufficiently inculcate, nevertheless, a rule of interpretation very different from that on which the bill rests. They condemn the exercise of any power, particularly a great and important power, which is not evidently and necessarily involved in an express power."[39]

Madison offered a distinction "which he said had not been sufficiently kept in view."[40] This is the distinction between (a) a power that is "necessary and proper for the Government or Union,"[41] and (b) power that is "necessary and proper for executing the enumerated powers."[42] The only powers that are necessary and proper for the national government are those that were enumerated; the only proper unenumerated powers are those derived from the nature of a power that was expressed. The expression of particular powers (and no others)

> constituted the peculiar nature of the Government; no power, therefore, not enumerated could be inferred from the general nature of Government. Had the power of making treaties, for example, been omitted, however necessary it might have been, the defect could only have been lamented, or supplied by an amendment of the Constitution.[43]

Madison then offered the crucial distinction between "necessity" and "convenience." "But the proposed Bank could not even be called necessary to the Government; at most it could be but convenient."[44] There were

---

[37] *Annals*, 2:1899.
[38] Ibid.
[39] Ibid.
[40] Ibid., 1900.
[41] Ibid.
[42] Ibid.
[43] Ibid., 1900–1901.
[44] Ibid., 1901.

many other ways, short of exercising this power to incorporate a bank, for the government to accomplish its enumerated objects or end.

Madison read portions of the ratification debates in which critics of the Constitution seized upon the Necessary and Proper Clause as evidence of the "dangerous latitude of its powers"[45] and the arguments by its supporters that this clause was to be interpreted as Madison had just done before Congress.

> The defence against the charge founded on the want of a bill of rights pre-supposed, he said, that the powers not given were retained; and that those given were not to be extended by remote implications. On any other supposition, the power of Congress to abridge the freedom of the press, or the rights of conscience, &c, could not have been disproved. The explanations in the State Conventions all turned on the same fundamental principle, and on the principle that the terms necessary and proper gave no additional powers to those enumerated.[46]

As was seen earlier in this chapter, the record bears out Madison's characterization.

Madison also made a crucial connection between the Necessary and Proper Clause and the protection of the rights and powers retained by the people by citing in support of this "rule of interpretation" the Ninth and Tenth Amendments. Of course, in February 1791 these amendments had yet to be ratified, and on that date were the eleventh and twelfth on the list of amendments then pending before states. Perhaps because he referred to them by these numbers, this use by Madison in a constitutional argument of the Ninth Amendment he himself had devised had, until recently, largely been ignored. "The latitude of interpretation required by the bill is condemned by the rule furnished by the Constitution itself."[47] As authority for this rule he offered this:

> The explanatory amendments proposed by Congress themselves, at least, would be good authority with them; all these renunciations of power proceeded on a rule of construction, excluding the latitude now contended for. . . . He read several of the articles proposed, remarking particularly on the 11th [the Ninth Amendment] and 12th [the Tenth Amendment]; the former, as guarding against a latitude of interpretation; the latter, as excluding every source of power not within the Constitution itself.[48]

Thus, for Madison, whether or not a proposed action of government that restricted the liberty of the people was necessary, and therefore within

[45] Ibid.
[46] Ibid.
[47] Ibid., 1899.
[48] Ibid., 1901.

the powers of Congress to enact, required some assessment of whether the means chosen were essential to the pursuit of an enumerated end. Without this assessment, the scheme of limited enumerated powers would unravel. In his words, allowing the exercise of a power that was neither specifically enumerated nor fairly inferred from one that is "involves the guilt of usurpation, and establishes a precedent of interpretation levelling all the barriers which limit the powers of the General Government. . . ."[49]

In Congress, Madison was joined by Representative Michael Stone of Maryland, a lawyer by training, who argued forcefully against the doctrine of implied powers, characterizing it "as a serpent which was to sting and poison the constitution."[50] Stone rested his argument in part on the ratification debates in which "all those who opposed the government, dreaded the doctrine—those who advocated it, declared it could not be resorted to—and all combined in the opinion that it ought not to be tolerated."[51] If the doctrine of implied powers was to be accepted, all the framers need have done was write the Preamble "and then said—here is your constitution! Here is your bill of rights! Do these gentlemen require anything more respecting the powers of Congress, than a description of the ends of government?"[52] Stone also stressed the fact that the Constitution was in writing. "The end of all government is the public good—and if the means were left to legislation, all written compacts were nugatory."[53] It was "the sober discretion of the legislature . . . [that] was the very thing intended to be curbed and restrained by the constitution."[54]

Another lawyer, James Jackson of Georgia, observed:

If the sweeping clause, as it is called, extends to vesting Congress with such powers, and *necessary* and *proper* means are an indispensable implication in the sense advanced by the advocates of the bill, we shall soon be in possession of all possible powers, and the charter under which we sit will be nothing but a name.[55]

Representative William Giles of Virginia defined "necessary" as "that mean without which the end could not be produced."[56] He rejected the suggestion that " 'necessary,' as applicable to a mean to produce an end, should be construed so as to produce the greatest quantum of public utility."[57] That definition,

---

[49] Ibid., 1902.
[50] *Documentary History of the First Congress*, 14:424
[51] Ibid.
[52] Ibid., 425.
[53] Ibid.
[54] Ibid.
[55] *Annals*, 2:1916–17.
[56] Ibid., 1941.
[57] Ibid.

if pursued, will be found to teem with dangerous effects, and would justify the assumption of any given authority whatever. Terms are to be so construed as to produce the greatest degree of public utility. Congress are to be the judges of this degree of utility. This utility, when decided on, will be the ground of Constitutionality. Hence any measure may be proved Constitutional which Congress may judge to be useful. These deductions would suborn the Constitution itself, and blot out the great distinguishing characteristic of the free Constitutions of America, as compared with the despotic Governments of Europe, which consist in having the boundaries of governmental authority clearly marked out and ascertained.[58]

In other words, "[i]f expediency constituted constitutionality; the House judged of the expediency; then every measure they could possibly enter into would be ipso facto constitutional: And what would then be the weight it was intended the Constitution should have; and where were its limits?"[59]

In the executive branch, President Washington solicited the views of Attorney General Edmond Randolph, Secretary of State Thomas Jefferson, and Secretary of the Treasury Alexander Hamilton on the measure's constitutionality. A few days after the close of debate in Congress, Randolph and Jefferson conveyed their formal opinions to the president that the bill was unconstitutional largely for the same reasons enunciated by Madison. Randolph, who had served as a delegate to the Constitutional Convention from Virginia, wrote, "let it be propounded as an eternal question to those who build new powers on this clause, whether the latitude of construction, which they arrogate will not terminate in an unlimited power in Congress."[60]

In his formal opinion, Jefferson drew the same distinction as had Madison between necessity and convenience:

[T]he constitution allows only the means which are "necessary," not those which are merely convenient for effecting the enumerated powers. If such a latitude of construction be allowed to this phrase, as to give any non enumerated power, it will go to every one; for there is no one, which ingenuity may not torture into a *convenience, in some way or other, to some one* of so long a list of enumerated powers: it would swallow up all the delegated powers. . . . Therefore it was that the constitution restrained them to the *necessary* means; that is to say, to those means, without which the grant of the power would be nugatory.[61]

---

[58] Ibid.

[59] *Documentary History of the First Congress*, 14:449.

[60] Edmund Randolph, "Opinion of Edmund Randolph," in *History of the Bank*, 89.

[61] Thomas Jefferson, "Opinion of Thomas Jefferson, Secretary of State, on the Same Subject," in *History of the Bank*, 93 (February 15, 1791); see also ibid.

Jefferson then allowed that "[p]erhaps, indeed, bank bills may be a more *convenient* vehicle than treasury orders." Despite this, "a little *difference* in the degree of *convenience* cannot constitute the *necessity*, which the constitution makes the ground for assuming any non enumerated power."[62]

As Madison summarized their argument, the construction of power exercised by the bank bill

> was condemned by the silence of the Constitution; was condemned by the rule of interpretation arising out of the Constitution; was condemned by its tendency to destroy the main characteristic of the Constitution; was condemned by the expositions of the friends of the Constitution, whilst depending before the public; was condemned by the apparent intention of the parties which ratified the Constitution; was condemned by the explanatory amendments proposed by Congress themselves to the Constitution; and he hoped would receive its final condemnation by the vote of this House.[63]

It did not.

"Necessary" Means "Convenient": Hamilton and Marshall

A week after Randolph and Jefferson issued their opinions, Hamilton, who had initially proposed the creation of the bank, defended the constitutionality of his proposal. As part of his lengthy opinion, he offered an alternative interpretation of the term "necessary." According to both the "grammatical" and "popular" senses of the term,

> *necessary* often means no more than *needful, requisite, incidental, useful,* or *conducive* to. It is a common mode of expression to say, that it is necessary for a government or a person to do this or that thing, when nothing more is intended or understood than that the interest of the Government or person require, or will be promoted by, the doing of this or that thing.[64]

Hamilton maintained that the "whole turn of the clause containing it, indicates that it was the intent of the convention, by that clause, to give a liberal latitude to the exercise of specified powers."[65] To adopt Jefferson's (and Madison's) interpretation, Hamilton wrote,

> would be to depart from its obvious and popular sense, and to give it a *restrictive* operation; an idea never before entertained. It would be to give it the same

---

[62] Ibid.

[63] *Annals*, 2:1902.

[64] "Opinion of Alexander Hamilton, on the Constitutionality of a National Bank," in *History of the Bank*, 97–98.

[65] Ibid., 98.

force as if the word *absolutely*, or indispensably, had been prefixed to it.

Such a construction would beget endless uncertainty and embarrassment. The cases must be palpable and extreme, in which it could be pronounced with certainty, that a measure was absolutely necessary; or one, without which the exercise of a given power would be nugatory.[66]

Hamilton also responded to the argument that a broad construction of this power would undermine the enumerated powers scheme. His argument highlights the distinction between interpretation and construction.

The same thing has been said, and may be said, with regard to every exercise of power, by *implication* or *construction*. The moment the literal meaning is departed from, there is a chance of error and abuse: and yet adherence to the letter of its powers would at once arrest the motion of Government. . . .

The truth is, that difficulties on this point are inherent in the nature of the federal constitution. They result inevitably from a division of legislative power. The consequences of this division is, that there will be cases clearly within the power of the National Government, others, clearly without its power; and a third class, which will leave room for controversy and difference of opinion, and concerning which a reasonable latitude of judgment must be allowed.[67]

In evaluating his argument, we should perhaps remember that Hamilton had four years earlier proposed to the Constitutional Convention a scheme of consolidated government in which the legislature of the United States would have been given "power to pass all laws whatsoever"[68] subject only to a nonoverridable veto power by the supreme executive authority. He contemplated no enumeration of powers or allocation of powers between state and national governments. Hamilton introduced his plan in a lengthy speech to the Convention, immediately after which the Convention adjourned without discussion. It was never explicitly considered thereafter. Later the Convention rejected the somewhat more qualified language proposed by Gunning Bedford of Delaware that would have given Congress power "to legislate in all Cases for the general Interests of the Union, and also in those Cases to which the States are separately incompetent, or in which the Harmony of the United States may be interrupted by the Exercise of individual Legislation."[69]

In the bank dispute, Hamilton gained the crucial support of the esteemed Washington and, as the behind-the-scenes leader of the fledgling

---

[66] Ibid.

[67] Ibid.

[68] Farrand, *Records*, 1:291. Although several different versions of Hamilton's proposal were recorded, none apparently differs on this point. See ibid., 3:617–19.

[69] Ibid., 2:131–32.

"Federalist" party that dominated Congress, prevailed on the bank.[70] Congress enacted the bank bill over the objections of congressmen noted above, and Washington signed it into law over the objections of Jefferson and Randolph. Still, though several members of Congress had argued that the bank was constitutional—and this position prevailed—we cannot be entirely sure whether this was because a majority in Congress rejected a narrow conception of necessity or because a majority of the members thought the bank met the more stringent standard put forward by Madison and others.[71]

The meaning of the Necessary and Proper Clause was first considered by the Supreme Court in 1803 in the case of *United States v. Fisher*. In his opinion, Chief Justice John Marshall interpreted the clause to give almost complete discretion to Congress, which, he said, "must possess the choice of means, and must be empowered to use any means which are in fact conducive to the exercise of a power granted by the constitution."[72] But Marshall gave his fullest, most careful, and best-known treatment of this clause some thirty years after the ratification of the Constitution in *McCulloch v. Maryland*,[73] a case involving the constitutionality of the legislation establishing a second national bank. In his 1819 opinion, still often cited by the Supreme Court, Marshall adopted, in some places almost word for word, the opinion Hamilton issued as secretary of the treasury.

In *McCulloch*, Maryland had challenged the constitutionality of the bank by asserting a narrow conception of necessity:

> But the laws which they are authorized to make, are to be such as are *necessary and proper* for this purpose. No terms could be found in the language more absolutely excluding a general and unlimited discretion than these. It is not "necessary or proper," but "necessary *and* proper." The means used must have both these qualities. It must be, not merely convenient—fit—adapted—proper, to the accomplishment of the end in view; it must likewise be *necessary* for the

---

[70] This controversy was among those that contributed to Jefferson's (and Madison's) eventually splitting from the Federalists and founding the competing "Republican" party. This party, dubbed "democrat" by the Federalists—a term of opprobrium as we saw in chapter 3—eventually took that name as its own and survives as the Democratic Party that exists today. The Federalist party eventually collapsed, was initially supplanted by the Whigs, and then by the abolitionist Republican party—the party we know by that name today. Until the twentieth century, the Democrats largely maintained their Jeffersonian commitment to "strict construction" of federal powers, with the Republicans favoring more expansive construction of those powers.

[71] Of course, a third possibility cannot definitively be disproved: the Federalist-dominated Congress knowingly exceeded its enumerated powers under the Constitution.

[72] *United States v. Fisher*, 6 U.S. (2 Cranch) 358, 396 (1805).

[73] 17 U.S. (4 Wheat.) 316 (1819).

accomplishment of that end. Many means may be *proper* which are not *necessary*; because the end may be attained without them. The word "necessary," is said to be a synonyme of "needful." But both these words are defined "*indispensably requisite;*" and most certainly this is the sense in which the word "necessary" is used in the constitution. To give it a more lax sense, would be to alter the whole character of the government as a sovereignty of limited powers. This is not a purpose for which violence should be done to the obvious and natural sense of any terms, used in an instrument drawn up with great simplicity, and with extraordinary precision.[74]

Echoing Hamilton, Marshall rejected this argument, adopting instead the meaning that Madison, Jefferson, and Maryland had posed as its opposite—"necessary" means convenient:

> If reference be had to its use, in the common affairs of the world, or in approved authors, we find that [the word "necessary"] frequently imports no more than that one thing is convenient, or useful, or essential to another. To employ the means necessary to an end, is generally understood as employing any means calculated to produce the end, and not as being confined to those single means, without which the end would be entirely unattainable.[75]

Marshall's textual and functional defense of this definition of "necessary" is well-known to law students. Unlike Madison's bank speech, Marshall's opinion is a central part of every casebook on constitutional law.[76]

Textually, Marshall contrasted the use of the term "necessary" in this clause with the term "absolutely necessary" used in Article I, Section 10,[77] arguing that it is "impossible to compare the sentences . . . without feeling a conviction that the convention understood itself to change materially the meaning of the word 'necessary,' by prefixing the word 'absolutely.' "[78] Thus, he argued it is a mistake, as a textual matter, to equate the term "necessary" with the term "absolutely necessary," as the State of Maryland purportedly did.[79] This textualist argument has greatly impressed later interpreters.

[74] Ibid., 366–67 (last emphasis added).

[75] Ibid., 413–14.

[76] Though one casebook unconventionally leads with Madison's speech, placing it before both *McCulloch* and *Marbury*. See Paul Brest, Sanford Levinson, Jack Balkin, and Akhil Amar, *Processes of Constitutional Decisionmaking: Cases and Materials*, 4th ed. (New York: Aspen Law and Business, 2000), 8–11.

[77] See U.S. Const., Art. I, § 10 ("No State shall, without the Consent of the Congress, lay any Imposts or Duties on Imports or Exports, except what may be absolutely necessary for executing its inspection Laws . . .").

[78] *McCulloch v. Maryland*, 17 U.S. at 414–15.

[79] In its brief, quoted above, the State of Maryland did not use this phrase, though it did use the phrase "indispensably requisite."

Functionally, Marshall argued:

> It must have been the intention of those who gave these powers, to insure, as far as human prudence could insure, their beneficial execution. This could not be done by confiding the choice of means to such narrow limits as not to leave it in the power of Congress to adopt any which might be appropriate, and which were conducive to the end. . . . To have declared that the best means shall not be used, but those alone without which the power given would be nugatory, would have been to deprive the legislature of the capacity to avail itself of experience, to exercise its reason, and to accommodate its legislation to circumstances.[80]

Marshall's functional argument depends upon the fear that the national government will fail without the sort of discretionary powers that his interpretation allows. As important, it assumes that this open-ended grant of discretionary powers will not eventually undermine the enumerated powers scheme as Madison predicted. He dismissed, almost casually, concerns about how such an open-ended grant of discretionary power squared with the theory of limited and enumerated powers.

> This government is acknowledged by all to be one of enumerated powers. The principle, that it can exercise only the powers granted to it, would seem too apparent to have required to be enforced by all those arguments which its enlightened friends, while it was depending before the people, found it necessary to urge. That principle is now universally admitted. But the question respecting the extent of the powers actually granted, is perpetually arising, and will probably continue to arise, as long as our system shall exist.[81]

And, just as Madison had given examples of enumerated powers that were not left to implication, Marshall offered three examples of unenumerated powers that had already been implied, even though they were arguably not "indispensably necessary" to the accomplishment of some enumerated purpose: the implied powers to carry mail between post offices and along post roads,[82] to punish any violations of its laws,[83] and to require congressional oaths of office.[84]

---

[80] *McCulloch v. Maryland*, 17 U.S. at 415–16.

[81] Ibid., 405.

[82] Ibid., 417 ("It may be said, with some plausibility, that the right to carry the mail, and to punish those who rob it, is not indispensably necessary to the establishment of a post office and post road").

[83] Ibid. ("The several powers of Congress may exist, in a very imperfect state to be sure, but they may exist and be carried into execution, although no punishment should be inflicted in cases where the right to punish is not expressly given").

[84] Ibid., 416 ("The power to exact this security for the faithful performance of duty, is not given, nor is it indispensably necessary").

There are any number of plausible responses to these examples that someone employing Jefferson and Madison's conception of necessity could make. The power to carry mail can surely be considered, in Madison's words, both requisite to and "incident to the nature"[85] of the postal power. Similarly, the power to punish violations is clearly incident, if not identical, to the nature of the lawmaking power. For many, a legislative enactment with no sanctions for disobedience can hardly be called a law. In contrast, the power to require congressional oaths of office may well be inessential to the performance of government.[86] Let candidates for office challenge their opponents to take such an oath or suffer the electoral consequences the way they now do with term limits and no-new-taxes pledges. If the inability to require congressional oaths be the price for holding Congress to its enumerated powers, a Madisonian might contend it is a price well worth paying.[87]

Although Madison, as president, had actually signed into law the bill establishing the national bank that Marshall upheld as constitutional,[88] it is significant that Madison took immediate exception to Marshall's opinion in *McCulloch*, renewing the argument he had made as a congressman nearly thirty years before:

[O]f most importance is the high sanction given to a latitude in expounding the Constitution, which seems to break down the landmarks intended by a specification of the powers of Congress, and to substitute, for a definite connection between means and ends, a legislative discretion as to the former, to which no practical limit can be assigned.[89]

[85] *Annals*, 2:1898 (1791).

[86] A mandatory congressional oath might be considered a qualification for holding office in addition to those mandated by Art. I, §§ 2 and 3, and thus beyond the powers of Congress to impose. See *Powell v. McCormack*, 395 U.S. 486 (1969) (limiting Congress to judging only the qualifications for membership enumerated in Art. I, § 2). On the other hand, an oath requirement might be considered a procedural rule within the powers of each house to determine for itself rather than a law. On either theory, an oath requirement is either permissible or impermissible independent of the Necessary and Proper Clause.

[87] Assuming Marshall was correct in claiming that a Madisonian conception of necessity would mean that a mandatory congressional oath to preserve, protect, and defend the Constitution lies outside the powers of Congress, a Madisonian might respond that a Congress that imposed such a requirement would be violating the terms of such an oath.

[88] Madison later justified his decision by citing the precedent established by the long-standing acquiescence to the claimed power as well as by the expediency of the bank: "A veto from the Executive, under these circumstances, with an admission of the expediency and *almost necessity* of the measure, would have been a defiance of all the obligations derived from a course of precedents amounting to the requisite evidence of the national judgment and intention." Letter from James Madison to Mr. Ingersoll (June 25, 1831), in *Letters*, 4:186 (emphasis added).

[89] Letter from James Madison to Judge Roane (September 2, 1819), in *Letters*, 3:143–44.

Madison then both acknowledged the supposedly modern insight that the national economy is interconnected and rejected this as a basis for a latitudinarian interpretation of "necessary":

> In the great system of political economy, having for its general object the national welfare, *everything is related immediately or remotely to every other thing*; and, consequently, a power over any one thing, if not limited by some obvious and precise affinity, may amount to a power over every other thing. Ends and means may shift their character at the will and according to the ingenuity of the legislative body.[90]

He concluded: "Is there a legislative power, in fact, not expressly prohibited by the Constitution, which might not, according to the doctrine of the court, be exercised as a means of carrying into effect some specified power?"[91]

Virginian John Taylor penned an entire book protesting the reasoning of *McCulloch*. In *Construction Construed and Constitutions Vindicated*, he argued that "There are two kinds of constructions; one calculated to maintain, the other to corrupt or destroy the principles upon which governments are established."[92] "Necessities," he argued, "are strictly, things unavoidable. . . . The plain question, divested of verbal evolutions is, whether congress are invested with the supreme power of altering or mending the constitution, should they imagine it to be expedient."[93] When necessity is taken to mean expedient, "this mode of construction completely establishes the position, that congress may pass any internal law whatsoever in relation to things, because there is nothing with which war, commerce and taxation may not be closely or remotely connected. . . ."[94]

Taylor further objected to Marshall's repeated reliance on the concept of "sovereignty" to justify discretionary congressional power.[95] "I do not know how it has happened," he writes,

> that this word has crept back into our political dialect. . . . Neither the declaration of independence, nor the federal constitution, nor the constitution of any

---

[90] Ibid. (emphasis added).

[91] Ibid.

[92] John Taylor, *Construction Construed and Constitutions Vindicated* (Richmond, Va.: Shepherd and Pollard, 1820), 21.

[93] Ibid., 169.

[94] Ibid., 170.

[95] See, e.g., *McCulloch v. Maryland*, 17 U.S. at 404 ("[W]hen, 'in order to form a more perfect union,' it was deemed necessary to change this alliance into an effective government, possessing great and sovereign powers, and acting directly on the people, the necessity of referring it to the people, and of deriving its powers directly from them, was felt and acknowledged by all"); ibid., 409 ("The original power of giving the law on any subject whatever, is a sovereign power").

single state, uses this equivocal and illimitable word. . . . In fact, the term "sovereignty," was sacrilegiously stolen from the attributes of God, and impiously assumed by kings. Though they committed the theft, aristocracies and republicks have claimed the spoil.[96]

Because sovereignty "is neither fiduciary nor capable of limitation," it results in the "new idea of 'sovereign servants,' [by which] our legislatures are converted into British parliaments, daily new-modelling the substance of our government, by bodies politick, exclusive privileges, pensions, bounties, and judicial acts, comprising an arbitrary power of dispensing wealth or poverty to individuals and combinations, at their pleasure."[97]

So Who Was Right? Perhaps They All Were

According to the originalist methodology described in chapter 4, we must ask what meaning a reasonable person would have attached to the term "necessary" when the Constitution was enacted. This question was addressed at some length by Gary Lawson and Patricia Granger. They note that the 1755 and 1785 editions of Samuel Johnson's *Dictionary of the English Language* define "necessary" as "1. Needful; *indispensably requisite*. 2. Not free; fatal; impelled by fate. 3. Conclusive; decisive by inevitable consequence." This definition explicitly includes the meaning attached to the term "necessity" by the State of Maryland in its brief. It does not include the terms "convenient or useful," which Marshall—following Hamilton—claimed to be a popular connotation of the term.

Nevertheless, although they abstain from a final position on the issue, Lawson and Granger express sympathy for Marshall's interpretation based on the usage of the term "necessary" in the Constitution itself. In particular, they concede that the contrast between the term "necessary" in the Sweeping Clause and the use of the term "absolutely necessary" in Article I, Section 10, Clause 2 "strongly suggests that 'necessary' by itself does not connote indispensability."[98] To this they add the language of Article II, Section 3, instructing the president to recommend to Congress "such Measures as he shall judge necessary and expedient." If "necessary" means "indispensable," they contend, "it is hard to understand how it would be conjoined with a term like 'expedient,' which suggests only a minimal requirement of usefulness."[99]

[96] Taylor, *Construction Construed*, 25–26.

[97] Ibid., 1–2.

[98] Gary Lawson and Patricia B. Granger, "The 'Proper' Scope of Federal Power: A Jurisdictional Interpretation of the Sweeping Clause," *Duke Law Journal* 43 (1993): 288.

[99] Ibid.

On the other hand, if "necessary" means merely "convenient or use-ful," as Hamilton and Marshall contended, it is hard to see what the term "necessary" adds to the term "expedient," in which case what "necessary and expedient" means is equally elusive. Perhaps this is why Marshall himself did not point to Article II, Section 3. Because it is equally incompatible with both meanings of "necessary," this passage does not help us distinguish between one meaning and the other.

What about Marshall's strongest textual argument: the contrast between "necessary" in the Necessary and Proper Clause, and the use of "absolutely necessary" in Article I, Section 10, Clause 2? Recall that Marshall said it was "impossible to compare the sentences . . . without feeling a conviction that the convention understood itself to change materially the meaning of the word 'necessary,' by prefixing the word 'absolutely.' "[100] But a review of the Convention notes suggests considerably less deliberation on this choice.

The Necessary and Proper Clause emerged from the Committee on Detail and was left unmodified by the Committee on Style. In contrast, Article I, Section 10, Clause 2 was proposed from the floor by George Mason (who sat on neither committee) on Saturday, September 15, the last day of deliberation and the very day that the Constitution was voted on and approved. (It was written up and signed two days later on Monday, September 17.) Mason's eleventh-hour proposal was adopted with no debate in the midst of a host of last-minute adjustments. This hardly suggests a deliberate change of meaning.

Moreover, Mason was seeking to qualify a previously agreed-to prohibition on the states' imposing any imposts or duties without the consent of Congress. Mason's language carves out an exception to this prohibition by granting the states the power to levy only those imposts that were necessary to pay for their inspection laws. Given that one of the prime reasons for the new Constitution was to prevent state interference with commerce, it is easy to understand why Mason would have proposed explicitly stringent restrictions on this exception.

Finally, Mason tended to favor the term "indispensably necessary" when speaking of grants of power and used the phrase frequently when speaking in the Virginia ratification convention. For example, although expressing concern about giving Congress the jurisdiction to govern the federal district, he stated that he "was very willing to give them, in this as well as in all other cases, those powers which he thought indispensably necessary."[101] Indeed, the official Journal of the Convention records Ma-

---

[100] *McCulloch v. Maryland*, 17 U.S. at 414–15.
[101] Elliot, *Debates*, 3:432.

son's proposal that became Article I, Section 10, Clause 2 as reading "indispensably necessary" rather than "absolutely necessary."[102]

All these factors, more than any deliberate distinction on the part of the Convention, explain the different usage in the two passages. Given its source, its last-minute nature, and its purpose, it is not at all clear that the choice of language "absolutely necessary" says much about the meaning of the unqualified term "necessary" conjoined with "proper" in the Necessary and Proper Clause.

On the other hand, my previous references to the Convention debates have been offered to illustrate the public meaning of words used by the framers. In contrast, perhaps this evidence about the origin of the phrase "absolutely necessary" in Article I, Section 10 reflects the sort of "secret usage" foreclosed by original meaning originalism. If the intratextual comparison of "necessary" with "absolutely necessary" conveyed the public meaning that "necessary" in the Necessary and Proper Clause meant something less than "absolutely necessary," then evidence of how the two phrases came to be incorporated in the text is immaterial if the legislative history was unknown, as it was, to the general public. Moreover, the phrase "indispensably necessary" was in common parlance at the time and was often used in the Convention and in other public statements. It would certainly have been possible for the Committee on Detail to have adopted that terminology in the Necessary and Proper Clause had it wished to convey unambiguously that meaning.

Nevertheless, the intratextual comparison of "necessary" in the Necessary and Proper Clause with "absolutely necessary" in Article I, Section 10 overlooks a significant fact. Although Madison strongly opposed equating necessity with mere convenience, in his bank speech he *also* rejected the suggestion that "necessary" meant "indispensably necessary." Instead, he favored a more "liberal construction" because "very few acts of the legislature could be proved essentially necessary to the absolute existence of government."[103]

Madison urged that the words be "understood so as to permit the adoption of measures the best calculated to attain the ends of government, and produce the greatest *quantum* of public utility."[104] His reason was that "[i]n the Constitution, the great ends of government were particularly enumerated; but all the means were not, nor could they all be, pointed out, without making the Constitution a complete code of laws: some discretionary power, and reasonable latitude, must be left to the judgment

[102] See "Journal of the Federal Convention," in Elliot, *Debates*, 1:313.
[103] Elliot, *Debates*, 4:417.
[104] Ibid.

of the legislature."[105] For example, although the Constitution had given Congress the power to lay and collect taxes, "the quantum, nature, means of collecting, &c., were of necessity left to the honest and sober discretion of the legislature."[106] Madison's final remark on the constitutionality of the bank was that "no power could be exercised by Congress, if the letter of the Constitution was strictly adhered to, and no latitude of construction allowed, and all the good that might be reasonably expected from an efficient government entirely frustrated."[107]

It seems, then, that Marshall—and most later commentators who rely solely upon his opinion in *McCulloch*—was considering a false dichotomy between mere "convenience" on the one hand and "absolute necessity" on the other. All parties to the first bank debate agreed that absolute necessity was not required, but at the same time all agreed that some degree of means-ends fit was needed. As Hamilton stated in a passage of his opinion to Washington that is not usually emphasized: "*The relation between the measure and the end*; between the nature of the mean employed towards the execution of a power, and the object of that power; *must be the criterion of constitutionality*; not the more or less of necessity or utility."[108] In modern terms, a showing of necessity should be neither so "strict" that no statute can pass muster nor so lenient than any statute can pass. The appropriate "level of scrutiny" of a measure's necessity must lie somewhere in between.[109]

Even Marshall's opinion in *McCulloch* can be read as taking a more circumspect view of congressional power than is commonly taught. I have already mentioned Marshall's earlier interpretation of the Necessary and Proper Clause in *United States v. Fisher*, where he contended that "Congress must possess the choice of means, and must be empowered to use any means which are in fact conducive to the exercise of a power granted by the constitution."[110] Here one indeed finds the open-ended interpretation attributed by others to Marshall's opinion in *McCulloch*.

Yet in *Fisher*, as constitutional historian David Currie notes, "Marshall's rejection of a straw man had led him unjustifiably to the opposite extreme: that Congress has some latitude in the choice of means need not mean it may employ any 'which are in fact conducive to the exercise of a power granted by the constitution.' Virtually anything Con-

[105] Ibid.
[106] Ibid.
[107] Ibid., 417–18.
[108] "Opinion of Alexander Hamilton," in *History of the Bank*, 98 (emphasis added).
[109] Levels of scrutiny will be discussed in chapter 13.
[110] *United States v. Fisher*, 6 U.S. (2 Cranch) 358, 396 (1805).

gress might want to do could meet that criterion. . . ."[111] By contrast, Currie contends that, in *McCulloch*, Marshall was more careful than he had been in *Fisher*:

> The means chosen must be "plainly" adapted to the end, not merely conducive to it; tenuous connections to granted powers will not pass muster. It must in addition be "appropriate," which implies some supervision of the reasonableness of the means. It must not, Marshall added in a later paragraph, be a mere "pretext . . . for the accomplishment of objects not entrusted to the government." Finally, and most important, it must consist with the "spirit" as well as the letter of the constitution.[112]

Currie concludes: "In light of earlier statements in his opinion, the implication seems unmistakable: incidental authority must not be so broadly construed as to subvert the basic principle that Congress has limited powers."[113] In other words, Marshall had come to sound more like Hamilton, who had admitted that a grant of power to make necessary laws was not unlimited after all. And both sound more like Madison and Jefferson than is now usually appreciated.

Perhaps the modern disregard of Marshall's more limited conception of Congress's implied powers in *McCulloch* can be explained by the fact that Marshall made little effort to apply his test to the case before him. Doing so "would have required a careful examination of the powers actually granted the Bank, of their relationship to the explicit powers of Congress, and of the degree to which they undermined the principle of limited federal powers."[114] In the end, Currie agrees that "Marshall devoted most of his effort to demolishing the straw man of indispensable necessity and slid over the real question of the propriety of the Bank itself. Moreover, in so doing he seems to have undermined the exemplary test he had just laid down."[115] This then became an open invitation for future generations to do the same. Marshall's "cavalier application of the test to the case before him, reinforced by his explicit refusal to examine the 'degree of . . . necessity' of any law 'really calculated to effect any of the objects entrusted to the government,' seemed to mean that the limits he had laid down should not be taken seriously."[116] And they have not been.

---

[111] David P. Currie, "The Constitution in the Supreme Court: State and Congressional Powers, 1801–1835," *University of Chicago Law Review* 49 (1982): 931.

[112] Ibid., 932.

[113] Ibid.

[114] Ibid., 933.

[115] Ibid., 933–34.

[116] Ibid. (quoting Marshall's opinion in *McCulloch*).

Judicial Deference and the Meaning of "Necessary"

This evidence suggests that, while it is a mistake to equate "necessary" with "convenient," neither was as stringent a standard as connoted by the terms "indispensably" or "absolutely" necessary. Instead, the original meaning of necessary creates the requirement of a degree of means-end fit somewhere between these two extremes. Considerations of constitutional construction also argue against a looser standard of "convenience."

Equating necessity with mere convenience or expediency—the view commonly, but perhaps mistakenly, attributed to Marshall—would make the application of this standard a matter of policy properly left to the discretion of the legislature. On the other hand, if one adopts the view of Jefferson and Madison—that "necessary" means that a given law must be incidental and closely connected to an enumerated power—then this is a matter of constitutional principle and within the purview of the courts to assess. Thus, the true debate is whether the original meaning of "necessary" was narrow enough to be enforced by courts or so open-ended that it became instead completely within the discretion of the legislature. If the Necessary and Proper Clause was generally thought justiciable, this further supports the conclusion that the public meaning of the term "necessary" was not equated with mere convenience or utility.

There is some textual support for the proposition that this clause, like all the other limits on congressional power, should be judicially enforceable. First is the fact that the clause says that laws *shall* be necessary and proper. In ordinary life, "shall" sometimes refers merely to a statement about what someone intends to do in the future. In the 1785 edition of *Dictionary of the English Language*,[117] Samuel Johnson notes that "[t]he explanation of *shall*, which foreigners and provincials confound with *will*, is not easy; and is not increased by poets, who sometimes give to *shall* an emphatical sense of *will*." Instead, Johnson repeatedly equates "shall" with "must." Then as now, in legal discourse the term "shall" is nearly always a mandatory command. "As used in statutes, contracts, or the like this word is generally imperative or mandatory."[118] When the law creates discretion, it uses the word "may" instead. Johnson defines "may" as "[t]o be at liberty; to be permitted; to be allowed."

The authors of the Constitution were careful to use "shall" and "may" properly. This strongly suggests that the injunction "to make all laws

---

[117] All references to Johnson's dictionary that appear here are to this edition, which is the closest in time to the drafting of the Constitution. Johnson's dictionary is not paginated, so page numbers cannot be provided.

[118] *Black's Law Dictionary*, 4th ed. (St. Paul, Minn.: West, 1968), 1541.

which *shall* be necessary and proper" was not discretionary on the part of the lawmaking authority to whom it is directed: Congress. It is mandatory, and like all other mandatory provisions, is presumptively enforceable by the other branches of government, including the courts.

Equally suggestive is the frequency with which the Constitution specifies the discretion it grants to particular actors, indicating that, when unreviewable discretion was granted over an important matter, it was done explicitly. Article I, Section 5 stipulates that "The Senate *shall have the sole Power* to try all Impeachments." Article I, Section 5 says that "Each House *shall be the Judge* of the Elections, Returns and Qualifications of its own Members" and that "Each House shall keep a Journal of its Proceedings, and from time to time publish the same, excepting such Parts *as may in their Judgment* require Secrecy." Article I, Section 9 speaks of "The Migration or Importation of such Persons as any of the States now existing *shall think proper* to admit."

The textual contrast between these provisions and the wording of the Necessary and Proper Clause severely undermines Joseph Lynch's thesis that the clause was so ambiguous that Congress was left "to determine whether, pursuant to that clause, they could legislate in the general interests of the country or whether they could merely implement the specifically enumerated powers."[119] To the contrary, a better presumption is that where the Constitution grants unlimited discretion, it does so explicitly.

Although many powers are granted solely to one actor by use of the phrase "shall have power"—such as the pardon power of the president[120]—without an explicit statement that the power is unreviewable, the Necessary and Proper Clause uses "shall" twice: once to say that "Congress shall have power . . . to make to make all laws . . ." and again to state that those "laws shall be necessary and proper. . . ." Only Congress is granted the power to make laws, but a mandatory standard for lawmaking is then imposed upon it.

Many examples where discretion is explicitly provided by the Constitution concern, not the allocation of power, but the application of a standard. Article II, Section 1 states that "Each State shall appoint [Electors], *in such Manner as the Legislature thereof may* direct." Article II, Section 2 states that "Congress may by Law vest the Appointment of such inferior Officers, *as they think* proper." Article II, Section 3 specifies that the president "shall from time to time give to the Congress Information of the

<hr />

[119] Lynch, *Negotiating the Constitution*, 100.

[120] See U.S. Const., Art. II, § 2 ("The President . . . shall have Power to grant Reprieves and Pardons for Offenses against the United States, except in cases of Impeachment").

State of the Union, and recommend to their Consideration such Measures *as he shall judge* necessary and expedient" and that "he may adjourn them to such Time *as he shall think* proper." Article V says that "Congress whenever two thirds of both Houses *shall deem it* necessary, shall propose Amendments to this Constitution."

In the Necessary and Proper clause, Congress is given no such discretion over the application of the standard it supplies. We need not imagine the outcry that such an expressed discretion would have engendered. Even in its absence, opponents of the Constitution protested that Congress was being given this discretion; whereas its proponents denied the charge repeatedly—a denial that would have been impossible in the face of discretionary language comparable to that found elsewhere in the text. This strongly suggests that whatever meaning the clause had, it must be one that is justiciable.

Although the justiciability of the Necessary and Proper Clause was not considered by the Constitutional Convention, where it received virtually no discussion, the issue did arise in ratification conventions. In Virginia, when discussing the Sweeping Clause, George Nicholas asked rhetorically, "Who is to determine the extent of such powers?" To this he replied: "I say, the same power which, in all well-regulated communities, determines the extent of legislative powers. If they exceed these powers, the judiciary will declare it void, or else the people will have a right to declare it void."[121]

Madison himself raised the issue of justiciability in his second speech to Congress on the national bank. To those who asserted that necessary meant merely expedient, he replied: "[W]e are told, for our comfort, that the Judges will rectify our mistakes. How are the Judges to determine in the case; are they to be guided in their decisions by the rules of expediency?"[122] This statement should not be interpreted as a rejection of judicial review, but as a rejection of a standard of constitutionality that would preclude judicial review.

Years later, in his critique of Marshall's opinion in *McCulloch*, Madison argued against an interpretation of "necessary" that takes the clause outside the province of the courts: "Does not the court also relinquish, by their doctrine, all control on the legislative exercise of unconstitutional powers?"[123] Madison objected to interpreting necessary as merely expedient or convenient, in part, because doing so would place the matter "beyond the reach of judicial cognizance. . . . By what handle could the court take hold of the case?"[124]

---

[121] Elliot, *Debates*, 3:442–43 (Virginia, June 16, 1788).
[122] Ibid., 1958.
[123] Madison, *Letters*, 3:144 (Letter to Judge Spencer Roane, September 2, 1819).
[124] Ibid.

Suppose Congress had expressly been given the power to pass "all laws that *it shall think* necessary and proper." One indication of how poorly received such wording would have been is an interesting exchange that occurred during the bank debate between Representatives Michael Stone of Maryland and William Smith of South Carolina. Stone accused Smith of holding the view that "all our laws proceeded upon the principle of expediency—that we were the judges of that expediency—as soon as we gave it as our opinion that a thing was expedient, it became constitutional."[125] To this, Smith revealingly replied:

> He had never been so absurd as to contend, as the gentleman had stated, that *whatever the Legislature thought expedient, was therefore Constitutional*. He had only argued that, in cases where the question was, whether a law was necessary and proper to carry a given power into effect, the members of the Legislature had no other guide but their own judgment, from which alone they were to determine whether the measure proposed was necessary and proper. . . . That, nevertheless, *it was still within the province of the Judiciary to annul the law*, if it should be by them deemed not to result by fair construction from the powers vested by the Constitution.[126]

Although Smith voted for the bank bill, at the same time he rejected the "absurd" accusation that Congress was the sole judge of a measure's necessity and propriety. By insisting on the appropriateness of judicial review, Smith was affirming a conception of necessity that was narrow enough to be justiciable. Smith's affirmation of judicial review also indicates that the bill's passage need not have represented an acceptance of the sort of open-ended discretion in Congress that has come to be associated with *McCulloch*. Instead, a majority of Congress may well have embraced the stricter meaning of necessary and simply concluded that the bank met this more demanding standard.

That exercises of power under the Necessary and Proper clause were thought subject to judicial review was also assumed by the author of the first scholarly work on the Constitution. St. George Tucker was professor of law at the College of William and Mary, one of the leading judges of the General Court in Virginia, and the American editor of *Blackstone's Commentaries*, the most influential and authoritative legal work of the period. In the 1803 edition of the *Commentaries*, he attached an appendix discussing the meaning of the U.S. Constitution. This work was drawn from the notes of his lectures given throughout the 1790s and contemporaneous with the earliest years of the Constitution.

---

[125] *Annals*, 2:1932 (1791).
[126] Ibid., 1936–37 (emphasis added).

Tucker's account of the Necessary and Proper Clause is nearly identical with that of Madison and Jefferson and with the views expressed in the ratification conventions:

> The plain import of this clause is, that congress shall have all the incidental or instrumental powers, necessary and proper for carrying into execution all the express powers; whether they be vested in the government of the United States, more collectively, or in the several departments, or officers thereof. It neither enlarges any power specifically granted, nor is it a grant of new powers to congress, but merely a declaration, for the removal of all uncertainty, that the means of carrying into execution those otherwise granted, are included in the grant.[127]

Tucker was gravely concerned about the use of the clause to justify an unwarranted expansion of congressional power: "But, notwithstanding this remarkable security against misconstruction, a design has been indicated to expound these phrases in the constitution, so as to destroy the effect of the particular enumeration of powers, by which it explains and limits them, which must have fallen under the observation of those who have attended to the course of public transactions."[128] In a footnote, he adds: "Witness, the act for establishing a bank."[129]

Tucker then offered the following method of construing the clause and other powers of Congress:

> Whenever, therefore, a question arises concerning the constitutionality of a particular power; the first question is, whether the power be expressed in the constitution? If it be, the question is decided. If it be not expressed, the next enquiry must be, whether it is properly an incident to an express power, and necessary to it's execution. If it be, it may be exercised by congress. If it be not, congress cannot exercise it.[130]

"[T]his construction of the words 'necessary and proper,' " he contended, "is not only consonant with that which prevailed during the discussions and ratifications of the constitution, but is absolutely necessary to maintain their consistency with the peculiar character of the government, as

---

[127] Tucker, appendix to *Blackstone's Commentaries*, vol. 1, pt. 1, 287.

[128] Ibid.

[129] Ibid. fn.* The footnote continues with further examples: "the act authorising the president to appoint officers to volunteer corps of militia; the act declaring that a paper not stamped agreeably thereto, shall not be admitted as evidence in a state court; the alien and sedition laws, &c." It concludes with the following: "not to multiply proofs on this subject, it may be sufficient to refer to the debates of the federal legislature, for several years, in which arguments have, on different occasions, been drawn with apparent effect from these phrases, in their indefinite meaning."

[130] Ibid., 288.

possessed of particular and defined powers, only; not of the general and indefinite powers vested in ordinary governments."[131]

This construction would constrain members of Congress through their oaths and is "indispensably necessary to support that principle of the constitution, which regards the judicial exposition of that instrument, as the bulwark provided against undue extension of the legislative power."[132] Like Madison, Tucker affirmed that this standard was within the competence of judges to apply.

> If it be understood that the powers implied in the specified powers, have an immediate and appropriate relation to them, as means, necessary and proper for carrying them into execution, questions on the constitutionality of laws passed for this purpose, will be of a nature sufficiently precise and determinate, for judicial cognizance and control. If on the one hand congress are not limited in the choice of the means, by any such appropriate relation of them to the specified powers, but may use all such as they may deem capable of answering the end, without regard to the necessity, or propriety of them, all questions relating to means of this sort must be questions of *mere policy*, and expediency, and from which the judicial interposition and control are completely excluded.[133]

Although David Currie suggests a more restrictive interpretation of *McCulloch* than it was given by its critics at the time, it is the latitudinarian gloss on the meaning of "necessary" that survives to this day largely unchallenged. While Marshall's fear of impotent government remains a matter of speculation (because he got his way), history seems to have borne out Madison's and others' expressed concern for the integrity of the enumerated powers scheme. With rare exception, the enumeration of powers has largely been vitiated as a limitation on the scope of the national government, owing in no small measure to the influence of Justice Marshall's opinion in *McCulloch*. As Stephen Gardbaum has observed, *McCulloch* is

> one of the handful of foundational decisions of the Supreme Court that are automatically cited as original sources for the propositions of constitutional law that they contain. But *McCulloch* has the further (and even rarer) distinction of being treated as providing a full and complete interpretation of a particular clause of the Constitution. Analysis of the Necessary and Proper Clause has historically begun and ended with *McCulloch* . . . [134]

---

[131] Ibid.
[132] Ibid.
[133] Ibid., 288–89 (emphasis added).
[134] Steven Gardbaum, "Rethinking Constitutional Federalism," *Texas Law Review* 74 (1996): 814.

Therefore, it is supremely ironic that, like the other leading figures already discussed, John Marshall, too, insisted that the courts should not cede unlimited discretion to Congress. In a practice we would today think bizarre, Marshall responded to the torrent of condemnation with a pseudonymously published defense of his own opinion in *McCulloch*. Writing as "A Friend of the Constitution," he took pains to emphasize that his interpretation of the Necessary and Proper Clause did not cede a complete discretion to Congress:

> In no single instance does the court admit the unlimited power of congress to adopt any means whatever, and thus to pass the limits prescribed by the Constitution. Not only is the discretion claimed for the legislature in the selection of its means, always limited in terms, *to such as are appropriate*, but the court expressly says, "should congress under the pretext of executing its powers, pass laws for the accomplishment of objects, not entrusted to the government, it would become the painful duty of this tribunal . . . to say that such an act was not the law of the land.[135]

True, Madison expressed his doubts about Marshall's assertion of a continued power of judicial nullification: "But suppose Congress should, as would doubtless happen, pass unconstitutional laws, not to accomplish objects not specified in the Constitution, but the same laws as means expedient, convenient, or conductive to the accomplishment of objects intrusted to the government; by what handle could the court take hold of the case?"[136] Although Madison's gloomy prediction proved prescient, Marshall had, nevertheless, conceded the point that the judiciary should maintain some control over the exercise of congressional power under the Necessary and Proper Clause.

The Meaning of "Proper": Means and Ends

Marshall's affirmation that congressional powers are limited to "such as are *appropriate*" emphasizes a portion of the Necessary and Proper Clause usually overlooked by those who assert that it is not justiciable: the meaning of the term "proper." In what respect could a measure that was shown to be truly necessary to the effectuation of an enumerated purpose ever be improper? Would a meaningful means-end scrutiny of

---

[135] John Marshall, "A Friend of the Constitution," *Alexandria Gazette*, July 15, 1819, reprinted in Gerald Gunther, ed., *John Marshall's Defense of McCulloch v. Maryland* (Stanford: Stanford University Press, 1969), 186–87 (emphasis added).

[136] Madison, *Letters*, 144. (Letter from James Madison to Judge Roane, September 2, 1819).

the necessity of a restriction on the liberties of the people make an assessment of its propriety superfluous?

One thing that stands out from the records of the Constitutional Convention was how frequently the term "necessary" was paired with "proper" (or "unnecessary" with "improper") in contexts suggesting each term has a distinct meaning. For example, when Rufus King of Massachusetts objected to one of the rules of the Convention authorizing any member to call for the Yeas and Nays and have them entered on the minutes, he urged "that as the acts of the Convention were not to bind the constituents, it was *unnecessary* to exhibit this evidence of the votes; and *improper*, as changes of opinion would be frequent in the course of the business, and would fill the minutes with contradictions."[137]

Although the distinction resonates throughout the Convention, it is often hard to figure out what was meant by it. Perhaps the clearest example is by Madison when he objected to the requirement that, to be a senator, one must have first been a citizen for fourteen years. While he agreed with some citizenship requirement, he

> thought any restriction however in the *Constitution* unnecessary, and improper;—unnecessary, because the National Legislature is to have the right of regulating naturalization, and can by virtue thereof fix different periods of residence as conditions of enjoying different privileges of citizenship;—improper, because it will give a tincture of illiberality to the Constitution; because it will put out of the power of the national Legislature even by special acts of naturalization to confer the full rank of citizens on meritorious strangers and because it will discourage the most desirable class of people from emigrating to the U.S.[138]

Madison's use of "unnecessary" here is relatively clear. The end can be accomplished by other less potentially intrusive means. His use of "improper" is harder to see, but seems to consist of a kind of wrong or injustice ("a tincture of illiberality") coupled with the idea that it was "properly" within the jurisdiction of the legislature to make this kind of decision. The injustice of such a restriction is underscored by his comment that, if the Constitution is successful in its aim, "great numbers of respectable Europeans: men who love liberty and wish to partake its blessings, will be ready to transfer their fortunes hither. All such would feel the mortification of being marked with suspicious incapacitations though they should not covet the public honors."[139]

---

[137] Madison, *Notes of Debates*, 25 (emphasis added).
[138] Ibid., 419 (emphasis added).
[139] Ibid.

Gary Lawson and Patricia Granger made an extensive examination of sources from the founding era and concluded that the following "jurisdictional" meaning of "proper" covers most instances of its actual use:

> In view of the limited character of the national government under the Constitution, Congress's choice of means to execute federal powers would be constrained in at least three ways: first, an executory law would have to conform to the "proper" allocation of authority within the federal government; second, such a law would have to be within the "proper" scope of the federal government's limited jurisdiction with respect to the retained prerogatives of the states; and third, the law would have to be within the "proper" scope of the federal government's limited jurisdiction with respect to the people's retained rights. In other words, . . . executory laws must be consistent with principles of separation of powers, principles of federalism, and individual rights.[140]

In other words, for a law to be "proper" it must not only be necessary, it must also be within the jurisdiction of Congress. This propriety of jurisdiction is determined in at least three ways: (1) according to principles of separation of powers; (2) according to principles of federalism; and (3) according to the background rights retained by the people. In light of the discussion of constitutional legitimacy in chapter 3, let me focus on the third: Laws are improper when they violate the background rights retained by the people.

If necessity is taken to mean "convenient," it is easy to see how an exercise of so discretionary a power could violate the background rights retained by the people, though taking this problem seriously reintroduces—under the rubric of "propriety"—many of the difficulties Marshall argued attach to a strict construction of necessity. Adopting a Madisonian conception of necessity, however, raises the following potential difficulty: If a restriction of liberty is shown to be a truly necessary means of executing an enumerated power or end, in what way can it be considered an "improper" infringement on these background rights? Have not the people surrendered to the national government the powers that were enumerated in Article I and any rights inconsistent with the exercise of such powers?

The answer to this rhetorical question is not as obvious as some may think. As was seen in chapter 3, the appropriate legal construct is not the surrender of rights to a master, but the delegation of powers to an agent. As Marshall himself wrote: "It is the plain dictate of common sense, and the whole political system is founded on the idea, that the departments of government are the agents of the nation, and will perform, within their

---

[140] Lawson and Granger, "The 'Proper' Scope of Federal Power," 297.

respective spheres, the duties assigned to them."[141] When a principal engages an agent, the agent can be empowered to act on behalf of and subject to the control of the principal, while at the same time the principal retains all his rights. So, for example, a principal can empower the agent to sell the principal's car, while retaining the right to sell it himself.

The fact that a principal retains rights is one reason that agents can be sued for failing to act on their principal's behalf or refusing to conform their actions to their principal's exercise of control. In normal agency relationships, the empowerment of an agent to act on the principal's behalf does not make the agent the sole judge of whether she is acting within the scope of her agency, as the discretionary conception of necessity seems to do. Moreover, the fact that some rights are inalienable suggests that those who purport to exercise them on behalf of another need to justify their assumption of such power.[142]

To see how a necessary law could still be improper, consider an example offered by Madison in his speech explaining his proposed amendments to the Constitution that became the Bill of Rights.

> The General Government has a right to pass all laws which shall be necessary to collect its revenue; the means for enforcing the collection are within the direction of the Legislature: may not general warrants be considered necessary for this purpose. . . ? If there was reason for restraining the State Governments from exercising this power, there is like reason for restraining the Federal Government.[143]

In other words, although using general warrants might "be considered necessary," their use would still be improper and unconstitutional. Nor would it be fair to conclude from this quotation that impropriety was limited to violations of express restrictions of power. There is little doubt that the use of general warrants would have been considered improper during the two-year hiatus between the ratification of the Constitution and that of the amendments. The impropriety of using general warrants stems from the need to protect a person and his property from unreasonable searches and seizures.[144]

[141] Marshall, "A Friend of the Constitution," reprinted in *John Marshall's Defense*, 211.

[142] See Randy E. Barnett, "Contract Remedies and Inalienable Rights," *Social Policy and Philosophy* 4 (1986): 179 (defining inalienable rights and providing four reasons why some rights are inalienable); Barnett, "Squaring Undisclosed Agency Law with Contract Theory," 1981 ("A principal who authorizes his agent to so act 'on his behalf' consensually empowers the agent to exercise certain rights that the principal alone would normally exercise").

[143] *Annals*, 1:456.

[144] A "general warrant" was one that did not specify the place or person to be searched and thus authorized government agents to search whom and where they pleased. Search warrants immunized a government agent from liability in trespass. The later rise of "sovereign immunity" made warrants less necessary for this purpose, and greatly undermined the

Another example of how the Necessary and Proper Clause confines Congress to using only those necessary means that are also proper was offered by St. George Tucker. "If, for example, congress were to pass a law *prohibiting* any person from bearing arms, as a means of preventing insurrections, the judicial courts, under the construction of the words necessary and proper, here contended for, would be able to pronounce decidedly upon the constitutionality of these means."[145] Giving Congress the power to choose any means it deems to be necessary would be to expand improperly its power to invade the rights retained by the people—in this case the enumerated right to keep and bear arms.

> But if congress may use *any means, which they choose to adopt*, the provision in the constitution which secures to the people the right of bearing arms, is a mere nullity; and any man imprisoned for bearing arms under such an act, might be without relief; because in that case, no court could have any power to pronounce on the necessity or propriety of the means adopted by congress to carry any specified power into complete effect.[146]

These are examples of improper *means* thought necessary to accomplish an enumerated end. Even a necessary means of pursuing a delegated power can "inappropriately" restrict the exercise of a right retained by the people. According to this view, although it may be necessary and proper to regulate a genuine exercise of liberty, it is inappropriate to prohibit its exercise altogether.[147] Whether or not a restriction on liberty is "inappropriate" would depend, therefore, not only on the degree of means-end fit, but on whether the measure is a regulation or a prohibition. While wrongful action can properly be prohibited, it would be improper to prohibit or deliberately subvert or discourage, as opposed to regulate and facilitate, rightful conduct.[148]

A law would also obviously be improper if it is enacted to accomplish an improper end. The powers enumerated in the Constitution, such as the

---

incentive of law enforcement to comply with the warrant requirement. At present the principal consequence of a warrantless illegal search is the suppression of evidence, which only helps the guilty. The original system of immunization from tort liability also helped the innocent as well as provided a greater deterrent against improper searches. See, generally, Randy E. Barnett, "Resolving the Dilemma of the Exclusionary Rule: An Application of Restitutive Principles of Justice," *Emory Law Journal* 32 (1983): 937–85.

[145] Tucker, appendix to *Blackstone's Commentaries*, vol. 1, pt. 1, 289 (emphasis added).

[146] Ibid. (emphasis added). Notice also that Tucker assumes here that the right of the people to keep and bear arms is an individual right that would restrict the disarmament of "any man" without reference to whether he was actively serving in the militia at the time.

[147] In contrast, if the action is an exercise of license (as opposed to liberty), it can be prohibited altogether.

[148] We shall consider the distinction between regulation and prohibition at greater length in chapters 10 and 11 in the context of Congress's power to "regulate trade" and the "police power" of the states.

power to raise and support armies, to establish post offices, or to grant monopolies for limited periods to authors can be viewed as objects or ends that are deemed by the text as proper. Such powers are "locked in," along with the other provisions of the written Constitution, as a matter of positive law whether or not they are truly among the proper ends of government.[149] In this respect, some ends-scrutiny is foreclosed by a written Constitution containing enumerated powers.[150]

Nevertheless, a judicial scrutiny of ends would be needed and warranted (or necessary and proper) when Congress purports to be pursuing an enumerated end, but is actually pursuing a purpose other than those included in the enumeration of its powers. A law actually enacted for a purpose or end that was not among those enumerated would exceed its jurisdiction under the Constitution and be improper regardless of the means it employed. Such a law would be, in the words of John Marshall in *McCulloch*, a mere "pretext . . . for the accomplishment of objects not entrusted to the government."[151]

If Congress were to enact such a law, Marshall insisted, "it would become the painful duty of this tribunal . . . to say that such an act was not the law of the land."[152] Wholly apart from the need to assess a measure's necessity, Congress cannot be the sole judge of whether it is acting within its powers because that would give it license to pursue objects or ends that are beyond its powers. In other words, an otherwise necessary law can still be improper if it employs improper *means*—such as by prohibiting or discouraging rather than regulating and facilitating rightful conduct—or is intended by Congress to accomplish an improper *end*—such as an end not enumerated in the Constitution.

Conclusion

Assuming judges have the power to nullify unconstitutional statutes, as most would concede, how much deference do they owe legislatures that enacted them? At the federal level, the answer turns in part on the meaning of the clause that is most often used to justify the constitutionality of con-

---

[149] Laws passed pursuant to an enumerated power that is actually improper, though authorized by positive law, may be as illegitimate as the powers created by the Fugitive Slave Clause of Article IV. Though a judge committed to a written constitution would not be free to declare such laws unconstitutional, their commands may not bind in conscience.

[150] As we shall see in chapter 11, this is not the case with the unenumerated "police power" claimed by the states.

[151] *McCulloch v. Maryland*, 17 U.S., at 423.

[152] Ibid. One way to understand the difference between Marshall and Madison is that while Marshall would limit judicial nullification to ends-scrutiny, Madison—and I think Hamilton as well—would also permit scrutiny of the means chosen in pursuit of a proper end.

gressional powers: the Necessary and Proper Clause. If you take the view attributed to Marshall that "necessary" means merely convenient or useful, then courts are generally unqualified to second-guess a congressional determination of expediency. On the other hand, if the clause requires (a) a showing of means-ends fit—as per Madison, Jefferson, and even Hamilton—together with a showing that (b) the means chosen do not prohibit the rightful exercise of freedom (or violate principles of federalism or separation of powers) and (c) the claim by Congress to be pursuing an enumerated end is not a pretext for pursuing other ends not delegated to it (as per Marshall in *McCulloch*), then an inquiry into each of these issues is clearly within the competence of courts. Given that the Necessary and Proper Clause applies only to Congress, what, then, is the proper stance of federal courts to laws exacted by states? It is to that issue I now turn.

CHAPTER EIGHT

Judicial Review of State Laws: The Meaning of the Privileges or Immunities Clause

> The right of a State to regulate the conduct of its citizens is undoubtedly a very broad and extensive one, and not to be lightly restricted. But there are certain fundamental rights which this right of regulation cannot infringe. It may prescribe the manner of their exercise, but it cannot subvert the rights themselves.
>
> —JUSTICE JOSEPH BRADLEY (1873)

TO THIS POINT we have examined whether the Necessary and Proper Clause precludes or invites the exercise of judicial review of a federal statute to see if it lies within the powers of Congress to enact. What stance should federal courts take toward state legislation? The original Constitution contained several explicit restrictions on state power. Article I, Section 10 stipulates, for example, that

> No State shall enter into any Treaty, Alliance, or Confederation; grant Letters of Marque and Reprisal; coin Money; emit Bills of Credit; make any Thing but gold and silver Coin a Tender in Payment of Debts; pass any Bill of Attainder, ex post facto Law, or Law impairing the Obligation of Contracts, or grant any Title of Nobility.[1]

In the early years of the Republic, federal courts actively scrutinized state enactments to ensure they did not violate these expressed prohibitions,

---

[1] U.S. Const, Art. I, § 10. The rest of the section adds these additional expressed restrictions:

> No State shall, without the Consent of the Congress, lay any Imposts or Duties on Imports or Exports, except what may be absolutely necessary for executing it's inspection Laws; and the net Produce of all Duties and Imposts, laid by any State on Imports or Exports, shall be for the Use of the Treasury of the United States; and all such Laws shall be subject to the Revision and Controul of the Congress.
>
> No State shall, without the Consent of Congress, lay any Duty of Tonnage, keep Troops, or Ships of War in time of Peace, enter into any Agreement or Compact with another State, or with a foreign Power, or engage in War, unless actually invaded, or in such imminent Danger as will not admit of delay.

especially the Contracts Clause. When it came to legislation not implicating these prohibitions, however, the courts deferred to states in their exercise of what was called their "police power." The nature and scope of this power will be examined at length in chapter 12.

Early on, the issue arose whether state laws were unconstitutional if they violated the rights enumerated in the Bill of Rights. In the 1833 decision of *Barron v. Baltimore*,[2] the Marshall Court ruled that the Bill of Rights did not apply to state governments, a decision that most likely reflected the original intent of those who wrote and ratified the first ten amendments. In the years leading up to the Civil War, unencumbered by any federal scrutiny, local officials routinely suppressed abolitionist speech and the freedom of the abolitionist press. They denied abolitionists and free blacks the equal protection of the laws from mob violence and terrorism. After the war, the black codes and other measures violated the right of blacks and Republicans to keep and bear arms to protect themselves from mobs and other violence, as well as the natural rights of blacks to hold property and enter into contracts. Under the Constitution as then construed, neither Congress nor federal courts had the power to offer relief from these violations of rights.

After the Republicans in Congress abolished slavery with the Thirteenth Amendment, they then set out to address these other abuses of rights by passing the Civil Rights Act of 1866. President Johnson vetoed the act on the ground that it was outside the enumerated powers of Congress. Although his veto was overridden, many in Congress worried that its constitutional authority was shaky and that, because it was only a statute, a future Congress might repeal the act. Republicans in Congress responded to all this by adopting the Fourteenth Amendment, thereby changing fundamentally the constitutional structure. Along with this change, as we shall see, came an increased responsibility of the federal courts to scrutinize the necessity and propriety of state as well as federal legislation.

THE RECONSTRUCTION ERA: PRIVILEGES OR IMMUNITIES AND *SLAUGHTER-HOUSE*

Prior to the Civil War, radical abolitionists continued to insist that the Bill of Rights applied to the states even after *Barron v. Baltimore*, contending that it was wrongly decided or ignoring it altogether. In addition, as was briefly touched upon in chapter 2, some abolitionists asserted that

[2] 32 U.S. 243 (1833).

the Bill of Rights applied to the states via the Privileges and Immunities Clause of Article IV, which reads: "The Citizens of each State shall be entitled to all Privileges and Immunities of Citizens in the several States."[3] This somewhat enigmatic provision was originally meant to protect the rights of out-of-state citizens from discrimination when they traveled to another state. It was not intended to protect citizens of a state from infringements of their liberties by their own state, but abolitionists were willing to seize upon a variety of textual provisions to advance their position, including this one.[4]

When their authority to enact the Civil Rights Act of 1866 was questioned, some members of Congress seemed unaware that *Barron* had limited the Bill of Rights to the national government. Others realized that a constitutional amendment was needed to reverse *Barron* and give Congress (and the courts) authority to protect the rights of citizens from violation by state governments and also to protect these rights from repeal by a future Congress. They proposed a provision in the Fourteenth Amendment that borrowed the language of the Privileges and Immunities Clause of Article IV, only this time making explicit the abolitionists' contention that the clause was not limited to preventing discrimination against citizens from out of state, but also protected the rights of citizens from abuses by their own state government.

In the House of Representatives, it fell to John Bingham of New York, the author of the Fourteenth Amendment, to explain that the absence of any power in Congress to protect the rights of citizens from state governments "makes plain the necessity of adopting this amendment."[5] After reading passages of Marshall's opinion in *Barron*, he passionately urged upon the House the necessity of a new amendment. "Is it not essential to the unity of the people," he asked, "that the citizens of each State shall be entitled to all the privileges and immunities of citizens of the several states?"[6] As it stands, he observed, Congress is empowered to protect Americans from tyranny abroad but is "powerless in time of peace, in the presence of the laws of South Carolina, Alabama, and Mississippi, . . . to enforce the rights of citizens of the United States *within their limits*."[7]

He lamented that the original Constitution did not provide this protection. Its framers, he argued, were content to make the Constitution the supreme law of the land, require all state officers to take an oath to the

---

[3] U.S. Const., Art. IV.

[4] Indeed, it was at this time that arguments based on original intent first became popular as a way of negating these creative textualist claims based on plain meaning made by abolitionists.

[5] *Congressional Globe*, 39th Cong., 1st sess., 1089 (February 29, 1866).

[6] Ibid., 1090.

[7] Ibid. (emphasis added).

Constitution, and then explicitly bind all state court judges to adhere to it. "Is it surprising," he asked,

> that essential as they held the full security to all citizens of all the privileges and immunities of citizens, and to all the people the sacred rights of persons, that having proclaimed them they left their lawful enforcement to each of the States, under the solemn obligation resting upon every State officer to regard, respect, and obey the constitutional injunction?[8]

What stopped them from going further and adding the additional grant of power represented by the Fourteenth Amendment? For Bingham, the answer was clear: slavery. "That is the only reason why it was not there. There was a fetter on the conscience of the nation; the people could not put it there and permit slavery in any State thereafter."[9] The matter was simple: "Gentlemen who oppose this amendment oppose the grant of power to enforce the bill of rights"[10] against the states.

As we saw in chapter 3, however, the term "privileges or immunities" was not limited to those listed in the Bill of Rights. It also included other legally protected natural rights—or "civil rights"—such as those listed in the Civil Rights Act itself.[11] Recall that when explaining the meaning of the Privileges or Immunities Clause, Senator Jacob Howard first read the well-known quotation from Justice Washington's opinion in *Corfield*, and then stated: "Such is the character of the privileges and immunities spoken of in the second section of the fourth article of the Constitution."[12] He then continued: "To these privileges and immunities, whatever they may be—for they are not and cannot be fully defined in their entire extent and precise nature—to these should be *added* the personal rights guaranteed and secured by the first eight amendments of the Constitution."[13]

When deference is based on trust, and trust is eroded, increased scrutiny follows. The enactment of the Fourteenth Amendment was specifically intended to subject state legislation to federal scrutiny to determine whether it violated the privileges or immunities of citizenship or whether it deprived any person of life, liberty, or property without due process of law. In essence, the exercise of power by state governments was now sub-

---

[8] Ibid.

[9] Ibid.

[10] Ibid.

[11] Those who argue that the Fourteenth Amendment was meant only to constitutionalize the Civil Rights Act—an overly restricted view of the amendment—are nonetheless conceding that the scope of rights it protects extends beyond those in the Bill of Rights given that the act clearly protected rights not enumerated in the first eight amendments.

[12] Ibid., 2765.

[13] Ibid. (emphasis added).

ject to new constitutional constraints in addition to those already provided for in Article I, Section 10. This alteration in the basic constitutional structure did not, however, go down well in the courts.

When the meaning of the Privileges or Immunities Clause was considered by the Supreme Court, its original meaning was set aside by a five-to-four decision in what are called *The Slaughter-House Cases*.[14] These cases arose when, in 1869, the legislature of Louisiana passed an act ordering all animals imported for consumption in the city to be landed at certain places, and all intended for food to be slaughtered there. The same law also conferred on seventeen persons the exclusive right to maintain landings for cattle and to erect slaughter-houses, chartering them under the name of The Crescent City Live-stock Landing and Slaughter-House Company. This law was challenged by the Live Stock Dealers' and Butchers' Association, whose members would be prohibited from competing with the new monopoly.

At the appellate court level, Supreme Court Justice Bradley, sitting as a circuit court judge,[15] indicated sympathy for a constitutional challenge based on the Privileges or Immunities Clause (although he ruled that the federal courts did not have power to enjoin state proceedings initiated by the Crescent City Company). Bradley began by distinguishing the new Privileges *or* Immunities Clause of the Fourteenth Amendment from the old Privileges *and* Immunities Clause of Article IV.[16] The new provision "is not identical with the clause in the constitution which declared that 'the citizens of each state shall be entitled to all privileges and immunities of citizens in the several states.' It embraces much more."[17] The "Privileges and Immunities" referred to in Article IV "were only such as each state gave to its own citizens. Each was prohibited from discriminating in favor of its own citizens, and against the citizens of other states."[18] But the Privileges or Immunities Clause of the Fourteenth Amendment "prohibits any state from abridging the privileges or immunities of the citizens of the United States, whether its own citizens or any others. It not merely requires equality of privileges; but it demands that the privileges and immunities of all citizens shall be absolutely unabridged, unimpaired."[19]

[14] 83 U.S. (16 Wall.) 36 (1873).

[15] In those days before the creation of the Circuit Courts of Appeals, justices themselves "rode circuit" to hear appeals.

[16] In what follows, I use "Privileges *or* Immunities Clause," to refer to the clause in the Fourteenth Amendment. When I refer to "Privileges *and* Immunities Clause," I mean the clause that appears in Article IV.

[17] *Live-Stock Dealers' and Butchers' Association v. Crescent City Live-Stock Landing and Slaughter-House Company*, 15 F. Cas. 649, 652 (1870).

[18] Ibid.

[19] Ibid.

In other words, while the Privileges and Immunities Clause of Article IV barred discrimination against out-of-staters, the Privileges or Immunities Clause of the Fourteenth Amendment barred states both from discriminating among different citizens within a state and from abridging or impairing the rights of all citizens even if the restrictions apply equally to all. Bradley then addressed the nature of these privileges a state cannot invade. "It may be difficult to enumerate or define them," he began.

> But so far as relates to the question in hand, we may safely say it is one of the privileges of every American citizen to adopt and follow such lawful industrial pursuit—not injurious to the community—as he may see fit, without unreasonable regulation or molestation, and without being restricted by any of those unjust, oppressive, and odious monopolies or exclusive privileges which have been condemned by all free governments. . . .[20]

According to Justice Bradley, this and other essential privileges

> cannot be invaded without sapping the very foundations of republican government. A republican government is not merely a government of the people, but it is a free government. Without being free, it is republican only in name, and not republican in truth, and any government which deprives its citizens of the right to engage in any lawful pursuit, subject only to reasonable restrictions, or at least subject only to such restrictions as are reasonably within the power of government to impose,—is tyrannical and unrepublican. And if to enforce arbitrary restrictions made for the benefit of a favored few, it takes away and destroys the citizen's property without trial or condemnation, it is guilty of violating all the fundamental privileges to which I have referred, and one of the fundamental principles of free government.[21]

When the various slaughter-house cases finally made their way to the full Supreme Court, Bradley's approach was rejected by a vote of five to four. Writing for the majority, Justice Miller distinguished between the privileges and immunities of *national* citizenship, which were created by the Constitution and protected by the Fourteenth Amendment, and the privileges and immunities or "civil rights" of *state* citizenship, which corresponded to what Justice Washington wrote in *Corfield* and were protected by the Privileges and Immunities clause of Article IV. The latter "are those which belong to citizens of the States as such, and . . . they are left to the State governments for security and protection, and not by this article placed under the special care of the Federal government."[22]

[20] Ibid.
[21] Ibid.
[22] 83 U.S. 36, 78.

In defense of this interpretation, Miller offered no direct evidence from the statements of those who proposed the Fourteenth Amendment. Such proof would have been impossible. Instead, he ignored the original meaning of the clause to rest his conclusion instead on the consequences of holding otherwise. If the "privileges or immunities" protected by the Fourteenth Amendment were as broad as the category of "civil rights," he contended, then

> not only are these rights subject to the control of Congress whenever in its discretion any of them are supposed to be abridged by State legislation, but that body may also pass laws in advance, limiting and restricting the exercise of legislative power by the States, in their most ordinary and usual functions, as in its judgment it may think proper on all such subjects.[23]

This, argued Miller, would be to give Congress a national police power that would supersede the traditional powers of the states in every area of legislation and would "radically change[ ] the whole theory of the relations of the State and Federal governments to each other and of both these governments to the people."[24] In the absence of "language which expresses such a purpose too clearly to admit of doubt,"[25] Miller concluded that "no such results were intended by the Congress which proposed these amendments, nor by the legislatures of the States which ratified them."[26] Because the privilege to pursue one's trade or occupation was a "civil right" and not a privilege of national citizenship it was, therefore, unprotected by the Fourteenth Amendment.

What then, according to Justice Miller, were the privileges and immunities of national citizenship protected by the amendment? He declined to elaborate since it was clear to him that the right asserted by the claimants was not among them. But he did list a few "which owe their existence to the Federal government, its National character, its Constitution, or its laws."[27] A citizen has the right

> to come to the seat of government to assert any claim he may have upon that government, to transact any business he may have with it, to seek its protection, to share its offices, to engage in administering its functions. He has the right of free access to its seaports, through which all operations of foreign commerce are conducted, to the subtreasuries, land offices, and courts of justice in the several States. . . .

[23] Ibid.
[24] Ibid.
[25] Ibid.
[26] Ibid.
[27] Ibid., 79.

Another privilege of a citizen of the United States is to demand the care and protection of the Federal government over his life, liberty, and property when on the high seas or within the jurisdiction of a foreign government. . . . The right to peaceably assemble and petition for redress of grievances, the privilege of the writ of *habeas corpus*, are rights of the citizen guaranteed by the Federal Constitution. The right to use the navigable waters of the United States, however they may penetrate the territory of the several States, all rights secured to our citizens by treaties with foreign nations, are dependent upon citizenship of the United States, and not citizenship of a State.[28]

The dissenting justices, in separate opinions, took strong issue with Miller's imputation of intent to Congress. On the majority's interpretation, wrote Justice Field, "it was a vain and idle enactment, which accomplished nothing, and most unnecessarily excited Congress and the people on its passage. . . . But if the amendment refers to the natural and inalienable rights which belong to all citizens, the inhibition has a profound significance and consequence."[29] What, then, did Field think were the privileges and immunities that were secured against abridgment by state legislation? Field's answer rested importantly on evidence of original meaning.

First were the civil rights protected by the Civil Rights Act including "the right 'to make and enforce contracts, to sue, be parties and give evidence, to inherit, purchase, lease, sell, hold, and convey real and personal property, and to full and equal benefit of all laws and proceedings for the security of person and property.' "[30] He also referenced the list recited by Justice Washington in *Corfield*:

Mr. Justice Washington said he had "no hesitation in confining these expressions to those privileges and immunities which were, in their nature, fundamental; which belong of right to citizens of all free governments, and which have at all times been enjoyed by the citizens of the several States which compose the Union, from the time of their becoming free, independent, and sovereign;" and, in considering what those fundamental privileges were, he said that perhaps it would be more tedious than difficult to enumerate them, but that they might be "all comprehended under the following general heads: protection by the government; the enjoyment of life and liberty, with the right to acquire and possess property of every kind, and to pursue and obtain happiness and safety, subject, nevertheless, to such restraints as the government may justly prescribe for the general good of the whole."[31]

---

[28] Ibid., 79–80 (quotation omitted).
[29] Ibid., 96.
[30] Ibid.
[31] Ibid., 97.

To Justice Field, this appeared to "be a sound construction of the clause in question. The privileges and immunities designated are those *which of right belong to the citizens of all free governments.*"[32] Unlike Miller, Field referred to the congressional debates, noting that

> repeated reference was made to this language of Mr. Justice Washington. It was cited by Senator Trumbull with the observation that it enumerated the very rights belonging to a citizen of the United States set forth in the first section of the act, and with the statement that all persons born in the United States, being declared by the act citizens of the United States, would thenceforth be entitled to the rights of citizens, and that these were the great fundamental rights set forth in the act; and that they were set forth "as appertaining to every freeman."[33]

In essence, the majority found there to be two classes of privileges and immunities: national and state. The national ones were those specifically designated in the Constitution or directly derivable from its national character; the state ones were the full panoply of natural or "civil rights" that pertain to all free persons. The Privileges or Immunities Clause of the Fourteenth Amendment protects the former absolutely, while the Privileges and Immunities Clause of Article IV protects the latter by protecting citizens from discrimination when they are residing or acting in other states. In contrast, Justice Field contended that there was just one set of privileges and/or immunities that formerly had been unprotected from state infringement, but which had been given national protection by the enactment of the Fourteenth Amendment. As between the two, the dissenters' position is clearly more consonant with the original meaning of "privileges or immunities" that I canvassed in chapter 3 and the origins of the clause described in this chapter.

Like Justice Field's opinion, which discussed the original meaning of "privileges or immunities," Justice Bradley's dissenting opinion elaborated the arguments he had made earlier while riding circuit concerning the meaning of this phrase and again quoted Justice Washington's opinion in *Corfield*. But Bradley also offered an important theoretical rebuttal to Justice Miller's contention that equating "privileges or immunities" with civil rights would be to establish a broad national power that would supersede those of the states.

> The right of a State to *regulate* the conduct of its citizens is undoubtedly a very broad and extensive one, and not to be lightly restricted. But there are certain

[32] Ibid.
[33] Ibid., 98.

fundamental rights which this right of *regulation* cannot infringe. It may prescribe the *manner* of their exercise, but it cannot *subvert* the rights themselves.[34]

In this neglected passage, Justice Bradley makes a crucial distinction I mentioned at the end of the previous chapter: the distinction between regulating the exercise of a civil right and improperly subverting or abridging its exercise; or between "regulating and facilitating" rightful conduct and "prohibiting or discouraging" it. States were free to regulate civil rights—that is, specify "the manner of their exercise"—and Congress was not empowered by the Fourteenth Amendment to do so. What the amendment did was to give the national government jurisdiction to protect these civil rights from being improperly abridged or subverted in the name of the "right of regulation." In the last portion of his dissent, Justice Bradley examined whether the monopoly at issue in *The Slaughter-House Cases* was a reasonable regulation and concluded that it was not.

Justice Bradley also offered a useful distinction between the Fourteenth Amendment's Privileges or Immunities Clause and its Due Process Clause. Among the most fundamental privileges or immunities protected by both provisions were those described by Blackstone as that of life, liberty, and property, and by the Declaration of Independence as that of life, liberty, and the pursuit of happiness. "These are the fundamental rights which can only be taken away by due process of law, and which can only be interfered with, or the enjoyment of which can only be modified, *by lawful regulations necessary or proper for the mutual good of all*; and these rights, I contend, belong to the citizens of every free government."[35]

The function of the Due Process Clause can be seen as prohibiting a state from depriving particular individuals, whether citizens or not, of their life, liberty, or property ("Nor shall the state deprive *any person* . . ."). The function of the Privileges or Immunities Clause is to protect the citizenry as a whole against unnecessary or improper legislation that infringes upon the exercise of their civil rights or liberty ("No state shall make or enforce *any law* . . ."). In other words, under the Due Process Clause of the Fourteenth Amendment, one cannot have his or her rights taken away without due process of law. And under the Privileges or Immunities Clause, Justice Bradley would require that legislation that purported to "regulate" or modify the exercise of any civil right—including that to life, liberty, and property—be both necessary and proper for the common good.

In this way, Justice Bradley resolved an obvious and long-standing tension between the two provisions. If the Privileges or Immunities Clause is

[34] Ibid., 114 (emphasis added).
[35] Ibid., 116 (emphasis added).

read to protect the rights found in the Bill of Rights, how is it that states may not abridge such rights as the right peaceably to assemble, but may abridge what appear to be the even more fundamental rights to life, liberty, and property provided only that "due process" is given? The answer is (a) that the Privileges or Immunities Clause includes the rights of life, liberty, and property in addition to those listed in the Bill of Rights, and (b) that legislation that improperly "abridges"—rather than regulates—any one of the entire set of civil rights is prohibited, whereas *even a proper law*[36] may not be used to deprive any particular person of her life, liberty, or property unless she is accorded due process. Whereas the Privileges or Immunities Clause protects a broad set of rights—including life, liberty, and property—of all citizens from improper *laws*, the Due Process Clause protects the life, liberty, or property of all persons from an improper *application* of an otherwise proper law.[37]

Bradley also responded to Justice Miller's claim that providing federal protection of fundamental civil rights would bring into federal courts the full panoply of cases now decided by state courts. "As the privileges and immunities protected are only those fundamental ones which belong to every citizen, they would soon become so far defined as to cause but a slight accumulation of business in the Federal courts. Besides, the recognized existence of the law would prevent its frequent violation."[38] By placing so much weight on consequences, the majority was, thought Bradley, putting the cart before the horse. "The great question is, What is the true construction of the amendment? When once we find that, we shall find the means of giving it effect. The argument from inconvenience ought not to have a very controlling influence in questions of this sort."[39]

Justice Miller's majority opinion has long been thought to have gutted the Privileges or Immunities clause of any real significance and, indeed, after *Slaughter-House* it ceased to play any important function. On the other hand, as has been pointed out by Kevin Newsom, Miller's opinion can be interpreted (though it has not been) as adopting the middle ground of protecting all the rights explicitly protected in the Constitution—including the Bill of Rights—but not the "civil rights" that are unmentioned

[36] A proper law is one that either regulates rightful or prohibits wrongful behavior.

[37] Because citizens may have more privileges than aliens, a law may treat them differently and still be proper under the Privileges or Immunities Clause—though citizens from other states are protected against discrimination within a state by the Privileges and Immunities Clause of Article IV. Nevertheless, all persons, whether or not they are citizens, have a right under the Due Process Clause to have otherwise proper laws applied to them with due process. In other words, if aliens are to be treated differently from citizens, it must be by a properly enacted law.

[38] 38 U.S. at 124.

[39] Ibid.

there.[40] The majority opinion's reference to the right in the First Amendment to peaceably assemble as a protected privilege or immunity of national citizenship supports Newsom's interpretation of the case. If Newsom is right, then the butchers lost because the right they asserted was not among those that were enumerated in the Constitution.

While a significant advance over the prevailing view of *Slaughter-House,* even this more expansive interpretation of Miller's opinion conflicts with the original meaning of "privileges or immunities." As we have seen, the framers of the Fourteenth Amendment, and its supporters in Congress, spoke often of protecting the Bill of Rights from infringement by states, but they clearly did not limit the meaning of this clause to these rights. They repeatedly referred to Justice Washington's expansive list of rights in *Corfield,* to the concept of natural or "civil" rights, in addition to the privileges contained in the Bill of Rights. Among these additional privileges or immunities rights were the rights listed in the Civil Rights Act of 1866. And they made no distinction whatever between classes of state and national privileges or immunities.

In his dissenting opinion, the third of the three dissents filed in the case, Justice Swayne made much the same originalist point:

> The construction adopted by the majority of my brethren is, in my judgment, much too narrow. It defeats, by a limitation not anticipated, the intent of those by whom the instrument was framed and of those by whom it was adopted. To the extent of that limitation it turns, as it were, what was meant for bread into a stone. By the Constitution, as it stood before the war, ample protection was given against oppression by the Union, but little was given against wrong and oppression by the States. That want was intended to be supplied by this amendment. Against the former this court has been called upon more than once to interpose. Authority of the same amplitude was intended to be conferred as to the latter. But this arm of our jurisdiction is, in these cases, stricken down by the judgment just given. Nowhere, than in this court, ought the will of the nation, as thus expressed, to be more liberally construed or more cordially executed. This determination of the majority seems to me to lie far in the other direction.[41]

Swayne concluded by expressing his earnest "hope that the consequences to follow may prove less serious and far-reaching than the minority fear they will be."[42]

---

[40] See Kevin Newsom, "Setting Incorporationism Straight: A Reinterpretation of the Slaughter-House Cases," *Yale Law Journal* 109 (2000): 643.

[41] Ibid., 129.

[42] Ibid., 130.

The Fourteenth Amendment was born of a newfound distrust of state governments. The immediate cause of this distrust was, of course, the imposition of chattel slavery by state governments in the South before the war and the resistance to reconstruction afterward. But while it was instigated by the experience of reconstruction, the Fourteenth Amendment was never intended to apply only to former slaves. Indeed, among the core of its concerns was the protection of free speech, peaceable assembly, and the right to keep and bear arms by white, as well as black, supporters of Reconstruction. Both before and after the Civil War, the civil liberties of white unionists and abolitionists were severely restricted in the South, much to the dismay of Northern Republicans.[43]

Moreover, the principles that were advanced against slavery applied to whites in another way. Abolitionists had developed a principle known as "free labor." The right to one's labor was one's own, they argued, and could be alienated only by consent. Even when a contract to work for another was made, such contracts could not be specifically or coercively enforced. As was explained in the 1865 case of *Ford v. Jermon,* "Is it not obvious that a contract for personal services so enforced would be but a mitigated form of slavery, in which the party would have lost the right to dispose of himself as a free agent, and be, for a greater or less length of time, subject to the control of another?"[44]

Like the Thirteenth Amendment, which prohibited involuntary servitude, the free labor principle protected whites as well as blacks. Although the facts in *Slaughter-House* did not concern African slavery or its vestiges, the dissent nonetheless understood the liberty to pursue an occupation to be a fundamental right closely related to "free labor." The monopoly granted by Louisiana, they argued, directly abridged the right to pursue the lawful occupation of butcher by depriving butchers of the requisite of maintaining a slaughter-house.

Soon after its adoption, then, the Fourteenth Amendment was invoked by citizens seeking protection of their liberties from improper restrictions by states that were not motivated by racial discrimination. While the decision in *Slaughter-House* effectively foreclosed using the Privileges or Immunities Clause for this purpose, the theories advanced by the four dissenters were later shifted to the Due Process Clause and, for a time, came to prevail.

---

[43] See Michael Kent Curtis, "The 1837 Killing of Elijah Lovejoy by an Anti-Abolition Mob: Free Speech, Mobs, Republican Government, and the Privileges of American Citizens," *UCLA Law Review* 44 (1997): 1109.

[44] *Ford v. Jermon,* 6 Phila. 6, 7 (Dist. Ct 1865). The suit concerned the specific performance of an actor. Plaintiff Ford was also the owner of the theater in which Lincoln was murdered.

THE PROGRESSIVE ERA: DUE PROCESS AND *LOCHNER*

The last decades of the nineteenth century witnessed the growth of social-ist, "progressive," and "populist" political movements throughout the United States and Europe. The roots of this political sea change are com-plex and I shall not offer a definitive account of them here. Perhaps they include the rise of scientific empiricism that made the abstract natural rights beliefs of the founders and authors of the Fourteenth Amendment seem archaic. Perhaps the change reflected a philosophical shift in the conception of liberty from the individualism of Locke to the utilitarianism of Bentham and Mill. Perhaps the new wealth made possible by the age of inventions and the free flow of capital and labor created a heretofore unprecedented disparity of incomes among the citizenry, and a newfound luxury of imagining that poverty could be ameliorated by enlightened state intervention. And perhaps the nouveau riche threatened the old-line families as well. These are only some of the possibilities.

New technologies of transportation, such as the steamship, greatly low-ered the cost of transoceanic travel, bringing waves of immigrants to the United States and, with them, more European political ideas. Americans also witnessed the appalling living conditions and breakdowns in public order that normally accompany mass migrations. Would these aliens with their many languages assimilate into American society? Undoubtedly the intellectual shift was greatly encouraged by the example of Otto von Bis-marck's new welfare state in Germany with its government schools, gov-ernment pensions, and government-mandated worker-compensation schemes. These, along with German accomplishments in the arts and sci-ences, made the German socialist model appear to be the wave of the future. (And well it might have been had it not been for the militarism that invariably accompanies collectivism and statism.)

All these influences, and many more, led to a movement away from a political culture in which government was considered a necessary evil—to be kept as limited in its power as possible consistent with the few essen-tial tasks it was needed to perform—and toward one in which government was viewed as the vital instrument for addressing social problems. As important as any of the other factors mentioned, the American Civil War provided encouragement to this shift, by enhancing the moral authority of the central government and undermining the moral appeal of true fed-eralism. By granting to the federal government unprecedented new pow-ers that were deemed necessary to preserve the union at gunpoint—includ-ing the first national military draft—in service of ending human bondage, the Civil War had reversed the American fear of "consolidation" and made the national government into a necessary force for good.[45] In the words of Jeffrey Hummel, "[t]he Civil War represents the simultaneous culmination and repudiation of the American Revolution."[46]

The word "liberalism" itself was transformed. No longer was it applied to the political philosophy based on individual rights of life, liberty, property, free trade, anti-imperialism, and limited constitutional government. Now it included the aggressive, but enlightened, use of government power to improve the material conditions of mankind to nurture "true" freedom, both domestically and internationally.

One way to understand this is as a shift in means. New liberals shared with classical liberals their concern for individual welfare and the pursuit of happiness, and their hostility toward aristocracy and privilege. But the new liberals viewed the means of limited constitutional government as entirely unsuited to the effective pursuit of these noble ends. Having lived their entire lives under the scheme of constitutional limitations, they viewed the old fears of government as quaint and even irrational. Moreover, had not an unprecedented expansion of government been the instrument of justice in the Civil War? Slavery was surely not the only injustice that required redress. Everywhere one turned, there were new or old "social" problems to be solved.

Substituting "Due Process" for "Privileges or Immunities"

There was of course a major legal barrier to using the government in this way: a written constitution drafted by generations of Americans who held fundamentally different beliefs about law and government coupled with those many Americans, both on and off the bench, who still hewed to these beliefs. At the national level where the principal source of revenue was excise taxes and tariffs, income redistribution was next to impossible. In the Senate, where senators were selected by state legislatures, states could effectively block the growth of federal power. At the state level, individuals and companies could bring suit in state and federal court to block new "progressive" state laws and such lawsuits would eventually find their way to the Supreme Court.

While the Supreme Court was not unmoved by the progressive zeitgeist, the limits provided by the written Constitution caused it to seek a middle ground. Checking the progressive enthusiasm even occasionally, however, would cast the Supreme Court as a highly visible enemy of enlightened change and make it the target of vicious attacks. In 1895, for example, it

---

[45] See Jeffrey Rogers Hummel, *Emancipating Slaves, Enslaving Free Men: A History of the Civil War* (Chicago: Open Court, 1996), 313–59.

[46] Ibid., 349.

held a national income tax of 2 percent to be unconstitutional on the grounds that it was a "direct" tax and therefore had to a be apportioned among the states according to population as was required by Article I, Section 8.[47]

It was not until 1913 that this limitation on national power was reversed by the Sixteenth Amendment, and it was in the same year that the Seventeenth Amendment was ratified, replacing the selection of senators by state legislatures with direct election by voters.[48] These were the first amendments to be enacted since the Fifteenth Amendment forty-three years earlier had extended the franchise to blacks. By eliminating two of the principal structural obstacles to the growth of national power, these two amendments altered the federal system far more than did the Fourteenth Amendment, especially as limited by *Slaughter-House*.

Although *The Slaughter-House Cases* left the Privileges or Immunities Clause to wither on the vine, it did not repeal the rest of the text. Litigants shifted their focus to the Due Process Clause, which reads, "nor shall any state deprive any person of life, liberty, or property, without due process of law." Unlike the Privileges or Immunities Clause, the Due Process Clause explicitly mentions the fundamental "privileges or immunities" of life, liberty, and property.

But also unlike the Privileges or Immunities Clause, it does not promise absolute protection; it promises only that individuals cannot be deprived of these rights without "due process of law." As such, the Due Process Clause seems to contain the negative implication that life, liberty, and property *may* be taken away *with* due process of the law. This is not surprising because, as was already seen, it was the Privileges or Immunities Clause that was designed to provide "absolute" protection from abridgment by legislation ("No State shall make or enforce *any law* . . ."), whereas the Due Process Clause was intended to protect individuals from the unjust application to them of otherwise permissible legislation ("nor shall *any person* be deprived . . .").

Because the Due Process Clause appears to protect only "process" or procedures, its use by courts to protect "substantive" privileges or immunities against any infringement invites ridicule. And it has been ridiculed ever since—first by Progressives and, in the last decades of the twentieth century, critics on the left were joined by political conservatives.

[47] *Pollack v. Farmers' Loan and Trust Company*, 157 U.S. 429 (1895).

[48] See Todd Zywicki, "Beyond the Shell and Husk of History: The History of the Seventeenth Amendment and Its Implications for Current Reform Proposals," *Cleveland State Law Review* 45 (1997): 165 ("The full story of the Seventeenth Amendment cannot be understood without examining the role of special interests seeking a more aggressive role by the federal government in passing legislation designed to redistribute wealth to those special interests").

Both groups dismissed as a contradiction in terms what they have dubbed "substantive due process"—a term devised, not by the courts applying the Due Process Clause to protect background rights from unreasonable regulations and restrictions, but derisively by the critics of these decisions.[49] They delight in lampooning the apparent redundancy of its supposed opposite, "procedural due process."

Once one gets past the distorted labels devised by critics, using the Due Process Clause to do the work of the Privileges or Immunities Clause has a powerful argument on its behalf that critics ignore: the due process of law includes judicial review. Unless all constitutional limitations on government are to be abandoned, courts exercising their power of nullification are entitled to ask if the law being applied to the person exceeds the constitutional powers of the legislature. Given that there is also a Due Process Clause in the Fifth Amendment, the same scrutiny is invited at the national level.

Put another way, a vital element of the "due process of law" is the judicial scrutiny of the necessity and propriety of legislation. Allowing legislatures to deprive any person of life, liberty, or property without providing a judicial forum in which the limits of legislative power can be contested and adjudicated is a denial of this due process. Moreover, the Fourteenth Amendment requires the due process of *law*. As was discussed in chapter 6, an unconstitutional statute violates the supreme law of the land—the Constitution itself. When such a conflict occurs, as Hamilton argued, it is the duty of the judicial branch to obey the superior law and ignore the inferior.

The criticism that "substantive due process" is contradictory (and "procedural due process" redundant) poses as a textual argument. But once the "due process of law" is viewed as including judicial review, as it unquestionably did, and once the Constitution is considered a law that supersedes ordinary statutes, as it unquestionably was, the textual argument evaporates. What remains is the criticism that this was not the original meaning of "due process of law" when the Fourteenth Amendment was enacted.

Aside from its ignoring the historical evidence that the term "due process" had long been used in this manner,[50] the irony in such a protest is patent. A judicial assessment of the necessity and propriety of state laws is entirely consistent with the original meaning of the Privileges or Immu-

---

[49] See James W. Ely, Jr., "The Oxymoron Reconsidered: Myth and Reality in the Origins of Substantive Due Process," *Constitutional Commentary* 16 (1997): 319 ("It bears emphasis that the phrase 'substantive due process' is anachronistic when used to describe decisions rendered during the nineteenth and early twentieth centuries").

[50] Ibid., 327–45.

nities Clause. For this reason, a doctrine of "substantive due process" restores rather than violates the original historical meaning of Section 1 of the Fourteenth Amendment taken as a whole from the damage done by *Slaughter-House*. Conversely, a sole reliance on "procedural due process," while continuing to disregard the Privileges or Immunities Clause, completely distorts the operation of Section 1.[51]

The Progressive Era Supreme Court Scrutinizes State Laws

In the spirit of the *Slaughter-House* dissenters and following the lead of many state courts, the Progressive Era Supreme Court eventually employed the Due Process Clause to establish some outer limits on government power. In *Meyer v. Nebraska*,[52] for example, the clause was used to nullify a statute mandating that no student, whether in government or private school, be taught in any language other than English until after completing the eight grade. The defendant was convicted under this statute for teaching the German language in a parochial school. The state claimed that this was within its police power and the Supreme Court of Nebraska agreed. The purpose of the statute was summarized by that court as follows:

> The legislature had seen the baneful effects of permitting foreigners, who had taken residence in this country, to rear and educate their children in the language of their native land. The result of that condition was found to be inimical to our own safety. . . . The enactment of such a statute comes reasonably within the police power of the state.[53]

The Supreme Court disagreed with the state's claim of power, holding that this statute "unreasonably infringes the liberty guaranteed to the plaintiff in error by the Fourteenth Amendment."[54] This liberty, explained Justice McReynolds,

---

[51] In addition to being a barrier against legislation that infringed everyone's rights, the Privileges or Immunities Clause was also meant to bar laws that favored or discriminated against particular classes. In contrast, the original emphasis of the Equal Protection Clause was to impose a duty on the executive and judicial branches of state governments to apply and enforce, in an evenhanded manner, nondiscriminatory legislation. Just as the "absolute" protection from laws that violate privileges or immunities of *all* citizens was shifted to the Due Process Clause, the protection against laws that discriminated against a particular class of citizens was shifted to the Equal Protection Clause. While "substantive due process" protection of absolute rights declined after the Progressive Era (before its partial revival), the nondiscrimination function that had been shifted to the Equal Protection Clause has grown.

[52] 262 U.S. 390 (1923).

[53] Ibid., 397–98.

[54] Ibid., at 399.

denotes not merely freedom from bodily restraint but also the right of the individual to contract, to engage in any of the common occupations of life, to acquire useful knowledge, to marry, establish a home and bring up children, to worship God according to the dictates of his own conscience, and generally to enjoy those privileges long recognized at common law as essential to the orderly pursuit of happiness by free men.[55]

In other words, McReynolds found that the Due Process Clause protected those "civil rights" or "privileges or immunities" that had been asserted by the framers of the Fourteenth Amendment when speaking of the meaning of the Privileges or Immunities Clause—the interpretation rejected by the five-judge majority in *Slaughter-House*. (So it is curious indeed that the first on the list of cases cited by McReynolds in support of this proposition is *Slaughter-House* itself.)

How did Justice McReynolds justify protecting this "privilege or immunity" under the Due Process Clause? "The established doctrine is that this liberty may not be interfered with, under the guise of protecting the public interest, by legislative action which is arbitrary or without reasonable relation to some purpose within the competency of the State to effect."[56] The Due Process Clause requires that the legislature not be the sole judge of such matters, but that any person whose liberty is abridged has a right to seek redress in a court of law to determine whether the action of the legislature exceeds its lawful constitutional power. As the Court made clear: "Determination by the Legislature of what constitutes proper exercise of police power is not final or conclusive but is subject to supervision by the courts."[57]

The Court concluded in this case that the statute exceeded the police power of the state of Nebraska by finding that the means chosen was unrelated to any appropriate end. The state claimed that its mandate was issued to promote civic development by inhibiting training and education of the immature in foreign tongues and ideals before they could learn English and acquire American ideals. The Court rejected the idea that the state could pursue this end by means that abridged the "fundamental rights" of "the individual."[58] In short, "a desirable end cannot be promoted by prohibited means."[59]

To illustrate this principle, McReynolds quoted from the *Republic*, in which Plato suggested that all children be taken from their parents and

[55] Ibid.
[56] Ibid., at 399–400.
[57] Ibid., at 400.
[58] Ibid., 401.
[59] Ibid.

raised by the State as Sparta had done with its male children. "Although such measures have been deliberately approved by men of great genius, their ideas touching the relation between individual and state were wholly different from those upon which our institutions rest; and it hardly will be affirmed that any legislature could impose such restrictions upon the people of a State without doing violence to both letter and spirit of the Constitution."[60] This was an interesting choice of words in an era in which more than a few "great geniuses" were proposing fundamental reconstructions of "the relation between individual and state." As interesting, perhaps, is the fact that Justice Oliver Wendell Holmes, Jr., dissented to this decision (without opinion) and would thus have upheld the power of states to prohibit the teaching of foreign languages.

In *Pierce v. Society of Sisters*,[61] the Due Process Clause was used by the Court to strike down a law mandating that all children attend public—that is, government—schools. As in *Meyer*, the issue for the Court was the relationship of means to ends. While the Court did not deny the power of the state to regulate schools, in another opinion by Justice McReynolds, it demanded that the state establish a legitimate reason to restrict both the liberty of parents to send their children to private schools as well as the liberty of the schools to operate. Private education, explained McReynolds, is "not inherently harmful, but long regarded as useful and meritorious."[62] The state had shown nothing to rebut this long-established view. "Certainly there is nothing in the present records to indicate that they have failed to discharge their obligations to patrons, students, or the State. And there are no peculiar circumstances or present emergencies which demand extraordinary measures relative to primary education."[63]

In *Pierce*, as in *Meyer*, the Court held that due process required legislatures to establish to the satisfaction of an independent tribunal that its restrictions on liberty were necessary and proper: "[R]ights guaranteed by the Constitution may not be abridged by legislation which has no reasonable relation to some purpose within the competency of the State."[64] Applied to the statute in *Pierce*, this principle led to the conclusion that

[60] Ibid., 402.
[61] 268 U.S. 510 (1925).
[62] Ibid., 534. The idea that an act must be "*inherently*" harmful to be justly prohibited—as opposed to regulated—under the "police power" of a state can be found in the writings of Christopher Tiedeman, which will be discussed in chapter 10.
[63] Ibid.
[64] Ibid., 535.

The fundamental theory of liberty upon which all governments in this Union repose excludes any general power of the state to standardize its children by forcing them to accept instruction from public teachers only. The child is not the mere creature of the state; those who nurture him and direct his destiny have the right, coupled with the high duty, to recognize and prepare him for additional obligations.[65]

The schools themselves had a right not to be deprived of their sometimes lucrative business without a showing of necessity and propriety. The business and property of these schools "are threatened with destruction through the unwarranted compulsion which appellants are exercising over present and prospective patrons of their schools. And this court has gone very far to protect against loss threatened by such action."[66]

Decisions like *Meyer* and *Pierce* were not what infuriated the progressive intelligentsia. Indeed, both cases remain good law to this day. No, what drove political progressives into a frenzy was the Court's application of the same means-ends scrutiny to legislative restrictions on what came to be called "economic" liberty. In this area, the Court protected the liberty of contract—or what was referred to in the Civil Rights Act of 1866 as the "right to make and enforce contracts." As in *Meyer* and *Pierce*, the Court found that the "due process of law" included judicial scrutiny to ensure that a deprivation of life, liberty, or property was within either the "police power" of the state or the enumerated powers of the national government.

Given the pervasiveness of political motives in conflict with the original constitutional scheme of limited powers, the Supreme Court would not simply take the legislature's word for its claim that some restriction of liberty was necessary to accomplish an appropriate end. The Court began requiring some proof that this was the case. It required states to show that legislation infringing upon the liberties of the people really was a necessary exercise of the state's police power—a power that it held, quite expansively, to include the protection of the health, safety, and morals of the general public. It seems clear that a majority of justices became suspicious that arguments of necessity were merely pretexts for transforming the original constitutional scheme of limited and enumerated constitutional powers into one that would make possible the growth of what we now know as the welfare/administrative state.

This skepticism of legislative motive was nowhere better exemplified than in the case of *Lochner v. New York*.[67] *Lochner* involved a statute

[65] Ibid.
[66] Ibid.
[67] 198 U.S. 45 (1905).

enacted by New York containing a myriad of regulations on the operations of bakeries—from the ceiling height (eight feet) to the types of floors ("an impermeable floor constructed of cement, or of tiles laid in cement, or an additional flooring of wood properly saturated with linseed oil")[68] to the fact that the walls must be whitewashed every three months. Only one of the many provisions of this act was examined by the Court for its constitutionality: a provision making it a criminal offence to employ a worker for more than sixty hours per week.[69] Defendant Joseph Lochner was indicted and convicted of this offense and sentenced to a fine of fifty dollars or fifty days in jail.

As in *Meyer* and *Pierce*, the issue for the court was whether this prohibition abridged the liberty protected by the Fourteenth Amendment and exceeded the police power of the state. The Court found that the statute did indeed infringe upon the liberty of both employer and employee to make and enforce contracts.

> The statute necessarily interferes with the right of contract between the employer and employees, concerning the number of hours in which the latter may labor in the bakery of the employer. The general right to make a contract in relation to his business is part of the liberty of the individual protected by the Fourteenth Amendment of the Federal Constitution.[70]

In words reminiscent of the "free labor" philosophy invoked by the dissenters in *Slaughter-House*, Justice Rufus Peckham wrote: "The right to purchase or to sell labor is part of the liberty protected by this amendment, unless there are circumstances which exclude the right."[71]

Justice Peckham proceeded to discuss the nature of "certain powers, existing in the sovereignty of each State in the Union, somewhat vaguely termed police powers, the exact description and limitation of which have not been attempted by the courts."[72] These powers of state government "relate to the safety, health, morals, and general welfare of the public. Both property and liberty are held on such reasonable conditions as may be imposed by the governing power of the state in the exercise of those

---

[68] Ibid., 46 n. 1.

[69] The statute read: "§ 110. *Hours of labor in bakeries and confectionery establishments.*—No employee shall be required or permitted to work in a biscuit, bread, or cake bakery or confectionery establishment more than sixty hours in any one week, or more than ten hours in any one day, unless for the purpose of making a shorter work day on the last day of the week; nor more hours in any one week than will make an average of ten hours per day for the number of days during such week in which such employee shall work" (ibid.).

[70] 198 U.S. at 53.

[71] Ibid.

[72] Ibid.

powers, and with such conditions the Fourteenth Amendment was not designed to interfere."[73] Peckham then listed many cases in which the Court had upheld restrictions on the freedom of contract that were legitimate exercises of the police power.

Nevertheless, the police power was not unlimited. "Otherwise the Fourteenth Amendment would have no efficacy and the legislatures of the States would have unbounded power, and it would be enough to say that any piece of legislation was enacted to conserve the morals, the health or the safety of the people."[74] Were such bare assertions deemed sufficient, "such legislation would be valid, no matter how absolutely without foundation the claim might be."[75]

In other words, the Court could not, under the Due Process Clause, merely take the legislature's word that it was acting pursuant to its police powers. For if such a claim was without foundation, it "would be a mere pretext" and "become another and delusive name for the supreme sovereignty of the State to be exercised free from constitutional restraint."[76] If the limitations imposed on state powers by the Fourteenth Amendment are to be respected, then the Court must ask: "Is this a fair, reasonable, and appropriate exercise of the police power of the State, or is it an unreasonable, unnecessary, and arbitrary interference with the right of the individual to his personal liberty or to enter into those contracts in relation to labor which may seem to him appropriate or necessary for the support of himself and his family?"[77]

Justice Peckham denied that judicial review of this sort put the Court's opinion of policy above that of the legislature. "This is not a question of substituting the judgment of the court for that of the legislature. If the act be within the power of the State it is valid, although the judgment of the court might be totally opposed to the enactment of such a law."[78] For Peckham and the majority, if the Fourteenth Amendment was to have its intended effect, the following question could not be avoided: Is a statute "within the police power of the State? and that question must be answered by the court."[79]

As for the maximum-hour prohibition in the bakery trade, the Court found no evidence that bakers were in peculiar need of assistance to look out for their own interests, nor that this prohibition was necessary to respond to some health and safety concern affecting the general public

[73] Ibid.
[74] Ibid., 56.
[75] Ibid.
[76] Ibid.
[77] Ibid.
[78] Ibid., 56–57.
[79] Ibid., 57.

and therefore within the state's police power. Of particular significance was the issue of proof and who was required to present it. The court viewed this, not as an issue of judicial supremacy, but as involving a clash between the rights of an individual and the power of the state. "It is a question of which of two powers or rights shall prevail—the power of the state to legislate or the right of the individual to liberty of person and freedom of contract."[80]

In a crucial passage for our purposes, the Court placed the burden on the state:

> The mere assertion that the subject relates though but in a remote degree to the public health does not necessarily render the enactment valid. The act must have a more direct relation, as a means to an end, and the end itself must be appropriate and legitimate, before an act can be held to be valid which interferes with the general right of an individual to be free in his person and in his power to contract in relation to his own labor.[81]

Thus, the doctrine of *Lochner*—and all the cases in which the court used the Due Process Clause of the Fourteenth Amendment to protect liberty— boils down a proposition that some today find shocking: When the liberty of the individual clashes with the power of the state, the Court would not accept the "mere assertion" by a legislature that a statute was necessary and proper. Instead, it required a showing that a restriction of liberty have a "direct relation, as a means to an end," and that "the end itself must be appropriate and legitimate." Having offered no such evidence, the State of New York lost.

Lochner is famous, not only for its holding, but for the dissenting opinion filed by Justice Holmes. From this and his other similar opinions, Holmes came to be known as the Great Dissenter and was a hero to a generation of progressive scholars and activists. Holmes took direct aim at the Court's assertion that it was protecting the liberty of the individual: "The liberty of the citizen to do as he likes so long as he does not interfere with the liberty of others to do the same, which has been a shibboleth for some well-known writers, is interfered with by school laws, by the Post Office, by every state or municipal institution which takes his money for purposes thought desirable, whether he likes it or not."[82] This principle he dismissed in one of the best-known of his many apho-

---

[80] Ibid.

[81] Ibid., 57–58.

[82] Ibid., 75. This, by the way, is a pragmatic objection to making exceptions to general principles in the first place. Someday someone like Holmes may argue that the presence of exceptions refutes the existence of a general rule. Then again, by ignoring the exceptional nature of exceptions, such an argument is obviously specious.

risms: "The Fourteenth Amendment does not enact Mr. Herbert Spencer's Social Statics."[83]

This charge was as unfair as it was memorable. The majority's position can most accurately be characterized as adopting the conception of civil rights or "privileges or immunities" held by the framers of the Fourteenth Amendment. The intellectual lineage of these rights is more directly traced to John Locke than to the nineteenth-century British writer Herbert Spencer. "The 14th Amendment does not enact Mr. John Locke's *Two Treatises of Government*" would not have conveyed quite the same sense of historical absurdity. But perhaps the suggested absurdity is itself unhistorical.

In 1866, in the immediate aftermath of the Fourteenth Amendment, Senator Benjamin Brown, Democrat of Mississippi in the Thirty-ninth Congress, specifically invoked Herbert Spencer's "law of equal freedom" and his *Social Statics* when defending the extension of the right to vote in the District of Columbia to blacks:

> The foundation upon which all free government rests, and out of which all natural rights flow as from a common center, has been well stated by Mr. Herbert Spencer in a late work on Social Statics, to be the "like liberty of each limited by the like liberty of all." As the fundamental truth originating and yet circumscribing the validity of laws and constitutions, it cannot be stated in a simpler form. As the rule in conformity with which society must be organized, and which distinguishes where the rightful subordination terminates, and where tyranny, whether of majorities or minorities, begins, it cannot be too much condemned. "Every man has freedom to do all that he wills, provided he infringes not the equal freedom of any other man," is stated as the law of just social relationships, and in it the rights of individual liberty of thought, of speech, of action find their complete expression.[84]

Brown observed that Spencer's principle also implied a fundamental equality among persons. "It will be observed that equality is the essence of it all. In fact any recognition of an inequality of rights is fatal to liberty."[85]

Unlike Senator Brown, for Holmes the issue was not the liberty of the individual but "the right of a majority to embody their opinions in law."[86] The majoritarianism of Holmes's position was also revealed near the end of his brief opinion when he stated that "I think that the word liberty in the Fourteenth Amendment is perverted when it is held to prevent the natural outcome of a dominant opinion. . . ."[87] The only test that Holmes

---

[83] Ibid.
[84] *Congressional Globe*, 39th Cong., 2d sess., 76 (December 12, 1866).
[85] Ibid.
[86] *Lochner v. New York*, 198 U.S., at 75.
[87] Ibid., 76.

would have used to uphold an exercise of majority will was whether "a rational and fair man necessarily would admit that the statute proposed would infringe fundamental principles as they have been understood by the traditions of our people and our law."[88] So long as any "[m]en whom I certainly could not pronounce unreasonable would uphold"[89] such a statute, it would be constitutional. This majoritarian vision also explains Holmes's dissent in *Meyer*, where he was willing to uphold the prohibition on teaching children a foreign language.

Holmes's ardent majoritarianism was articulated in a later opinion in *Noble State Bank v. Haskell*.[90] "It may be said in a general way that the police power extends to all public needs," wrote Holmes. "It may be put forth in aid of what is sanctioned by usage or held by the prevailing majority or strong and preponderant majority to be greatly and immediately necessary to the public welfare."[91] His overriding commitment to legislative majoritarianism helps explain another Holmes dissent that is rarely discussed.

In the 1911 case of *Bailey v. Alabama*[92] the "Lochner" Court struck down as unconstitutional a state statute criminalizing breach of employment contracts by creating a presumption of fraud whenever a worker quits his job after receiving any advanced payment of wages. Such statutes were aimed at black workers as part of "Jim Crow." The Court found in this scheme a surreptitious effort to revive peonage and involuntary servitude in violation of the Thirteenth Amendment. This was just one of several examples of how the Progressive Era Court's skepticism about legislation aided much-beleaguered black workers.[93]

Holmes, in contrast, ignored both the fiction and effect of the statutory presumption of fraud and dissented from the decision. "If the contract is one that ought not to be made, prohibit it. But if it is a perfectly fair and proper contract, I can see no reason why the State should not throw its weight on the side of performance."[94] Here, as elsewhere, Holmes sides with the "preponderant majority."

Despite the contrast, it is the majority in *Lochner*, not the majoritarianism of Holmes, that academic commentators have found shocking for all these years. While Holmes remains a revered figure, "Lochnerizing" is

[88] Ibid.

[89] Ibid.

[90] 219 U.S. 104 (1911).

[91] Ibid., 111.

[92] 219 U.S. 219 (1911)

[93] See David Bernstein, *Only One Place of Redress: African Americans, Labor Regulations, and the Courts from Reconstruction to the New Deal* (Durham, N.C.: Duke University Press, 2001).

[94] 219 U.S. at 247.

considered a venial, if not a mortal, judicial sin. For all the rhetorical fireworks of Holmes's opinion in *Lochner*, however, it was Justice John Harlan's dissent that more directly addressed the doctrine established by the Court. Unlike Holmes, Harlan did not disparage the nature of the fundamental liberty articulated by the majority.

> Speaking generally, the State in the exercise of its powers may not unduly interfere with the right of the citizen to enter into contracts that may be necessary and essential in the enjoyment of the inherent rights belonging to everyone, among which rights is the right "to be free in the enjoyment of all his faculties; to be free to use them in all lawful ways; to live and work where he will; to earn his livelihood by any lawful calling; to pursue any livelihood or avocation."[95]

Indeed, in the 1908 case of *Adair v. United States*,[96] Harlan wrote the opinion of the Court, declaring that legislative prohibitions on contract terms barring union membership (dubbed "yellow dog contracts" by union supporters) were unconstitutional. "The right of a person to sell his labor upon such terms as he deems proper is, in its essence," wrote Harlan, "the same as the right of the purchaser of labor to prescribe the conditions upon which he will accept such labor from the person offering to sell."[97] He then affirmed that "the employer and the employee have equality of right, and any legislation that disturbs that equality is an arbitrary interference with the liberty of contract which no government can legally justify in a free land."[98]

For Harlan, the issue was who bears the burden of showing the necessity and propriety of restrictions upon this liberty. The Court in *Lochner* required that the legislature had to assert some evidence or proof on behalf of a restriction on liberty. By contrast, Harlan thought the presumption ought to run the other way.

> If there be doubt as to the validity of the statute, that doubt must therefore be resolved in favor of its validity, and the courts must keep their hands off, leaving the legislature to meet the responsibility for unwise legislation. If the end which the legislature seeks to accomplish be one to which its power extends, and if the means employed to that end, although not the wisest or best, are yet not plainly and palpably unauthorized by law, then the court cannot interfere. In other words, *when the validity of a statute is questioned, the burden of proof, so to speak, is upon those who assert it to be unconstitutional.*[99]

[95] 198 U.S. at 65.
[96] 208 U.S. 161
[97] Ibid., 174.
[98] Ibid., 175.
[99] 198 U.S. at 68 (emphasis added).

As authority for this presumption of constitutionality, Harlan cited *McCulloch v. Maryland*.

Holmes, and to a lesser extent Harlan, criticized the majority for claiming the existence of a fundamental liberty of contract in the face of prior precedents restricting its exercise. But this was to attack a straw man, given that the Court never claimed this right to be absolute. In *Adkins v. Children's Hospital of the District of Columbia*,[100] it made this clear:

> There is, of course, no such thing as absolute freedom of contract. It is subject to a great variety of restraints. But freedom of contract is, nevertheless, the general rule and restraint the exception; and the exercise of legislative authority to abridge it can be justified only by the existence of exceptional circumstances.[101]

In *Adkins*, the court attempted to rationalize numerous exceptions it had made to the general rule. Notwithstanding these exceptions, the existence of the right meant that the legislature had the burden of justifying to the satisfaction of an independent tribunal any additional restrictions on liberty.

For Holmes, in dissent, the concept of an exception eluded him here, as it had in *Lochner*. For him, the bare existence of exceptions was alone enough to refute the general rule, and no further justification was required. "[P]retty much all law consists in forbidding men to do some things that they want to do, and contract is no more exempt from law than other acts."[102] It was thus to be left entirely to the legislature to decide whether or not any restriction was warranted.

In response to the Progressive Era Court's demand for some proof that the legislation in question was a reasonable means of pursuing an appropriate end, lawyers began presenting courts with empirical support for particular legislation. The most famous of these litigators was future justice Louis Brandeis, whose extensive citations of the social science literature became known as "Brandeis Briefs."[103] Upon being presented with Brandeis's ninety-five page brief in *Muller v. Oregon*,[104] the Court upheld a statute mandating maximum working hours for women. In addition to listing similar state and foreign statutes, the brief

[100] 261 U.S. 525 (1923).

[101] Ibid., 546.

[102] Ibid., 568.

[103] See John W. Johnson, "Brandeis Brief," in Hall et al., *The Oxford Companion*, 85.

[104] 208 U.S. 412. See ibid., 419 ("In the brief filed by Mr. Louis D. Brandeis, for the defendant in error, is a very copious collection of all these matters, an epitome of which is found in the margin").

contained "extracts from over ninety reports of committees, bureaus of statistics, commissioners of hygiene, inspectors of factories, both in this country and in Europe, to the effect that long hours of labor are dangerous for women, primarily because of their special physical organization."[105] Thus, the presumption of liberty established by the Progressive Era Court was rebuttable. It was perfectly willing to find statutes constitutional in light of facts made known to it, though *Muller* was later cited as a precedent for upholding restrictions on liberty even in the absence of such information.

The Progressive Era Supreme Court Scrutinizes Federal Laws

Although this chapter primarily concerns the judicial review of state laws, the discussion of the Progressive Era Court's willingness to scrutinize legislation would be incomplete without mention of its treatment of federal laws. In the early years of the era, progressive and populist legislation emanated primarily from the states, and therefore implicated the Due Process Clause of Fourteenth Amendment. With the election of Franklin Roosevelt in 1932, Congress began passing ambitious statutes, which then came under the scrutiny of the Supreme Court under the rubric of the Due Process Clause of the Fifth Amendment.

As in the state cases, the Court examined both the necessity and the propriety of the challenged statutes. By necessity, I mean the degree of means-end fit. By propriety, I mean whether the statutory restriction fell within one of the enumerated powers—usually the commerce power—or was a pretext for the exercise of other powers it had not been delegated.[106] Typical of these cases was *Railroad Retirement Board et al. v. Alton R. Co.*,[107] in which the Court evaluated the constitutionality of a statute requiring railroads to give retirement pensions to their employees (and former employees as well) on terms determined by Congress.

In evaluating the constitutionality of the act, the Court distinguished between its necessity and its propriety. As to the first issue, the Court stated:

> If we assume that under the power to regulate commerce between the States Congress may require the carriers to make some provision for retiring and pensioning their employees, then the contention that various provisions of the Act

[105] Ibid., 420 n. 1.

[106] As we shall see in chapter 11, the Progressive Era Court extended the power to regulate commerce to the power to prohibit it as well. See discussion there of *Champion v. Ames*, 188 U.S. 321 (1903).

[107] 295 U.S. 330 (1935).

are arbitrary and unreasonable and bear no proper relation to that end must be considered.[108]

After a lengthy analysis of the complexities of the statutory requirements, the Court concluded that they did not meet this test.

On the second issue of "propriety" the Court concluded that "The Act is not in purpose or effect a regulation of interstate commerce within the meaning of the Constitution."[109] Distinguishing between "constitutional power" and "social desirability,"[110] the court examined the rationales on behalf of the statute and found them to be too distant from the regulation of commerce to be acceptable. Instead, the purpose of the statute was not the regulation of commerce but the enhancement of the social welfare of workers beyond their voluntary terms of employment.

> The catalogue of means and actions which might be imposed upon an employer in any business, tending to the satisfaction and comfort of his employees, seems endless. Provision for free medical attendance and nursing, for clothing, for food, for housing, for the education of children, and a hundred other matters, might with equal propriety be proposed as tending to relieve the employee of mental strain and worry. Can it fairly be said that the power of Congress to regulate interstate commerce extends to the prescription of any or all of these things? Is it not apparent that they are really and essentially related solely to the social welfare of the worker, and therefore remote from any regulation of commerce as such?[111]

The Court's conclusion makes clear the constitutional standard it was applying: "This is neither a *necessary nor an appropriate* rule or regulation affecting the due fulfillment of the railroads' duty to serve the public in interstate transportation."[112]

The reason for the Court's insistence that laws be proper as well as necessary was stated in the 1935 case of *Schechter Poultry Corporation v. United States*,[113] which concerned the constitutionality of the National Recovery Act. The act authorized the president to approve "codes of fair competition" for a trade or industry upon application by one or more trade or industrial associations or groups. These codes became law without any additional action of Congress. In essence, the act encouraged the formation of legally enforced industry cartels.

---

[108] Ibid., 347–48.

[109] Ibid., 362. In chapter 9, I will consider the proper interpretation of the Commerce Clause.

[110] Ibid., 367.

[111] Ibid., 368.

[112] Ibid., 374 (emphasis added).

[113] 295 U.S. 495 (1935).

The defendants, Joseph, Martin, Alex, and Aaron Schechter, operated a poultry slaughterhouse that purchased live poultry from suppliers in New York, and furnished live or slaughtered poultry to dealers and butchers selling directly to consumers. They sold no poultry to buyers in other states. The Schechters were convicted for several violations the "Code of Fair Competition for the Live Poultry Industry of the Metropolitan Area in and about the City of New York."[114] They challenged the act as beyond Congress's power to regulate commerce among the states.

In considering its constitutionality, the Court emphasized that the act did not merely foster cooperation among members of industry or immunize their cooperation from normal antitrust restrictions. Rather,

> [i]t involves the coercive exercise of the law-making power. The codes of fair competition which the statute attempts to authorize are codes of laws. If valid, they place all persons within their reach under the obligation of positive law, binding equally those who assent and those who do not assent. Violations of the provisions of the codes are punishable as crimes.[115]

In other words, it enabled industry to promulgate codes that would legally restrict the liberty of its "members."

The Court, without dissent, found the act unconstitutional both because it was an inappropriate delegation of legislative power from Congress to the president and private industry groups and because it inappropriately permitted the regulation of commerce wholly within a state. "Defendants held the poultry at their slaughterhouse markets for slaughter and local sale to retail dealers and butchers who in turn sold directly to consumers. Neither the slaughtering nor the sales by defendants were transactions in interstate commerce."[116] Nor did their actions "directly" affect interstate commerce either by injuring interstate commerce or by interfering with persons engaged in that commerce. As difficult as it was to draw a precise line between interstate and intrastate commerce, or between direct or indirect effects on interstate commerce, such line drawing is necessary if Congress is to be held within its constitutionally enumerated powers.

---

[114] These included violation of the minimum wage and maximum hour provisions of the code, permitting retail dealers and butchers to make individual selections of birds rather than accept birds solely on the basis of their grade, sale to a butcher of an unfit chicken, failing to have the poultry inspected or approved in accordance with regulations or ordinances of the city of New York and making false reports or the failure to make reports relating to the range of daily prices and volume of sales for certain periods, and selling to slaughterers or dealers who were without licenses required by the city of New York.

[115] Ibid., 529.

[116] Ibid., 543.

Responding to the argument that the act was made necessary by the "grave national crisis," the court observed:

> The Constitution established a national government with powers deemed to be adequate, as they have proved to be both in war and peace, but these powers of the national government are limited by the constitutional grants. Those who act under these grants are not at liberty to transcend the imposed limits because they believe that more or different power is necessary. Such assertions of extra-constitutional authority were anticipated and precluded by the explicit terms of the Tenth Amendment,—"The powers not delegated to the United States by the Constitution, nor prohibited by it to the States, are reserved to the States respectively, or to the people."[117]

Shocking indeed.

Conclusion

In *Lochner* and other such cases, the Progressive Era Supreme Court began to require proof that both federal and state legislatures restricting the retained liberties of the people were actually pursuing a legitimate purpose rather than merely purporting to do so. At the state level, an act must be within the police powers of a state, while at the national level it must be within an enumerated power. As Madison had urged, they began requiring of legislation a showing of actual means-end fit, rather than merely deferring to legislative judgment that measures were necessary to achieve a proper purpose. When judicial deference is based on trust and trust is eroded, increased scrutiny follows.

Yet these decisions came to be reviled, first by political progressives and populists, and most recently by judicial conservatives. Condemnation of *Lochner* has become de rigueur among law professors of nearly all stripes. One claim commonly made by progressives was that the Progressive Era Court was deviating from the original meaning of the Constitution.[118] Later critics hailed the New Deal Court's rejection of these doctrines as a "restoration" rather than a constitutional revolution. These positions have been effectively challenged by Howard Gillman[119] and are also refuted by the evidence of original meaning presented here.

---

[117] Ibid., 528–29.

[118] See, e.g., Walton H. Hamilton and Douglas Adair, *The Power to Govern: The Constitution—Then and Now* (New York: Norton, 1937).

[119] See Howard Gillman, *The Constitution Besieged: The Rise and Demise of Lochner Era Police Powers Jurisprudence* (Durham, N.C.: Duke University Press, 1993). Gillman contends that the Court was attempting to identify what the founders would have considered "class legislation," which benefited a faction at the expense either of another class or

Be this as it may, the difference between the approach of *Lochner* and that which came later turns primarily on the choice among presumptions that one uses when assessing the constitutionality of statutes. Since the Constitution does not explicitly establish any presumption, this is largely a matter of constitutional construction. The question then becomes which construction is truer to the meaning of what the Constitution does say in a passage the Court has largely treated as lost: the Ninth Amendment.

---

of the general public. Although his analysis represents an important advance, he underplays the ongoing commitment to liberty, which is continuous with the tradition of natural rights that animated both the founders and those who wrote the Fourteenth Amendment. The fact that a bill was special interest or class legislation could be viewed as evidence that it infringed the rights of others.

CHAPTER NINE

The Mandate of the Ninth Amendment: Why Footnote Four Is Wrong

> It has been objected also against a bill of rights, that, by enumerating particular exceptions to the grant of power, it would disparage those rights which were not placed in that enumeration; and it might follow, by implication, that those rights which were not singled out, were intended to be assigned into the hands of the General Government, and were consequently insecure. This is one of the most plausible arguments I have ever heard urged against the admission of a bill of rights into this system; but I conceive, that it may be guarded against.[1]
>
> —JAMES MADISON

AS ANYONE who has studied constitutional law knows, the era in which the Court attempted to scrutinize the necessity and propriety of state and federal restrictions on liberty came to a close as the perceived legitimacy of legislative activism continued to grow. What is not well known today is that the doctrinal vehicle used by the New Deal Court to overturn the Progressive Era precedents was the adoption of a presumption of constitutionality. In this chapter, I describe the revival of the presumption of constitutionality, its almost immediate qualification in the form of the most famous footnote in constitutional history, and the incompatibility of this judicial doctrine with the text of the Constitution—in particular, with the Ninth Amendment.

THE FALL AND PARTIAL REVIVAL OF MEANS-ENDS SCRUTINY

The presumption of constitutionality had been advocated some thirty years earlier by Harvard Law professor James Thayer. In his influential 1893 article, "The Origin and Scope of the American Doctrine of Consti-

---

[1] *Annals*, 1:456 (statement of Rep. Madison).

tutional Law,"[2] Thayer reproduced a number of examples of judicial unwillingness to second-guess legislative judgment. The earliest was the 1811 opinion of Chief Justice Tilghman, of Pennsylvania:

> For weighty reasons, it has been assumed as a principle in constitutional construction by the Supreme Court of the United States, by this court, and every other court of reputation in the United States, that an Act of the legislature is not to be declared void unless the violation of the constitution is so manifest as to leave no room for reasonable doubt.[3]

What are these "weighty reasons" for this "constitutional construction"? Thayer offered the following:

> This rule recognizes that, having regard to the great, complex, ever-unfolding exigencies of government, much which will seem unconstitutional to one man, or body of men, may reasonably not seem so to another; that the constitution often admits of different interpretations; that there is often a range of choice and judgment; that in such cases the constitution does not impose upon the legislature any one specific opinion, but leaves open this range of choice; and that whatever choice is rational is constitutional. This is the principle which the rule that I have been illustrating affirms and supports.[4]

According to Thayer, because assessing constitutionality is so uncertain, a judgment by a legislature that it is acting within its proper powers should be respected unless it is clearly wrong. Exactly this position would be articulated by Justice Harlan in his *Lochner* dissent eight years later.

At much the same time Thayer was writing, Louis Brandeis was filing his "Brandeis Briefs," providing the empirical support the Court required for progressive legislation. After his appointment to the Supreme Court, however, Brandeis took the lead in advocating the presumption of constitutionality that both Thayer and Harlan had urged upon the Court. In his 1931 opinion in *O'Gorman & Young, Inc. v. Hartford Fire Insurance Co.*,[5] Brandeis used the presumption of constitutionality to put the burden of proof on those challenging a statute:

> The statute here questioned deals with a subject clearly within the scope of the police power. We are asked to declare it void on the ground that the specific

---

[2] James B. Thayer, "The Origin and Scope of the American Doctrine of Constitutional Law," *Harvard Law Review* 7 (1893): 129. On the one hundredth anniversary of its publication, an entire symposium was devoted to the legacy of this one article. See "One Hundred Years of Judicial Review: The Thayer Centennial Symposium," *Northwestern University Law Review* 88 (1993): 1.

[3] Thayer, "Origin and Scope of the American Doctrine," 140 (quoting *Commonwealth v. Smith*, 4 Binn. 117 [1811]).

[4] Ibid., 144.

[5] 282 U.S. 251 (1931).

method of regulation prescribed is unreasonable and hence deprives the plaintiff of due process of law. As underlying questions of fact may condition the constitutionality of legislation of this character, the presumption of constitutionality must prevail *in the absence of some factual foundation of record for overthrowing the statute.*[6]

One contemporary of Brandeis, Professor Walton Hamilton, wrote glowingly of this maneuver in the *Columbia Law Review*, noting that the rejection of the assessment of necessity and propriety was accomplished merely through the adoption of a presumption in favor of the legislature. His paean is worth quoting at length:

> The demand is to find an escape from the recent holdings predicated upon "freedom of contract" as "the rule," from which a departure is to be allowed only in exceptional cases. The occasion calls not for the deft use of tactics, but for a larger strategy. The device of presumption is almost as old as law; Brandeis revives the presumption that acts of a state legislature are valid and applies it to statutes regulating business activity. *The factual brief has many times been employed to make a case for social legislation*; Brandeis demands of the opponents of legislative acts a recitation of fact showing that the evil did not exist or that the remedy was inappropriate. He appeals from precedents to more venerable precedents; reverses the rules of presumption and proof in cases involving the control of industry; and sets up a realistic test of constitutionality. It is all done with such legal verisimilitude that a discussion of particular cases is unnecessary; it all seems obvious—once Brandeis has shown how the trick is done. It is attended with so little of a fanfare of judicial trumpets that it might have passed almost unnoticed, save for the dissenters, who usurp the office of the chorus in a Greek tragedy and comment upon the action. Yet an argument which degrades "freedom of contract" to a constitutional doctrine of the second magnitude is compressed into a single compelling paragraph.[7]

In the passage italicized, it is not clear whether Hamilton was wryly noting or simply missing the profound irony. Here was the attorney, lauded to this day for bringing "realism" to judicial proceedings via the "Brandeis Brief," adopting a presumption as a justice that would fictitiously impute a rational basis to any legislative decision. After all, who "realistically" is in the best position to present a court with empirical information for or against the necessity of a statute: agencies of government who proposed it or an affected individual or company on whom it is imposed? Those who have already succeeded in lobbying Congress to enact legislation or those who lost?

---

[6] Ibid., 257–58 (footnote omitted) (emphasis added).
[7] Walton H. Hamilton, "The Jurist's Art," *Columbia Law Review* 31 (1931): 1074–75 (footnotes omitted) (emphasis added).

As Hamilton notes, the dissenters in *O'Gorman* made it clear that the presumption of constitutionality was being used to avoid the showing of necessity that the Court had previously required. After rejecting the suggestion that "the burden of establishing any underlying disputable fact rests upon the appellant before it can successfully challenge the validity of the questioned enactment,"[8] the dissent argued: "In order to justify the denial of the right to make private contracts, some special circumstances sufficient to indicate the necessity therefor must be shown by the party relying upon the denial."[9]

Although constitutional scholars are accustomed to thinking that the New Deal Court expansively interpreted the Commerce Clause, Stephen Gardbaum has argued that it actually expanded the Necessary and Proper Clause instead. "[T]he New Deal Court's own constitutional justification for its radical expansion of the scope of federal power over commerce," he writes, "was that the congressional measures in question were valid exercises of the power granted by the Necessary and Proper Clause and were not direct exercises of the power to regulate commerce among the several states."[10] That is, "the Court did not simply and directly enlarge the scope of the Commerce Clause itself, as is often believed. Rather, it upheld various federal enactments as necessary and proper means to achieve the legitimate objective of regulating interstate commerce."[11] Gardbaum offers several examples to support this claim.

One is the 1941 case of *United States v. Darby*,[12] in which *McCulloch v. Maryland* is cited by Justice Stone in support of the following position:

> The power of Congress over interstate commerce is not confined to the regulation of commerce among the states. It extends to those activities intrastate which so affect interstate commerce . . . as to make regulation of them appropriate means to the attainment of a legitimate end, the exercise of the granted power of Congress to regulate interstate commerce. See McCulloch v. Maryland . . . . [13]

Later in this opinion, Stone makes clear that he favors deference to Congress's assessment of a measure's necessity:

> Congress, having by the present Act adopted the policy of excluding from interstate commerce all goods produced for the commerce which do not conform to the specified labor standards, it may choose the means reasonably adapted

---

[8] O'Gorman, 282 U.S. at 265 (Justice Van Devanter dissenting).
[9] Ibid., 269.
[10] Gardbaum, "Rethinking Constitutional Federalism," 807 (footnotes omitted).
[11] Ibid., 807–8.
[12] 312 U.S. 100 (1941).
[13] Ibid., 118–19 (citations omitted). *McCulloch* concerns the Necessary and Proper Clause.

to the attainment of the permitted end, even though they involve control of intrastate activities. Such legislation has often been sustained with respect to powers, other than the commerce power granted to the national government, when the means chosen, although not themselves within the granted power, were nevertheless deemed appropriate aids to the accomplishment of some purpose within an admitted power of the national government. [14]

Gardbaum also notes that among "the relatively few observers to acknowledge the basis upon which the New Deal Court expanded federal power"[15] was Justice O'Connor in her dissent in *Garcia v. San Antonio Metropolitan Transit Authority*:[16]

The Court based the expansion [of the commerce power] on the authority of Congress, through the Necessary and Proper Clause, "to resort to all means for the exercise of a granted power which are appropriate and plainly adapted to the permitted end." It is through this reasoning that an intrastate activity "affecting" interstate commerce can be reached through the commerce power. . . . [A]nd [this] reasoning . . . underlies every recent decision concerning the reach of Congress to activities affecting interstate commerce.[17]

The only thing Gardbaum fails to mention is that this expansive reading of the Necessary and Proper Clause was facilitated doctrinally by adopting a presumption of constitutionality in favor of congressional judgment.

Until recently, most observers have marked the 1937 case of *West Coast Hotel v. Parish* as the end of *Lochner*-type scrutiny of legislation. The fact that it was 1931 when Brandeis, in *O'Gorman*, applied the presumption of constitutionality should raise some question about this timing. Barry Cushman has persuasively defended the thesis that, beginning around 1930, new justices appointed by President Hoover shifted the Court into a middle position that was not definitively rejected until 1941 when Roosevelt appointees took complete control of the Court.[18] He also stresses how the Court's Due Process and Commerce Clause jurisprudence were distinct, but ultimately linked.

Cushman's account shows that, from 1931 to 1941, the Supreme Court adopted a method akin to Justice Harlan's dissent in *Lochner*: Legislation would be presumed constitutional, but this presumption could, at least in principle, still be rebutted. During this period, though more state and federal statutes were upheld than previously, some were still nullified. Al-

---

[14] Ibid., 121 (citations omitted).

[15] Gardbaum, "Rethinking Constitutional Federalism," 810.

[16] 469 U.S. 528 (1985).

[17] Ibid., 584–85 (Justice O'Connor dissenting) (citations omitted).

[18] See Barry Cushman, *Rethinking the New Deal Court: The Structure of a Constitutional Revolution* (New York: Oxford University Press, 1998).

though *West Coast Hotel* in 1937 marked the complete abandonment of scrutiny of state laws under the Due Process Clause, it was not until 1941 in the case of *United States v. Darby* that the Court ceased holding Congress to its enumerated Commerce Power. At this point, the Court had essentially supplanted Harlan's method with that favored by Holmes in his *Lochner* dissent: legislative majorities would get their way without any scrutiny at all unless their actions were expressly prohibited by the Constitution.

The harbinger of this approach had been announced in the wake of the Court's abandonment in 1937 of "substantive due process." After *West Coast Hotel*, it became necessary to establish limits on this burden-shifting technique lest it swallow the entire constitutional practice of judicial review. This feat was accomplished one year later in *United States v. Carolene Products Co.*,[19] a case that concerned legal restrictions on the sale of a milk substitute that competed with the products of dairy farmers.[20]

The *Carolene Products* case became one of the most influential Supreme Court opinions of the twentieth century on the strength of its fourth footnote. This footnote is so famous that lawyers and law professors refer to it, not by its case name, but solely as "Footnote Four."[21] To appreciate the significance of this passage, one must first read the portion of Justice Stone's opinion that immediately preceded it where he clearly asserts the presumption of constitutionality. "[T]he existence of facts supporting the legislative judgment is to be presumed," wrote Stone,

> for regulatory legislation affecting ordinary commercial transactions is not to be pronounced unconstitutional unless in the light of the facts made known or generally assumed it is of such a character as to preclude the assumption that it rests upon some rational basis within the knowledge and experience of the legislators.[22]

With this in mind, we are now in a better position to appreciate fully the theory of Footnote Four, which began as follows:

> There may be narrower scope for operation of the presumption of constitutionality when legislation appears on its face to be within a specific prohibition of the Constitution, such as those of the first ten amendments, which are deemed equally specific when held to be embraced within the Fourteenth.[23]

---

[19] 304 U.S. 144 (1938).

[20] See Geoffrey P. Miller, "The True Story of Carolene Products," *Supreme Court Review* (1987): 397.

[21] The fame of this footnote is also illustrated by the fact it merits its own entry in *The Oxford Companion to the Supreme Court of the United States*. See Dean Alfange, Jr., "Footnote Four," in Hall et al., *The Oxford Companion*, 306–7.

[22] *United States v. Carolene Products Co*, 304 U.S. at 152.

[23] Ibid., 152 n. 4.

Thus, in Footnote Four we have enunciated the modern theory of constitutional rights that, by 1941, was to apply to both state and federal restrictions on liberty: Adopt a loose conception of necessity and presume all
acts of legislatures to be valid, except when an enumerated right listed in
the Bill of Rights is infringed (or when legislation affects the political
process or discrete and insular minorities),[24] in which event the Court will
employ a strict conception of necessity and put the burden on legislatures
to show that their actions were both necessary and proper.

Subsequent cases made the presumption of constitutionality virtually
irrebuttable.[25] As Justice Douglas explained in *Williamson v. Lee Optical
Co.*: "It is enough that there is an evil at hand for correction, and that it
might be thought that the particular legislative measure was a rational
way to correct it."[26] Any restriction on liberty will be upheld under this
standard if there is a hypothetical reason why "a legislature *might* have
concluded"[27] that the restriction was necessary—unless a "fundamental"
enumerated right is at issue, in which event few statutes will withstand
the "strict scrutiny" of both means and ends that will then be applied.

This reversal of constitutional presumptions, as qualified by the first
paragraph of Footnote Four, required for the first time that courts develop
a means of distinguishing fundamental rights from other liberties that

---

[24] The rest of Footnote Four adds:

It is unnecessary to consider now whether legislation which restricts those political
processes which can ordinarily be expected to bring about repeal of undesirable legislation, is to be subjected to more exacting judicial scrutiny under the general prohibitions
of the Fourteenth Amendment than are most other types of legislation.

Nor need we enquire whether similar considerations enter into the review of statutes
directed at particular religious, . . . or national, . . . or racial minorities . . . ; whether
prejudice against discrete and insular minorities may be a special condition, which
tends seriously to curtail the operation of those political processes ordinarily to be
relied upon to protect minorities, and which may call for a correspondingly more
searching judicial inquiry.

Ibid., 152–53 n. 4 (citations omitted). In what follows I will dwell exclusively on the first
of these three paragraphs. This is not meant to deny these other justifications offered in
Footnote Four for rebutting the presumption of constitutionality.

[25] The theory of Footnote Four was not needed prior to 1937 because the presumption
of constitutionality announced in *Gorman* could, at least in theory, be rebutted by a showing
that the legislation was unnecessary. After *West Coast Hotel*, such a showing would not be
permitted and the power of judicial nullification would be completely abrogated in Due
Process cases. The narrow three-part formula of Footnote Four thus preserved some role
for judicial review.

[26] 348 U.S. 483, 488 (1954) (emphasis added).

[27] Ibid., at 487 (emphasis added). For emphasis, Douglas repeats the phrase "might have
concluded" or "may have concluded" three times in a single paragraph.

would be left to the mercy of legislative majorities. As Howard Gillman has explained:

> While it is generally realized that footnote 4 of *Carolene Products* signaled a substantive redirection of the Court's role in the political system, it is not often recognized that this shift also required the Court to do something unprecedented; that is, to enumerate the specific freedoms and privileges that should be considered inviolate even in a regime of expanded powers. In the nineteenth century it was assumed that government should leave individuals alone unless the state could convince a court that the exercise of power advanced a valid public purpose. By contrast, under the contemporary model, it has been assumed that the government's power should be left undisturbed unless an individual can convince a court that the law infringed on a discrete fundamental right.[28]

And so stood constitutional theory and doctrine for some thirty years, until 1965, when the Court decided the landmark case of *Griswold v. Connecticut*.[29]

Griswold concerned a Connecticut statute that criminalized the use of "any drug, medicinal article or instrument for the purpose of preventing conception."[30] Connecticut's statute on accountability also outlawed the actions of anyone who "assists, abets, counsels, causes, hires or commands another"[31] to commit an offense. Under both these statutes, Estelle Griswold, the executive director of the Planned Parenthood League of Connecticut, and C. Lee Buxton, a physician at the Planned Parenthood clinic, were arrested and charged for prescribing and distributing contraceptive devices. The law was challenged as unconstitutional under the Fourteenth Amendment and the Court sustained the challenge.

Writing for the Court, Justice Douglas took pains to distance himself from *Lochner v. New York* and to reaffirm the deferential stance he articulated in *Williamson*. "We do not sit as a super-legislature," he wrote "to determine the wisdom, need, and propriety of laws that touch economic problems, business affairs, or social conditions."[32] Nevertheless the Court, citing with approval the two *Lochner*-era cases of *Meyer v. Nebraska* and *Pierce v. Society of Sisters*, found that the statute in question violated the right of privacy, a right not explicitly enumerated in the Constitution.

---

[28] Gillman, *The Constitution Besieged*, 104.
[29] 381 U.S. 479 (1965).
[30] Ibid., 480.
[31] Ibid.
[32] Ibid., 482.

What made this case so controversial among constitutional scholars when it was decided was not that it protected the use and distribution of contraceptives. Most legal academics would have favored that. Rather, what bothered them in the extreme about both this case and *Roe v. Wade*[33] was that this unenumerated right to privacy was the first right since *Carolene Products* to be protected as fundamental that was not "within a specific prohibition of the Constitution"—the formulation of Footnote Four.

In his opinion, one can see Justice Douglas struggling mightily to reconcile the right of privacy with the theory of Footnote Four by grounding it, not squarely on the Ninth Amendment as urged by Justice Goldberg,[34] but on the "penumbras, formed by emanations" from the "specific guarantees in the Bill of Rights."[35] Douglas's attempt to shoehorn an unenumerated right of privacy into the confines of Footnote Four, however, satisfied no one. Consequently, the right of privacy was controversial from the start, not because it ran afoul of the original meaning of either the initial Constitution or the Fourteenth Amendment, but because it violated the post–New Deal jurisprudence of Footnote Four.

Griswold represents a repudiation of the purified Footnote Four. No longer would the liberty rights that justify reversing the presumption of constitutionality be strictly limited to those that are specifically enumerated. Under what we might call Footnote Four-Plus, some judicially favored unenumerated rights could also be used to shift the burden to the government to justify its restrictions on liberty.

The 1992 decision in *Planned Parenthood v. Casey*[36] was significant, therefore, because it showed that a majority of the Rehnquist Court was still committed to the Footnote Four-Plus approach. In *Casey*, the Court strongly asserted: "It is a promise of the Constitution that there is a realm of personal liberty which the government may not enter. We have vindicated this principle before."[37] In support of this assertion, the Court cited several cases including *Pierce v. Society of Sisters* and *Meyer v. Nebraska*, each of which scrutinized legislation infringing unenumerated rights.

Relying explicitly and appropriately on the Ninth Amendment, Justices O'Connor, Kennedy, and Souter wrote in their rare jointly authored opinion that "Neither the Bill of Rights nor the specific practices of States at the time of the adoption of the Fourteenth Amendment marks the outer limits of the substantive sphere of liberty which the Fourteenth Amend-

---

[33] 410 U.S. 113 (1973).
[34] See 410 U.S. at 486 (Justice Goldberg concurring).
[35] 410 U.S. at 484 (Justice Douglas).
[36] 505 U.S. 833 (1992).
[37] Ibid., 847.

ment protects. See U.S. Const., Amdt. 9."[38] In *Casey*, the justices wrote of "liberty"—a term that appears in the text of the Constitution—rather than "privacy," which does not. It is significant, therefore, that the majority opinion in *Lawrence v. Texas*,[39] striking down a sodomy statute aimed at homosexuals, was based entirely on "liberty" rather than on a right to privacy.[40]

Casey exemplifies the current approach to constitutional rights: Adopt the formulation of Footnote Four, but then add protection for the right of privacy and perhaps other selected unenumerated rights deemed by the Court to be "fundamental." But while Footnote Four-Plus improves upon Footnote Four by acknowledging the potential significance of unenumerated rights and thereby taking the Ninth Amendment's recognition of unenumerated rights seriously, it has a striking weakness.

With Footnote Four-Plus, judges now find themselves having to pick and choose among the unenumerated liberties of the people to find those that justify switching the presumption and those that do not. Courts are placed in the uneasy position of making essentially moral assessments of different exercises of liberty. A liberty to use birth control pills is protected, but a liberty to use marijuana is not. The business of performing abortions is protected, but the business of providing transportation is not. What "protected" means in this context is that a particular exercise of liberty is sufficient to rebut the presumption of constitutionality and that the government then must establish that such legislation is both necessary and proper.

The Footnote Four-Plus approach of protecting some unenumerated rights has long been criticized by some modern judicial conservatives. Ironically, no group has been more faithful to the pure Footnote Four approach invented by the New Deal Court than these conservative proponents of original intent. As Robert Bork, for example, has written of Justice Stone's opinion in Footnote Four:

> [O]ne hardly knows what to make of the tentativeness with which Stone suggests that the Court might be less deferential to the legislature if the legislation appears to be specifically prohibited by the Constitution. Of course, review should be more stringent if the Constitution reads on a subject than if it does not. That distinction should spell the difference between review and no review.[41]

Should it really?

[38] Casey, 505 U.S. at 848..

[39] 123 S. Ct. 2472 (2003).

[40] As I explain in chapter 12, Justice Kennedy's opinion seems to reject the Footnote Four-Plus approach in favor of a presumption of liberty. See Randy E. Barnett, "Justice Kennedy's Libertarian Revolution," *Cato Supreme Court Review 2002–2003* (2003).

[41] Bork, *The Tempting of America*, 60.

Why it is that only the specific prohibitions of the Constitution may shift the presumption of constitutionality, when the Ninth Amendment declares: "The enumeration in the Constitution, of certain rights, *shall not be construed to deny or disparage* others retained by the people"? Disparaging the liberties or rights retained by the people that are not "within a specific prohibition of the Constitution" is exactly what Footnote Four accomplishes. As such, Footnote Four runs afoul of the text of the Constitution, as does the modern Footnote Four-Plus variation that lets judges pick those unenumerated liberties they deem fundamental from those they dismiss as mere liberty interests.

The Mandate of the Ninth Amendment

The Ninth Amendment has proved mysterious to many. For example, when asked about it at his confirmation hearings, Judge Bork was at a loss to explain its meaning or significance. As he memorably testified:

> I do not think you can use the ninth amendment unless you know something of what it means. For example, if you had an amendment that says "Congress shall make no" and then there is an ink blot, and you cannot read the rest of it, and that is the only copy you have, I do not think the court can make up what might be under the ink blot.[42]

In this opinion Bork was, sadly, well within the mainstream of legal thought. When he testified, the Ninth Amendment could still be called "forgotten,"[43] though his testimony provoked a serious scholarly reconsideration of the Ninth Amendment.[44] Still, to this day courts have rarely

[42] *Nomination of Robert H. Bork to Be Associate Justice of the Supreme Court of the United States: Hearings before the Senate Committee on the Judiciary,* 100th Cong., 1st sess.(1987), 249. In *The Tempting of America,* Bork adopted the view of Ninth Amendment skeptic Russell Caplan that the rights "retained by the people" referred solely to state law rights. See Bork, *The Tempting of America,* 184–85. I respond to Caplan's argument below. Bork then shifted his ink blot metaphor to the Privileges or Immunities Clause. "No judge is entitled to interpret an ink blot on the grounds that there must be something under it. So it has been with the clause of the fourteenth amendment prohibiting any state from denying citizens the privileges and [*sic*] immunities of citizens of the United States. The clause has been a mystery since its adoption and in consequence has, quite properly, remained a dead letter" (ibid., 166). As we have seen, evidence of the original meaning of this clause is plentiful.

[43] See, e.g., Bennett B. Patterson, *The Forgotten Ninth Amendment: A Call for Legislative and Judicial Recognition of Rights under Social Conditions of Today* (Indianapolis: Bobbs-Merrill, 1955).

[44] For a collection of post–Bork hearing scholarship, see Randy E. Barnett, *The Rights Retained by the People: The History and Meaning of the Ninth Amendment,* vol. 2 (Fairfax, Va.: George Mason University Press, 1993).

been willing to rely upon it when assessing the constitutionality of statutes, which is another reason why the *Casey v. Planned Parenthood* case was significant.[45]

The fear of the Ninth Amendment, even by committed textualist/originalists, results in part from its apparently open-ended reference to unenumerated rights. What are these rights and is it proper for courts to identify and protect them? Given this uncertainty, courts fear opening a Pandora's box of limitless claims that are impossible to adjudicate in a principled fashion. The overarching thesis of this book is that a practical method exists to implement this crucial passage.

To begin with, as with the Privileges or Immunities Clause, ample historical evidence exists to ascertain the original meaning of the Ninth Amendment. In chapter 2, we began by examining the original meaning of the phrase "others retained by the people." We saw that this was a reference to the natural or liberty rights that are retained by the people when forming a government. Thus, not any rights claim is justified under the Ninth Amendment, but only the liberty to act free of unjustified interference.

The Ninth Amendment does more than merely refer to these unenumerated natural rights and affirm their existence, however. It also mandates how they are to be treated: they are not to be "denied or disparaged." On its face, this wording strongly suggests that unenumerated liberties are to be treated the same as those that were enumerated. To the degree that enumerated rights receive protection from Congress, so should those that were left unenumerated. This historical evidence strongly supports this interpretation, and undercuts the Footnote Four approach to the presumption of constitutionality when liberty is at issue.

The Original Meaning of the Ninth Amendment

The Ninth Amendment was the creation of James Madison. Both his reason for devising it and his use of the amendment in constitutional argument support the most obvious textual meaning. Recall the problem that the Ninth Amendment was intended to solve. Until the Bill of Rights was enacted two years after the ratification of the Constitution, with a few exceptions, all of the rights retained by the people were unenumerated. There was no explicit protection for the rights of free speech and assembly or the rights of freedom of religion and of the press. During this period

---

[45] For a brief summary of how the Ninth Amendment has been treated by the courts in recent decades, see Randy E. Barnett, "The Ninth Amendment," in Leonard W. Levy, Kenneth L. Karst, and Adam Winkler, eds., *The Encyclopedia of the American Constitution, Supplement II* (New York: Macmillian, 2000), 1813–15.

no one argued that the federal government had the power to abridge or deny these and other liberties. In the absence of explicit mention in the Constitution, how were these rights to be protected?

The most obvious way was by the political constraints of federalism and separation of powers, which required a convergence of opinions before laws could be enacted and enforced. Their protection also came from the fact that the powers of Congress were limited and enumerated. Even when Congress was ostensibly acting within its powers, the means it chose to employ might still be unnecessary or improper. Finally, the judiciary was to be the guardian of the Constitution when Congress exceeded its powers, including its lawmaking power under the Necessary and Proper Clause. Taken together these structural and textual constraints prevent whole categories of rights violations without having to discuss the rights themselves and contributed importantly to the legitimacy of the original constitution.

When the opponents of the Constitution objected to the absence of a bill of rights, the Federalists argued that this additional protection was unnecessary because the Congress was not given any power to violate the rights retained by the people. "Why, for instance," asked Hamilton, "should it be said that the liberty of the press shall not be restrained, when no power is given by which restrictions may be imposed?"[46] As we have already seen, the Federalists also argued that adding a bill of rights would be dangerous because the rights or liberties of the people were unenumerable and any rights that would be omitted would be rendered insecure.

Despite their arguments, the Federalists were forced to promise a bill of rights to obtain enough support for ratification. When James Madison sought to honor this commitment in the first Congress, he was faced with solving the difficulty that he and his Federalist allies had noted just two years earlier. As soon as any particular rights or liberties were explicitly enumerated, the status of those left out of the enumeration became unclear. Were only the enumerated rights to be protected and the unenumerated rights left unprotected? By "unprotected" I mean subject to being surrendered up to Congress to be abridged or denied at its sole discretion.

Here, once again, is how Madison stated the problem when he introduced his proposed amendments to the House:

> It has been objected also against a bill of rights, that, by enumerating particular exceptions to the grant of power, it would disparage those rights which were not placed in that enumeration; and it might follow, by implication, that those rights which were not singled out, were intended to be assigned into the hands of the General Government, and were consequently insecure. This is one of the

---

[46] *Federalist* 84, 513–14 (Hamilton).

most plausible arguments I have ever heard urged against the admission of a bill of rights into this system; but I conceive, that it may be guarded against.[47]

Madison then referred the members to the portion of his proposal that read:

> The exceptions here or elsewhere in the constitution, made in favor of particular rights, shall not be so construed as to diminish the just importance of other rights retained by the people, or as to enlarge the powers delegated by the constitution; but either as actual limitations of such powers, or as inserted merely for greater caution.[48]

Eventually, all of Madison's proposals were referred to a Select Committee of the House, which decided to list the amendments after the body of the original Constitution rather than insert them within the text. From this committee emerged the current text of the Ninth Amendment, which replaced the "diminish the just importance" language with the stronger phrase "deny or disparage." While there is much that is controversial about the Ninth Amendment, this story of its origin and enactment is not.

What do Madison's original proposal, and his explanation of it, add to our understanding of the Ninth Amendment? First of all, Madison's placement of this provision is revealing. He put it at the end of the list of specific individual rights that he proposed be inserted in Article 1, Section 9, immediately after the two individual rights already listed there—the rights of habeas corpus and the rights against bills of attainder and ex post facto laws—but before the other prohibitions of government power listed in Section 9 that are not easily conceived as individual rights, such as the prohibition on granting titles of nobility. This supports a conclusion that it refers to the same sorts of individual liberty rights that were explicitly enumerated in the Constitution and that it was to be accorded the same importance as the other provisions in that section.

Then there are the words of the original proposal, which convey information about the nature of both enumerated and unenumerated rights omitted from the otherwise stronger final version. Owing to his tendency to run parallel ideas together in a single sentence, Madison's original proposal is a bit difficult to follow. When disentangled, however, it shows clearly that the rights enumerated in the Bill of Rights were of at least two kinds.

First were those enumerated rights that provided additional or "actual limitations" on the delegated powers beyond those that already existed. For example, prior to its amendment, the Constitution did not require

---

[47] *Annals*, 1:456 (statement of Rep. Madison).
[48] Ibid., 452.

jury trials in civil cases. In his speech to the House, Madison categorized these actual limitations as "positive rights" and gave the example of trial by jury.[49] Second were those rights that were enumerated "merely for greater caution." As Madison explained, these refer to "those rights which are retained when particular powers are given up to be exercised by the Legislature."[50] Crucially, in his handwritten notes to this speech, Madison refers to these "rights which are retained" as "natural rights" and gives as an example of such a natural right the freedom of speech.[51]

Thus, according to how Madison used the term "retained" rights, we know that the "other" unenumerated rights "retained by the people" mentioned in the Ninth Amendment fall into the second category of his original proposal. They are the natural rights "which are retained when particular powers are given up to be exercised by the Legislature."[52] A few of these rights were included in the Bill of Rights "for greater caution" but most were left unenumerated. They were not left textually unprotected, however. The textual source of that protection was, initially, the limited powers scheme and the Necessary and Proper Clause, and soon thereafter the enumeration of certain rights coupled with the Ninth Amendment for the others.

Madison's speech to the House also clarifies how constitutional rights, whether enumerated or unenumerated, relate to the delegated powers. Constitutional rights can limit both the ends of government as well as the means by which the legitimate ends of government are executed. As Madison explained (in another sentence combining parallel ideas), "the great object in view is to limit and qualify the powers of Government, by excepting out of the grant of power those cases in which the Government ought not to act, or to act only in a particular mode."[53] Disentangling this passage, we find that *ends* constraints "*limit* . . . the powers of Government" by specifying when "the Government *ought not to act.*" *Means* constraints "*qualify* the powers of Government" by specifying when "Government ought . . . to *act only in a particular mode.*"

As an example of improper means, Madison offered the use of general warrants we discussed in chapter 7: "The General Government has a right to pass all laws which shall be necessary to collect its revenue; the means for enforcing the collection are within the direction of the Legislature: may not general warrants be considered necessary for this purpose

---

[49] *Annals*, 1:454. For this item, Madison's notes read: "4. positive rights resultg. as trial by jury."

[50] Ibid.

[51] Madison's notes read: "Contents of Bill or Rhts. . . . 3. natural rights retained as speach."

[52] *Annals*, 1:454.

[53] Ibid.

• •

. . . ?"[54] As Madison's example suggests, the Necessary and Proper Clause exacerbates the means-end problem within a scheme of delegated powers. Authorizing the Congress "[t]o make all Laws which shall be necessary and proper for carrying into Execution the foregoing Powers, and all other Powers vested by this Constitution in the Government of the United States, or in any Department or Officer thereof" heightens the prospect that Congress or some department or officer of the general government may pursue a delegated enumerated end by means that infringe upon the rights retained by the people. Therefore, some regulation of the means employed to achieve enumerated governmental ends must supplement the device of enumerating powers.

In his speech, Madison explicitly linked the abuse of the Necessary and Proper Clause with the need for constitutional rights to constrain the means chosen by the general government:

> It is true, the powers of the General Government are circumscribed, they are directed to particular objects; but even if Government keeps within those limits, it has certain discretionary powers with respect to the means, which may admit of abuse to a certain extent, . . . because in the constitution of the United States, there is a clause granting to Congress the power to make all laws which shall be necessary and proper for carrying into execution all the powers vested in the Government of the United States, or in any department or officer thereof. . . .[55]

As the Supreme Court stated in *Dennis v. United States*,[56] "[t]he question with which we are concerned here is not whether Congress has such *power*, but whether *the means which it has employed* conflict with the First and Fifth Amendments to the Constitution."[57]

In addition to placing "actual" or additional limits on the means by which government can accomplish its legitimate ends, Madison identifies a second power-constraining function of constitutional rights: constitutional rights provide a "redundant" or cautionary safeguard in the event that delegated powers of government are given an overly expansive interpretation. Constitutional rights can help hold government to its legitimate enumerated ends in two ways. Rights can prevent the adoption of an expansive interpretation of enumerated powers in the first instance. Failing this, once a power has been expansively interpreted, the direct judicial protection of enumerated and unenumerated rights holds government within some limits.

---

[54] *Annals*, 1:456.

[55] Ibid., 455.

[56] 341 U.S. 494 (1951).

[57] Ibid., 501 (emphasis added). See also *Barenblatt v. United States*, 360 U.S. 109, 112 (1959) ("Congress . . . must exercise its powers subject to the . . . relevant limitations of the Bill of Rights").

Madison himself used the Ninth Amendment to check an expansive construction of delegated powers during the debate over the constitutionality of the national bank. Near the end of his speech in which he argued that the powers to incorporate a bank and grant it a monopoly were beyond those granted to Congress under the Necessary and Proper Clause, he observed: "The *latitude of interpretation* required by the bill is condemned by the rule furnished by the Constitution itself."[58] As one authority for this "rule" of interpretation, Madison cited the Ninth Amendment:

> The explanatory amendments proposed by Congress themselves, at least, would be good authority with them; all these renunciations of power proceeded on a rule of construction, excluding the latitude now contended for. . . . He read several of the articles proposed, remarking particularly on the 11th [the Ninth Amendment] and 12th [the Tenth Amendment], *the former, as guarding against a latitude of interpretation*; the latter, as excluding every source or power not within the Constitution itself.[59]

Thus, Madison viewed the Ninth and Tenth Amendments as playing distinct roles. Madison viewed the Tenth Amendment as authority for the rule that Congress could exercise only a delegated power. For example, Congress could not establish a post office or raise and support armies without a delegation of power to pursue these ends.[60] In contrast, Madison viewed the Ninth Amendment as providing authority for a rule against the loose construction of these powers—especially the Necessary and Proper Clause—when legislation affected the rights retained by the people. As Madison concluded in his bank speech: "In fine, if the power were in the Constitution, the immediate exercise of it cannot be essential; if not there, the exercise of it involves the guilt of usurpation. . . ."[61]

---

[58] *Annals*, 1:1899 (statement of Rep. Madison) (emphasis added).

[59] Ibid., 1901 (emphasis added). The numbering of the amendments changed because the first two amendments proposed by Congress were not ratified by the states. So what came to be called the First Amendment was originally the third amendment on the list submitted to the states. At the time Madison spoke, however, this outcome was not yet known. One of these two moribund proposals—which regulated congressional pay increases—became the Twenty-seventh Amendment in 1992 when it was finally ratified by a sufficient number of states.

[60] The Tenth Amendment is redundant of the list of enumerated powers coupled with the first sentence in Article I, which begins: "All legislative Powers *herein granted* shall be vested in a Congress of the United States. . . ." U.S. Const., Art. I, § 1 (emphasis added). For this reason, whereas Madison highlighted the importance of the Ninth Amendment in his Bill of Rights speech, he viewed the Tenth Amendment as largely superfluous: "Perhaps other words may define this more precisely than the whole of the instrument now does. I admit they may be deemed unnecessary; but there can be no harm in making such a declaration. . . ." Ibid., 441.

[61] Ibid., 1902.

Three years later, in 1794, Madison would again argue in Congress that the unenumerated rights retained by the people directly constrained congressional power. When Congress sought to censure the activities of certain self-created societies for their participation in the Whiskey Rebellion earlier that year, Madison contended that "When the people have formed a Constitution, they retain those rights which they have not expressly delegated."[62] Here Madison was asserting that the unenumerated retained right to hold opinions constrained the power of Congress to issue a censure, in the same manner as "the liberty of speech, and of the press."[63] Indeed, "the censorial power is in the people over the Government, and not in the Government over the people."[64] Strong words on behalf of supporters of insurrection.

Madison's uses of the Ninth Amendment show that, like the natural rights that were enumerated, the unenumerated rights retained by the people provide a twofold check on government power. Their existence argues against a latitudinarian interpretation of enumerated powers when those powers are used to restrict the liberties of the people; and the direct protection of the liberties of the people also effectively limits both the ends of government and the means by which these ends can legitimately be pursued. This from the man who devised the Ninth Amendment.

In his treatise on the Constitution, St. George Tucker offered a similar interpretation of the Ninth Amendment (while it was still referred to as the Eleventh). He begins his explanation of the Ninth and Tenth Amendments by connecting them with the enumeration of powers and the Necessary and Proper Clause. "All the powers of the federal government," he wrote, were "either expressly enumerated, or necessary and proper to the execution of some enumerated power."[65] He then described, as "one of the rules of construction which sound reason has adopted," the principle "that, as exception strengthens the force of a law in cases not excepted, so enumeration weakens it, in cases not enumerated." This meant that, because the powers of government are enumerated, the inference from the text is that government is to have no powers beyond those expressly provided.

Tucker then offers a rule of construction that follows from this inference. "[I]t follows, as a regular consequence, that *every power which concerns the right of the citizen, must be construed strictly, where it may operate to infringe or impair his liberty*; and liberally, and for his benefit,

---

[62] *Annals*, 4:934 (statement of Rep. Madison).

[63] Ibid.

[64] Ibid.

[65] Tucker, "Of the Constitution of the United States," in appendix to *Blackstone's Commentaries* (1), 307–8.

where it may operate to his security and happiness, the avowed object of the constitution. . . ."[66] Tucker shared with Madison the view that the Ninth Amendment provided an argument against a latitudinarian interpretation of the delegated powers, but he also made even clearer that the end of constitutional construction is the protection of individual liberty: both a "strict construction" of powers and "liberal construction" of rights. Tucker was proposing something very much like what I will call a "Presumption of Liberty."

In other words, both the plain and original meanings of the Ninth Amendment require the strict construction of any power that restricts the exercise of individual liberty, whether that liberty is enumerated or unenumerated. The Ninth Amendment is, therefore, violated by the Footnote Four approach that limits protection solely to those retained rights that happen to be enumerated. It is violated as well by the Footnote Four-Plus approach that extends protection to unenumerated liberties but only those few that courts have deemed to be "fundamental."

Before examining how the equal protection of unenumerated liberties can be accomplished, I turn to the alternative interpretations of the Ninth Amendment that have been offered as a way of diminishing the just importance of the "other" rights retained by the people.

The Views of Ninth Amendment Skeptics

In the 1980s, when the Ninth Amendment was almost entirely forgotten by scholars, Russell Caplan proposed a theory that the rights to which the Ninth Amendment referred were "those individual rights contained in the state constitutions, statutes, and common law."[67] Because these laws could be changed by state legislative or constitutional processes, and because federal law supersedes state law, the rights "retained by the people" provide no constraint whatever on government power. The Ninth Amendment merely affirmed that state laws and state constitutional rights were not repealed by the Bill of Rights. This is the view of the Ninth Amendment that Robert Bork endorsed in *The Tempting of America* after his ill-fated attempt to analogize the Ninth Amendment to an ink blot.[68]

Caplan's evidence for this assertion was circumstantial and rather sparse. To appreciate the weakness of his historical evidence requires a distinction between objections to the Constitution and objections to the enumeration of certain rights. Neither at the time of the founding nor at

[66] Ibid., 307 (emphasis added).
[67] Russell L. Caplan, "The History and Meaning of the Ninth Amendment," *Virginia Law Review* 69 (1983): 259.
[68] See Bork, *The Tempting of America*, 184–85.

the time the Bill of Rights was proposed and debated did anyone suggest that such an enumeration of rights would have so bizarre an effect on state law rights. The few statements Caplan presents were made during ratification of the Constitution when opponents argued that it (not "the enumeration in the Constitution of certain rights") would jeopardize state-protected liberties. Indeed, many of these critics of the Constitution urged the adoption of an enumeration in the Constitution of certain rights—over Federalist objections that such an enumeration would be dangerous. In other words, Anti-Federalist statements expressing fear about *the Constitution*'s effect on state constitutional rights have nothing to do with the meaning of the Ninth Amendment, which concerns the effect of enumerating rights, something the Anti-Federalists favored.

Caplan discusses none of the evidence examined here that the Ninth Amendment refers to natural liberty rights, including Roger Sherman's draft of a bill of rights, which included the following passage: "The people have certain natural rights which are retained by them when they enter into Society."[69] He also neglects to mention Madison's use of the Ninth Amendment in his bank speech in a context that had nothing to do with state law rights, or St. George Tucker's explication of the Ninth Amendment, which makes no reference to state laws or constitutions. In short, Caplan ignores nearly every contemporaneous explanation and usage of the Ninth Amendment.[70]

Moreover, there is another indication that the rights "retained by the people" was not a reference to state law rights. After Madison devised it as a solution to an inevitably incomplete enumeration, many states attached similar provisions to their constitutions.[71] Such references in state constitutions to rights "retained by the people" would be incoherent if the phrase referred solely to state-created and state-protected rights rather than to natural rights.

The existence of these state provisions also undercuts another interpretation of the Ninth Amendment: that it was intended solely to underscore the limited nature of federal power. As John Yoo has observed, "These provisions stunningly demonstrate that the people, speaking through the

[69] "Roger Sherman's Draft of the Bill of Rights," in Barnett, *Rights Retained by the People*, 1:351.

[70] In fairness to Caplan, so, too, did nearly all other constitutional scholars and judges who had up to that point discussed the Ninth Amendment.

[71] See Ala. Const., Art. I, § 30 (1819); Ark. Const., Art. II, § 24 (1836); Calif. Const., Art. I, § 21 (1849); Iowa Const., Art. I, § 25 (1846); Kans. Const., Art. I (1855); Kans. Const., Bill of Rights, § 24 (1857); Me. Const., Art. I, § 24 (1820); Md. Const., Declaration of Rights, Art. 42 (1851); Minn. Const., Art. I., § 16(1857); N.J. Const., Art. I, § 19 (1844); Ohio Const., Art. I, § 20 (1851); Ore. Const., Art. I, § 34 (1857); R.I. Const., Art. I, § 23 (1842).

states, considered the Ninth Amendment a declaration of rights, rather than a limitation on enumerated powers."[72] And John Ely noted, "The fact that the constitution-makers in, say, Maine and Alabama in 1819 saw fit to include in their bills of rights provisions that were essentially identical to the Ninth Amendment is virtually conclusive evidence that they understood it to mean what it said and not simply to relate to the limits of federal power."[73]

The leading and most thoughtful proponent of the view that the "other" rights referred to by the Ninth Amendment are solely defined by the extent of enumerated powers is Thomas McAffee. Although his arguments and the rejoinders to them may become abstruse at times, it is necessary to examine them here because McAffee's writings have received a sympathetic reception from judicial conservatives who wish to dismiss the relevance of the Ninth Amendment to any aspect of judicial review.

According to McAffee, the Ninth Amendment was originally intended solely to prevent later interpreters of the Constitution from exploiting the incompleteness of the enumeration of rights to expand federal powers beyond those delegated by the Constitution.[74] So, for example:

> If the government contended in a particular case that it held a general power to regulate the press as an appropriate inference from the first amendment restriction on that power, or argued that it possessed a general police power by virtue of the existence of the bill of rights, the ninth amendment would provide a direct refutation.[75]

In other words, in McAffee's view, the exclusive function of the Ninth Amendment is to protect the scheme of delegated powers by arguing against this specific sort of inference:

> The Ninth Amendment reads *entirely* as a "hold harmless" provision: *it thus says nothing about how to construe the powers of Congress or how broadly to read the doctrine of implied powers*; it indicates *only* that no inference about those powers should be drawn from the mere fact that rights are enumerated in the Bill of Rights.[76]

[72] John Choon Yoo, "Our Declaratory Ninth Amendment," *Emory Law Journal* 42 (1993): 1008–9.

[73] John H. Ely, *Democracy and Distrust* (Cambridge.: Harvard University Press, 1980), 204 n. 87.

[74] As Thomas McAffee explains: "On the residual rights reading, the ninth amendment serves the unique function of safeguarding the system of enumerated powers *against a particular threat* arguably presented by the enumeration of limitations on national power" ("The Original Meaning of the Ninth Amendment," *Columbia Law* Review 90 [1990]: 1306–7; emphasis added).

[75] Ibid., 1307.

[76] Ibid., 1300 n. 325 (emphasis added).

McAffee denies that what he terms the "residual rights" retained by the people "are to be defined independently of, and may serve to limit the scope of, powers granted to the national government by the Constitution."[77] Instead, he maintains that "the other rights retained by the people are *defined* residually from the powers granted to the national government."[78]

Given that, according to his interpretation, the Ninth Amendment addresses the problem of enumerating rights rather than objections to enacting the original constitution, McAffee's theory is both a refutation of and an improvement over Russell Caplan's "state law" theory of the Ninth Amendment. Nonetheless, McAffee's "residual rights" theory, too, conflicts with the available evidence of original meaning.

Although McAffee's historical sources show beyond peradventure that the framers of the Constitution intended the structure of separate and enumerated powers to be the primary means of protecting the rights retained by the people, his evidence falls short of demonstrating that these were the exclusive means to this end. Despite heroic efforts, he fails to prove, in particular, that the framers specifically excluded the possibility that unenumerated rights could be identified and protected independent of structural protections provided by the separation and enumeration of powers.

Perhaps the most telling evidence to the contrary is James Madison's own use of the Ninth Amendment in his speech concerning the national bank (discussed above) in which Madison applied the amendment he had devised to a real constitutional controversy. In his bank speech, Madison was in no way responding to an argument for expanded federal powers based on the incomplete enumeration of rights. Rather, Madison used the Ninth Amendment entirely outside the only context in which, according to McAffee, the Ninth Amendment was meant to be relevant.

Although Madison stressed the fact that an enumerated power to charter a national bank could be found nowhere in the Constitution, he also used the Ninth Amendment precisely and explicitly as authority for more strictly construing enumerated powers. In particular, and in contrast to McAffee's thesis, Madison used the Ninth Amendment to attempt to cabin the Necessary and Proper Clause—that is, to restrict the means by which delegated powers can be exercised. Moreover, contrary to what McAffee's theory would predict, Madison rested his argument against the claimed power to grant a monopoly charter in part on the fact that such a power violates the "equal rights of every citizen." In other words, these "equal rights" restrict the scope of the Necessary and Proper Clause.

---

[77] Ibid., 1222.
[78] Ibid., 1221 (emphasis added).

If all this were not enough, Madison's concluding observation definitively refutes McAffee's thesis: "In fine, *if the power were in the Constitution*, the immediate exercise of it cannot be essential; if not there, the exercise of it involves the guilt of usurpation. . . ."[79] Madison is arguing that the Ninth Amendment is authority for limiting the exercise of enumerated powers that "were in the Constitution" to those restrictions on liberty that are "essential." According to McAffee's "residual rights" thesis, if a power were in the Constitution, its exercise could not conceivably violate a "residual" right. Madison's own use of the Ninth Amendment, therefore, refutes McAffee's thesis as clearly as evidence ever can.

Unfortunately, a "residual rights" view of the rights retained by the people was once adopted by the Supreme Court as a way to render the Ninth Amendment without function. In the 1947 case of *United Public Workers v. Mitchell*,[80] which McAffee cites with approval,[81] Justice Reed asserted: "If granted power is found, necessarily the objection of invasion of those rights reserved by the Ninth and Tenth Amendments, must fail."[82] To the contrary, Madison's speech belies this "residual rights" interpretation. Rather than looking exclusively to the delegation of powers to define as well as to protect the rights retained by the people, as McAffee and Justice Reed would have it, Madison also looked to the rights retained by the people in his effort to interpret and define the delegated-powers provisions. If McAffee's "residual rights" theory about original understanding was correct, Madison would never have thought to make the constitutional argument he did.

McAffee also questions the relevance of Sherman's draft bill of rights that explicitly refers to the "natural rights which are retained by" the people. He argues that because Madison proposed his precursor to the Ninth Amendment to Congress before Sherman drafted his proposal as a member of the Select Committee, "it is not likely that Madison's draft or the committee's work owed anything to Sherman's particular choice of language."[83]

McAffee's denial of any connection is undercut, however, by his acknowledgment in a different context that both North Carolina and Virginia proposed to Congress language virtually identical to Sherman's and these proposals preceded Madison's speech.[84] It is obvious that Sherman's

---

[79] *Annals*, 2:1902 (emphasis added).

[80] 330 U.S. 75, 95–96 (1947).

[81] See McAffee, "Original Meaning of the Ninth Amendment," 1220 n. 20, 1245 n. 121.

[82] 330 U.S., at 96.

[83] Thomas McAffee, "The Bill of Rights, Social Contract Theory, and the Rights 'Retained' by the People," *Southern Illinois University Law Journal* 16 (1992): 300.

[84] See ibid., 301 ("Several state ratifying conventions had proffered similar amendments . . .").

draft includes verbatim portions of these proposals.[85] Thus the fact that Sherman's draft was written after Madison's initial proposal concerning rights retained by the people in no way diminishes the likelihood of their common ancestry in these state proposals.[86]

The discovery in 1987 of Sherman's draft is significant, and I have focused on it rather than on the North Carolina and Virginia proposals, because Sherman explicitly used the word "retained" when referring to these natural rights, thus depriving Ninth Amendment skeptics of the argument that "retained" was a term of art that referred only to state-law rights (Russell Caplan's thesis) or to those which were reserved residually by the enumeration (McAffee's thesis), and not to natural rights.

Sherman's proposal demonstrates that the term "retained" was used to refer to natural rights by a member of the same committee that drafted the Ninth Amendment. Better historical evidence of original meaning is hard to come by. Just as Sherman used the word "retained" when speaking of natural rights, there is no reason to think that Madison used the term in some different and idiosyncratic manner. Indeed, as was noted earlier, Madison's notes for his amendments speech refer to "natural rights *retained* as speach."[87]

McAffee has also argued that another portion of Sherman's draft, rather than this one, connects to the Ninth Amendment. Because of this, McAffee contends that Sherman's reference to "retained" natural rights connects only to Madison's proposed prefix to the Constitution or what McAffee calls "the language of first principle."[88] Note that this argument contradicts his other claim that because Sherman's draft came after Madison's speech and proposal, it cannot be used to explain it.

But what is this other passage from Sherman that, according to McAffee, supposedly connects up with the Ninth Amendment? Here it is:

[85] The Virginia and North Carolina proposals read: "1st. That there are certain natural rights, of which men, when they form a social compact, cannot divest their posterity, among which are the enjoyment of life and liberty, with the means of acquiring, possessing, and protecting property, and pursuing and obtaining happiness and safety." See "Amendments to the United States Constitution Proposed by State Ratification Conventions," in Barnett, *Rights Retained*, 364, 380.

[86] This is not to concede, however, the validity of McAffee's other efforts to limit the meaning of the Ninth Amendment to various formulations in these state proposals.

[87] Madison, *Notes for Amendments Speech*, 1789, in Barnett, *Rights Retained*, 64 (emphasis added).

[88] As I noted earlier, Madison proposed a declaration be prefixed to the constitution that "all power is originally vested in, and consequently derived from, the people. That Government is instituted and ought to be exercised for the benefit of the people; which consists in the enjoyment of life and liberty, and the right of acquiring and using property, and generally of pursuing and obtaining happiness and safety. That the people have an indubitable, unalienable, and indefeasible right to reform or change their Government, whenever it be found adverse or inadequate to the purposes of its institution" (*Annals*, 1:451).

And *the powers* not delegated to the Government of the united States by the Constitution, nor prohibited by it to the particular States, are retained by the States respectively, nor shall any [*sic*] *the exercise of power* by the Government of the united States particular instances here in enumerated by way of caution, be construed to imply the contrary.[89]

But this provision refers only to delegated powers, not the implications of enumerating rights. McAffee sees the invisible word "rights" somewhere in this passage, for he asserts that "Sherman's draft appears to describe *rights* provisions as purely cautionary without even acknowledging that they might operate as exceptions to granted powers."[90] Moreover, this passage refers only to the states and not to the people, a distinction established by the Tenth Amendment.

Now compare Sherman's proposal to the words of the Tenth Amendment: "The powers not delegated to the United States by the Constitution, nor prohibited by it to the States, are reserved to the States respectively, or to the people." This language is virtually identical with Madison's original proposal that "[t]he powers not delegated by this constitution, nor prohibited by it to the States, are reserved to the States respectively."[91] McAffee never denies that this proposal, made by Madison, is the precursor to the Tenth Amendment. Indeed, when it suits other purposes, he insists upon it.[92] Yet, despite the fact that Sherman's proposal includes an almost verbatim rendition of both the actual Tenth Amendment and Madison's precursor to it, we are nonetheless urged to conclude that this "powers not delegated" passage—and not the "natural rights . . . retained" passage—is the part of Sherman's proposal that connects to the Ninth Amendment. (I warned you this gets abstruse.)

McAffee's positivist reading of the Ninth Amendment is also undermined by the debate between representatives Sedgwick and Page discussed in chapter 3. Sedgwick, you will recall, argued that the right to peaceably

[89] "Roger Sherman's Draft of the Bill of Rights," reprinted in Barnett, *Rights Retained*, 352 (emphasis added).

[90] McAffee, "Original Meaning of the Ninth Amendment," 1303 n. 33 (emphasis added). In contrast, Madison's precursor to the Ninth Amendment—which McAffee stresses preceded Sherman's formulation—referred to the implications of enumerated *rights* ("The exceptions here or elsewhere in the constitution, made in favor of particular *rights* . . ."); see ibid., 1283. If, as McAffee suggests, Sherman's draft was merely his suggestion as to how Madison's amendments could be appended at the end of the text (see McAffee, "Bill of Rights, Social Contract Theory"), it makes no sense that Sherman would drop Madison's reference to "particular rights" and substitute "delegated powers."

[91] *Annals*, 1:453 (statement of Rep. Madison).

[92] See McAffee, "Original Meaning of the Ninth Amendment," 1300 n. 326 ("The Virginia state proposal that became the Ninth Amendment goes no further than the precursors to the tenth amendment in Madison's proposal for a bill of rights").

assemble was "a self-evident, unalienable right which the people possess; it is certainly a thing that never would be called into question; it is derogatory to the dignity of the House to descend to such minutiae. . . ."[93] According to the reading of the Constitution urged by McAffee, in making this argument Sedgwick would have known that the government was free to infringe this right unless and until the Constitution was amended. Page replied to Sedgwick that "that such rights have been opposed, and . . . people have . . . been prevented from assembling together on their lawful occasions, therefore it is well to guard against such stretches of authority, by inserting the privilege in the declaration of rights."[94] According to McAffee, Page would have believed that "such stretches of authority" would be permissible in the absence of such insertions in the declaration of rights.

However, as was seen above, Madison described the amendments serving "either as actual limitations of such powers, or as inserted merely for greater caution."[95] Like Page, Madison viewed the amendments as helping guard against "stretches of authority." Ninth Amendment skeptics have always seemed to think that when a provision is "inserted merely for greater caution," this means it has no function apart from serving as some sort of unenforceable warning.[96] They consistently overlook how such "cautionary" rights can serve as a redundant or secondary line of defense when other primary constraints on government power fail.

Lastly, McAffee's historical claim that the Ninth Amendment "says nothing about how to construe the powers of Congress or how broadly to read the doctrine of implied powers" is completely refuted by St. George Tucker's contemporaneous explication of the Ninth Amendment. In Tucker's view, the Ninth Amendment justified the principle "that *every power which concerns the right of the citizen, must be construed strictly, where it may operate to infringe or impair his liberty*; and liberally, and for his benefit, where it may operate to his security and happiness, the avowed object of the constitution. . . ."[97]

With all this in mind we can fruitfully revisit the only other explicit reference that Madison is known to have made to the Ninth Amendment. While it was pending ratification in the states, Madison wrote to George

[93] *Annals*, 1:759 (statement of Rep. Sedgwick).

[94] Ibid., 760 (statement of Rep. Page).

[95] Ibid., 452.

[96] Indeed, as was seen above, Madison more likely viewed the Tenth Amendment, of which some Ninth Amendment skeptics are more fond, in this way. Yet this did not prevent Madison from appealing to the Tenth Amendment as authority for his argument against the national bank.

[97] Tucker, "Of the Constitution of the United States," in appendix to *Blackstone's Commentaries* (1), 307–8 (emphasis added).

Washington in reply to a criticism of the Ninth Amendment that had been made by Edmund Randolph—an objection Madison had learned about in a letter from Hardin Burnley.[98] Madison related Randolph's objection as follows:

> [Randolph's] principal objection was pointed against the word retained in the eleventh proposed amendment, and his argument if I understood it was applied in this manner, that as the rights declared in the first ten of the proposed amendments were not all that a free people would require the exercise of; and that as there was no criterion by which it could be determined whether any other particular right was retained or not, it would be more safe, & more consistent with the spirit of the 1st. & 17th. amendments proposed by Virginia, that this reservation against constructive power, should operate rather as a provision against extending the powers of Congress by their own authority, than as a protection to rights reducable to no definitive certainty.[99]

Madison's now much-noted, and somewhat confusing, response was as follows:

> The difficulty stated agst. the amendments is really unlucky, and the more to be regretted as it springs from [Randolph,] a friend to the Constitution. It is a still greater cause of regret, if the distinction be, as it appears to me, altogether fanciful. If a line can be drawn between the powers granted and the rights retained, it would seem to be the same thing, whether the latter be secured ["whether" stricken out] by declaring that they shall ["be not be abridged violated" stricken out], or that the former shall be not be extended. If no line can be drawn, a declaration in either form would amount to nothing.[100]

Ninth Amendment skeptics, especially Raoul Berger, have read this passage to mean that the rights retained by the people are the logical obverse of the delegated powers, so that if a delegated power is found to exist, this automatically means that no right remains by which such power could be challenged.[101] Taken in context, we can see that they are wrong.

In this letter, Madison is once again seen combining in a single sentence two parallel ideas that require disentangling. In this instance, he is speaking of two complementary strategies for accomplishing the single objec-

---

[98] See Bernard Schwartz, *The Bill of Rights: A Documentary History*, vol. 2 (New York: Chelsea House, 1971), 1188 (letter from Burnley to Madison, November 28, 1789).

[99] Ibid., 1188. Notice how similar Randolph's alternative proposal is to McAffee's interpretation of the Ninth Amendment—the provision to which Randolph is *objecting*.

[100] Ibid., 1190 (letter from Madison to President Washington, December 5, 1789).

[101] See, e.g., Raoul Berger, "The Ninth Amendment: The Beckoning Mirage," *Rutgers Law Review* 42 (1990): 966 ("Self-evidently, a specific grant of power overrides an unenumerated right. How can an undescribed right present an obstacle to the exercise of a granted power?").

tive of protecting the retained rights of the people: (a) enumerate powers and (b) protect rights. An expressed declaration of "rights retained . . . that shall not be abridged" has the same *purpose* as an expression that "powers granted . . . shall not be extended." The object of both strategies is that "the rights retained . . . be secure." Given this object, if one provision has teeth, so must the other. They are, after all, "the same thing." In other words, rights can be protected from improper extensions of government power either by enumerating those powers, by protecting rights, or (for greater caution) by both devices.

This interpretation of Madison's argument is bolstered by Hardin Burnley's response to Randolph's objection that he included in his report to Madison.

> But others among whom I am one see not the force of the distinction, for by preventing an extension of power in that body from which danger is apprehended safety will be insured if its powers are not too extensive already, & so by protecting the rights of the people & of the States, an improper extension of power will be prevented & safety made equally certain.[102]

Even more clearly than Madison, Burnley is here assessing two competing strategies. According to Burnley, "*by protecting* the rights of the people & of the States, an improper extension of power will be prevented & safety made equally certain." That is, Burnley advocates *protecting rights* as a means of preventing an *improper extension of power*—exactly how Madison used the Ninth Amendment in his bank speech. The other method of ensuring safety is "*by preventing* an extension of power."

Bear in mind that in his letter advocating the strategy of "protecting the rights of the people," Burnley was not referring to the enumerated rights, but was defending the Ninth Amendment's reference to "retained" rights from Randolph's criticism. The Ninth Amendment provides no such protection, however, if the unenumerated retained rights have a constitutional status inferior to those that were enumerated. Burnley's letter assumes that unenumerated rights provide the same constitutional restrictions as those enumerated—an understandable assumption in light of what the Ninth Amendment actually says.

McAffee's rejection of this analysis is weak. He asks how, if there were two distinguishable strategies and Madison preferred one to the other, Madison could dismiss Randolph's distinction as "altogether fanciful." Why would he not instead defend the superiority of his chosen method rather than assert there was no difference between the two?[103] But

---

[102] Schwartz, *The Bill of Rights*, 1188 (letter from Burley to Madison, November 28, 1789).

[103] See McAffee, "Bill of Rights, Social Contract," 241.

Madison was not committed to a single strategy for protecting the rights retained by the people; all his writings and speeches suggest his commitment to the dual strategy of limiting powers *and* protecting rights. Indeed, in his bank speech delivered within fourteen months of his letter to Washington, Madison argues both that the power to incorporate the bank is not in the enumeration and also that, if there, the exercise of the power is not essential. McAffee fails to explain why the unenumerated rights protected by the Ninth Amendment are confined merely to being "the fruit of structural protection,"[104] and do not provide their own "limitations in the scope of power" as Madison argued in his speech and suggested in his letter to Washington.

Madison's actual use of the Ninth Amendment in his bank speech helps clarify the sentence in his letter to Washington that has been exploited by Ninth Amendment skeptics. And his bank speech flatly contradicts Thomas McAffee's elaborately defended "residual rights" thesis that the Ninth Amendment "says nothing about how to construe the powers of Congress or how broadly to read the doctrine of implied powers. . . ."[105] We are left to choose whom to believe about the Ninth Amendment, McAffee or Madison.

Conclusion

The Ninth Amendment mandates that unenumerated rights be treated the same as those that are listed. While an across-the-board presumption of constitutionality would meet this formal standard, not even the New Deal Supreme Court posed so deferential a stance, a position that would conflict with the textual provisions that argue for judicial review. But the doctrine currently in place, the presumption of constitutionality except where certain judicially favored liberties are abridged, fails to provide the equal protection of liberties required by the Ninth Amendment. It is a construction that runs afoul of the text—unlike a Presumption of Liberty.

[104] Ibid., 1297 n. 310.
[105] Ibid., 1300 n. 325.

CHAPTER TEN

The Presumption of Liberty: Protecting Rights without Listing Them

> If we are committed to anything, it is the idea of "liberty."
> If that commitment doesn't really refer to anything except
> a good inner feeling, we ought to shut up about it.[1]
>   —CHARLES L. BLACK, JR.

THERE ARE at least four distinguishable approaches that judges may take toward legislation restricting the retained liberties of the people. First is the laissez-faire approach of complete judicial deference: Adopt a general presumption of constitutionality toward all legislation affecting any liberties of the people. To adopt the laissez-faire approach would be to make Congress the sole judge of its own powers in every dispute between it and a citizen concerning the necessity and propriety of a legislative interference with the citizen's rightful exercise of freedom.[2] Essentially, this approach would eliminate judicial nullification of legislation infringing on constitutional liberties, including those enumerated in the Bill of Rights. Consequently, few advocate this position and it has never been accepted as the correct approach to judicial review at any time in our history.

Second is the original Footnote Four approach: Reverse the presumption of constitutionality when legislation infringes upon those liberties—and only those liberties—that are specified in the Bill of Rights. Although some judicial conservatives, such as Robert Bork, advocate this approach, it, too, is problematic. To begin with, it flies in the face of the many unenumerated rights that have received protection from the Supreme Court for well over a hundred years—such as the right to travel within the United States (which had been enumerated in the Articles of Confederation),[3]

---

[1] Charles L. Black, Jr., "On Reading and Using the Ninth Amendment," in Barnett, *Rights Retained*, 1:345.

[2] Note on terminology: By my usage, the term "liberty" refers to rightful exercises of freedom whereas "license" refers to wrongful exercises of freedom. Hence liberty is a bounded concept that includes some freedoms and excludes others. When I refer here to "rightful exercises of freedom," I mean liberty as opposed to license. See Barnett, *Structure of Liberty*, 1–26.

[3] *Shapiro v. Thompson*, 394 U.S. 618 (1969); *Crandall v. Nevada*, 73 U.S. (6 Wall.) 35 (1868).

the right to provide one's children with religious education,[4] the right to educate one's children in one's native language,[5] the right to associate with others,[6] the right to choose and follow a profession,[7] the right to marry or not to marry,[8] the right to decide whether or not to have children,[9] the right to decide how to rear one's children,[10] and the unenumerated right to privacy that has been explicitly protected for over thirty-five years.[11] Perhaps some of these cases were wrongly decided. Certainly some were decided on the wrong basis. But the pure Footnote Four approach would deem them all wrongly decided.[12]

Far more importantly, the pure Footnote Four approach is undercut by the original meaning of both the Ninth and Fourteenth Amendments. The Ninth Amendment mandates that unenumerated natural rights be treated the same as those that were enumerated. The Privileges or Immunities Clause mandates that no state shall abridge the unenumerated retained natural rights of citizens. Yet Footnote Four calls for protecting only those rights that happened to be enumerated in the Constitution. Also inconsistent with the Ninth Amendment is the third and current Footnote Four-Plus approach that elevates some unenumerated rights to the exalted status of "fundamental" while disparaging the other liberties of the people as mere "liberty interests."

A fourth approach—the one I advocate—would be to protect *all* the rights retained by the people equally whether enumerated or unenumerated. But how would one identify the unenumerated rights retained by the people? How does one define, in the words of the Court in *Casey*, the "substantive sphere of liberty" that is protected by the Privileges or Immunities clause of the Fourteenth Amendment? The uncertainty of specifying unenumerated rights is the crucial issue that prevents some from taking the Ninth Amendment and Privileges or Immunities Clause as seriously as the text would seem to require. As Robert Bork observed

---

[4] *Pierce v. Society of Sisters*, 268 U.S. 510 (1925).

[5] *Meyer v. Nebraska*, 262 U.S. 390 (1923).

[6] *National Association for the Advancement of Colored People v. Alabama*, 357 U.S. 449 (1958); *De Jonge v. Oregon*, 299 U.S. 353 (1937).

[7] *Gibson v. Berryhill*, 411 U.S. 564 (1973); *Allgeyer v. Lousiville*, 165 U.S. 578 (1897).

[8] *Zablocki v. Redhail*, 434 U.S. 374 (1978); *Loving v. Virginia*, 388 U.S. 1 (1967).

[9] *Carey v. Population Services*, 431 U.S. 678 (1977); *Eisenstadt v. Baird*, 405 U.S. 438 (1972).

[10] *Troxel v. Granville*, 530 U.S. 57 (2000).

[11] *Griswold v. Connecticut*, 381 U.S. 479 (1965).

[12] To avoid confusion, let me emphasize that my argument against the approach of Footnote Four is based on the mandate of the Ninth Amendment as well as the meaning of the Privileges or Immunities Clause—not on the existence of Supreme Court cases that protected various unenumerated rights. That the Supreme Court has recognized these rights should, however, give pause to anyone who would accept an unqualified Footnote Four approach.

about using the Ninth Amendment: "Senator, if anybody shows me historical evidence about what they meant, I would be delighted to do it. I just do not know."[13]

Most would agree with Bork that, if the uncertainty surrounding their content can be resolved, unenumerated rights should be enforceable. Otherwise, although the Congress and the executive branch could be prevented from violating enumerated rights, both could violate the unenumerated rights with impunity. Surely this would disparage, if not entirely deny, the unenumerated rights. But many also fear that opening the door to protecting unenumerated rights will empower courts to protect spurious along with valid rights claims. Rather than risk this, they would prefer judges to protect no unenumerated rights at all.

Because ignoring all unenumerated rights violates the mandate of the Ninth Amendment, it must be an option of last resort. Before it is adopted, two alternatives deserve serious consideration, the originalist and presumptive methods.

Using Originalism to Identify Specific Unenumerated Rights

One way to identify unenumerated rights that merit legal protection is suggested by Robert Bork's call for historical evidence. Originalists no more need to discern the content of actual or real rights than they need to discern activity that is "really" commerce. Instead, they can seek either the original intent of the framers or the original meaning of the text. However difficult it may be, interpreting the Ninth Amendment in this way is no different from the task of interpreting other provisions of the Constitution.

We have already seen how the "rights . . . retained by the people" referred, not to any conceivable claim of right, but to liberties. This is an important constraint imposed by the original meaning of the Ninth Amendment. To discover the exact contours of these liberties, we could protect only those unenumerated rights, privileges, or immunities that are revealed by an originalist inquiry. Even if moral skeptics are correct and unenumerated rights are nonexistent, determining the content of the rights that the founders believed to be natural would not be impossible and would give meaning to the text they ratified.

Just as those concerned with original meaning and/or intent consult such materials as Madison's notes on the Constitutional Convention, we may also consult the lengthy lists of proposed amendments sent to Congress by several state ratification conventions. Virginia, for example, pro-

---

[13] *Nomination Hearings*, 249.

posed twenty provisions for "a declaration or bill of rights asserting, and securing from encroachment, the essential and unalienable rights of the people."[14] Only a handful of the many proposed rights were incorporated into the Bill of Rights.[15] In addition, the rights expressly stipulated by state constitutions at the time of the Constitution's ratification are potentially significant.[16] Some of these rights were conceived of as retained by the people against state government. Certainly natural rights retained against state governments were not surrendered to the general government.

These various lists cannot be definitive. Many of these rights were left out of the Bill of Rights and it is nearly impossible to know the motivation behind every decision to include or exclude a particular right. Moreover, as we have already seen, the Ninth Amendment was intended to remove the need to enumerate every right retained by the people. Thus, the mere fact that a right was excluded from the enumeration does not support a strong negative implication.

Further, just as those concerned with original intent consult such theoretical writings as *The Federalist* to interpret passages of the text, they may also consult the framers' theoretical writings on natural rights that were contemporaneous with the Ninth Amendment. Some of these writings are comprehensive and specific. In his lectures on jurisprudence, James Wilson, for example, summarized his analysis of natural rights as follows:

> In his unrelated state, man has a natural right to his property, to his character, to liberty, and to safety. From his peculiar relations, as a husband, as a father, as a son, he is entitled to the enjoyment of peculiar rights, and obliged to the performance of peculiar duties. These will be specified in their due course. From his general relations, he is entitled to other rights, simple in their principle, but, in their operation, fruitful and extensive. . . . In these general relations, his rights are, to be free from injury, and to receive the fulfilment of the engagements, which are made to him; his duties are, to do no injury, and to fulfil the engagements, which he has made. On these two pillars principally and respectively rest the criminal and the civil codes of the municipal law. These are the pillars of justice.[17]

Of course, some may contend that any discussion of natural rights based on this sort of historical inquiry would be too open-ended to provide judges with adequate guidance. Originalists such as Robert Bork and

---

[14] Elliot, *Debates*, 3:657.

[15] For a complete list, see Barnett, *Rights Retained*, 1:353–85.

[16] For a comprehensive tabulation and analysis of the proposals to Congress that compares them with rights then protected in state constitutions, see Donald S. Lutz, "The States and the U.S. Bill of Rights," *Southern University Law Review* 16 (1992): 251–62.

[17] Wilson, "Of the Natural Rights of Individuals," 308.

Raoul Berger, however, cannot make such an argument. Their position requires that we engage in just such an enterprise to interpret the rest of the Constitution—such as the open-ended Necessary and Proper Clause, Due Process Clauses, and the Eighth Amendment's prohibition of "cruel and unusual" punishments. Abandoning the originalist method only when considering the Ninth Amendment may eliminate spurious rights claims but only at the price of a consistent originalist methodology.

There is, then, no shortage of historical materials contemporaneous with ratification of the Ninth Amendment that would permit us to elaborate the original understanding of the rights retained by the people. These materials are comparable in every respect to those traditionally used to interpret the original meaning (or intent) of other provisions and no ink blot prevents us from reading them.

One scholar who has attempted this is Jeffrey Rosen, who concludes that "[t]he documentary sources of the Bill of Rights reveal that conceptions of natural rights were much more determinate two hundred years ago than both commentators and courts suppose today."[18] They are "so determinate, in fact, that only three groups of rights are repeatedly called natural or unalienable in the Revolutionary declarations and state ratifying conventions."[19] Rosen identifies these as the individual right to "worship God according to the dictates of conscience";[20] the individual right of "defending life and liberty, acquiring, possessing and protecting property, and pursuing and obtaining happiness and safety";[21] and the

---

[18] Jeff Rosen, "Was the Flag Burning Amendment Unconstitutional?" *Yale Law Journal* 100 (1991): 1078. The citations presented in the next six footnotes are taken from this article.

[19] Ibid.

[20] The Virginia, New York, North Carolina, and Rhode Island ratifying conventions proposed amendments to the Constitution declaring that the people have an "equal, natural, and unalienable right" to the free exercise of religion, according to the dictates of conscience. Elliot, *Debates*, 3:659 (Virginia); ibid., 4:244 (North Carolina); Schwartz, *The Bill of Rights*, 2:912 (New York); H.R. Doc. No. 398, 69th Cong., 1st sess., 1052 (1927) (Rhode Island). Five Revolutionary declarations of rights call the right to worship God according to the dictates of conscience "unalienable." Pa. Const. (1776), § 2, reprinted in Benjamin Poore, *Federal and State Constitutions; Colonial Charters, and Other Organic Laws of the United States*, vol. 2 (Washington, D.C.: Government Printing Office, 1878), 1541; Del. Declaration of Rights (1776), § 2, reprinted in Schwartz, *The Bill of Rights*, 1:277; N.C. Const. (1776), § XIX, reprinted in Poore, *Federal and State Constitutions* 2: 1410; Vt. Const. (1777), Ch. I, § III, reprinted in ibid., 1859; N.H. Const. (1784), Art. I, § IV, reprinted in ibid., 1280–81.

[21] Pa. Const (1776), Art. I, reprinted in ibid., 1541; Va. Bill of Rights (1776), § 1, reprinted in ibid., 1908; Mass. Const. (1780), Pt. I, Art. I, reprinted in ibid., 1:957; N.H. Const. (1784), Art. I, § II, reprinted in ibid., 2:1280. Two state ratifying conventions proposed amendments declaring the rights of life, liberty, property, and happiness to be "natural." See Elliot, *Debates*, 3:657 (Virginia); ibid., 4:243 (North Carolina).

right of a majority of the people to "alter and abolish" their government.[22] Three other rights are also called natural in the documentary sources: the right to emigrate or to form a new state,[23] the rights of assembly,[24] and the freedom of speech.[25] No originalist of any stripe should accept less than the protection of all these liberties. Nor should those whose interpretive methodology takes original meaning as its starting point.

While it may improve upon current approaches, there is a telling objection to relying solely upon originalist sources to identify specific fundamental rights. As was discussed in chapter 4, we are bound to interpret the text at its original level of generality. The Ninth Amendment was written at a higher level of abstraction or generality—that of natural liberty rights—than any specific list of liberties and deliberately so. The Ninth Amendment and Privileges or Immunities Clause referred to natural rights because it was impossible to specify them all in advance. Any approach that overlooks this in favor of particular historically situated liberties runs afoul of original meaning.

As we have seen, natural liberty rights define a sphere of moral jurisdiction that persons have over certain resources in the world—including their bodies. This jurisdiction establishes boundaries within which persons are free to do as they wish. So long as persons are acting within their respective jurisdictional spheres, their acts are deemed to be "rightful" (as distinguished from "good") and others may not use force to interfere.

[22] Madison's proposed amendment, calling the right to "reform or change" government "unalienable," *Annals*, 1:452, relied on the language of four Revolutionary constitutions. See Va. Bill of Rights (1776), § 3, reprinted in Poore, *Federal and State Constitutions*, 2:1908–9; Pa. Const. (1776), Art. V, reprinted in ibid., 1541; Vt. Const. (1777), Ch. I, Art. VI, reprinted in ibid., 2:1859; Mass. Const. (1780), Pt. I, Art. VII, reprinted in ibid., 1:958.

[23] Pa. Const. (1776), Art. XV, reprinted in ibid., 2:1542; Vt. Const. (1777), Ch. I, Art. XVII, reprinted in ibid., 1860.

[24] "If people freely converse together," said Mr. Sedgwick, "they must assemble for that purpose; it is a self-evident, unalienable right which the people possess. . . ." *Annals*, 1:759 (August 15, 1789).

[25] In addition to Madison's and Sherman's references to speech as a "retained" natural right, the rights of speech were called "inherent" during the debate in the First Congress. "The committee who framed this report," said Mr. Benson, "proceeded on the principle that these rights [of free expression, speech, press, assembly, and of redress of grievances] belonged to the people; they conceived them to be inherent; and all that they meant to provide against was their being infringed by the Government." *Annals*, 1:759 (August 15, 1789); see also St. George Tucker's notes on the American edition of Blackstone's Commentaries: "Thought and speech are equally the immediate gifts of the Creator, the one being intended as the vehicle of the other: they ought, therefore, to have been wholly exempt from the coercion of human laws in all speculative and doctrinal points whatsoever: liberty of speech in political matters, has been equally proscribed in almost all the governments of the world, as liberty of conscience in those of religion" (in appendix of *Blackstone's Commentaries*, vol. 1, pt. 1, 11).

At this level of generality, while the concept of liberty rights excludes other types of rights claims, the specific liberty rights it includes are as numerous as the various acts we may perform within our respective jurisdictions. Our actions must remain within proper jurisdictional bounds but, within those bounds, our rights are as varied as our imaginations. Given this conception of rights, it is impossible to specify in advance all the rights we have. Recall James Wilson's statement (from chapter 3) that

> there are very few who understand the whole of these rights. All the political writers, from Grotious and Puffendorf down to Vattel, have treated on this subject; but in no one of those books, nor in the aggregate of them all, can you find a complete enumeration of rights appertaining to the people as men and as citizens.
>
> . . . Enumerate all the rights of men! I am sure, sir, that no gentleman in the late Convention would have attempted such a thing.[26]

Therefore, and somewhat paradoxically, the original meaning of the rights retained by the people cannot be confined to the specific liberties identified by originalist materials. The Ninth Amendment was added to the Constitution precisely because it was impossible to enumerate all the liberties we have and undesirable even to try. Any effort to do so using originalist methods would give rise to the very danger the Ninth Amendment is there to prevent.

The effort to identify specific liberties in the historical record is not only dangerous; it is also unnecessary. We can protect the unenumerable rights retained by the people by shifting the background interpretive presumption of constitutionality whenever legislation restricts the liberties of the people. We can adopt a Presumption of Liberty.

THE PRESUMPTION OF LIBERTY

To respect the original meaning of the Ninth and Fourteenth Amendments from national or state abridgment, we need a way to protect the rights retained by the people without having to list them. Both Madison and Tucker intimated such a method in their arguments for a strict construction of government powers when such powers are used to restrict individual liberty. Instead of authorizing a search for particular rights, the Ninth Amendment and the Privileges or Immunities Clause can be viewed as establishing a general Presumption of Liberty, which places the burden

---

[26] Elliot, *Debates*, 2:454 (remarks of Justice Wilson).

on the government to establish the necessity and propriety of any infringement on individual freedom.

The Equal Protection of the Rights Retained by the People

A Presumption of Liberty would place the burden on the government to
show why its interference with liberty is both necessary and proper rather
than, as now under Footnote Four-Plus, imposing a burden on the citizen
to show why the exercise of a particular liberty is a "fundamental right."
The Constitution makes no distinction between fundamental rights and
mere liberty interests. This is a pure construction that conflicts with the
mandate of the Ninth Amendment that no right be denied or disparaged
just because it was not enumerated. But the Constitution does say that all
laws shall be both necessary and proper.

A general Presumption of Liberty can be justified, not only on the
grounds that it gets the courts out of the business of picking and choosing
among the liberties of the people to decide which is fundamental, and
not only on the grounds that it is more harmonious with the text (and
original meaning) of the Ninth and Fourteenth Amendments. It can also
be justified as a more realistic presumption in light of what we know of
legislative behavior.

The original justification of the presumption of constitutionality rested,
in part, on a belief that legislatures would consider carefully, accurately,
and in good faith the constitutional protections of liberty before infringing it. This belief assumed that legislatures really do assess the necessity
and propriety of laws before enacting them. In recent decades, however,
we have remembered the problem of faction that (at least some of) the
framers never forgot. We now understand much better (or are more willing to admit) than our post–New Deal predecessors on the left and on
the right that both minorities and majorities can successfully assert their
interests in the legislative process to gain enactments that serve their own
interests rather than being necessary and proper.

In short, our understanding of the facts on which the presumption of
constitutionality rests have changed. And, with this change in its factual
underpinnings, the presumption—which appears nowhere in the constitutional text—must fall. Statutes that emerge from the legislative process
are not entitled to the deference they now receive unless there is some
reason to think that they are a product of necessity, rather than mere
interest. And a statutory restriction of liberty should not blindly be presumed to be a "proper" regulation.

A Presumption of Liberty would place unenumerated rights on a par
with enumerated rights—no more, no less. For example, courts have
not construed the First Amendment as literally barring any restriction of

"the freedom of speech." Ancient common law torts, such as fraud and defamation, provide boundaries beyond which the rightful exercise of free speech may not go. If speech is fraudulent—which I hasten to add is not the same as false—it is wrongful and may be prohibited, not merely regulated. Nevertheless, the First Amendment establishes a constitutional presumption in favor of any rightful speech that is within these common law boundaries.

When legislation operates to restrict speech, such legislation is now subjected to meaningful judicial scrutiny. The executive branch of government must justify to the judiciary any legislative or executive interference with free speech. The fact that such legislation reflects a majority preference is insufficient to overcome the presumption established by the First Amendment. Moreover, the bare assertion that legislation abridging freedom of speech serves a legitimate legislative end is also insufficient. When the First Amendment is implicated we maintain a healthy skepticism of legislative motivations.

Given its original meaning, the Ninth Amendment is best construed as establishing the same constitutional presumption in favor of other rightful activities. This presumption requires the executive branch of the government to justify to the judiciary any legislative or executive interference. The fact that such legislation reflects a majority preference is insufficient to overcome the presumption established by the Ninth Amendment. Moreover, the bare assertion that such legislation serves a legitimate legislative end would also be insufficient. As with restrictions on speech, skepticism of legislative motivations is warranted when unenumerated rights are abridged.

Statutes do not create a duty of obedience in the citizenry simply because they are enacted. The only way that statutes may create a prima facie duty of obedience in the citizenry is if some agency not as affected by interest (or affected by different interests) will scrutinize them to ensure that they are both necessary and proper. However imperfect they may be, only courts are presently available to perform this function. Without some meaningful assurance of necessity and propriety, statutes are to be obeyed merely because the consequences of disobedience are onerous. Without judicial review, statutes are mere exercises of will, and are not entitled to the same presumption of respect that attaches to statutes surviving meaningful scrutiny.

Distinguishing Rightful from Wrongful Conduct

In the absence of actual consent, a law must be shown to be necessary and proper for it to bind in conscience. To be proper it must, among other things, not violate the rights retained by the people. There are two ways a law can restrict freedom of action without violating the background natural rights that define one's liberty.

First, if a particular action violates the rights of others, then it is not a rightful exercise of freedom. It is not liberty but license. Prohibiting such actions, though it restricts a person's freedom to do as he wills, does not violate the rights retained by the people. To the contrary, such prohibitions protect the liberty rights of others. Second, when the rightful exercise of freedom involves more than one person, it can be "regulated" or made regular to facilitate its exercise and, if necessary, to protect the rights of others. A regulation of liberty is not an improper infringement of liberty if a legal system merely says that, to obtain its protection, contracts or other transactions must take a certain form (if such a regulation is also found to be necessary).

In short, laws that are necessary to prohibit wrongful or regulate rightful activity would satisfy the Presumption of Liberty. Laws that prohibit or unnecessarily regulate rightful behavior would not. In part IV, I examine how the Presumption of Liberty may be rebutted. First, however, a threshold question needs to be addressed: To apply the presumption requires a distinction be made between rightful and wrongful conduct. What exactly is a "rightful" exercise of freedom and by whom is this decision to be made? Does not the need to distinguish rightful from wrongful behavior require unelected federal judges with lifetime tenure to speculate about the Rights of Man? What qualifies them to determine what learned philosophers cannot agree upon? Where in their legal education or experience did they gain expertise in distinguishing rightful from wrongful conduct? A moment's reflection should dissipate such concerns.

A "rightful" exercise of freedom roughly corresponds to what courts today refer to as a "liberty interest." No court today would find an action that violated the rights of others to be a "liberty interest." As Chief Justice Earl Warren explained: "Although the Court has not assumed to define 'liberty' with any great precision, that term is not confined to mere freedom from bodily restraint. Liberty under law extends to the full range of conduct which the individual is free to pursue, and it cannot be restricted except for a proper governmental objective."[27] Of course, at present, liberty interests are not protected unless they are also deemed to be fundamental rights, but at this juncture what is important is that, by identifying liberty interests, courts have in practice routinely distinguished rightful from wrongful exercises of freedom.

Nor does it require philosophical speculation to do so. In our legal order, distinguishing rightful from wrongful conduct is generally done every working day at the state level. Indeed, at least a quarter of a law

[27] *Bolling v. Sharpe*, 347 U.S. 497, 499–500 (1954).

student's legal education is devoted to this subject in courses such as contracts, torts, property, agency and partnership, secured transactions, commercial paper, and portions of criminal law. In contrast with constitutional law, which provides rules for the conduct of government agents, these private law subjects provide principles to regulate the conduct of persons toward each other. Ever since the forms of action were abolished, concepts within these subject areas have been used to assess the merits of claims that one person has violated the rights of another and therefore acted wrongfully. For example, when one person injures another and this injury is considered to be "tortious," then it is deemed to be wrongful and a duty to compensate is held to exist. It is also wrongful to breach a valid contract without a valid defense.

At the time of the founding, this body of rules and principles was judge-made, and largely remains so today. Moreover, in the United States's federal system it was (and still is) primarily made by state court judges. When federal judges today decide civil actions between two parties pursuant to their powers in diversity cases, they distinguish rightful from wrongful behavior by discerning state law. When federal judges make these decisions on state law, their rulings may even be "overruled" by subsequent state court decisions.

Thus, today there is a healthy functioning division of labor between state law assessments of the rights the people have against each other, and federal constitutional adjudication that protects these rights of the people from infringement by government. It is only when federal judges are asked to distinguish protected fundamental rights from unprotected "liberty interests," as they currently do under the Footnote Four-Plus approach, that they arguably exceed the boundaries of their competence.

Distinguishing rightful from wrongful behavior is exactly what common law courts have been doing for centuries (with occasional assistance from legislatures). The freedom to act within the boundaries provided by one's common law or "civil" rights may be viewed as a central background presumption of the Constitution—a presumption reflected in both the Ninth Amendment and the Privileges or Immunities Clause. There is no constitutional privilege to commit a tort or breach of contract; but so long as one is acting rightfully, one should presumptively be immune from government interference.

This does not mean that all legislative alterations of common law rights are constitutionally prohibited. Common law processes assumed that legislation can occasionally be used to correct doctrinal errors perpetuated by a strong doctrine of precedent, to establish needed conventions, and to achieve uniformity among diverse legal systems. Judges make mistakes and act out of interest. Legislatures can provide a popular "check" against such abuses. Under a Presumption of Liberty, legislative alteration of common law rights is permissible, but such legislation must be scrutinized by independent tribunals of justice to see whether, in the guise of performing these permissible functions, the legislature is seeking instead to invade individual rights.

Legislation that is necessary to achieve ends deemed by the Constitution to be appropriate—and defined at the federal level by the enumerated powers provisions—may rebut the presumption in favor of rightful activity when such legislation passes the sort of meaningful scrutiny we associate with the infringement of other constitutional rights. Further, state legislation and popular referenda expanding the sphere of liberty and protecting it from judicial encroachment are to be treated far differently from legislation restricting the exercise of otherwise rightful conduct.

Still, though legislative alterations of common law rights complicate the story a bit, it is important to bear in mind that such legislative interventions were originally supposed to be, and in fact were, comparatively rare. Determination of private rights was traditionally, and still remains, overwhelmingly the province of state court judges. Even with sweeping statutory innovations such as the Uniform Commercial Code,[28] legislative alterations of private law rights are relatively rare. Common law has been far more frequently affected by the opinions of the nonprofit American Law Institute through their authoritative series, *Restatements of the Law.* As legislative activity becomes less extraordinary, however, increased skepticism of the purported justifications of legislation is warranted. Legislative inflation results in a general diminution of legislative value.

I am not suggesting that I agree with all the rules and principles that currently define a person's "civil" or common law rights—that is why I teach and write about contract law. Moreover, I can think of entirely new causes of action that have been devised by judges in recent years that are manifestly unjust violations of liberty. Nor do I necessarily endorse the exact process by which all such matters are currently decided by judges. Rather, I am answering the question of how, as a practical matter, we distinguish between rightful and wrongful conduct when protecting unenumerated liberties from legislative infringement. My answer: Such decisions should be made, for better or worse, the way these distinctions are made at present.

So emerges the great outline of an institutional allocation of responsibility in discerning and protecting the background natural rights of all persons: State common law processes determine the rights that each citi-

---

[28] The broad principles of the Uniform Commercial Code require much judicial interpretation and construction. In many cases where they are not merely determining useful conventions, they can be considered as providing only general principles that require additional judicial doctrine to apply to specific cases.

zen enjoys against others, whereas state and federal judges are authorized to protect citizens from having their "civil" rights infringed by state and federal governments. When assessing the practicality of this traditional allocation of institutional responsibility, one must keep two facts in mind.

First, courts will rarely need to determine the rightfulness of an exercise of liberty because little legislation at the federal or state level even purports to define and/or prohibit wrongful behavior—that is, behavior by one person that supposedly violates the rights of another. Rather, legislation restricting "liberty interests" is typically defended, not on the ground that such liberty is wrongful, but because the restrictions achieve some desirable social policy or "legitimate state interest." Nor is it the case that every claim of government power can plausibly be recast in terms of vindicating some individual person's rights.

Second, and equally important, not all legislation restricts the liberties of the people in any way. The many laws that regulate the internal operation of government agencies or the dispensation of government funds, for example, would be unaffected by a Presumption of Liberty. When the post office sets its hours of operation or the price of its postage stamps, it is not restricting the rightful freedoms of the citizenry any more than a private organization that does the same. If heightened scrutiny of the necessity and propriety of such laws is warranted, as it may very well be,[29] it would for some other reason than that the laws in question may infringe upon the rights retained by the people.[30]

On the other hand, when Congress asserts that to effectuate its power "[t]o establish Post Offices,"[31] it is necessary and proper to grant a legal monopoly to its post office, those companies that wish to carry first-class mail are entitled to demand that Congress or the executive branch demonstrate the necessity and propriety of such a restriction on liberty. As Madison argued with respect to the national bank: "It involves a monopoly,

---

[29] I do not address here when, if ever, conditioning the receipt of government benefits or employment on the waiver of one's background rights should be protected by a presumption of unconstitutionality. See, generally, Richard A. Epstein, *Bargaining with the State* (Princeton: Princeton University Press, 1993) (discussing the appropriate limits on the power of government to bargain with its citizens). Whether or not such so-called unconstitutional conditions violate the rights retained by the people, they may be insidious or "improper" enough in their own right to justify shifting the presumption of constitutionality and thereby placing the burden on the government to show that such conditions are both necessary and proper.

[30] For example, heightened scrutiny of the necessity of laws that tell state governments how they are to behave might be justified as infringing the powers reserved to the states or to the people mentioned by the Tenth Amendment. Heightened scrutiny of laws might also be warranted when laws appear to violate the Equal Protection Clause of the Fourteenth Amendment. Neither doctrine would follow from the Ninth Amendment, or the Privileges or Immunities Clause, and the Presumption of Liberty that effectuates them.

[31] U.S. Const., Art. I, § 8, Cl. 7.

which affects the equal rights of every citizen."[32] Similarly when Congress asserts that to effectuate its power "to raise and support Armies,"[33] it is necessary and proper to draft young men or women to serve in the military, those who are subject to this form of involuntary servitude are entitled to demand that Congress or the executive branch demonstrate to the satisfaction of an independent tribunal of justice that armies cannot be raised through the use of volunteers.

Perhaps there are times when post offices cannot be provided without a grant of a monopoly, or when an all-volunteer army is insufficient for the defense of the United States. However, when Congress seeks to put postal competitors out of business or to draft young men or women, a Presumption of Liberty would put the onus on Congress to demonstrate that this is one of those times. There is every reason to expect that, when pressed with cases of genuine necessity, courts would not hesitate to uphold legislation that is truly necessary and proper. Indeed, even were a Presumption of Liberty to be adopted, I have little doubt that government-employed judges would more likely uphold unnecessary restrictions on liberty than strike down a law that is truly necessary. To counteract this tendency, it is important to restore another lost provision of the Constitution: the original meaning of the term "trial by jury," which includes the right of juries to refuse to enforce criminal laws they deem unjust or unjustly applied a particular defendant.[34]

Will Judges Have Too Much Power?

Some may object that a Presumption of Liberty would place altogether too much power in judges. A reliance on judges, however, is unavoidable in a constitutional system in which only courts are available to stand between individual citizens and majority and minority factions operating through representative government. As Madison observed in *Federalist* 10:

> No man is allowed to be the judge in his own cause, because his interest would certainly bias his judgment, and, not improbably, corrupt his integrity. With equal, nay with greater reason, a body of men are unfit to be both judges and parties at the same time; yet what are many of the most important acts of legisla-

---

[32] *Annals*, 2:1900 (1791); see also Lysander Spooner, "The Unconstitutionality of Laws of Congress, Prohibiting Private Mails" (New York: Tribune Printing Establishment, 1844), reprinted in vol. 1 of Spooner, *The Collected Works*.

[33] U.S. Const., Art. I, § 8, Cl. 12.

[34] For an examination of the historical origins and practical application of the right of "jury nullification," see Clay S. Conrad, *Jury Nullification: The Evolution of a Doctrine* (Durham, N.C.: Carolina Academic Press, 1998).

tion but so many judicial determinations, not indeed concerning the rights of single persons, but concerning the rights of large bodies of citizens? And what are the different classes of legislators but advocates and parties to the causes which they determine? . . . Justice ought to hold the balance between them.[35]

When legislation encroaches upon the liberties of the people, only review by an impartial judiciary can ensure that the rights of citizens are protected and that justice holds the balance between the legislature or executive branch and the people. Without judicial review to see that Congress stays within its powers and refrains from violating the rights retained by the people, there is little reason to believe that legislation is binding in conscience on the people.

From the standpoint of constitutional legitimacy, it is woefully inadequate to insist that legislatures or executive branch officials may be the judge in their own cases when their actions are alleged to infringe upon the rightful freedom—or Liberty—of a citizen. The whole purpose of natural rights in this context is to protect persons from legislative or executive abuses. Unless these rights are protected by what Madison called "independent tribunals of justice,"[36] they are virtually worthless. As Jeffrey Reiman has observed, "the Court's decisions must be legally binding [on the other branches] precisely because they are decisions about the conditions of legitimate governance by the other branches, conditions whose determination cannot be left up to those branches."[37] Without judicial review, "a necessary condition of legitimacy, namely, a built-in mechanism for not only monitoring but effectively correcting the conditions of legitimacy, is lacking."[38]

Of course, if legislatures do take pains to regulate the rights of citizens only when it is necessary and proper to do so, we can expect them to be able to justify their actions. Regrettably, our actual experience with legislatures has not been so utopian. For this reason, meaningful scrutiny of legislative and executive branch actions by an impartial magistrate is required if the laws imposed on the citizens are to bind in conscience.

Moreover, the problem of judicial power, although real, is usually overstated. Most instances of "judicial activism" cited by judicial conservatives involve latitudinarian interpretation of sweeping and indefinite *statutory* language. Congress is free to correct such judicial interpretations if

---

[35] *Federalist* 10, 79–80 (Madison).

[36] The phrase is taken from Madison's speech to the first House of Representatives in defense of his proposed amendments to the Constitution: "If they are incorporated into the constitution, independent tribunals of justice will consider themselves in a peculiar manner the guardians of those rights. . . ." *Annals*, 1:457 (statement of James Madison).

[37] Reiman, "The Constitution, Rights, and the Conditions of Legitimacy," 144.

[38] Ibid.

it wishes. That it often does not evidences Congress's all-too-common strategy of passing vaguely worded statutes so that administrative agencies or courts provide the rules of law that Congress would not.

In the event that Congress disagrees with an assessment by the Supreme Court that a particular enactment is either unnecessary or improper, and there is strong popular support for the statute, Congress has the power to propose a constitutional amendment. A majority of the Supreme Court may well protect rights at variance from the opinion of the overwhelming majority of the people for a time, but life is, alas, all too short. As Barry Friedman has noted, this fact plus our method of judicial selection assures that, for better or worse, in the not-so-long run any Supreme Court opinion about the rights of the people that is opposed by an overwhelming majority of the people will be reversed.[39] The president may take any disagreement (or agreement) with past Supreme Court rulings into account in selecting judicial nominees, and the Senate may express its views during the confirmation process.

These various mechanisms by which Supreme Court rulings protective of liberty can be challenged mean that sooner or later a sustained majoritarian preference will eventually overcome any judicial resistance. That this takes some time and effort to happen is, in most instances, salutary. In any event, such delay is absolutely essential if legislatures are not to be judges in their own cases when they restrict the liberty of citizens. The more likely practical deficiency of a Presumption of Liberty is that government judges are not sufficiently independent of government or of a majority faction to provide "an impenetrable bulwark against every assumption of power in the legislative or executive."[40] For this reason prior Supreme Court rulings upholding the exercise of such powers should always be subject to reconsideration when circumstances have changed.

CONCLUSION

As a practical matter, we must choose between two fundamentally different constructions of the Constitution, each resting on a different presumption. We either accept the presumption that in pursuing happiness persons may do whatever is not justly prohibited or we are left with a presumption

---

[39] See Barry Friedman, "Dialogue and Judicial Review," *Michigan Law Review* 91 (1993): 577 (arguing that courts are not systematically less majoritarian than the political branches of government).

[40] The phrase is, once again, Madison's. See *Annals*, 1:457 (statement of James Madison), See, e.g., *Korematsu v. United States*, 323 U.S. 214 (1944) (upholding the constitutionality of confining citizens of Japanese ancestry in detention camps).

that the government may do whatever is not expressly prohibited.[41] The presence of the Ninth Amendment in the Constitution strongly supports the first of these two presumptions. The Constitution established what Steven Macedo has called islands of governmental powers "surrounded by a sea of individual rights." It did not establish "islands [of rights] surrounded by a sea of governmental powers."[42] The Ninth Amendment is sometimes dismissed as a mere "rule of construction," but this in no way undermines its supreme importance. For it directly refutes the second of these presumptions and affirms the first: the Presumption of Liberty.

[41] See, e.g., Lino Graglia, "Judicial Review on the Basis of 'Regime Principles': A Prescription for Government by Judges," *Southern Texas Law Journal* 26 (1985): 436 ("Very few occasions for . . . [judicial review] would arise, because the Constitution contains few limitations on self-government, and those limitations are almost never violated").

[42] Stephen Macedo, *The New Right v. the Constitution* (Washington, D.C.: Cato Institute, 1987), 97.

PART IV

Constitutional Powers

Respecting the Ninth Amendment and the Privileges or Immunities Clause means according protection to the unenumerated rights, privileges, and immunities retained by the people equal to that accorded to enumerated rights. A Presumption of Liberty accomplishes this. Just as the rightful exercise of speech is presumptively immune from government restriction, so any other rightful activity should be. Only by establishing a presumption in favor of any rightful exercise of freedom can we hope to protect the unenumerated rights retained by the people as we do those rights that were listed.

Even the enumerated rights of free speech and assembly are not absolute, however. Wrongful exercises of speech—for example, fraud or threats of violence—are justly prohibited. Speech and assembly can also be regulated, provided that such regulations are shown to be necessary and not a pretext for prohibiting speech that the legislature dislikes or with which it disagrees. Time, place, and manner regulations—such as the requirement to get a parade license or the prohibition on loud sound trucks in residential neighborhoods—can be proper if they are not pretextual.

Unenumerated rights are no more absolute than enumerated rights. The Presumption of Liberty allows the government to meet the burden placed upon it by establishing the necessity and propriety of its restrictions on liberty. Because a judicial assessment of necessity requires a particularistic fact-dependent appraisal of the means chosen by a legislature in pursuit of a proper end, it is preferable to consider the requirement of propriety to be the threshold issue. If a particular law is shown to be beyond the powers of federal or state legislatures, an inquiry into the particulars of the means chosen is rendered unnecessary.

In chapter 11, I discuss the propriety of federal laws under the power most often invoked to justify restrictions on liberty: the power to regulate commerce among the several states. In chapter 12, I examine the propriety of state laws under what is known as the "police powers" of the states, before considering, in chapter 13, the sort of inquiry that is needed to establish an otherwise proper measure as also "necessary." I conclude that chapter by discussing how the Presumption of Liberty would handle particular cases and controversies, although I caution that this should not be the ultimate touchstone of its acceptability.

CHAPTER ELEVEN

The Proper Scope of Federal Power: The Meaning of the Commerce Clause

> Agriculture, manufacturers and commerce are acknowledged
> to be the three great sources of wealth in any state. By the
> first we are to understand not only tillage, but whatever re-
> gards the improvement of the earth; as the breeding of cattle,
> the raising of trees, plants and all vegetables that may contrib-
> ute to the real use of man; the opening and working of mines,
> whether of metals, stones, or mineral drugs; by the second,
> all the arts, manual or mechanic; by the third, the whole ex-
> tent of navigation with foreign countries.
> —*PENNSYLVANIA GAZETTE* (January 13, 1790)

THE PROPRIETY OF FEDERAL POWERS

The Necessary and Proper Clause commands that all laws passed by Congress shall be proper. When a government restriction of liberty is challenged by an affected citizen, a Presumption of Liberty means that the
citizen wins, unless the government can justify its restrictions as proper.
A "proper" exercise of power is one that is within the jurisdiction of the
branch or department in question and that does not violate the rights
retained by the people.[1] In Article I, the Constitution lists a number of
powers that the Congress may exercise.[2]

The enumeration of congressional powers was adopted by the Convention after the delegates rejected more general grants of legislative power
as overly vague. For example, when it was proposed to grant Congress
all powers then exercised by the Confederation and "moreover to legislate
in all cases to which the separate states are incompetent; or in which
the harmony of the U.S. may be interrupted by the exercise of individual
legislation,"[3] Pierce Butler of South Carolina objected: "The vagueness of
the terms rendered it impossible for any precise judgment to be formed."[4]
In response, Nicholas Ghorum of Massachusetts explained: "The

---

[1] See Lawson and Granger, "The 'Proper' Scope of Federal Power."
[2] This list appears at the beginning of chapter 7.
[3] Farrand, *Records*, 2:17.
[4] Ibid.

vagueness of the terms constitutes the propriety of them. We are now establishing general principles, to be extended hereafter into details which will be precise & explicit."[5] Fellow delegate from South Carolina John Rutledge renewed Butler's objection "and moved . . . that a specification of the powers comprised in the general terms, might be reported."[6]

The demand for specificity immediately followed the decision that morning (by a bare majority) of the Convention to allocate equal representation to every state in the Senate. As explained by Edmund Randolph of Virginia, "The vote of this morning (involving an equality of suffrage in 2nd branch) had embarrassed the business extremely. All the powers given in the Report from the Come. of the whole, were founded on the supposition that a Proportional representation was to prevail in both branches of the Legislature."[7] Though they had earlier supported the so-called Virginia Plan putting sweeping powers in the hands of Congress, it has been suggested that Virginia and the other Southern states began pressing for a specificity of powers when they lost the assurance that they would dominate both houses of the future Congress.[8] Whatever the motivation, the insistent demand eventually resulted in the list of enumerated powers drafted initially by the Committee of Detail.

The vote over the composition of the Senate was so disruptive to the prior stances of various delegates and states concerning the scope of federal powers that when, later the same day, Edmund Randolph urged adjournment because "we were unprepared to discuss this matter further,"[9] more than one delegate took him to be calling for an adjournment of the entire Convention so that members might return home for consultation.[10] By the next day, and after a meeting of delegates from the larger states to discuss the "proper steps to be taken in consequence of the vote in favor of an equal Representation in the [Senate],"[11] the previously offered broad statement of congressional powers was characterized by Gouveneur Morris as "the abstract of the powers necessary to be vested in the general Government"[12] and by his fellow Pennsylvanian James Wilson as "the general principle."[13] Roger Sherman read to the Convention an enumeration of powers he had drafted, though it was not approved (and Madison did not record its contents).

---

[5] Ibid.
[6] Ibid.
[7] Ibid.
[8] See Lynch, *Negotiating the Constitution*, 17–19.
[9] Farrand, *Records*, 2:18.
[10] See ibid. Randolph protested that he had been "strangely misinterpreted."
[11] Ibid., 19.
[12] Ibid., 25 (Governeur Morris).
[13] Ibid., 26 (James Wilson).

Significantly, weeks later, during its consideration of the precise enumeration of powers to be adopted, the Convention rejected the following language that the Committee on Detail proposed be added to the list:

> and to provide, as may become necessary, from time to time, for the well managing and securing the common property and general interests and welfare of the United States in such a manner as shall not interfere with the Governments of individual States in matters which respect only their internal police, or for which their individual authorities may be competent.[14]

By making this proposal, the Committee confirmed that so general a power was not implicit in the rest of the enumeration already proposed. By rejecting it, the Convention affirmed what seems apparent: that Congress lacked a general power to legislate in the public interest and possessed only the enumerated "Powers herein granted"[15] to it.

Ordinarily I place little emphasis on provisions that fail to be adopted. What matters is the original meaning of the text that *was* adopted. However, when what has been adopted is later argued to be the equivalent of something quite different that was explicitly rejected, the evidence becomes pertinent. In this case, the Convention was faced with a clear choice between a general grant of power to be exercised at Congress's discretion and a specific enumeration by which Congress's power was to be defined textually and thereby limited. It chose the latter.

What, then, is the connection between the enumeration of powers and the "propriety" of laws passed by Congress? According to the theory of legitimacy advanced in part I, in the absence of unanimous consent to the delegation of these powers, these powers must not violate the rights retained by those who never consented to their alienation. Of course, it may be that some powers granted Congress by the Constitution are proper and others not. Most of the powers on the original list are not problematic in this regard. They simply authorize the Congress to engage in certain activities, such as establishing post offices, or raising and supporting armies, that do not of themselves directly restrict the liberties of the people and therefore cannot violate their retained rights.

To completely evaluate the legitimacy of the Constitution would therefore require a detailed analysis of each of these powers and whether it violates the rights of nonconsenting persons. Though one of the most glaring defects of the Constitution was its failure to prohibit slavery in the states, the framers carefully avoided mentioning slavery by name or empowering Congress to enslave any person. Suppose, however, that it had. Although the exercise of such a power, if enumerated, would be le-

---

[14] Ibid., 367.
[15] U.S.Const., Art. I, § 1.

gally "valid," it would still be improper, as would any laws passed under its authority. Such laws would also be illegitimate as there would be no constitutional assurance that they are just and, as a consequence, such laws would not bind in conscience.

Despite this, courts are not empowered to disregard expressly enumerated powers, even those that violate the rights of the people. They are authorized only to interpret the meaning of these powers, and where this meaning is underdeterminate, to construe them in a manner that is consistent with original meaning and that would render their exercise as legitimate as possible. Assuming, *arguendo*, that the power to impose a tax on incomes authorized by the Sixteenth Amendment was unjust and improper, and consequently any laws passed to execute this power did not bind the citizenry in conscience, for better or worse, judges who swear to uphold the Constitution would not, in our system, be free to disregard this power or these laws. Such is the price we pay for the benefits of a written constitution. "Locking in" the good parts of the Constitution, it "locks in" any bad parts as well.[16]

Of course, it would be better for the sake of constitutional legitimacy if the powers granted to Congress were in fact proper. If the original meaning of a power does not violate the rights of nonconsenting persons, then the government need only show that a particular law lies within that delegated power to establish its propriety. Where the original meaning of a particular power is vague, a court can and should construe it to ensure it does not violate the liberty rights of persons who did not consent to the Constitution. A law justified in either manner would bind in conscience regardless of whether the Constitution also contained other enumerated powers, the original meaning of which improperly violates the rights retained by the people.

With this in mind, I now turn my attention to the enumerated power that has most often been used by Congress to restrict the liberties of the people: the power "to regulate Commerce with foreign Nations, and among the several States, and with the Indian Tribes." The evidence is overwhelming that the original meaning of this power renders it entirely consistent with the background rights retained by the people even in the absence of their consent. Adopting this interpretation would also narrow the legislative powers now claimed by Congress and accepted as constitutional by the courts.

---

[16] That is why a commitment to originalism depends on the prior assessment that the constitution to be interpreted is "good enough" to provide a legitimate lawmaking process. This, in turn, is why a rejection of originalism also entails a rejection of the written constitution being interpreted. See chapter 4.

THE FEDERAL POWER TO REGULATE COMMERCE AMONG THE STATES

The Commerce Clause raises three questions that must be answered by interpretation, construction, or both: What is the meaning of "Commerce"? What is the meaning of "among the several States"? And what is the meaning of "to regulate"? Some have claimed that each of these terms of the Commerce Clause had, at the time of the founding, both an expansive and a more limited meaning in common discourse.

"Commerce" might be limited to trade or exchange of goods, which would exclude, for example, agriculture, manufacturing, and other methods of production, or it might be interpreted expansively to refer to any gainful activity. "To regulate" might be limited to "make regular," which would subject a particular type of commerce to a rule and would exclude, for example, any prohibition on trade as an end in itself, or it might be interpreted expansively to mean "to govern," which would include prohibitions as well as pure regulations. "[A]mong the several States" might be limited to commerce that takes place between the states (or between people of different states), as opposed to commerce that occurs between persons of the same state. Or "among the states" might be interpreted expansively to refer to commerce "among [the people of] the States," whether such commerce occurs between people in the same state or in different states.

Although it is often difficult to be sure of the meaning intended by a speaker from the context of a particular statement, there are good textual and contextual reasons to accept the narrower definition of each of these terms as their original meaning at the time of the founding. Because the meaning of the term "commerce" has been the most contentious, I will spend more time evaluating the evidence of its original meaning than that of the others.

The Original Meaning of "Commerce"

The use of the term "commerce" in the drafting and ratification process was remarkably uniform. Indeed, I have found not a single example from the reports of these proceedings that unambiguously used a broad meaning of "commerce" and many instances where the context makes clear that the speaker intended a narrow meaning.

ORIGINALIST SOURCES

The Text.   The first place to look for the original meaning of the text is the text itself, both the immediate text at issue and any other text in the Constitution that may shed light on the meaning of the relevant portion. Does the Constitution serve as its own dictionary on the meaning of a particular word?

When we consider the meaning of the term "commerce," it is tempting to argue that "commerce" must mean trade, and not manufacturing or agriculture, because it would make no sense to refer to a congressional power "to regulate manufacturing with foreign nations" or "to regulate agriculture with Indian tribes." This temptation should be resisted, however. If we plug the broadest alleged meaning of "commerce"—that is, "gainful activity"—into the sentence so it reads Congress shall have power "to regulate gainful activity with foreign nations," the sentence makes perfect grammatical sense. True, so interpreted the clause would be referring only to that subset of gainful activity that can be conducted "with foreign nations" and "with the Indian tribes" and this would exclude manufacturing and agriculture. This narrowed application would not, however, be due to the narrow meaning of the word "commerce," but would result from the interpretive effect of "with foreign nations" and "with Indian tribes." In other words, the word "commerce" could still be used in its broadest sense in a manner that does grammatical justice to the sentence as a whole. Therefore, grammar alone does not tell us in which sense, narrow or broad, the word "commerce" is being used in the Commerce Clause, and we must look elsewhere for guidance.

A bit more assistance is provided by the way "commerce" is used in Article I, Section 9, which reads: "No Preference shall be given by any Regulation of Commerce or Revenue to the Ports of one State over those of another. . . ." Here, as Richard Epstein has written, "[t]he term 'commerce' is used in opposition to the term 'revenue,' and seems clearly to refer to shipping and its incidental activities; this much seems evident from the use of the term 'port.' "[17] Moreover, unlike the Commerce Clause, we cannot here comfortably substitute "gainful activity" for the term "commerce." "No Preference shall be given by any Regulation of gainful activity to the Ports of one State over those of another" is too awkward to be an accurate translation. But though the term "commerce," standing alone in Article I, Section 9,[18] is clearly being used in a much narrower sense than "any gainful activity," we cannot be sure from this usage exactly what this sense is. For that we need to appeal to extrinsic evidence of original meaning that lies outside the four corners of the Constitution.

---

[17] Richard A. Epstein, "The Proper Scope of the Commerce Power," *Virginia Law Review* 73 (1987): 1388, 1395.

[18] By this I mean the narrowing sense is not provided by some other phrase such as "with foreign Nations."

Contemporary Dictionaries. "Commerce" is defined in the 1785 edition of Samuel Johnson's *Dictionary of the English Language* as "1. Intercourse; exchange of one thing for another; interchange of any thing; trade; traffick." In contrast, "manufacture" is defined as "1. The practice of making any piece of workmanship. 2. Any thing made by art." "Agriculture" is defined as "[t]he art of cultivating the ground; tillage; husbandry, as distinct from pasturage." If Johnson is accurate, commerce referred predominantly to exchange or trade as distinct from the agricultural or manufacturing production of those things that are subsequently traded. Johnson's definition of "commerce" is borne out by other dictionaries of the time.[19] It is also the usage most closely associated with the drafting and adoption of the Constitution.

Constitutional Convention. In Madison's notes for the Constitutional Convention, the term "commerce" appears thirty-four times in the speeches of the delegates.[20] Eight of these are unambiguous references to commerce with foreign nations, which can consist only of trade. In every other instance, the terms "trade" or "exchange" could be substituted for the term "commerce" with the apparent meaning of the statement preserved. In no instance is the term "commerce" clearly used to refer to "any gainful activity" or anything broader than trade. One congressional power proposed by Madison, but not ultimately adopted, suggests that the delegates shared the limited meaning of "commerce" described in Johnson's dictionary. Madison proposed to grant Congress the power "[t]o establish public institutions, rewards, and immunities for the promotion of agriculture, commerce, trades and manufactures,"[21] strongly indicating that the members understood the term "commerce" to mean trade or exchange, as distinct from the productive processes that made the things to be traded.

The Federalist. Nor was this a secret usage confined to the Convention. In several of his contributions to *The Federalist*, ardent nationalist Alexander Hamilton repeatedly made clear the commonplace distinction between commerce, or trade, and production. In *Federalist* 11, he also

---

[19] See e.g., Nathan Bailey, *An Universal Etymological English Dictionary*, 26th ed. (Edinburgh: Neill & Co., 1789) ("trade or traffic"); T. Sheridan, *A Complete Dictionary of the English Language*, 6th ed. (Philadelphia: W. Young, Mills and Son, 1796), 585–86 ("Exchange of one thing for another; trade, traffick").

[20] This is apart from the sixteen times in which it appears in quotations from various proposals.

[21] Madison, *Notes of Debates*, 478 (August 18, 1787) (emphasis added). The term "trades" connotes crafts and other types of trades, not trade or exchange.

explained the purpose of the Commerce Clause, a purpose entirely consistent with the prevailing "core" meaning of the term "commerce":

> An unrestrained intercourse between the States themselves will advance the trade of each by an interchange of their respective productions, not only for the supply of reciprocal wants at home, but for exportation to foreign markets. The veins of commerce in every part will be replenished and will acquire additional motion and vigor from a free circulation of the commodities of every part. Commercial enterprise will have much greater scope from the diversity in the productions of different States.[22]

In *Federalist* 12, he referred to the "rivalship," now silenced, "between agriculture and commerce,"[23] while in *Federalist* 17, he distinguished between the power to regulate such national matters as commerce and "the supervision of agriculture and of other concerns of a similar nature, all those things, in short, which are proper to be provided for by local legislation."[24] In *Federalist* 21, Hamilton maintained that causes of the wealth of nations were of "an infinite variety," including "[s]ituation, soil, climate, the nature of the productions, the nature of the government, the genius of the citizens, the degree of information they possess, the state of commerce, of arts, of industry."[25] In *Federalist* 35, he asked, "Will not the merchant understand and be disposed to cultivate, as far as may be proper, the interests of the mechanic and manufacturing arts to which his commerce is so nearly allied?"[26]

In none of the sixty-three appearances of the term "commerce" in *The Federalist* is it ever used to refer unambiguously to any activity beyond trade or exchange. At the time of the framing, then, even for a proponent of broad national powers such as Hamilton, the term "commerce" in the Constitution referred to trade or exchange, not to the production of items to be traded, and certainly not to all gainful activity. Even later, with the contentiousness of the Constitution's adoption behind him, Hamilton's usage did not change. As secretary of the treasury, Hamilton's official opinion to President Washington advocating a broad congressional power to incorporate a national bank repeatedly referred to Congress's power under the Commerce Clause as the power to regulate the "trade between the States."[27]

---

[22] *Federalist* 11, 89 (Hamilton).
[23] *Federalist* 12, 91 (Hamilton).
[24] *Federalist* 17, 118 (Hamilton).
[25] *Federalist* 21, 141 (Hamilton).
[26] *Federalist* 35, 216 (Hamilton).
[27] Alexander Hamilton, "Final Version of an Opinion on the Constitutionality of an Act to Establish a Bank" (February 23, 1791), in Harold C. Syrett et al., eds., *The Papers of Alexander Hamilton*, vol. 8 (New York: Columbia University Press, 1965), 97, 100. See also ibid., 118 (referring to "the regulation of trade between the states").

Ratification Conventions. Having examined every use of the term "commerce" that appears in the reports of the state ratification conventions, I found that the term was uniformly used to refer to trade or exchange. I found no example where it unambiguously referred to all gainful activity. Of course, people used the word "commerce" to convey its accustomed meaning, so they neither defined it nor often gave contextual clues as to what it meant to them. Nevertheless, some public speeches make clear that "commerce" was used as a synonym for trade or exchange— and did not include agriculture, manufacturing, or other business; every speech is consistent with such a narrow meaning (though two statements can be misinterpreted as connoting a broader meaning of "commerce"). I will present this evidence state by state.

In the records of the Massachusetts convention, the word "commerce" is used nineteen times—every use consistent with its meaning trade, mostly foreign trade; and no use clearly indicating a broader meaning. The most explicit distinction was made by Thomas Dawes, a prominent revolutionary and legislator, who began his discussion on the importance of the national taxation powers. "We have suffered," said he, "for want of such authority in the federal head. This will be evident if we take a short view of our agriculture, commerce, and manufactures."[28] He then expounded at some length, giving separate attention to each of these activities and the beneficial effect the Constitution would have on them. Under the heading of "commerce," he referred to "our own domestic traffic that passes from state to state."[29]

Only two other speakers in the Massachusetts convention implicitly distinguished between "commerce" and other economic activities. Charles Turner referred to "the deplorable state of our navigation and commerce, and various branches of business thereon dependent."[30] Making much the same point, James Bowdoin argued that the existing confederation lacked the power to retaliate against foreign nations who placed restrictions on American exports:

> Hence a decrease of our commerce and navigation, and the duties and revenue arising from them. Hence an insufficient demand for the produce of our lands, and the consequent discouragement of agriculture. Hence the inability to pay debts, and particularly taxes, which by that decrease are enhanced. And hence, as the necessary result of all these, the emigration of our inhabitants.[31]

[28] Elliot, *Debates*, 2: 57.
[29] Ibid., 58.
[30] Ibid., 170.
[31] Ibid., 83.

While each of these further consequences flowed from a decrease of "our commerce and navigation," they were not the same thing as commerce.

In the few fragments that survive of the Maryland, Connecticut, and New Hampshire ratification debates, the term "commerce" is mentioned only once. In the opening address to the Connecticut convention, Oliver Elsworth referred to the Swiss, who "[t]ill lately," he said, "had neither commerce nor manufactures. They were merely a set of herdsmen."[32] By contrast, in the more extensive records of the New York convention, the term appears thirty times. Governor Clinton referred to "[t]he situation of [each state's] commerce, its agriculture, and the system of its resources."[33] Another delegate questioned the need for the new central government by noting the rapid economic progress: "How [the country's] agriculture, commerce, and manufactures have been extended and improved!"[34]

The New York delegate who repeatedly made the clearest distinction between commerce and other economic activity was Alexander Hamilton. As part of a lengthy speech, he observed: "The Southern States possess certain staples,—tobacco, rice, indigo, &c.,—which must be capital objects in treaties of commerce with foreign nations."[35] The same distinction is implicit in his denial that the regulation of commerce was outside the competency of a central government: "What are the objects of the government? Commerce, taxation, &c. In order to comprehend the interests of commerce, is it necessary to know how wheat is raised, and in what proportion it is produced in one district and in another? By no means."[36] Later, in defending the power of direct taxation, Hamilton predicted that in its absence, the "general government . . . will push imposts [on our commerce] to an extreme."[37] As a result, "[o]ur neighbors, not possessed of our advantages for commerce and agriculture, will become manufacturers: their property will, in a great measure, be vested in the commodities of their own productions; but a small proportion will be in trade or in lands. Thus, on the gentleman's scheme, they will be almost free from burdens, while we shall be loaded with them."[38]

Although there is no example in New York of a clear use of "commerce" in any sense broader than trade or exchange, two statements might mistakenly be so interpreted. In one, Hamilton argued that "one man can be as fully acquainted with the general state of the commerce,

[32] Ibid., 188.
[33] Ibid., 261.
[34] Ibid., 336.
[35] Ibid., 237.
[36] Ibid., 255.
[37] Ibid., 369.
[38] Ibid.

manufactures, population, production, and common resources of a state, which are the proper objects of federal legislation."[39] Although here, as elsewhere, he uses the term "commerce" narrowly, this passage might be read to indicate that the entire list of activities fell within the power of Congress to regulate commerce among the states. Taken in context, this would be a misreading. Hamilton is contending here, as he did throughout his career and as did many others, that the advancement of all these economic activities was the proper goal of national legislation. He is not speaking of the specific powers granted to Congress by the Constitution to pursue these goals, such as the power of taxation and the power to regulate commerce with foreign nations or among the states.[40]

Referring to the same problem of knowledge, Anti-Federalist Melancton Smith asserted:

> To understand the true *commercial interests* of a country, not only requires just ideas of the general *commerce* of the world, but also, and principally, a knowledge of the *productions* of your own country, and their value, what your soil is capable of producing, the nature of your *manufactures*, and the capacity of the country to increase both.[41]

Although this statement employs the term "commercial interests" broadly, it still uses the narrow conception of "commerce" as distinct from "productions" and "manufactures" as included among these "commercial" interests.

Smith's statement is especially useful because some of the quotations employed by those who have claimed a broader meaning for the term "commerce" actually refer to "commercial interest," not "commerce."[42]

[39] Ibid., 265–66.

[40] The same is true of Chancellor Livingston's argument that "Some gentlemen suppose that, to understand and provide for the general interests of commerce and manufactures, our legislators ought to know how all commodities are produced, from the first principle of vegetation to the last polish of mechanical labor; that they ought to be minutely acquainted with all the process of all the arts. If this were true, it would be necessary that a great part of the British House of Commons should be woollen-drapers; yet we seldom find such characters in that celebrated assembly" (ibid., 275).

[41] Ibid., 245 (emphasis added).

[42] See, e.g., Grant S. Nelson and Robert J. Pushaw, Jr., "Rethinking the Commerce Clause: Applying First Principles to Uphold Federal Commercial Regulations but Preserve State Control over Social Issues," *Iowa Law Review* 85 (1999): 1 at 40 n. 163 (citing Charles Pinckney's reference at the Constitutional Convention to the five "commercial interests" of the American states as including staple crops such as "wheat," "tobacco," and "Rice & Indigo," as well as "fisheries" and "trade," as evidence that he held a broad view of "commerce"). Pinckney's statement can be read as enumerating the different sources of various articles of commerce throughout the states. In no way does his list comprehend all gainful activities. In addition, we shall see below that Pinckney publicly used the term "commerce" in the narrow sense.

By explicitly using "commercial interests" to convey a broader meaning than the term "commerce," we can see that statements using the phrase "commercial interest" should not be viewed as synonymous with "commerce" itself. The original meaning of the regulatory powers granted to Congress might have been broader had Article I, Section 8 granted it the power "to regulate the commercial *interests* of the States" rather than the power to regulate only "commerce."[43]

The term "commerce" appears only eight times in the report of the Pennsylvania ratification convention. All uses are consistent with the narrow meaning of "commerce"; none clearly uses a broader meaning. Only three uses add any context to the term, and all are by James Wilson, a member of the Constitutional Convention. Wilson referred to "the objects of commerce,"[44] suggesting items being traded. Later he asked, "Is it not an important object to extend our manufactures and our commerce? This cannot be done, unless a proper security is provided for the regular discharge of contracts. This security cannot be obtained, unless we give the power of deciding upon those contracts to the general government."[45] His most revealing comment suggesting a strong distinction between "commerce" and other economic activities was this:

> Suppose we reject this system of government; what will be the consequence? Let the farmer say, he whose produce remains unasked for; nor can he find a single market for its consumption, though his fields are blessed with luxuriant abundance. Let the manufacturer, and let the mechanic, say; they can feel, and tell their feelings. Go along the wharves of Philadelphia, and observe the melancholy silence that reigns. . . . Let the merchants tell you what is our commerce.[46]

In the North Carolina debates, "commerce" is mentioned eighteen times (including two instances in proposed amendments). As elsewhere, there are no clear uses of it in any sense broader than "trade" or "exchange" and a few clear examples of its use in the narrow sense in speeches by William Davie. Davie defined the "general objects of the union" to be "1st, to protect us against foreign invasion; 2nd, to defend us against internal commotions and insurrections; 3rd, to promote the commerce, agriculture, and manufactures, of America."[47] Later, he explained why the regulation of commerce, though distinct from agriculture and manufacturing, promoted them: "Commerce, sir, is the nurse of both. The merchant furnishes the planter with such articles as he cannot manu-

---

[43] Although, as will be seen below, the original meaning of "between the States" might still have greatly limited the scope of this power.

[44] Elliot, *Debates*, 467.

[45] Ibid., 492.

[46] Ibid., 524.

[47] Ibid., 4:17.

facture himself, and finds him a market for his produce. Agriculture cannot flourish if commerce languishes; they are mutually dependent on each other."[48] Davie also distinguished between the interests "of agriculture and commerce" and how the Constitution would protect just claims of "the merchant or farmer."[49] Merchants were those who bought and sold goods; it was they, not farmers or artisans, who engaged in commerce.

In the reports of the South Carolina convention, the word "commerce" is used twenty-six times. Charles Pinckney, who had been a delegate to the Constitutional Convention, equated "the regulation of commerce" and mere "privileges with regard to shipping," when he asked, "[i]f our government is to be founded on equal compact, what inducement can [the Eastern states] possibly have to be united with us, if we do not grant them some privileges with regard to their shipping?"[50] Later, he distinguished between those "people [who] are employed in cultivating their own lands" and "the rest [who are] in handicraft and commerce."[51] And he immediately expanded upon this by discussing the different "classes" of society comprising the "commercial men," the "professional men," those engaged in "the mechanical," and the "landed interest—the owners and cultivators of the soil."[52] Although Pinckney contended that all the other classes should be subservient to the promotion of the last, he defended commerce from the criticism that it was "generally cheating."[53] No other use of the term in South Carolina connoted a broader meaning of "commerce"; all uses were entirely compatible with the terms "trade" or "exchange."

Virginia wins the prize for the most mentions of the word: seventy-four. Here, as elsewhere, there is not a single instance of "commerce" being used unambiguously in the broader sense. To the contrary, the most striking evidence is the dominance of a conception of commerce that is even narrower than "trade" or "exchange"—also manifested by Pinckney's reference in the South Carolina debates to "privileges with regard to shipping." In Virginia, I count at least seventeen references that link "commerce" in some way to ports, shipping, navigation, or the "carrying trades." In other words, on these occasions, the term "commerce" is lim-

---

[48] Ibid., 20.

[49] Ibid., 159.

[50] Ibid., 284.

[51] Ibid., 321.

[52] Ibid., 321–22.

[53] Ibid., 322 (stating that "there are some kinds of commerce not only fair and valuable, but such as ought to be encouraged by government").

ited to conveying or transporting the articles of trade, rather than to the entire act of trading.[54]

For example, Richard Henry Lee asked those who doubted the need for the Constitution to "go to our seaports; let him see our commerce languishing—not an American bottom to be seen."[55] Edmund Randolph urged members to "[c]ast your eyes to your seaports: see how commerce languishes."[56] He observed that "Virginia is in a very unhappy position with respect to the access of foes by sea, though happily situated for commerce,"[57] and that "[a]s it is the spirit of commercial nations to engross as much as possible the carrying trade, this makes it necessary to defend our commerce."[58] Like Lee and Randolph, Francis Corbin also referred to those ports

> where we had every reason to see the fleets of all nations, he will behold but a few trifling little boats; he will every where see commerce languish; the disconsolate merchant, with his arms folded, ruminating, in despair, on the wretched ruins of his fortune, and deploring the impossibility of retrieving it.[59]

Future Chief Justice John Marshall asked whether "the Algerines . . . and every other predatory or maritime nation, [cannot] pillage our ships and destroy our commerce, without subjecting themselves to any inconvenience?"[60] Madison asserted that "American vessels, if they can do it with advantage, may carry on the commerce of the contending nations."[61] William Grayson stated that the riches of all those "maritime powers of Europe . . . come by sea. Commerce and navigation are the principal sources of their wealth."[62] And, echoing Marshall, James Innes asked, "Is it not in the power of any maritime power to seize our vessels, and destroy our commerce, with impunity?"[63]

I do not present these quotations to show that the original meaning of the term "commerce" was limited to shipping. Surely shipping was so

---

[54] On the other hand, these usages could be construed as somewhat expanding the scope of "commerce" to include trade and exchange, as well as transporting for these purposes. Even so expanded, however, the original meaning of "commerce" would not embrace agriculture, manufacturing, or other productive activity. I will discuss this at greater length below in the context of *Gibbons v. Ogden*.

[55] Eliot, *Debates*, 3:43.
[56] Ibid., 66.
[57] Ibid., 72.
[58] Ibid., 78.
[59] Ibid., 105.
[60] Ibid., 235.
[61] Ibid., 249.
[62] Ibid., 428.
[63] Ibid., 635.

closely identified with commerce because it was at that time the indispensable means for the movement of goods. One could easily extend this preoccupation with what is now called the "channels and instrumentalities" of commerce to railroads, canals, and air transport. But this close connection reinforces the narrow meaning of commerce and the purpose for granting Congress the power to regulate it. It also explains why the earliest cases involving the commerce power had to do with boats.[64]

Moreover, these were not the only references to "commerce" in Virginia. Others of the sort I have canvassed from elsewhere appear here as well. Edmund Pendleton, for instance, viewed "commerce" as the means by which "the people may have an opportunity of disposing of their crops at market, and of procuring such supplies as they may be in want of."[65] So synonymous was "commerce" with "trade" that William Grayson worried that "the whole commerce of the United States may be exclusively carried on by merchants residing within the seat of government."[66] He surely could not have been including agriculture or manufacturing in his definition of commerce.

Despite the strength and consistency of all this evidence, it is also true that persons participating in the process of drafting and ratifying the Constitution frequently used the phrase "trade and commerce."[67] In the absence of the evidence already presented, this might suggest that these terms were not identical. On the other hand, if "commerce" is given its broadest connotation as "gainful activity," it would include "trade" within its meaning, and this phrase would still make little sense. Instead, it appears that the phrase "trade and commerce" was something of a couplet like "cease and desist" or, as they say in Disney World, a "full and complete" stop. The couplet "trade and commerce" refers to a single activity that could be, and usually was, called either trade or commerce. Indeed, on two occasions, state convention delegates referred to the power to "regulate trade" rather than to the power to regulate "commerce."[68]

Should there be any doubt about my interpretation of these statements, go back to the quotations in which there is a context provided and replace

[64] See, e.g., *Gibbons v. Ogden*, 22 U.S. (9 Wheat.) 1 (1824) (invalidating an exclusive navigation license granted by the New York state legislature). I shall discuss *Gibbons* at greater length below.

[65] Elliot, *Debates*, 3:295.

[66] Ibid., 291.

[67] See. e.g., Farrand, *Records*, 1:243, 263.

[68] See Elliot, *Debates*, 2:80 ("Why not give Congress power only to regulate trade?"); ibid., 4:70 ("[I]t was well known he was for giving power to Congress to regulate the trade of the United States"). It is possible, although I think implausible given the context, to infer that these two speakers were advocating a power narrower than the power to regulate "commerce."

the term "commerce" with the term "gainful activity." All of these sentences would be rendered incoherent. Nor are these statements to be dismissed because they occur in partisan debate. Remember, we are not asking what purposes or intentions these delegates are expressing. We are just asking how they used the term "commerce." So far as these records permit us to judge, both proponents and opponents of the Constitution used the term in the same way.

From these findings, we can conclude that if anyone in the Constitutional Convention or the state ratification conventions used "commerce" to refer to something more comprehensive than "trade" or "exchange," either they failed to make explicit that meaning or their comments were not recorded for posterity. The surviving evidence on this point is entirely consistent and confirms the observation made by Madison late in his life that "[i]f, in citing the Constitution, the word *trade* was put in the place of *commerce*, the word *foreign* made it synonymous with commerce. Trade and commerce are, in fact, used indiscriminately, both in books and in conversation."[69]

General Usage: The Pennsylvania Gazette.   One practical problem of establishing the historical meaning of a particular term is the inability to discern whether particular examples are aberrations or represent the mainstream use of a term. Language, after all, is susceptible of many uses, some commonplace, others idiosyncratic, metaphoric, or poetic. Until recently it was difficult to know whether the evidence of usage offered by a particular historian was typical or cherry-picked.[70] For this reason, I surveyed every use of the term "commerce" in the Constitutional Convention, Ratification Debates, and *The Federalist*. I did not expect usage to be uniform, but hoped rather to be able to detect what usage was normal and what usage was aberrational. Hence my surprise at finding that usage was consistently narrow where the context supplied meaning.

Some may respond that the general public would have taken the word in its broader sense notwithstanding how participants in the drafting or ratification processes might have used the term. They might claim that "many of the citizens who ratified the Constitution likely understood 'commerce' in this larger sense."[71] To assess this claim, I designed a survey of every use of the term "commerce" in the *Pennsylvania Gazette* that

---

[69] Madison, *Letters*, 4:233 (letter to Professor Davis, not sent, 1832).

[70] By "cherry-picked" I do not mean to suggest any impropriety. Until the advent of electronic searches it was impractical to conduct comprehensive empirical surveys of the sort I present here.

[71] Robert J. Pushaw, Jr., and Grant S. Nelson, "A Critique of the Narrow Interpretation of the Commerce Clause," *Northwestern University Law Review* 96 (2002): 695, at 700.

appeared from 1728 to 1800.[72] The *Pennsylvania Gazette*, which from 1729 to 1766 was published by Benjamin Franklin,[73] "in its essential character, although not in its unusual longevity, . . . was representative of the great majority of the newspapers of the provincial period."[74] If the term "commerce" had a readily understood broad meaning, one would expect it to have made its appearance in this typical newspaper whose publication spanned the colonial and postcolonial period. If the term "commerce" was indeed ambiguous, one could detect which of the multiple meanings of "commerce" was most common.

From 1728 to 1800, the term "commerce" appeared 1,594 times.[75] The earliest use of the term appeared in 1728 and referred to "commerce" as "the Affairs of Merchandize."[76] One of the latest in 1798 refers to a 1765 caricature in which the messenger god Mercury was used to signify commerce. A 1787 entry defines the term explicitly: "[B]y commerce I mean the exports as well as the imports of a country. . . ."[77] A 1773 entry notes the existence of "the Royal College of Physicians, and the Society for the Encouragement of Arts, Manufactures and Commerce."[78] But these are mere pinpricks of data.

As with the data I reported from the drafting and ratification proceedings, the term "commerce" was routinely used to refer to trade or exchange, including shipping. Indeed, so identified was "commerce" with

[72] For details of the survey methodology, see Randy E. Barnett, "New Evidence of the Original Meaning of the Commerce Clause," *Arkansas Law Review* 55 (2003), at 865–57.

[73] Clarence S. Brigham, *History and Bibliography of American Newspapers, 1690–1820* (Worcester, Mass.: American Antiquarian Society, 1947), 2:933–34. Although the electronic archives end at 1800, Brigham dates the demise of the paper as 1815. Ibid., 934.

[74] Charles E. Clark and Charles Wetherell, "The Measure of Maturity: The Pennsylvania Gazette from 1728–1765," *William and Mary Quarterly* 46 (1989): 279–80.

[75] A brief note on the methodology employed. When this survey was made, the Accessible Archives database was divided into the following periods, 1728–50, 1751–65, 1766–83, and 1784–1800. At the time of this study, each period had to be searched separately and, if there were more than five hundred hits during any period, only a random selection of five hundred results would be displayed. The periods before 1750 each had fewer than five hundred hits, but after 1750 the number of hits per period exceeds five hundred. Therefore, to ensure that every example was surveyed, it was necessary to search the periods after 1750 year by year with a search string of the following type: <commerce & 1766>. Extraneous references to articles containing somewhere within them the date searched for, for example, 1766, but that were published in some other year were easily identified by their heading and ignored. I was told by Accessible Archives that they will be redesigning the search engine to make this sort of effort unnecessary.

[76] October 1, 1728 (#1). Citations to the database will be by date and the unique item number of each entry. Any entry cited here can be retrieved through a search for <commerce & [item number]> (except for item #1, which can be found through a search for <commerce & "october 1 1728">).

[77] March 7, 1787 (#73694).

[78] December 29, 1773 (#54627).

shipping that ninety-nine of the references were to ships named *Commerce*. Commerce was also routinely distinguished from agriculture and manufacturing. As shown by the passage from the January 13, 1790, issue at the head of this chapter, no redundancy or "couplet" could possibly have been intended by the use of this triad. As with the evidence surrounding the drafting and ratification of the Constitution, each is considered a distinct activity. With these data, as before, commerce is typically associated with merchants, which should come as no surprise since both terms share the same common root, "*merci*" or merchandise. For example, "As a Merchant, it was thought that no Person amongst us understood Commerce in general, and the trading Interests of this Province in particular, better than he. . . ."[79]

Even those claiming that "commerce" had a broad meaning agree it had a narrow meaning as well. For this reason, it was necessary to survey every use of the term to see how often, if ever, a broad meaning was conveyed. If this occurred only rarely, then the public would not have been deceived by the framers' decision to employ "commerce" to convey a narrow meaning. As before, the evidence of original meaning is overwhelming. A reasonable speaker of English would have understood the term "commerce" in the Commerce Clause in its narrow sense.

JUDICIAL INTERPRETATIONS OF COMMERCE, 1824–1935

The Marshall Court. Thirty-five years after ratification, in the 1824 case of *Gibbons v. Ogden*,[80] John Marshall was called upon to decide whether navigation was included in the power of Congress to regulate commerce among the states. He held that it was. From the perspective of original intent, this holding is unremarkable. The above sources, and others unmentioned,[81] make clear the intention to subject shipping and navigation to the regulation of Congress. The interpretive challenge is in determining exactly how, if at all, navigation is included in the original meaning of the text. Was it a part of the term "commerce" itself? Or was the regulation of navigation incidental to the regulation of commerce and therefore authorized by the Necessary and Proper Clause? Then there is always the possibility that the framers used words the original meaning

[79] December 5, 1754 (#17724).

[80] 22 U.S. (9 Wheat.) 1 (1824).

[81] Several proposals in the Constitutional Convention to require a supermajority for the passage of navigation acts make it clear that such acts were thought to be within the powers of Congress even after the Convention moved to an enumeration of powers. See, for example, Farrand, *Records*, 2:143 (proposal in Edmund Randolph's handwriting to the Committee of Detail); ibid., 169 (proposal in James Wilson's handwriting to Committee of Detail); ibid., 183 (proposal of Committee of Detail). The Committee eventually struck the proposal. See ibid., 400.

of which did not accurately express their intentions, and so they failed to include a power over "navigation" though they believed they had.

Although the sources I have examined do not provide indisputable answers to these questions, on balance, I think navigation appears to be included within the meaning of the term "commerce" because of its intimate connection to the activity of trading. Indeed, the etymology of the term "commerce" is "with" (*com*) "merchandise" (*merci*),[82] a phrase that could accurately be applied to the "carrying trade," which is how the object of navigation laws was frequently described. Perhaps the strongest evidence that "commerce" included navigation is in Article I, Section 9, where Congress is forbidden to enact any "Regulation of Commerce" that gives preference "to the Ports of one State over those of another: nor shall Vessels bound to, or from, one State, be obliged to enter, clear, or pay Duties in another." Although regulations concerning imports that might favor one port over another could be considered simply rules governing trade or exchange, laws governing the movement of vessels, the enactment of which are partially restricted by this clause, would appear to be rules concerning navigation or the transportation of articles of commerce.

In the Philadelphia convention, the extensive debate over whether "navigation acts" should require a supermajority occurred explicitly in the context of the power to regulate commerce.[83] For instance, John Rutledge of South Carolina contended that "[i]t did not follow from a grant of the power to regulate trade, that it would be abused. At the worst a navigation act could bear hard a little while only on the S[outhern] States."[84] The sort of navigation act contemplated here was an "act encouraging American bottoms & seamen"[85] that would incidentally raise the price of freight[86] and so impact adversely exporting interests.

Moreover, there is a hint that the term "commerce" included navigation in the fact that—like "commerce and trade"—the couplet "commerce and navigation" appears, by my count, four times during the ratification debates, twice in Massachusetts and twice in Virginia.[87] On two of these

[82] See *Oxford English Dictionary*, 2d ed., vol. 3 (Oxford: Oxford University Press, 1989), 552 (*com*—"with"; *merci*—"merchandise").

[83] See Farrand, *Records*, 2:449–53.

[84] Ibid., 452 (statement of John Rutledge).

[85] Ibid., 450 (statement of Gouverneur Morris).

[86] See ibid., 451 (statement of James Madison that "the disadvantage to the S[outhern] States from a navigation act, lay chiefly in a temporary rise of freight").

[87] See Elliot, *Debates*, 3:428 (statement of Mr. Grayson of Virginia that "Commerce and navigation are the principal sources of" the wealth of the maritime nations of Europe); ibid., 604 (statement of Mr. Mason of Virginia referring to the opinion expressed by another delegate that "with respect to commerce and navigation, . . . their regulation, as it now stands, was a sine qua non of the Union, and that without it the states in Convention would never concur").

occasions, "commerce and navigation" was distinguished from "various branches of business thereon dependent"[88] as well as specifically from agriculture.[89] Even expanded to include navigation or transportation, then, commerce is still distinguishable from production. If the public at the time of ratification understood the term "commerce" in the Constitution to include trade, exchange, and navigation, then that is its original meaning.

On the other hand, though enactment of "navigation laws" was widely thought to be within the power of Congress, several statements suggest that such laws were considered by some at least to be distinct from regulations of commerce and that the term "navigation" was neither synonymous with nor subsumed within the term "commerce." The Virginia and North Carolina ratification conventions formally proposed that the Constitution be amended to state "That no navigation law, or law regulating commerce, shall be passed without the consent of two thirds of the members present, in both houses."[90] This proposed amendment both assumes that Congress has power to pass navigation laws and distinguishes such laws from regulations of commerce.

If this and other like evidence is accepted, the admitted power to pass navigation laws is most accurately conceived as an implied power that was embraced by the Necessary and Proper Clause. In which case, the congressional power to regulate transportation is proper only insofar as it is necessary to effectuate the regulation of trade and exchange between state and state. Even statements warmly supporting the enactment of navigation laws suggest that such laws were thought a necessary means to protect commerce rather than the regulation of commerce itself. As Edmund Randoph observed to the Virginia convention:

> As it is the spirit of commercial nations to engross as much as possible the carrying trade, this makes it necessary to defend our commerce. But how shall we compass this end? England has arisen to the greatest height, in modern times, by her navigation act, and other excellent regulations. The same means would produce the same effects.[91]

But even this statement could be read as including navigation in the definition of "commerce."

---

[88] Ibid., 2:170 (statement of Mr. Turner of Massachusetts referring to "the deplorable state of our navigation and commerce, and various branches of business thereon dependent").

[89] Ibid., 83 (statement of Mr. Bowdoin of Massachusetts referring to "a decrease of our commerce and navigation, and the duties and revenue arising from them. Hence an insufficient demand for the produce of our lands, and the consequent discouragement of agriculture").

[90] Elliot, *Debates*, 3:660 (proposal of Virginia); ibid., 4:245 (proposal of North Carolina). See also ibid., 2:552–53 (same amendment disapproved by Maryland convention).

[91] Ibid., 3:78.

In *Gibbons*, Marshall reached his conclusion that navigation was included in the term "commerce" by relying on the definition of "commerce" as "intercourse."[92] This was indeed the first definition of "commerce" offered in Johnson's dictionary. Johnson, however, defines "intercourse" as "1. Commerce; exchange" and "2. Communication: followed by *with*," so it is not at all clear that the meaning of "intercourse" (especially when not "followed by with") was itself much broader than trade and exchange. Moreover, it is difficult to imagine that John Marshall, much less the founders, believed that the term "commerce" in the Constitution embraced noncommercial intercourse or every form of intercourse. Although the term "intercourse" appears sixty-three times in the records of the ratification debates (sometimes with a broader meaning), on each of the six times it is used in conjunction with "commercial," it is a clear reference to foreign trade—though these examples of usage might also be broad enough to include transport for purposes of trade.[93] And while "intercourse" sometimes had a broader meaning, we must never forget that the Constitution speaks of "commerce," not the "regulation of intercourse" among the states.

The Progressive Era Court. By the time of the Progressive Era, the meaning of commerce had not changed and the Supreme Court accepted the limited conception of commerce as "trade and exchange." As early as the 1895 case of *United States v. E.C. Knight Co.*[94] and as late as the 1936 case of *Carter v. Carter Coal Co.*,[95] the Court drew a distinction between "production"—such as manufacturing, agriculture, or mining—and "commerce" or trade in the things produced. As Chief Justice Fuller wrote in *E.C. Knight*: "Commerce succeeds to manufacture, and is not a part

---

[92] 22 U.S. (9 Wheat) at 189–90 ("Commerce, undoubtedly, is traffic, but it is something more: it is intercourse. It describes the commercial intercourse between nations, and parts of nations, in all its branches, and is regulated by prescribing rules for carrying on that intercourse"). It is worth noting that Chief Justice Marshall did not suggest that navigation was covered because "commerce" included the trade or exchange of services for money.

[93] The term "commercial intercourse" is used six times by four speakers at two conventions. See Elliot, *Debates*, 3:344 (statement of Mr. Monroe of Virginia referring to "a commercial intercourse between the United States and Spain"); ibid., 365 (statement of Mr. Corbin of Virginia referring to treaties "being a regulation of commercial intercourse between different nations"); ibid., 4: 119 (statement of Mr. Davie of North Carolina referring to "that commercial intercourse, which, founded on the universal protection of private property, has, in a measure, made the world one nation"); ibid., 221 (statement of Mr. Iredell of North Carolina that "At the beginning of the late war with Great Britain, the Parliament thought proper to stop all commercial intercourse with the American provinces").

[94] 156 U.S. 1 (holding that the Sherman Act did not apply to manufacturing trusts).

[95] 298 U.S. 238, 298 (1936) (ruling that Congress could not regulate the conditions under which coal is produced before it became an article of commerce).

of it. . . . The fact that an article is manufactured for export to another State does not of itself make it an article of interstate commerce."[96] And in *Carter Coal*, Justice Sutherland defined "commerce" as "the equivalent of the phrase 'intercourse for the purpose of trade.' "[97] "Mining" he explained, "brings the subject matter of commerce into existence. Commerce disposes of it."[98] Sutherland's definition harks back to Marshall's use of "intercourse" without the unwarranted suggestion that "commerce" embraces every form of intercourse. It also seems a reasonable definition of the term "commercial intercourse."

With this conception of "commerce," the power of Congress to regulate the economy was sharply restricted. It is no surprise, therefore, that these decisions were roundly condemned by political and academic proponents of national control of the entire economy.[99] As was to be expected, the Court was criticized for its failure to acknowledge that the meaning of the Constitution must evolve to meet changing circumstance.[100] More surprisingly, however, in light of the historical evidence presented here, the Court was also harshly criticized for distorting the original meaning of "commerce."

ACADEMICS DISPUTE THE ORIGINAL MEANING OF "COMMERCE"

In their influential little book, *The Power to Govern: The Constitution—Then and Now*, published in 1937, Walton Hamilton and Douglass Adair castigate the Court for imposing its conception of commerce on the founding generation in defiance of the historical understanding. "A narrowing of the concept 'commerce,' " they confidently assert, "is at odds with [the Fathers'] contemporary usage."[101] But though they pick quotations from the ratification debates reflecting the demand for stronger national governance, they reveal little of the evidence of usage also to be found there[102] or in the notes of the Philadelphia convention that I have summarized here. Instead, they rely primarily on five pages of quotations from a pamphlet by Tench Coxe, written before the Constitutional Convention, in which he argues for a sweeping national control over the economy, and on Hamilton's 1791 Report on Manufactures, which Coxe is reputed to have helped draft.

[96] 156 U.S. at 12–13.

[97] 298 U.S. at 298.

[98] Ibid., 304.

[99] See, for example, Hamilton and Adair, *The Power to Govern*, 184–94.

[100] Ibid., 191–94.

[101] Ibid., 181.

[102] But see ibid., 163 (quoting William Davie's reference to "commerce, agriculture, and manufactures of America" and his assertion that "Commerce, sir, is the nurse of both" without commenting on the distinction explicit in Davie's usage).

Hamilton, it will be recalled, proposed to the Constitutional Convention a plan of government in which the legislature would have the power to pass all laws "whatsoever"[103] subject only to a negative by the president. His plan was never considered and, as we have seen, a general grant of powers to the Congress was rejected by the Convention in favor of an enumeration. For the rest of his career, Hamilton never wavered in his efforts on behalf of expanding the power of the national government. Despite this, when he wrote as Publius in *The Federalist*, when he spoke at the New York ratification convention, and in his opinion supporting the constitutionality of a national bank, Hamilton used the word "commerce" in its ordinary narrow sense.

In 1953, this originalist criticism of the Supreme Court's definition of "commerce" during the Progressive Era was picked up and greatly expanded by William Crosskey in his massive book, *Politics and the Constitution in the History of the United States*.[104] Like Adair and Douglass, Crosskey deliberately avoids consulting the Philadelphia or state conventions for evidence of usage, focusing instead on an extensive canvass of pre-Revolutionary and pre-Constitutional sources, such as John Dickinson's 1765 pamphlet, *The Late Regulations Respecting the British Colonies Considered*.[105] "The samples of word-usage and juristic and political discussion . . . will . . . all be drawn . . . from sources not connected with the Constitution."[106] Indeed, Crosskey claims this omission as a virtue:

> For, by using such materials, a dictionary can be made which will not, it is conceived, be open to the many natural suspicions that arise from the known or suspected political bias of speakers and writers on the Constitution. And in consequence of this, it should lead to constitutional conclusions having a very high and singular cogency.[107]

Unfortunately, Crosskey omits to tell readers how convenient to his thesis was his methodological choice since he remains silent on how the excluded sources differ from the evidence he emphasized. Moreover, when considering evidence of word usage, as Crosskey purports to do, this omission was completely unnecessary because these words were used to convey the same meaning by both proponents and opponents of the Constitution.

---

[103] Farrand, *Records*, 1:291.

[104] William Winslow Crosskey, *Politics and the Constitution in the History of the United States* (Chicago: University of Chicago Press, 1953).

[105] Dickenson's pamphlet was written at a time when the plenary power of England to govern the affairs of the colonies was politically difficult to question. Late in life Jefferson recalled his opposition to what he called "the half-way house of John Dickinson who admitted that England had a right to regulate our commerce, and to lay duties on it for the purposes of regulation, but not of raising revenue." *Writings of Thomas Jefferson*, 1:14.

[106] Crosskey, *Politics and the Constitution*, 5.

[107] Ibid., 5–6.

It is striking the degree to which these authors, whose tone is nothing if not self-righteous toward those who do not share their views, completely ignore the evidence of usage that the records of the drafting and ratification process reveal. I do not dispute that many before and after the Constitution strongly favored a national government powerful enough to govern all "gainful activities." I dispute only, on the strength of the evidence of usage presented here, that a government of so unlimited a power was adopted in 1789. Owing to their highly selective treatment of the evidence, neither of these works calls this conclusion into serious question.

The Original Meaning of "Among the Several States"

Even if "commerce" had a meaning as broad as any "gainful activity," the implications of this may be less than is commonly believed. The reach of even a broad conception of "commerce" is confined by the meaning of the rest of the clause—that is, by the phrases "among the several States" and "to regulate."

ORIGINALIST EVIDENCE

The Text. Textual analysis of the Commerce Clause strongly supports a conclusion that the phrase "among the several States" refers to "between people of different states." If this phrase included commerce between people of the same state that takes place wholly within a single state, the Commerce Clause would then embrace all commerce. This interpretation would render the phrase "among the several States" superfluous. The only reason for listing the three commerce powers of Congress is to exclude some type of commerce from the power of Congress, and the only commerce that is excluded is commerce that occurs within a single state. Therefore, barring some extrinsic evidence that suggests another plausible possibility, we can safely conclude that the original meaning of "among the several States" to those who used and heard this phrase in the Constitution was commerce that occurred, in Hamilton's words, "between the States."[108] As Chief Justice Marshall wrote in *Gibbons v. Ogden*:

> The enumeration presupposes something not enumerated; and that something, if we regard the language or the subject of the sentence, must be the exclusively internal commerce of a State. . . . The completely internal commerce of a State, then, may be considered as reserved for the State itself.[109]

[108] *Federalist* 23, 153 (Hamilton) ("The principal purposes to be answered by union are these—the common defense of the members; the preservation of the public peace, as well as against internal convulsions as external attacks; the regulation of commerce with other nations and between the States; the superintendence of our intercourse, political and commercial, with foreign countries").

[109] 22 U.S. 1, 195 (1824).

Other evidence of usage confirms this conclusion.

The Federalist.   In *Federalist* 42, Madison clarifies that the purpose of the power to regulate commerce "among the several States" was to manage trade between people of different states and facilitate the essential power of regulating trade with foreign nations:

> The defect of power in the existing Confederacy to regulate the commerce between its several members is in the number of those which have been clearly pointed out by experience. . . . [W]ithout this *supplemental provision*, the great and essential power of regulating foreign commerce would have been incomplete and ineffectual. A very material object of this power was the relief of the States which import and export through other States from the improper contributions levied on them by the latter. Were these at liberty to *regulate the trade between State and State*, it must be foreseen that ways would be found out to load the articles of import and export, during the passage through their jurisdiction, with duties which would fall on the makers of the latter and the consumers of the former.[110]

In no way would such a power reach purely intrastate activities, whether gainful or not, a point that he emphasized again in *Federalist* 45:

> The powers delegated by the proposed Constitution to the federal government are few and defined. Those which are to remain in the State governments are numerous and indefinite. The former will be exercised principally on external objects, as war, peace, negotiation, and foreign commerce; with which last the power of taxation will, for the most part, be connected. The powers reserved to the several States will extend to all the objects which, in the ordinary course of affairs, concern the lives, liberties, and properties of the people, and the internal order, improvement, and prosperity of the State.[111]

Trade "between the States" was a usage that Hamilton would continue to employ when referring to the Commerce Clause while advocating, in his opinion to President Washington, that Congress had the power to incorporate a national bank.

Both the meaning of the term and the well-known purpose of the clause were made clear by Hamilton in *The Federalist*. Under the Articles of Confederation, the states had "fettered, interrupted and narrowed"[112] the flow of commerce from one state to another by protective legislation of all sorts.

---

[110] *Federalist* 42, 267–68 (Madison) (emphasis added).

[111] *Federalist* 45, 292–93 (Madison). See also ibid., 293 ("The regulation of commerce, it is true, is a new power; but that seems to be an addition which few oppose and from which no apprehensions are entertained").

[112] *Federalist* 11, 90 (Hamilton).

Apart from the need to negotiate treaties of commerce with other nations, the principal purpose for adopting a new Constitution was to deprive the states of the power to interfere with productive exchanges.

> An unrestrained intercourse *between the States* themselves will advance the trade of each by an *interchange* of their respective productions, not only for the supply of *reciprocal* wants at home, but for exportation to foreign markets. The veins of commerce in every part will be replenished and will acquire additional motion and vigor from a free circulation of the commodities of every part. Commercial enterprise will have much greater scope from the diversity in the productions of different States. When the staple of one fails from a bad harvest or unproductive crop, it can call to its aid the staple of another. The variety, not less than the value, of products for exportation contributes to the activity of foreign commerce. It can be conducted upon much better terms with a large number of materials of a given value than with a small number of materials of the same value, arising from the competitions of trade and from the fluctuations of markets.[113]

The Ratification Debates. At the New York convention, John Lansing, who had been a delegate in Philadelphia, praised the Commerce Clause and complained about "[t]he languishing situation of our commerce [that] has also been attributed to the impotence of Congress."[114] He then asserted that "all the states, excepting two, had passed laws to enable Congress to regulate commerce, and that those two were not indisposed to vest that power."[115] Lansing was referring here to the 1784 Act of Congress asking the states for the power to regulate the trade between different states.[116] In no way did this proposed act reach commerce or trade that lay solely within any state.[117]

Finally, the silence from the Southern states during ratification supports this interpretation. It can be asserted with certainty that the Southern states would never have ratified the Constitution if the power to regulate commerce among the states included the power to regulate the slave trade within a particular state, which was unquestionably and reprehensibly thought to be a form of commerce.[118] In my view, asking whether a partic-

---

[113] Ibid., 89–90 (emphasis added).

[114] Elliot, *Debates*, 2:218.

[115] Ibid.

[116] The act was ineffectual because most of the states that accepted the recommendation of Congress made their consent contingent on the unanimous acceptance of all the other states. When this did not occur, the measure failed. See Report of the States on the Regulation of Commerce, &c. Elliot, *Debates*, 1:108–9 (March 3, 1786).

[117] In fact, the act appears to have focused entirely on foreign commerce. See ibid., 106–8.

[118] See *Scott v. Sandford*, 60 U.S. 393, 408 (1858) ("Dred Scott") (describing the English government as "extensively engaged in this commerce"). See also ibid., 425 (describing slaves

ular meaning would have been agreed to by one group or another is not the best indication of the original meaning of any constitutional provision. At issue should be the public meaning of the term to which they did agree. Nonetheless, when supported by other types of evidence of original meaning, the fact that the slave trade was considered outside the power of Congress to regulate commerce "among the several States" bolsters our understanding of that phrase's public meaning.

Other Commentators.   Although this interpretation of "among the states" has been contested, most vigorously by William Crosskey,[119] there remains a scholarly and judicial consensus in favor of this as the original meaning.[120] Consistent with the scheme of federalism that motivated the granting to Congress of a power to regulate commerce among the states, trade that occurs wholly within a state was not commerce "among the states" and, therefore, the regulation of such commerce was not among the powers of Congress. As St. George Tucker explained: "The constitution of the United States does not authorise congress to regulate, or in any manner to interfere with, the domestic commerce of any state."[121] Tucker offered as, an example of such intrastate commerce, "a vessel wholly employed in that domestic commerce, seems not to be subject to the control of the laws of the United States."[122] Tucker allowed that federal law could punish or seize the vessels of persons who gave "aid or assistance to any fraudulent commerce, either with foreign parts, or between the states."[123] Congress "may also prescribe, or limit the terms and conditions, upon which vessels may be permitted to trade with foreign parts, or with other states."[124] Nevertheless, citing the Tenth Amendment, Tucker concluded that Congress, under its power to regulate commerce among the states, has "no constitutional right to control the intercourse between any two or more parts of the same state."[125]

---

as "subjects of commerce"). Below I shall also discuss the relationship between the Commerce Clause and the restriction on Congress's power to restrict the slave trade with other nations.

[119] See Crosskey, *Politics and the Constitution*, 50–83 (noting the difference between "among" and "between" and asserting that the natural meaning of "among the several states" included all commerce occurring within any state).

[120] See, for example, Nelson and Pushaw, "Rethinking the Commerce Clause," 42–49 (discussing deficiencies in Crosskey's interpretation of "among the States" and concluding: "Although Crosskey's interpretation is defensible, he did not marshal evidence strong enough to overcome the presumption that the regulation of commerce, like all federal power, does not extend purely to internal state affairs").

[121] Tucker, in appendix of *Blackstone's Commentaries*, 250, n.*.

[122] Ibid. Notice once again the close connection between "commerce" and navigation.

[123] Ibid.

[124] Ibid. By referring to a navigation law that limits "the terms and conditions, upon which vessels may be permitted to trade," Tucker's usage again suggests that navigation is subsumed within the meaning of trade or commerce.

[125] Ibid.

Adopting the narrower meaning of "among the several States" also reduces the significance of whether "commerce" is interpreted broadly to include any gainful activity or limited only to trade or exchange. For if Congress can regulate only gainful activity that takes place between people of different states, even the broader definition of commerce will not encompass much more than trade or exchange.

Thus, supposing the Progressive Era courts were wrong to exclude manufacturing, agriculture, and mining from the category of "commerce," they were onto something nonetheless. It is hard even to imagine either a good being manufactured or a crop being grown "among the states" or "between state and state" unless the factory or farm physically straddles a state line. Of course, when a company that manufactures goods or raises crops then sells them or transports them for gain from one state to another, this aspect of its operation is commerce "among the states" under even the narrow definition of commerce and is subject to federal regulation. Thus, ordinarily, manufacturing, agriculture, and mining—even when "commercial" in the broadest sense—do not occur between states and therefore are outside the regulatory powers of Congress.

I say "ordinarily" because one can imagine industrial, agricultural, or mining processes which, though otherwise within a state, extend beyond that state by emitting harmful substances into the air or water that are carried into neighboring states, as one can imagine a person standing in Indiana and shooting a bullet into Illinois. Therefore, just as the regulation of a shipment of products to other states is "proper" under the Commerce Clause, the "commercial" production of harmful emissions that cross state lines would be included under the broader definition of "commerce," even though manufacturing, agriculture, and mining usually occur within a single state.[126]

MARSHALL'S OVERLY BROAD CONSTRUCTION IN *GIBBONS V. OGDEN*

In *Gibbons*, John Marshall contended that "among the states" meant "concerns more states than one"[127] and his formulation has been accepted by courts ever since.[128] This substitution of language has been used to justify extending the power of Congress from regulating commerce that

---

[126] Because I think the evidence of the narrow original meaning of "commerce" is overwhelming, in chapter 13 I cite the failure of the Constitution to grant Congress the power to regulate interstate emissions as a genuine defect in the written Constitution. It is one of the few examples where the founders failed to anticipate modern developments, but the flaw would swiftly be repaired by a constitutional amendment were the narrow definition of commerce adopted by the courts.

[127] Gibbons, 22 U.S. (9 Wheat) at 194–95.

[128] See, for example, *United States v. Lopez*, 514 U.S, 549, 553 (citing *Gibbons*).

actually moves between the states to commerce that occurs within a state and has external effects.

The Commerce Clause grants Congress the power to regulate commerce that occurs "among the several States," which we have seen meant "between state and state" or between persons in one state and persons in another. It does not speak of a power to regulate commerce that "concerns" more than one state, or even commerce between persons of the same state that somehow "concerns" other states. By the same token, the Commerce Clause also empowers Congress to regulate commerce "with foreign Nations, . . . and with the Indian Tribes." It does not empower Congress to regulate commerce that concerns or affects foreign nations or that concerns or affects Indian tribes.[129]

Marshall's formulation has improperly permitted the expansion of the power to regulate commerce beyond that which actually crosses state lines. The interpretive issue is not whether it might be "necessary and proper" to regulate either noncommercial actions or all intrastate commerce that has a direct impact upon commerce that *does* cross state lines. The issue here is whether Congress's power under the Commerce Clause extends to commerce that occurs wholly within one state but still can be said to "concern" more states than one. The original meaning of "among the several States" provides no warrant for this extension of power.

Determining the constitutionality of a particular regulation of activity that is not "commerce . . . among the several States"—that is, trade between state and state—requires an assessment not only of the Commerce Clause but of the Necessary and Proper Clause as well. As we have seen, the original meaning of the Necessary and Proper Clause requires a showing of means-end fit, whereas "propriety" requires a showing that Congress is not asserting its power over interstate commerce as a pretext for assuming powers it was not delegated, such as a power over intrastate conduct.

The Meaning of "To Regulate"

THE ORIGINAL MEANING OF "TO REGULATE" DID NOT GENERALLY INCLUDE THE POWER TO PROHIBIT

Dictionaries.   Samuel Johnson defines "to regulate" as "1. To adjust by rule or method. . . . 2. To direct." In other words, the term "to regu-

---

[129] This is not to deny Richard Epstein's contention that all commerce takes place in one state or another. See Epstein, "Proper Scope," 1403. Rather, it is to insist that Congress has power only to regulate those activities that are part of a transaction between persons of different states (or with foreign nations or Indian tribes), not a transaction between persons of the same state.

late" means "to make regular." The power to regulate is, in essence, the power to say, "if you want to do something, here is how you must do it." For example, the making of contracts and wills is "regulated" by the law of contracts and estates. To make an enforceable agreement for a sale of goods over five hundred dollars requires that the agreement be in writing. To make a will requires a specified number of witnesses to one's signature. These requirements regulate—or "make regular"—the making of contracts and wills by subjecting them to a rule or method. The power to regulate the making of contracts or wills is not the power to prohibit such activity, even though contracts or wills that do not conform to the regulation are necessarily unenforceable. A pure regulation of commerce, then, is a set of rules that tells people, "If you want to trade or exchange with others, here is how you must go about it."

In contrast, Johnson defines "to prohibit" as "1. To forbid; to interdict by authority. . . . 2. To debar; to hinder." Forbidding, interdicting, and hindering are not the same thing as regulating, or "making regular," or adjusting by rule or method. It does not tell you how to do something, but instead tells you that you may not do it at all. Moreover, in Johnson's dictionary, neither "to regulate" nor "to prohibit" is defined in terms of the other; each seems quite distinct. Indeed, both terms appear in the Constitution and the context in which they are used suggests that their meanings differ sharply.

Usage in the Constitution. Apart from the Commerce Clause, the terms "regulate" or "regulation" appear seven times in the body of the Constitution and three times in the amendments proposed by Congress to the states, though only once in the Bill of Rights as ratified. The term "prohibit" is used once in the body of the Constitution and twice in the Bill of Rights. Article I, Section 4 gives Congress the power to "alter such Regulations" on the time, place, and manner of elections prescribed by state legislatures. Clearly, the power to regulate or facilitate elections is not the power to prohibit them. Article I, Section 8 gives Congress the power "[t]o . . . regulate the Value" of money, not to prohibit the use of money or to "regulate" its value to zero.

In two places the Constitution makes an explicit distinction between prohibition and regulation. Article III, Section 2 gives the Supreme Court appellate jurisdiction, as to both law and fact, "with such Exceptions, and under such Regulations as the Congress shall make." By distinguishing "exceptions" from "regulations," the Constitution distinguished Congress's power to regulate or subject to rule the Court's appellate jurisdiction and its power to prohibit the Court from exercising its jurisdiction by making "exceptions" thereto. If the power to make regulations included the power to prohibit that which is regulated, there would have been no need to give explicit power to Congress to make "exceptions" to appellate jurisdiction.

That the Constitution does not adopt the broader meaning of regulation as "to govern" is also reflected in Article I, Section 8, which gives Congress the power "[t]o make Rules for the Government and Regulation of the land and naval Forces." Here, the term "government" is coupled with "regulation" in a manner that makes clear that Congress has complete power to command or govern the army and navy, not merely the power to regulate them.

Less clear, but still consistent with the distinction between "to regulate" and "to govern," is Congress's power in Article IV, Section 3 "to dispose of and make all needful Rules and Regulations respecting the Territory or other Property belonging to the United States." Congress clearly has the power to govern the territories, and the term "rules and regulations" suggests strongly that its powers are broader than merely regulatory, although it includes the power to make "regulations" as well as other needful "rules."

That the Constitution uses the term "to regulate" in this sense is made plain by the Second Amendment, the first portion of which reads, "A well-regulated Militia, being necessary to the security of a free State." A "well-regulated" militia is not a prohibited militia but one that is well drilled.[130] Even those who read the Second Amendment as a "collective" rather than an individual right on the basis of this preface concede—indeed their theory requires them to insist—that the power to regulate the militia that the Constitution elsewhere confers upon Congress[131] does not include the power to forbid or prohibit the militia. By their interpretation, the sole purpose of the Second Amendment was to protect the continued existence of the state militias.[132] By the same token, the power of Congress

---

[130] This is implicit in Hamilton's observation that "To oblige the great body of the yeomanry and of the other classes of the citizens to be under arms for the purpose of going through military exercises and evolutions, as often as might be necessary to acquire the degree of perfection which would entitle them to the character of a well-regulated militia, would be a real grievance to the people and a serious public inconvenience and loss." *Federalist* 29, 184 (Hamilton).

[131] See U.S. Const., Art. I, § 8, Cl. 16 (referring to the power of Congress: "To provide for organizing, arming, and disciplining, the Militia, and for governing such Part of them as may be employed in the Service of the United States"). Even here the distinction between regulation and governance is implicit. Congress has the general power to regulate the militia by "organizing, arming, and disciplining" it (but not the power to abolish it), and has the stronger power "to govern" only that "part" of the militia that is in actual service.

[132] See, for example, Keith A. Ehrman and Dennis A. Henigan, "The Second Amendment in the Twentieth Century: Have You Seen Your Militia Lately?" *University of Dayton Law Review* (1989): 5, 57 (arguing that the framers' intent behind the Second Amendment was to protect independent state militias).

to "well-regulate" commerce among the states does not include the power to forbid or prohibit commerce.[133] James Madison described a direct parallel between the regulation of the militia and the regulation of commerce when he asked:

> How can the trade between the different States be duly regulated without some knowledge of their relative situations in these and other points? . . . How can uniform regulations for the militia be duly provided without a similar knowledge of some internal circumstances by which the States are distinguished from each other? These are the principal objects of federal legislation and suggest most forcibly the extensive information which the representatives ought to acquire.[134]

Ratification Debates. How do the debates in the state ratification conventions bear out this distinction between the power "to regulate" and the power "to prohibit"? The term "regulate" appears fifty-five times in all the records we have of the deliberations in the states.[135] In every case where the context makes the meaning clear, the term connotes "subject to a rule" or "make regular" in the sense that "if you want to do something, here is how you should do it." As with the word "commerce," the term "regulate" is used with stunning uniformity—so much so that it would be tedious to reproduce the quotations here. Moreover, it is unnecessary because the term appears overwhelmingly in the context of regulatory powers that, as we observed in the intratextual discussion above, could not plausibly have included the power to prohibit such activities. These are references to the powers to regulate elections (18), jury trials (6), courts (5), militias (2), taxes (1), treaties (1), and the deliberations of the Senate (1).[136] In the rest, the term "regulate" is used in its ordinary sense, in some context other than the Constitution of the new govern-

---

[133] The first amendment originally proposed by Congress, which was never ratified, is entirely consistent with regulate's meaning "make regular." It directed that the number of representatives "shall be so regulated by Congress" that the number of representatives shall not fall below a specified proportion of the population.

[134] *Federalist* 53, 333 (Madison). Notice here the reference to the Commerce Clause as regulating "trade between the different States." In *Federalist* 4, John Jay drew a like parallel between the power of Congress over the militia and commerce when he referred to "our trade prudently regulated, our militia properly organized and disciplined." *Federalist* 4, 49 (Jay).

[135] Massachusetts (13), Connecticut (1), New York (9), Pennsylvania (2), Virginia (16), North Carolina (11), and South Carolina (3).

[136] I have, of course, omitted from this list discussions of the power to regulate commerce (5), trade (2), or contracts (1) because it is the scope of this power that is at issue here. Nevertheless, the two references to regulating "trade" support the narrow meaning of "commerce."

ment.[137] Nothing in these materials supports the conclusion that a power to regulate includes the power to prohibit.

The Pennsylvania Gazette. Usage was equally consistent in the *Pennsylvania Gazette.* The term "regulate" appears 393 times. The term "regulation" appears 410 times. Rarely, if at all, was either term used to mean something other than "make regular." No unambiguous examples of these terms referring to prohibitions were found. Of course, as with "commerce," a great many uses are unclear, but wherever context provides any clue, the intended meaning seems clearly a reference to rules stipulating the method or mode by which particular activities should be conducted.[138]

THE POWER "TO REGULATE" MIGHT SOMETIMES INCLUDE THE POWER "TO PROHIBIT"

Of course even a narrow power "to regulate" commerce among the states, properly construed, would include a limited power to prohibit some activities related to trade. A power to specify the manner by which trade is to be conducted includes a power to prohibit, for example, fraud in the conduct of trade between states. This suggests that Congress, not the states, has a power to police wrongful conduct with respect to commerce between states. That is, Congress may protect the rights of persons engaged in commerce among the states or the rights of third persons that are violated by such commerce.

In other words, a narrow power to regulate rightful commerce includes the power to prohibit wrongful acts with respect to commerce between state and state. Properly conducted, commerce itself can rarely violate the rights of another, although one type of objectionable contract is clear: a contract for the purchase and sale of human beings. Such commerce is surely wrongful. Given that a prohibition on such commerce would not violate in any way either the rights "retained by the people" or the powers reserved to the states and would therefore be proper, we should not be surprised to find the framers assuming that such powers were subsumed within the power "to regulate."

---

[137] See, for example, Elliot, *Debates*, 2:16 ("[W]e ought to consult the sentiments of wise men, who have written on the subject of government, and thereby regulate our decision on this business."); ibid., 252 ("[T]he general sense of the people will regulate the conduct of their representatives."); ibid., 301 ("[T]here should be, in every republic, some permanent body to correct the prejudices, check the intemperate passions, and regulate the fluctuations, of a popular assembly."); ibid., 384 (referring to "making laws to regulate the height of fences and the repairing of roads"); ibid., 3:137 ("There are certain maxims by which every wise and enlightened people will regulate their conduct."); ibid., 227 ("We may now regulate and frame a plan that will enable us to repel attacks").

[138] For a more detailed account of the findings, see Barnett, "New Evidence," 863–65.

Article I, Section 9 stipulates that the "Migration or Importation of such Persons as any of the States now existing shall think proper to admit, shall not be prohibited by the Congress prior to the Year [1808]." This suggests that, but for this section, Congress would have the power to prohibit the slave trade with foreign nations as part of either its taxing power or its power to regulate commerce.

Edmund Randolph discussed this clause as part of his argument to the Virginia ratification convention that the exceptions to congressional powers that appeared in the Constitution in no way implied a power to legislate generally. To rebut the contrary suggestion, Randolph endeavored to show how every exception modified an enumerated power: "To what power in the general government is the exception made respecting the importation of negroes? Not from a general power, but from a particular power expressly enumerated. This is an exception from the power given them of regulating commerce."[139] In this way, Randolph explicitly linked the power to prohibit the slave trade to the commerce power. Randolph's recollection is borne out by the draft sketch of a constitution he had submitted during the Convention to the Committee of Detail. In his sketch, the prohibition is listed explicitly as the second exception to the power to regulate commerce.[140]

Ironically, just as the South's commitment to slavery undermines the inference that Congress had the power to regulate intrastate trade, thereby supporting the narrow meaning of "among the states," here the slavery issue provides evidence that Congress's power "to regulate" commerce with foreign nations was broad enough to include the power to prohibit at least some kinds of commerce.[141] But this is not the only reason to believe that the power to regulate commerce included the power to prohibit at least some types of trading.

Perhaps the most important reason to grant Congress the power to regulate commerce was not the power to eliminate trade barriers among the several states (which Madison referred to in *Federalist* 42 as a "supplemental provision"), but the power to place restrictions on foreign access to American markets to facilitate the opening of European trade to Ameri-

---

[139] Elliot, *Debates*, 3:464.

[140] See James H. Hutson, ed., *Supplement to Max Farrand's The Records of the Federal Convention of 1787* (New Haven: Yale University Press, 1987), 187.

[141] The Supreme Court later held that although the foreign slave trade was subject to congressional legislation—see *Groves v. Slaughter*, 40 U.S. 449 (1841)—the federal government clearly lacked the power to regulate the domestic slave trade. See ibid., 508 (Justice Taney concurring) ("[T]he power over this subject is exclusively with the several states."); ibid., 514 (Justice Baldwin concurring) (asserting that the regulation of slavery "depended on the law of each state," and that "no power [over this] is granted of the Constitution to Congress").

cans as well as to promote domestic production. Thus, it was envisioned that the power to regulate trade with foreign nations included the power to prohibit certain types of trade by means of, for example, tariffs.[142]

However, even if it is conceded that the original meaning of "to regulate" included a power to restrict foreign commerce in negotiating treaties to lower foreign barriers to American goods as well as to protect some domestic markets from foreign competition, this aspect of the power to regulate does not necessarily extend to domestic commerce. Article I, Section 9 expressly bars Congress from using any "Regulation of Commerce" to favor the ports of one state over those of another,[143] and Article I, Section 8 mandates that "all Duties, Imposts and Excises shall be uniform throughout the United States."[144] These provisions deny Congress the same degree of regulatory power over domestic commerce that it has over commerce with foreign nations. And they provide some circumstantial textual evidence that the domestic portion of the Commerce Clause lacked the prohibitory aspect that was included in the power to regulate commerce with foreign nations and was instead intended to eliminate and prevent any state-imposed barriers to trade between the states.

This is precisely the distinction offered by James Madison long after ratification in correspondence with Joseph Carrington Cabell, a post-Revolutionary intellectual and cofounder, with Thomas Jefferson, of the University of Virginia. Madison contended that the "meaning of the power to regulate commerce is to be sought in the general use of the phrase; in other words, in the objects generally understood to be embraced by the power when it was inserted in the Constitution."[145] And, as is well known, the purposes of granting Congress the power to regulate trade "with foreign nations" differed markedly from the purpose for regulating trade "among the several States." Given the need for a broader power over the former, Madison said he "always foresaw"[146] difficulty properly interpreting the latter.

---

[142] Another means to promote American trade by requiring that trade be carried in American ships could be viewed as a regulation rather than a prohibition, as it states, "if you want to trade with the United States, here is how you must do it."

[143] Although this power applies to both domestic and foreign commerce, it does not prevent the Congress from enacting "regulations of commerce" that give preference to trade with one foreign nation over that with another.

[144] To the extent that duties and imposts are proper means for regulating commerce with foreign nations (as opposed to raising revenues) by favoring one nation over another or one type of good over another, this clause operates to prohibit Congress from using its power to regulate commerce among the states to impose duties or imposts to favor one state over another.

[145] *Writings*, 3:571 (letter to Joseph C. Cabell, March 22, 1827).

[146] Ibid., 4:14 (letter to Joseph C. Cabell, February 13, 1829).

Being in the same terms with the power over foreign commerce, the same extent, if taken literally, would belong to it. Yet it is very certain that it grew out of the abuse of the power by the importing States in taxing the non-importing, and was intended as a negative and preventive provision against injustice among the States themselves, rather than as a power to be used for the positive purposes of the General Government, in which alone, however, the remedial power could be lodged. And it will be safer to leave the power with this key to it, than to extend to it all the qualities and incidental means belonging to the power over foreign commerce, as is unavoidable.[147]

In other words, the use of tariffs and other forms of "prohibitory regulation[s]"[148]—the term itself a concession to the normal meaning of "regulation"—while necessary to effectuate the purposes of the power to regulate commerce with foreign nations, would directly contradict the purpose for regulating commerce among the states.[149] The former power was supposed to protect and promote domestic economic activities by restricting imports, as well as to levy the types of restrictions that would induce foreign nations to open their markets to American shipping and goods. By contrast, within the United States, the purpose of the power was the reverse: to eliminate trade barriers at the state level that were thought entirely proper at the national level. And this last purpose is manifested in the textual prohibitions of preferential regulations of commerce and nonuniform duties or imposts—textual provisions that support an inference that the original meaning of "to regulate" varied with the subject of the regulation.

When the known purposes of the founders suggest that a single use of a word has two different meanings depending on the noun to which it refers, is this consistent with the objective approach to original meaning? Yes. In contracts, objective ambiguity can occur when a word has more

[147] Ibid., 15. Madison's account would also explain why "[n]o serious and sustained effort . . . was ever made to employ against the domestic slave trade the power of Congress to regulate interstate commerce." Arthur Bestor, "The American Civil War as a Constitutional Crisis," *American Historical Review* 69 (1964): 327, 342. According to Bestor, "[p]ublic opinion seems to have accepted as virtually axiomatic the constitutional principle" that Congress had no power to prohibit or obstruct the trade in slaves between the slaveholding states. Ibid.

[148] *Writings*, 4:14 (letter to Joseph C. Cabell, February 13, 1829).

[149] It may be argued that admitting evidence of such purposes is a reversion to original intent rather than original meaning. I discuss this evidence, however, to put in perspective the express textual restriction on Congress's power to restrict the slave trade with foreign nations; see U.S. Const., Art. I, § 9, and its possible effect on the meaning of "to regulate" in the Commerce Clause. But the same evidence of purpose that helps explain this broadening of the power "to regulate" also includes evidence that this broadening was limited to foreign trade. This is an example of how evidence of publicly known purposes helps to shape the original public meaning of words and phrases.

than one reasonable or public meaning. For example, to take a famous contracts case, each party can use the name *Peerless* to refer to one of two different ships bearing the same name.[150] If the name *Peerless* reasonably describes both ships, then the parties' use of the term *Peerless* is ambiguous from an objective standpoint. Owing to the objective ambiguity, though they used the same word, as Oliver Wendell Holmes, Jr., put it, "[each party] said a different thing."[151]

Likewise, a group of persons can use a single ambiguous verb to signify objectively two different activities depending on the noun to which it refers. When two people attach different meanings to the same word in a contract, we consider this to be a "misunderstanding" and assent can fail. But when a group of people agrees to use one word to connote, depending on the circumstances, two different meanings, they have objectively manifested their intentions, albeit in an awkward manner that makes the objective meaning of their words sometimes difficult to discern.

Although it is generally preferable to avoid reliance on teleological considerations or evidence of purpose when interpreting the objective meaning of constitutional terms, when it comes to the powers of government, this will frequently be unavoidable. As we have already seen, the Constitution requires that all laws be both necessary and proper. For there to be an assessment of the necessity of a particular means, there must be some understanding of the proper end. Unless the propriety of the exercise of a power includes some purposive element, then, it will sometimes be difficult, if not impossible, to assess its necessity. We shall return to this issue, when considering the requirement of "necessity" in chapter 13.

That the power to regulate rightful commerce includes the power to prohibit wrongful commerce helps explain the case of *Champion v. Ames*.[152] In *Champion*, the Progressive Era Court upheld, in a 5–4 decision, the power of Congress to prohibit the interstate shipment of lottery tickets. After concluding that lotteries were "commerce" and that this commerce was being conducted "among the states,"[153] the Court considered the question of "whether regulation may not *under some circumstances* properly take the form or have the effect of prohibition. . . ."[154] Finding that a prohibition was proper in light of "the nature of the interstate traffic which it was sought by the act . . . to suppress,"[155] the Court

[150] See *Raffles v. Wichelhaus*, 2 H & C 906, 159 Eng Rep 375 (Ex 1864).
[151] Oliver Wendell Holmes, Jr., *The Common Law* (1881; reprint, Boston: Little, Brown, 1963), 242.
[152] 188 U.S. 321 (1903).
[153] Ibid., 353–55, 363.
[154] Ibid., 355 (emphasis added).
[155] Ibid.

allowed Congress the discretion to ban such commerce altogether, not as a means to protect commerce between the states, but as an end in itself.

Champion can be understood as recognizing a police power in Congress over commerce between the states analogous to the police power of a state within its borders.

> If a State, when considering legislation for the suppression of lotteries within its own limits, may properly take into view the evils that inhere in the raising of money, in that mode, why may not Congress, invested with the power to regulate commerce among the several States, provide that commerce shall not be polluted by the carrying of lottery tickets from one State to another?[156]

After all, states do not have such a power to prohibit wrongful interstate commerce. Over the dissent of four justices, the Court reasoned that this power must reside in Congress or there is an unexplained gap in the allocation of power between state and federal authorities. As the Court stated, "We should hesitate long before adjudging that an evil of such appalling character, carried on through interstate commerce, cannot be met and crushed by the only power competent to that end . . . because Congress alone has the power to occupy, by legislation, the whole field of interstate commerce."[157]

The four dissenters denied that the power to regulate commerce included "the absolute power to prohibit it."[158] They contended that when the states "surrendered the power to deal with commerce as between themselves to the general government it was undoubtedly in order to form a more perfect union by freeing such commerce from state discrimination, and not to transfer the power of restriction."[159] They also contended that the scope of the power over commerce with foreign nations was not necessarily the same as the power over interstate commerce. To the contrary,

> the latter was intended to secure equality and freedom in commercial intercourse as between the states, not to permit the creation of impediments to such intercourse; while the former clothed Congress with that power over international commerce, pertaining to a sovereign nation in its intercourse with foreign nations, and subject, generally speaking, to no implied or reserved power in the states. The laws which would be necessary and proper in the one case would not be necessary or proper in the other.[160]

---

[156] Ibid., 356.
[157] Ibid., 357–58.
[158] Ibid., 371.
[159] Ibid., 372.
[160] Ibid., 373.

Be this as it may, the majority in *Champion* did not extend the power of Congress to prohibit wrongful commerce to commerce that occurs wholly within the boundaries of a state. "Besides, Congress, by that act, does not assume to interfere with traffic or commerce in lottery tickets carried on exclusively within the limits of any State, but has in view only commerce of that kind among the several States."[161]

Whether or not the Court in *Champion* erred in its interpretation of the Commerce Clause—and I find this a close question—in upholding this particular prohibition it wrongly assumed the police power of the states to be improperly broad. As will be discussed in the next chapter, though the unenumerated police power should be construed to include the power to prohibit wrongful acts, to be wrongful such acts must involve the violation of the rights of others. If this is the proper scope of the police power, then *Champion* was wrongly decided. The prohibition on the interstate sale of lottery tickets is neither a necessary regulation of the manner by which trade may be carried on, nor a prohibition of activity that violates the rights of others.

Upon all the evidence it looks as though today's equation of the power of regulation with a power of prohibition represents a euphemistic use of the term "regulate," the original meaning of which was much narrower. Indeed, notwithstanding the holding in *Champion*, as late as 1919, it was still thought necessary to enact the Eighteenth Amendment, by which "the manufacture, sale, or transportation of intoxicating liquors within, the importation thereof into, or the exportation thereof from the United States and all territory subject to the jurisdiction thereof for beverage purposes is hereby *prohibited*."[162] Even this prohibition did not reach mere possession or noncommercial transfers of alcohol. And a proposed, but unratified, 1926 amendment made the distinction between regulation and prohibition abundantly clear when it declared: "The Congress shall have power to limit, *regulate*, and *prohibit* the labor of persons under eighteen years of age."[163]

THE SURPRISING LIMITS OF AN EXPANDED MEANING OF THE COMMERCE POWER

The historical evidence overwhelmingly supports a narrow original meaning of Congress's power "to regulate Commerce . . . among the several States," though interpreting the precise meaning of "regulate" is tricky.

[161] Ibid., 357.
[162] U.S. Const., Amend. XVIII (emphasis added).
[163] H.J. Res. 184, 68th Cong., 1st sess. (June 2, 1924, in 43 Stat 670) (emphasis added).

"Commerce" means the trade or exchange of goods including the means of transporting them; "among the several States" means between persons of one state and another; and the term "to regulate," when applied to domestic commerce, means "to make regular"—that is, to specify how a rightful activity may be transacted—and the power to prohibit wrongful acts. Were the evidence in equipoise between the narrow and broad meanings of these terms, the most that could be claimed is that we must establish a construction of this clause that is consistent with the rest of the constitutional scheme. In the face of such ambiguity, we are obligated to adopt a narrower construction if that fits better with the rest of the constitutional scheme, including the principles of federalism and limited enumerated powers, as I think it does.

Suppose, however, that we decide to adopt the broadest possible original meaning of the power to regulate commerce among the several states: that Congress is empowered to make regular or prohibit any gainful activity that occurs anywhere in the United States. Even this interpretation constrains the "propriety" of Congress's power to a greater degree than is currently acknowledged and would leave Congress with less power than it currently claims. Such a power would unquestionably exclude entirely noncommercial—or nongainful—activities from the scope of Congress's regulatory powers. That is, any activity that is not being done for profit or gain is completely untouched by Congress's power to regulate commerce among the states even under the most expansive interpretation of this provision's original meaning.

These limits have been examined in some detail by Grant Nelson and Robert Pushaw.[164] Examples of the types of activities that Congress may not regulate or prohibit, provided that they are not done for profit or gain are: the transmission of information of any kind between persons via telephone or computer; the movement of persons across state lines "for immoral purposes" (say for purposes of adultery or fornication); the mere possession of any good whatsoever because mere possession is not gainful (unless it is possession for purposes of sale), which would include the mere possession of any firearm, therapeutic or intoxicating drug, or erotic literature. This last distinction was adopted in the Eighteenth Amendment, which barred the manufacture and sale of alcoholic bever-

---

[164] See Nelson and Pushaw, "Rethinking the Commerce Clause," 1. While recognizing the limits of the broadest meaning of "commerce," Nelson and Pushaw accept—wrongly, in my view—the idea that Congress has nearly unlimited discretion to determine those actions that in any way affect commerce between more states than one. And they also mistakenly accept Crosskey's broad interpretation of "commerce." In addition to the evidence of original meaning presented here, which they do not consider, I offer some additional criticisms of their analysis in Randy E. Barnett, "The Original Meaning of the Commerce Clause," *University of Chicago Law Review* 68 (2001): 101, 119–20.

ages, but not their mere possession, by consumers. Because it, too, is non-commercial, Congress could make no law respecting transfer of ownership or possession of any of these or other goods, provided that their transfer was not for profit or gain.

Even under the broad conception of commerce, Congress may not control the nongainful use or destruction of any object, just because it had once been in commerce. The fact that a particular item may once have been the subject of commerce or gainful activity does not make it perpetually so—or the powers of Congress under the Commerce Clause would know no limit whatsoever. So any laws prohibiting or even regulating the private possession or use of firearms of any kind are beyond the powers of Congress "to regulate commerce among the states," as are laws restricting the burning of the American flag.

Therefore, under the broadest original meaning of every term in the Commerce Clause, federal laws prohibiting the possession and use of alcohol, tobacco, firearms, drugs, sexual literature, or any other items are improper and unconstitutional. One need not reach the issue of the alleged necessity of such laws. Consequently, even the broadest meaning of Congress's power to regulate commerce among the states would leave untouched most of the natural rights retained by the people to possess, use, and dispose of their property however they may choose, provided these activities are not done for profit or gain. The regulation or prohibition of these activities would be within the purview of the states.

If the most expansive original meaning of the power to regulate commerce among the states would greatly restrict the powers currently claimed by Congress, how do the courts justify Congress's current exercise of even broader powers? The rationale is not based on original meaning at all,[165] but from how the courts have construed the term "among the states." While long affirming that "among the states" means "between state and state," they have also construed "among the states" to permit the regulation of, not merely commerce itself, but any activity that affects the commerce of more states than one. Then, to determine whether any particular action has this effect, they aggregate the effects of all similar actions. Under the "aggregate affects" doctrine, then, any activity that affects commerce among the states, though it may be wholly intrastate and noncommercial, is brought under the commerce power.

The "aggregate affects" test also allows the commerce power to reach actions each of which has minuscule or no effect upon interstate commerce at all. Of course, most of what we do, indeed all our actions in the

---

[165] As was already seen, the primary source of expanded power associated with the Commerce Clause comes not from an interpretation of the Commerce Clause but from an expansive interpretation of the Necessary and Proper Clause.

market, have effects that extend beyond our immediate vicinity, especially when considered in the aggregate. Each of our decisions to buy or refrain from buying gasoline, for example, certainly determines its national price when taken in the aggregate. By allowing Congress the power to regulate any activity that, when aggregated, "affects" commerce between the states, courts have granted Congress a near plenary power to do anything it wills and thus have nearly destroyed the system of limited enumerated powers.

One of the most extreme examples of this was the 1942 case of *Wickard v. Filburn*.[166] In *Wickard*, the Supreme Court found that Congress had the power to regulate the production and consumption of wheat grown by a farmer and used to feed his own livestock and family because such activity, in the aggregate, "affects" the national wheat market. In *Wickard*, as Chief Justice Rehnquist explained forty years later,

> the Court expanded the scope of the Commerce Clause to include the regulation of acts which taken alone might not have a substantial economic effect on interstate commerce, such as a wheat farmer's own production, but which might reasonably be deemed nationally significant in their cumulative effect, such as altering the supply-and-demand relationships in the interstate commodity market.[167]

By this rationale the distinction between interstate and intrastate commerce is destroyed.

Such expansive doctrinal constructions are often defended as an unavoidable implication of an increasingly interconnected national economy that was unforeseen by the founders. If we want the Constitution to keep up with an increasingly integrated national economy, the argument goes, we have no choice but to construe the Commerce Clause in this way. Yet an interconnected economy was far from unforeseen by the founders. As Madison stated in his letter responding to Justice Marshall's loose construction of the Necessary and Proper Clause in *McCulloch*: "In the great system of political economy, having for its general object the national welfare, *everything is related immediately or remotely to every other thing*; and consequently, a power over any one thing, if not limited by some obvious and precise affinity, may amount to a power over every other thing."[168]

Moreover, the founders certainly distinguished between commerce and activities that affect or are benefited by commerce. As was explained by

---

[166] 312 U.S. 111 (1942).

[167] *Hodel v. Virginia Surface Mining Association*, 452 U.S. 264, 308 (1981) (Justice Rehnquist concurring).

[168] James Madison, "Letter to Judge Roane" (September 2, 1819), in Madison, *Letters*, 3:143–44 (emphasis added).

Jefferson in his objections to the constitutionality of the first national bank:

> To erect a bank, and to regulate commerce, are very different acts. He who erects a bank, creates a subject of commerce in its bills; so does he who makes a bushel of wheat, or digs a dollar out of the mines; yet neither of these persons regulates commerce thereby. To make a thing which may be bought and sold, is not to prescribe regulations for buying and selling.[169]

Jefferson also objected that, even if it could be considered a regulation of commerce, it would not be limited to commerce among the several states:

> Besides, if this was an exercise of the power of regulating commerce, it would be void, as extending as much to the internal commerce of every State, as to its external. For the power given to Congress by the Constitution does not extend to the internal regulation of the commerce of a State, (that is to say of the commerce between citizen and citizen,) which remain exclusively with its own legislature; but to its external commerce only, that is to say, its commerce with another State, or with foreign nations, or with the Indian tribes.[170]

For Jefferson, then, there was a constitutional distinction between "a regulation of trade" and a measure that is "productive of considerable advantages to trade." Under current doctrines, this distinction has been dissolved.

Were the "aggregate effects" maneuver not bad enough, the courts have also adopted an "articles of commerce" doctrine under which Congress has power to regulate any activity that makes use of any product that once traveled in interstate commerce. Using this doctrine, the Supreme Court upheld the power of Congress to control the sale of drugs by a local pharmacist to his customer because the package lacked warnings required of drugs traded between states.[171] The Court also upheld the federal prosecution of a person for possessing a prohibited firearm merely because it once had moved in interstate commerce.[172] David Engdahl calls this the "herpes theory" of interstate commerce in that "some lingering federal power infects whatever has passed through the federal dominion."[173] Under this doctrine, Congress claims the power to criminalize any conduct that involves the use a credit card, telephone, or fax machine that was sold in interstate commerce.

---

[169] *The Writings of Thomas Jefferson*, 6:198–99 (opinion against the constitutionality of a National Bank, February 15, 1791).

[170] Ibid., 199.

[171] See *United States v. Sullivan*, 332 U.S. 689 (1948).

[172] See *Scarborough v. United States*, 431 U.S. 563 (1977).

[173] David E. Engdahl, "The Necessary and Proper Clause as an Intrinsic Restraint on Federal Lawmaking Power," *Harvard Journal of Law and Public Policy* 22 (1998): 120.

By use of these constructions, Congress has claimed, and the Supreme Court has permitted, what amounts to a general plenary power to legislate in any manner it wishes. In 1995, however, the Supreme Court began again to place some limit on the commerce power by requiring that any affect on interstate commerce be "substantial,"[174] and by limiting the application of the aggregate affects doctrine to intrastate economic activity.[175] In a concurring opinion in *United States v. Lopez*, Justice Thomas warned that "our case law has drifted far from the original understanding of the Commerce Clause."[176] He urged the Court "to temper our Commerce Clause jurisprudence in a manner that both makes sense of our more recent case law and is more faithful to the original understanding of that Clause."[177] The most persuasive evidence of original meaning— statements made during the drafting and ratification of the Constitution as well as dictionary definitions and *The Federalist*—strongly supports Justice Thomas's and the Progressive Era Supreme Court's narrow interpretation of Congress's power "To regulate Commerce with foreign Nations, and among the several States, and with the Indian Tribes."

CONCLUSION

The Presumption of Liberty places the burden on Congress to justify the propriety of its actions by pointing to the enumerated power it is employing. When considering the legitimacy of the powers granted to Congress by the Constitution, we must note that, standing alone, the narrowest construction of either "commerce" or "among the states" would not reduce the scope of government power over private activity but would merely shift power from the national to the state governments. If Congress is barred from regulating agriculture and manufacturing, it would fall to the states to regulate these activities. The same is true if "among the states" is interpreted as "between persons of different states," in which case states would have the power to regulate wholly intrastate trade.

The most crucial issue with respect to the legitimacy of the commerce power turns out to be the meaning of "to regulate." Empowering either Congress or the states to prohibit the wrongful exercise of freedom, which

---

[174] *United States v. Lopez*, 514 U.S. 549, 559 (1995) ("We conclude . . . that the proper test requires an analysis of whether the regulated activity 'substantially affects' interstate commerce").

[175] *United States v. Morrison*, 529 U.S. 598, 611 (2000) ("in those cases where we have sustained federal regulation of intrastate activity based upon the activity's substantial effects on interstate commerce, the activity in question has been some sort of economic endeavor").

[176] *United States v. Lopez*, 514 U.S. at 584.

[177] Ibid.

can be characterized as license, as opposed to liberty does not violate the rights retained by the people. Thus, it would be perfectly proper to prohibit the slave trade. If, however, "to regulate" grants Congress (or states) the power to impose any restriction it pleases on gainful activity that is rightful, then this power authorizes the violation of the rights retained by the people and is illegitimate. Given such a meaning, there is no reason to believe that laws enacted pursuant to this power are actually proper even though they are deemed "proper" by the (alleged) original meaning of the text.

On the other hand, if "to regulate" means "to make regular" or, as was defined in Johnson, "to subject to a rule," then there need be no inherent conflict between this grant of power and the rights of the people. For it is entirely proper to regulate the exercise of one's natural rights. The proper regulation of contract and property is nearly as essential to ensuring the ability of the people to pursue happiness as the requirements of justice defined by natural rights. Thus, a grant of power to Congress to regulate commerce in this sense complements and enhances the rights of the people. Laws that effectuate this power are perfectly proper and constitutional—if they are also necessary.

CHAPTER TWELVE

The Proper Scope of State Power: Construing the "Police Power"

> The conservation of private rights is attained by the imposi-
> tion of a wholesome restraint upon their exercise, such a
> restraint as will prevent the infliction of injury upon others
> in the enjoyment of them. . . . The power of the government
> to impose this restraint is called Police Power.[1]
> —CHRISTOPHER TIEDEMAN

IF THE PRESUMPTION of Liberty were adopted, how could state laws be shown to be proper? Unlike the enumerated powers of Congress, the powers of states are unwritten. This makes determining their proper limits one of the most challenging and vexatious issues in constitutional theory. Answering this question will require a reliance on many of the concepts and distinctions we have examined in previous chapters, so I begin with a brief review of the terrain we have crossed to reach this point.

THE NEED TO CONSTRUE THE PROPRIETY OF STATE LAWS

We have seen how a written constitution is used to "lock in" certain rights and procedures so they are not easily changed by majority or minority factions. Lock-in requires that the original meaning of these provisions be maintained until the writing is amended. If this original meaning creates a lawmaking process that is good enough to produce laws that are binding in conscience, then the original scheme is legitimate. The Necessary and Proper Clause dictates that a federal law must be both necessary and proper. According to the original meaning of "proper," reinforced by the Tenth Amendment, a federal law must be a means to the achievement of an object or power enumerated in the text. Most of the enumerated powers are inoffensive to the background rights or liberties retained by the

---

[1] Christopher Tiedeman, *Treatise on the Limitations of Police Power in the United States* (St. Louis, Mo.: F. H. Thomas, 1886), 1–2.

people. Even the one power that most often is relied upon to justify legislation affecting liberty, the commerce power, interpreted according to its original meaning, is consistent with the rights retained by the people.

Because the states are not restricted by a similar enumeration of powers, ascertaining the propriety of state laws is a more difficult endeavor. Nor are the contours of their powers written in the Constitution. This does not mean that state lawmaking powers are unlimited. First, they are constrained by their own written constitutions, and by some additional prohibitions contained in the original Constitution. Before the Civil War, however, unless a state law violated one of these expressed prohibitions, it could not be challenged in federal court. In 1833, the Supreme Court, in *Barron v. Mayor of Baltimore*,[2] held that the Bill of Rights applied only to the federal government and did not constrain the states (notwithstanding that the text of some of the first ten amendments contains no such limitation). Thus, at the founding period and for decades thereafter, the propriety of state laws received minimal federal scrutiny.[3]

Upon passage of the Fourteenth Amendment, however, the constitutional structure changed. States were now prohibited from abridging any of the "privileges or immunities" of their citizens, a phrase that included the background natural rights of the people along with other rights and privileges of citizenship expressly created by the Constitution. In addition, states could not deprive persons of life, liberty, or property without due process of law or deny them the equal protection of the laws. Federal courts were now required to assess whether states had violated any of these prohibitions.

Although the Privileges or Immunities Clause was largely gutted by the conventional interpretation of *The Slaughter-House Cases*,[4] there are signs that it is not yet a dead letter.[5] Moreover, after *Slaughter-House*, the courts began using the Due Process and Equal Protection Clauses to provide much the same constraint on state power that was originally intended to result from the Privileges or Immunities Clause, albeit with less textual justification. The "absolute" protection against laws that violate the privileges or immunities of all citizens has been shifted to the Due Process

---

[2] 32 U.S. (7 Pet.) 243 (1833).

[3] Though, as will be noted below, state court judges began to scrutinize the propriety of state legislation under the "law of the land" provisions in state constitutions to ensure that such legislation served the general public, as opposed to a faction or special interest. See Gillman, *The Constitution Besieged*, 45–60.

[4] Though, as was discussed in chapter 8, this interpretation may have exaggerated the degree to which the majority opinion in *The Slaughter-House Cases* undercut the application of the Bill of Rights to the states. See Newsom, "Setting Incorporationism Straight."

[5] See *Saenz v. Roe*, 526 U.S. 489 (1999) (Justice Stevens) (grounding the unenumerated right to travel in the Privileges or Immunities Clause).

Clause, although not to the degree warranted by the original meaning of the Privileges or Immunities Clause. Likewise, the protection against laws that discriminated against a particular class of citizens was shifted to the Equal Protection Clause, the original purpose of which was to require the state judiciary and executive branch officials to apply and enforce laws equally.

Owing to the Fourteenth Amendment, therefore, state governments no longer can claim a plenary power to restrict the liberties of the people subject only to their constitutions and any express restrictions in the original Constitution. Rather, any state abridgment of the privileges or immunities should be subject to challenge in federal court. When state legislatures restrict the liberties of the people, they are no more entitled to be the judge in their own case than is Congress. The exercise of liberty by the citizen should not be restricted unless the state can show, to the satisfaction of an independent tribunal of justice, that such a restriction is both necessary and proper.

However, because there is no list of enumerated powers the original meaning of which can be used to distinguish proper from improper exercises of power, determining the necessity and propriety of state laws is problematic. Indeed, there is nothing in the Constitution that speaks to the issue of the proper scope of state powers. The Tenth Amendment reads: "The powers not delegated to the United States by the Constitution, nor prohibited by it to the states, are reserved to the states respectively, or to the people." While this provision establishes that federal powers are limited to those that are enumerated, it does not say whether any other power is in the hands of the states or the people. As Justice Thomas has correctly observed, "With this careful last phrase, the Amendment avoids taking any position on the division of power between state governments and the people of the States."[6] To answer that question we must look elsewhere.

Originally, the obvious place to look was state constitutions to see what powers a particular state had been granted,[7] but as was already mentioned, the passage of the Fourteenth Amendment complicated this by forbidding states to improperly violate the privileges or immunities of its own citizens even where permitted by their constitutions. In the absence of a written enumeration of state powers in the U.S. Constitution, we have no original meaning to apply to the problem at hand and so are thrown back upon the technique of constitutional construction. How are

---

[6] *United States Term Limits v. Thornton*, 514 U.S. 779, 848 (1995) (Justice Thomas dissenting).

[7] See ibid. ("It is up to the people of each State to determine which 'reserved' powers their state government may exercise").

we to construe the propriety of state power in the absence of an express enumeration? The traditional term for appropriate state power is the "police power" and, as we shall see, to understand this concept requires an understanding of and respect for natural rights.

CONSTRUING THE POLICE POWER OF THE STATES

The Original Meaning of "Police"

The idea that the states possess a power of "police" existed at the time of the framing. The phrase "internal police" was used seven times by delegates to refer to the power of state governments; once this power was referred to as "their police." The issue of the police power of states arose when the Convention was still considering making a general grant of power to the national government, but wished to ensure that the "[National Legislature should] not . . . interfere with the governments of the individual States in any matters of internal police, [in] which the general welfare of the United States is not concerned."[8] In *The Federalist*, Hamilton employs the term "domestic police" twice in essays denying that the national government was a threat to state power.[9]

The term "police" was rarely used in the state ratification conventions. On two occasions in New York it was used to refer to the power of states. John Williams insisted that "[t]he constitution should be so formed as not to swallow up the state governments: the general government ought to be confined to certain national objects; and the states should retain such powers as concern their own internal police."[10] Hamilton contended that there might be more force in this type of objection, "[w]ere the laws of the Union to new-model the internal police of any state; were they to alter, or abrogate at a blow, the whole of its civil and criminal institutions; were they to penetrate the recesses of domestic life, and control, in all respects, the private conduct of individuals. . . ."[11] Elsewhere, the term was used during the debate over the powers of Congress to control the national capital. In Pennsylvania, it was proposed that the Constitution be amended so that the powers of Congress "be qualified by a proviso that such right of legislation extend only to such regulations as respect the

---

[8] "Journal of the Convention," Farrand, *Records*, 2:21 (July 17, 1787) (from resolution proposed to the convention).

[9] See *Federalist* 17, 118 (Hamilton) ("The regulation of the mere domestic police of a State appears to me to hold out slender allurements to ambition"). See *Federalist* 34 , 309 (Hamilton) (referring to "expenses arising from those institutions which are relative to the mere domestic police of a state").

[10] Elliot, *Debates*, 2:241.

[11] Ibid., 267.

police and good order thereof."[12] The term "police" was also used in the same manner several times in the Virginia convention.

Only slight elaboration is added by St. George Tucker in his treatise on the Constitution: "The congress of the United States possesses no power to regulate, or interfere with the domestic concerns, or police of any state: it belongs not to them to establish any rules respecting the rights of property; nor will the constitution permit any prohibition of arms to the people; or of peaceable assemblies by them, for any purposes whatsoever, and in any number, whenever they may see occasion."[13] In none of these uses, however, is the scope of this power made clear. What, then, did it mean?

In one sense, the term is almost completely open-ended. Samuel Johnson defined "police" as "[t]he regulation and government of a city or country, so far as regards the inhabitants." Apart from reinforcing the distinction discussed in chapter 11 between "regulate" and "govern," this definition adds only the idea that the police power is a power over individuals (as opposed to a power over subsidiary governmental units). It adds little to an understanding of the scope of the power to regulate and govern individuals. The same can be said about the early Supreme Court opinions by John Marshall distinguishing the "regulations of interstate commerce" from "police power regulations." As Laurence Tribe has noted, "these labels appear to have been largely conclusory; whatever their internal coherence or their predictive value for those who used them, they reveal little of the analysis underlying the decisions in which they played a role."[14]

The Lockean Theory of the Police Power

The absence of an articulated theory of "police power" reflected the lack of any need for such a theory so long as federal courts had little responsibility for protecting the rights of citizens from being violated by their state governments. With the enactment of the Fourteenth Amendment in 1868, however, a theory was required and such a theory was swiftly produced. In that same year the first edition of Thomas M. Cooley's *A Treatise on the Constitutional Limitations Which Rest Upon the Legislative Power of the United States of the American Union* was published.[15] Cooley, then

---

[12] Ibid., 545.

[13] Tucker, in appendix of *Blackstone's Commentaries*, 1:315–6. Notice also Tucker's statement that the right to arms forbids disarming the people—this is an equivalent to the individual right of assembly—and his use of the term "prohibition" to denote what the right to keep and bear arms bars.

[14] Laurence H. Tribe, *American Constitutional Law*, 3d ed. (New York: Foundation Press, 2000), 1047.

[15] Thomas M. Cooley, *A Treatise on Constitutional Limitations Which Rest Upon the Legislative Power of the United States of the American Union* (Boston: Little, Brown, 1868).

a justice on the Michigan Supreme Court and the Jay Professor of Law at the University of Michigan, sought to address the question of "conflict between national and State authority" as well as the question of "whether the State exceeds its just powers in dealing with the property and restraining the actions of individuals."[16] The answers to these questions turned on the content of the police power, which he defined in light of previous judicial opinions as follows:

> The police of a State, in a comprehensive sense, embraces its system of internal regulation, by which it is sought not only to preserve the public order and to prevent offences against the State, but also to establish for the intercourse of citizen with citizen those rules of good manners and good neighborhood which are calculated to prevent a conflict of rights, and to insure to each the uninterrupted enjoyment of his own, so far as is reasonably consistent with a like enjoyment of rights by others.[17]

The last part of this definition can be conceptualized as the power of a state to protect the rights of each of its citizens from being violated by any other person in society and to permit the exercise of one's rights in such a manner as to prevent such exercise from intruding upon the like rights of others. Whereas the protection afforded common-law rights by adjudication occurs *after* they have been violated, police power regulations seek to facilitate the exercise of these rights and prevent their infringement before the fact.[18] Whereas damage actions compensate for past violations of rights, the police power regulations permit laws to prevent rights violations from occurring. As we saw with *Champion v. Ames*, it is consistent with this conception of police power to acknowledge that "Congress may establish police regulations, as well as the States; confining their operation to the subjects over which it is given control by the Constitution."[19]

There is no enumeration or list of specific state powers for much the same reason the founders thought rights could not be comprehensively listed. Just as all the ways that liberty may be exercised rightfully cannot be enumerated in advance, neither can all the specific ways that people may transgress upon the rights of others:

> It would be quite impossible to enumerate all the instances in which this power is or may be exercised, because the various cases in which the exercise by one

---

[16] Ibid., 572.

[17] Ibid.

[18] I refer to "police power regulation" because, in Lockean theory, adjudication is also an exercise of the police power.

[19] Ibid., 586.

individual of his rights may conflict with a similar exercise by others, or may be detrimental to the public order or safety, are infinite in number and in variety.[20]

Like the modern doctrine that views content-neutral "time, place, and manner" regulations of speech to be consistent with the First Amendment, the police power permits the states the authority "to make extensive and varied regulations as to the time, place, and circumstances in and under which parties shall assert, enjoy, or exercise their rights, without coming into conflict with any of those constitutional principles which are established for the protection of private rights or private property."[21]

Cooley's conception of the police power descended from the same Lockean political theory on which the rest of the Constitution was based. In the prepolitical "state of nature" people are in possession of all their natural rights, including the right to execute or enforce their rights against other persons. "[I]n the state of Nature," wrote Locke, "every one has the Executive Power of the Law of Nature."[22] However, in such a state, it can be objected that "it is unreasonable for Men to be Judges in their own Cases, that Self-love will make Men partial to themselves and their Friends. And on the other side, that Ill Nature, Passion and Revenge will carry them too far in punishing others."[23] For this reason, "nothing but Confusion and Disorder will follow," and government is needed "to restrain the partiality and violence of Men."[24]

Locke readily allowed "that *Civil Government* is the proper Remedy for the Inconveniences of the State of Nature, which must certainly be Great, where Men may be Judges in their own Case, since 'tis easily to be imagined, that he who was so unjust as to do his Brother an Injury, will scarce be so just as to condemn himself for it."[25] For this reason, "the Community government comes to be Umpire, by settled standing Rules, indifferent, and the same to all Parties; and by Men having Authority from the Community, for the execution of those Rules, decides all the differences that may happen between any Members of that Society, concerning any matter of right; and punishes those Offences which any Member hath committed against the Society, with such Penalties as the Law

---

[20] Ibid., 594. Ironically, modern judicial conservatives extol the open-ended police power, while shunning unenumerated rights because they are too uncertain. See, e.g., Bork, *The Tempting of America*, 44–45 ("The better view of state legislative power is that . . . it encompasses the power to make any enactment whatever that is not forbidden by a provision of a constitution").

[21] Ibid., 597.

[22] Locke, *Two Treatises*, 316.

[23] Ibid.

[24] Ibid.

[25] Ibid.

has established."[26] For Locke, an impartial judiciary applying a common law defines "civil society" :

> Those who are united into one Body, and have a common establish'd Law and Judicature to appeal to, with Authority to decide Controversies between them, and punish Offenders, *are in Civil Society* one with another: but those who have no such common Appeal, I mean on Earth, are still in the state of Nature, each being, where there is no other, Judge for himself, and Executioner; which is, as I have before shew'd it, the perfect *state of Nature*.[27]

Thus, according to Lockean political theory, the first duty of government is to provide standing general rules for the equal protection of the rights retained by each person, and these rights, in turn, provide the baseline against which to assess the propriety of government actions and the justice of positive rules of law. But Locke also cautioned those who saw government as the solution to the inconveniences of the state of nature that these inconveniences did not justify a Leviathan with unlimited power of the sort advocated by Hobbes:

> ... *Absolute Monarchs* are but Men; and if Government is to be the Remedy of those Evils, which necessarily follow from Mens being Judges in their own Cases, and the State of Nature is therefore not to be endured, I desire to know what kind of Government that is, and how much better it is than the State of Nature, where one Man, commanding a multitude, has the Liberty to be Judge in his own Case, and may do to all his Subjects whatever he pleases, without the least liberty to any one to question or controle those who Execute his Pleasure? And in whatsoever he doth, whether led by Reason, Mistake or Passion, must be submitted to?[28]

From this Locke concluded that the state of nature with no government is preferable to an "absolute" or unlimited government, because at least in the state of nature, "Men are not bound to submit to the unjust will of another: And if he that judges, judges amiss in his own, or any other Case, he is answerable for it to the rest of Mankind."[29]

The propriety of the laws made by the legislature is dictated by the rationale for yielding the lawmaking power to the government. ". . . Men, when they enter into Society, give up the Equality, Liberty, and Executive Power they had in the State of Nature, into the hands of the Society, to be so far disposed of by the Legislative, as the good of the Society shall require."[30] This "good of society," however, is no open-ended grant of

---

[26] Ibid., 367.
[27] Ibid.
[28] Ibid., 316–17.
[29] Ibid., 317.
[30] Ibid., 398.

power simply to do good; it is defined and limited by the rights retained by the people when they surrender their powers of enforcement, and this is what makes it a genuine common good or good for everyone, not merely a segment or faction of society. "[I]t being only with an intention in every one the better to preserve himself his Liberty and Property; (For no rational Creature can be supposed to change his condition with an intention to be worse), the power of the Society, or *Legislative* constituted by them, *can never be suppos'd to extend farther than the common good.*"[31] And to secure this "common good," the legislature "is obliged to secure every ones Property by providing against those three defects . . . that made the State of Nature so unsafe and uneasie."[32]

These three defects are (1) "the want of an *establish'd*, settled, known Law, received and allowed by common consent to be the Standard of Right and Wrong, and the common measure to decide all Controversies between them" (§ 124); (2) the want of "a *known and indifferent Judge*, with Authority to determine all differences according to the established Law" (§ 125); and (3) the want of the "Power to back and support the Sentence when right, and to *give* it due *Execution*" (§ 126). Therefore, "whoever has the legislative or Supreme Power of any Common-wealth, is bound to govern by establish'd Standing Laws, promulgated and known to the People, and not by Extemporary Decrees; by *indifferent* and upright *Judges*, who are to decide Controversies by those Laws; And to imploy the force of the Community at home, *only in the Execution of such Laws. . . .*"[33]

According to Lockean political theory, then, because people form government to secure their rights of liberty and property more effectively than they can secure them on their own, the executive or police power must be limited to the advancement of the common good, which is accomplished by protecting those same retained rights. In this way, Lockean theory provides both a powerful rationale for and an important limit upon the powers of government that is reflected in the police power doctrine. The police power is the legitimate authority of states to *regulate rightful* and *prohibit wrongful* acts. As Hamilton explained in *Federalist* 17, "[t]he administration of private justice between the citizens of the same State, the supervision of agriculture and of other concerns of a similar nature, all those things, in short, which are proper to be provided for by local legislation, can never be desirable cares of a [national] jurisdiction."[34]

[31] Ibid.
[32] Ibid.
[33] Ibid., 399.
[34] *Federalist* 17, 118 (Hamilton).

Construing the Police Power of States

Because the original meaning of the Fourteenth Amendment makes it necessary to distinguish legitimate from illegitimate exercises of state power, it requires the construction of some such doctrine as the police power of the states. No judicially created construction of state power, however, can properly grant state governments a completely plenary power limited only by whatever express prohibitions may exist in its constitution or in Article I, Section 10 of the U.S. Constitution. Granting so unlimited a power would conflict with the original meaning of the Privileges or Immunities, the Due Process, and the Equal Protection Clauses of the Fourteenth Amendment. In this manner, the original meaning of the text dictates some constructions of state power and excludes others.

Unsurprisingly, the Lockean theory of the police power adopted by Cooley and others to identify when states violate the injunctions of the Fourteenth Amendment is generally consistent with the conception of natural rights to which the framers of the Constitution and Fourteenth Amendment adhered. Natural rights define the boundary or space within which people are at liberty to do as they please provided their actions do not interfere with the rightful actions of others operating within their own boundaries or spaces. Just as it is proper to prohibit wrongful or rights-violating conduct, proper police power regulations specify the manner in which persons may exercise their liberties so as to prevent them from accidentally interfering with the rights of others.

After Cooley, the leading nineteenth-century theorist of the police power was Professor Christopher Tiedeman. In his 1886 *Treatise on the Limitations of Police Power in the United States*, he repeatedly relied on the power to prevent rights violations to identify reasonable—and therefore constitutional—exercises of the police power. To explain the police power and its limits he began with the concept of natural rights.

> The private rights of the individual, apart from a few statutory rights, which when compared with the whole body of private rights are insignificant in number, do not rest upon the mandate of municipal law as a source. They belong to man in a state of nature; they are natural rights, rights recognized and existing in the law of reason.[35]

Like Locke, Tiedeman defines the legitimate purpose of government as the protection of these rights. "The object of government is to impose that degree of restraint upon human actions, which is necessary to the uniform and reasonable conservation and enjoyment of private rights. Government and municipal law protect and develop, rather than create,

---

[35] Tiedeman, *Treatise on the Police Power*, 1.

private rights."[36] Government protects and develops these rights by preventing people from violating the rights of others. "The conservation of private rights is attained by the imposition of a wholesome restraint upon their exercise, such a restraint as will prevent the infliction of injury upon others in the enjoyment of them. . . . The power of the government to impose this restraint is called POLICE POWER."[37]

While the Lockean theory of the police power, as developed by Cooley, Tiedeman, and others, was generally consistent with the background rights retained by the people, this power was sometimes construed more broadly than was proper. In particular, the police power was typically construed to empower states to protect, not only the "health and safety" of the general public, but its "morals" as well. For example, in the 1887 case of *Mugler v. Kansas*, Justice Harlan, the author of the opinion in *Champion v. Ames*, rejected a Fourteenth Amendment challenge to the prohibition of manufacturing and selling of alcohol on the ground that "It cannot be supposed that the states intended, by adopting that amendment, to impose restraints upon the exercise of their powers for the protection of the safety, health, *or morals* of the community."[38] By this rationale, courts upheld the power of states to prohibit gambling, the consumption of alcohol, prostitution, doing business on the Sabbath, and other types of activities that did not violate the rights of others.

Some of these expansions were recognized by leading police power theorists as improper even at the time. Christopher Tiedeman, for example, contended that legislation prohibiting gambling "would be open to serious constitutional objections. Gambling or betting of any kind is a vice and not a trespass, and inasmuch as the parties are willing victims of the evil effects, there is nothing that calls for public regulation."[39] According to this view, "[n]o law can make vice a crime, unless it becomes by its consequence a trespass upon the rights of the public."[40] For Tiedeman, the protection of rights is the measure of proper police power regulations.

[36] Ibid.

[37] Ibid., 1–2 (capitals in original).

[38] *Mugler v. Kansas*, 123 U.S. 623, 664 (1887) (emphasis added). In *Mugler* Harlan explained why judicial review was essential to cabin the police power. "If . . . a statute purporting to have been enacted to protect the public health, the public morals, or the public safety, has no real or substantial relation to those objects, or is a palpable invasion of rights secured by the fundamental law, it is the duty of the courts to so adjudge, and thereby give effect to the Constitution" (ibid., 661).

[39] Tiedeman, *Treatise on the Police Power*, 260.

[40] Ibid., 291. Tiedeman also thought that "when they pursue gambling *as a business*, and set up a gambling house, like all others who make a trade of vice, they may be prohibited and subjected to severe penalties" (ibid.; emphasis added). An explicit rationale for this distinction is not provided, but most likely it stems from Tiedeman's conception of "public harm." While private vice, of itself, works no necessary harm to the general public, Tiede-

Tiedeman discusses at some length why temperance laws were not only bad policy, but also beyond the state's police power. "[N]o trade can be subjected to police regulation of any kind," wrote Tiedeman, "unless its prosecution involves some harm or injury to the public or to third persons, and in any case the regulation cannot extend beyond the evil which is to be restrained."[41] Moreover, "no trade can be prohibited altogether, unless the evil is inherent in the character of the trade, so that the trade, *however conducted*, and whatever may be the character of the person engaged in it, must *necessarily* produce injury upon the public or upon individual third persons."[42]

After a lengthy examination of the effects of the use and sale of alcohol, Tiedeman concluded that prohibition was not constitutionally justified under these principles of the police power. "[T]he liquor trade can not . . . be prohibited entirely, unless its prosecution is essentially and necessarily injurious to the public. Even the prohibition of saloons, that is, where intoxicating liquor is sold and served, to be drunk on the premises, cannot be justified on these grounds."[43] Although the courts of his day rejected this view, Tiedeman contended that it was "the duty of a constitutional jurist to press his views of constitutional law upon the attention of the legal world, even though they place him in opposition to the current of authority."[44]

What Tiedeman could not justify was the prohibition of the liquor trade on private property. In contrast, when a state is acting as an owner of property, such as its own offices and buildings, or as the guardian of public spaces such as streets and parks, it may properly constrain conduct there, such as public fornication or intoxication. Immoral actions like these, though permitted behind closed doors, can wrongfully interfere with the use and enjoyment of the public sphere by reasonable members of the community and their children. Provided such restrictions on freedom were shown to be necessary to this end—and not violative of some

man appears to have thought that the business of supplying such vices does. He seems not to have understood that the legal suppression of such private business created enormous harm to the general public.

[41] Ibid., 301.

[42] Ibid., 301–2 (emphasis added).

[43] Ibid., 307.

[44] Ibid., 311. Thus I believe it is wrong to claim that "Cooley and Tiedeman, with the characteristic dogmatism of treatise writers, asserted that their views were 'the law.' " Paul Brest, Sanford Levinson, Akhil Reed Amar, and J. M Balkin, *Processes of Constitutional Decisionmaking: Cases and Materials* (New York: Aspen Law & Business, 2000), 350. While Cooley hewed closely to precedent, Tiedeman was a bit more normative though he stated clearly where his views differed with the cases. As a result, Tiedeman's thesis was somewhat more radical than Cooley's. Of course, both attempted to synthesize "the law" and in so doing emphasized some authorities while de-emphasizing others.

other constitutional prohibition[45]—these sorts of protection of "public morals" would be within the Lockean construction of the police power of the states identified here.

On the other hand, were the state allowed the power to prohibit any purely private activity *on the sole ground* that a majority of the legislature deems it to be immoral, there would be no limit on state power since no court could review the rationality of such a judgment. As between the legislature and a citizen, the legislature would improperly be the judge in its own case. Imposing so unlimited a power on nonconsenting citizens would be an illegitimate construction of state power that would violate the original meaning of the Fourteenth Amendment.

How can a proper regulation of rightful activity be distinguished from an improper abridgment of the private rights of the people? As with the federal laws, the key is whether state laws are a pretext for purposes other than the prevention of future or rectification of past rights violations. One sign that a law is pretextual is when it benefits a particular group rather than the general public. This type of inquiry was emphasized and developed by the courts during the Reconstruction and Progressive Eras.

Building on the Lockean idea of the "common good," courts examined whether a particular law benefited every person in the community as a whole or whether it instead was implemented for the benefit of a majority or minority faction (what today would be called a "special interest" group). As was stated by Justice Bradley in his *Slaughter-House* dissent: "[F]undamental rights . . . can only be interfered with . . . by lawful regulations necessary or proper for the mutual good of all."[46] The paradigm of a law that exceeded the police power to regulate rightful or prohibit wrongful conduct was a law that, in the words of Justice Samuel Chase in *Calder v. Bull*, "takes property from A. and gives it to B"[47] or from group A to group B.

"An exercise of legislative powers would be considered valid," explains Howard Gillman, "only if it could reasonably be justified as contributing to the general welfare. The adjudicative task was to give meaning to this standard."[48] Gillman has shown how great effort was expended by federal and state courts throughout the Progressive Era to develop sophisticated doctrines by which special interest legislation could be distinguished from general interest legislation that served a common good.

---

[45] Laws that improperly discriminate against some class of citizens, for example, would still be barred by the original meaning of the Privileges or Immunities Clause, or by the modern interpretation of the Equal Protection Clause.

[46] 83 U.S. 36, 116.

[47] 3 U.S. 386, 388 (1798).

[48] See Gillman, *The Constitution Besieged*, 49.

Specifically, it came to be determined, first, that laws that singled out specific groups or classes for special treatment would withstand constitutional scrutiny only if they could be justified as really related to the welfare of the community as a whole . . . and were not seen as corrupt attempts to use the powers of government to advance purely "private" interests; and second, that acts that interfered with an individual's property or market liberty would be considered legitimate so long as they were not designed to advance the interests of just certain groups or classes.[49]

This project actually originated in state courts decades before the enactment of the Fourteenth Amendment, when interest groups began organizing to obtain special benefits from early state legislatures.[50] Policing the vast array of legislative initiatives consistently from statute to statute was not always easy in a system in which a Supreme Court composed of nine justices oversaw numerous lower federal and state courts comprising innumerable judges. Gillman demonstrates that, despite the difficulties of such an inquiry, these efforts were remarkably coherent and also consistent with the political principles of the founding generation.

Gillman's important work has two major themes. The first is that "Lochner-Era police powers jurisprudence" was both coherent and continuous with the underlying principles of the founding. This makes the New Deal rejection of this constitutional jurisprudence a revolution, not a restoration. After this revolution, unless a right deemed by the Court to be fundamental is violated, "Congress need not justify intervention itself, . . . need not justify intervening to favor some participants in the economy over others, . . . [and] need not justify its choice of favorites."[51] And neither must the states.

Gillman's second theme is that the animating principle of the "Lochner Era" was an aversion to class legislation, not an adherence to "laissez-faire." "But 'public purpose' as a limit on the powers of government did not mean 'laissez-faire'; it meant by and large, class-neutral legislation—legislation that did not impose special burdens or benefits on certain market competitors."[52] Although Gillman's evidence shows that resistance to class-based legislation was undoubtedly a touchstone by which reasonable regulation was distinguished from arbitrary interference with liberty, I have two small quarrels with this last claim.

---

[49] Ibid., 49–50.

[50] See ibid., 45–60.

[51] Martin Shapiro, "The Supreme Court's 'Return' to Economic Regulation," in Karen Orren and Stephen Skowronek, eds., *Studies in American Political Development* (New Haven: Yale University Press 1986), 134.

[52] Gillman, *The Constitution Beseiged*, 55.

Because Gillman misunderstands "laissez-faire," he is rejecting a straw man. Laissez-faire was never a claim that liberty could not be regulated. The writings of Cooley and Tiedeman testify to this. Therefore, finding that "reasonable" regulations on liberty were upheld is no evidence that courts were rejecting laissez-faire as a political end. Courts that are completely committed to laissez-faire would still uphold reasonable regulations of liberty.

Gillman also underestimates the degree to which the resistance to class-based legislation was seen as a means to the protection of natural rights, rather than an end in itself. That is, the identification of class-based legislation could well have been thought to be a workable standard or doctrine by which infringements on natural rights could be detected and corrected. Although Gillman never really disputes this last point, his continued refrain about the rejection of laissez-faire in favor of an aversion to class-based legislation sets up an opposition that goes beyond his evidence.

CONCLUSION

We can sum up this analysis of the police power of states as follows: A Presumption of Liberty puts the burden upon states to justify any interference with liberty as both necessary and proper. Because the nature of state powers differs from federal power, the assessment of propriety will differ as well. The Fourteenth Amendment does not bar states from prohibiting wrongful exercises of freedom. There is no privilege to violate the rights of others, nor any immunity from liability should one do so. In nearly all instances, the Constitution leaves the general power to prohibit wrongful conduct where it was before its ratification: in the hands of states. It does, however, give Congress the power to prohibit and set the punishment for certain identifiable offenses, such as treason and piracy. The powers that came to be called the "police power" of the state are far from being inconsistent with the rights retained by the people. To the contrary, the protection of individual rights is at the core of a state's police power.

A state may also justify its laws by showing that it is merely regulating liberty in a way that protects the rights of others. The Fourteenth Amendment bars states from "abridging" or violating the privileges or immunities of citizenship. It does not bar them from subjecting these privileges to publicly accessible "standing rules" of law, provided that such rules are also shown to be necessary to protect the rights that everyone possesses. In this manner, although the Fourteenth Amendment bars the abridgment of liberty and permits liberty-restricting laws to be challenged in federal court, it does not prevent legislatures from reasonably regulating the exercise of private rights.

Finally, in addition to prohibiting wrongful and regulating rightful private behavior that may injure the rights of others, the state may also manage government-controlled public space so as to enable members of the public to enjoy its use, and may restrict the use of its own property—provided these regulations and restrictions do not improperly violate other constitutional prohibitions on state power.

The Supreme Court's decision in *Lawrence v. Texas*[53] striking down a statute criminalizing homosexual "sodomy" illustrates these principles. In *Lawrence*, the government's sole justification for the statute was that the legislature found this conduct to be "immoral." The protection of "morals" is the most dubious aspect of the traditional construction of the police power—although typically this power was used to prohibit conduct that took place *in public places* where it could interfere with the use and enjoyment of public property by other citizens. Only very rarely was the power to protect "morals" used to reach wholly private conduct. In other words, the traditional police power would more accurately be defined as giving states power to protect the "health, safety, and *public* morals" of the populace.[54]

A police power to reach purely private "immoral" acts could always be asserted by a legislature whenever it decides to prohibit any form of conduct. By providing no judicially enforceable limit whatsoever on the police power of states, such a construction would violate the original meaning of the Fourteenth Amendment. Because it would permit legislatures to abridge the privileges or immunities of citizens, and because it appears nowhere in the text of the Constitution, such a claim of power is illegitimate.

It is significant, therefore, that the Court in *Lawrence* found this exercise of power to be improper. The actions banned neither harmed others nor took place in the public sphere where government must balance competing uses by different citizens. Justice Kennedy's opinion in *Lawrence* is especially noteworthy because it protects *liberty*, rather than privacy, without any discussion of whether that liberty was "fundamental." Having identified the conduct as liberty (not license), it then placed the burden on the government to justify its restriction. In this way, *Lawrence* can be viewed as escaping the Footnote Four-Plus framework described in chapter 9, and employing in its place a Presumption of Liberty.[55]

[53] 123 S. Ct. 2472 (2003).

[54] See Randy E. Barnett, "The Police Power," *Notre Dame Law Review* 79 (forthcoming). See also *Brief of the Institute for Justice as* Amicus Curiae *in Support of Petitioners*, submitted in *Lawrence v. Texas*.

[55] See Barnett, "Justice Kennedy's Libertarian Revolution."

CHAPTER THIRTEEN

Showing Necessity: Judicial Doctrines and Application to Cases

> Freedom is a blessing. Regulation is sometimes necessary, but is always a burden. A decision *not to regulate* the way in which an owner chooses to enjoy the benefits of an improvement to his own property is adequately justified by a presumption in favor of freedom.[1]
>
> —JUSTICE JOHN PAUL STEVENS

ASSESSING the propriety of state or federal legislation is a legal question. Courts must determine whether the purpose of a particular statute falls within the enumerated powers of the federal government or the police power of a state. The Presumption of Liberty places the burden of establishing the propriety of laws on the government. The government may meet its burden by showing that any restrictions on individuals are either prohibitions on wrongful conduct or proper regulations of rightful activity.

To be justified under the Commerce Power, federal laws must be regulating or protecting trade between the states. They may not seek to regulate intrastate trade or an activity that is not commerce at all, unless such actions themselves interfere directly with commerce and regulation is needed to protect and facilitate commerce between people of different states. Wrongful acts involving fraud or the physical interference with trade may be prohibited. State laws may properly protect the rights of A from infringement by B. The actual infringement of rights by private parties is wrongful and may justly be prohibited. Actions that do not inherently or inevitably violate rights but that create a substantial risk of violating the rights of others may only be regulated rather than prohibited altogether. Prohibitions and regulations that cannot be justified in terms of these principles are improper and unconstitutional.

Judicial review requiring the government to show that a law is consistent with a properly circumscribed conception of propriety would go a long way toward establishing the binding nature, or legitimacy, of such commands. Constitutional legitimacy, however, also requires a demon-

---

[1] F.C.C. v. Beach Communications, 508 U.S. 307, 320 (Justice Stevens concurring).

stration of a law's necessity. Restrictions on liberty that are unnecessary to accomplish an enumerated end or power, or the state power of police, are not binding in conscience.

Because the issue of necessity will depend on the myriad facts and circumstances of particular laws and the problems they are allegedly needed to handle, assessing the necessity of legislation is trickier than establishing its propriety. Consequently, many have favored a presumption of constitutionality by which courts defer to the legislature's judgment that its laws are necessary. Such a presumption would, however, largely make legislatures the judge of their own laws and would encourage them to pass unnecessary laws to satisfy particular factions rather than to serve the common good.

How, then, can necessity be assessed by courts? Courts actually have a good deal of experience assessing the necessity of statutes that violate express restrictions on legislative power, such as those provided by the Equal Protection Clause of the Fourteenth Amendment or by the free speech guarantees of the First Amendment. Although far from perfect, these techniques can be extended to apply to any infringement of liberty.

JUDICIAL DOCTRINES TO ASSESS NECESSITY

Taking the First Amendment as a model, when law is used to accomplish a proper purpose by restricting the liberties of the people, the Presumption of Liberty imposes a burden on those defending the necessity of these restrictions to show two things: First, the government must show that there is a sufficient "fit" between the liberty-restricting means it chose and the proper purposes it was seeking to attain. Second, the government must show that there were no less restrictive alternatives to the liberty-restricting means that were chosen.

Requiring Means-End Fit

The first debate over the meaning of the Necessary and Proper Clause concerned the constitutionality of the national bank. This debate involved whether the power to create a bank was incidental or "necessary" to an enumerated power and therefore a proper exercise of congressional power. Although John Marshall characterized this as a choice between "absolute" or "indispensable" necessity on the one hand, and a completely open-ended "convenience" on the other, we saw in chapter 7 that Madison's and Hamilton's positions were actually much closer to each other than this dichotomy suggests. Madison rejected as overly restrictive the idea of indispensable necessity whereas Hamilton allowed that some degree of actual necessity, not mere convenience, must be shown to exist.

The way courts now deal with the infringement of a "fundamental" right, or a denial of equal protection of the laws, is instructive. They require that a degree of fit be shown to exist between the "legitimate state interest" to be served by the statute and the means chosen to accomplish this end. For example, when assessing the reasonableness of regulations aimed at one person or group, as opposed to the general public, the courts have asked the government agency to articulate the problem they say such regulations are necessary to solve. They then see whether the need to solve these problems justifies the discrimination contained in the statute.

In the 1984 case of *City of Cleburne v. Cleburne Living Center*, the city had required the operator of a group home for mentally retarded persons to obtain a special permit under the zoning laws that operators of other group homes were not required to obtain. This special permit was denied and the construction of the group home was prohibited. The federal district court required the city to articulate the reasons for such a restriction and the city gave four: First, the city was concerned about the negative reactions of neighboring property owners. Second, the city was concerned that the facility was near a school and it feared that students might either be jeopardized by or ridicule the occupants of the home. Third, the city claimed that the home was situated on a flood plain. Fourth, the city expressed concern about the size of the home and the number of persons who would occupy it.

The Supreme Court rejected the first two of these concerns as based on "mere negative attitudes, or fear, unsubstantiated by factors which are *properly* cognizable in a zoning proceeding. . . ."[2] In essence, these were improper bases "for treating a home for the mentally retarded differently from apartment houses, multiple dwellings, and the like."[3] The court also rejected the flood plain, size, and density rationales because these same considerations would apply equally to other group homes that were not required to obtain a special permit. In essence, the city had not shown why it was *necessary* to restrict only this particular type of group home to prevent flooding or to reduce population density. Applying a restriction only to this type of group home and no other suggests that some other unstated motivation may lie behind the statute.

Notice that placing the burden on the city merely to articulate its purposes and the necessity for its restrictions on liberty revealed the tenuousness of the city's claim of power. This and the inability of the city to show the necessity of the restriction to accomplish its articulated purpose

---

[2] 473 U.S. 432, 448 (1984) (emphasis added).
[3] Ibid.

also bolstered the conclusion that the real motivation for this restriction was not the public or common good but the good of a faction of the community who disliked having a group home in their neighborhood. In other words, requiring that the city's actions be necessary to accomplish a proper purpose revealed that the true purpose for the restriction was most likely improper. This close functional connection between necessity and propriety helps to explain why the founders used them so often in tandem.

To enforce the requirement of equal protection, the Court in *Cleburne* did not defer to the city's own judgment concerning the necessity or propriety of its restriction on liberty, but instead attempted to identify and evaluate the purposes for its actions. This allowed the Court to assess whether the classification represented a means to accomplish a proper end. While *Cleburne* did not reject the presumption of constitutionality that gives government actions the benefit of the doubt, neither did it blindly defer to the judgment of the city as it now does when mere "liberty interests" are restricted by state and federal laws. The Presumption of Liberty would make the government articulate its purposes for a particular restriction of liberty and would also place the burden on the government to show that restricting liberty was necessary to accomplish a proper end.

Requiring the Least Restrictive Alternative

To show a restriction on liberty is truly necessary, it is not enough for the government to show it is a means to accomplish a constitutionally proper purpose. The government should also have to show that it could not achieve its purpose by other means that do not so restrict the liberties of the people or by means that were less restrictive of such liberty. Courts are prepared to require this when a fundamental right, such as the right of freedom of speech, is being infringed. Requiring that the government choose the less restrictive alternative is closely related to the requirement that any restriction be "narrowly tailored" to achieve the proper purpose, or that it not be "overbroad."

This requirement is exemplified in the case of *United States v. Playboy Entertainment Group* (2000).[4] Congress had enacted a statute requiring either that the audio and video of sexually explicit cable channels be completely scrambled or that, where this could not be assured, their transmission be completely blocked from 6 A.M. until 10 P.M. to prevent children from viewing or hearing the programming. Most cable companies complied with the statute by restricting the times that the Playboy Channel was transmitted. The Playboy Entertainment Group challenged the stat-

---

[4] 529 U.S. 803.

ute as unnecessarily restrictive content-based legislation that violated their First Amendment right of freedom of speech.

The issue of whether the restriction was "content-based" went to its propriety. Rules specifying the time, place, and manner of all speech can be a proper regulation that does not infringe upon the rightful exercise of freedom. Their purpose is to facilitate speech and to prevent the actions of speakers from infringing the rights of other persons. Think of a group of protesters who attempt to parade up a public street during the middle of the day. The interference with automobile traffic the parade would cause has nothing to do with the message the protesters intend to convey. The same would be true of a truck with a loudspeaker in a quiet residential neighborhood.

In contrast, a content-based restriction on speech is aimed at the communication of a particular message. Speech does not ordinarily interfere with the liberty of others because of its content, and therefore content restrictions infringe upon the right of free speech unless they are adequately justified by the government.[5] As the Court explained: "Laws designed or intended to suppress or restrict the expression of specific speakers contradict basic First Amendment principles."[6]

In *Playboy*, the Playboy Channel was being restricted in what it could say because of what it was saying. Therefore, the Court found that imposing a restriction on the hours that the Playboy Channel could be transmitted to all cable subscribers was an infringement on the freedom of speech of the Playboy Channel, a fundamental right,[7] and was improper unless justified. "It is of no moment," wrote Justice Kennedy, "that the statute does not impose a complete prohibition. The distinction between laws burdening and laws banning speech is but a matter of degree. The Government's content-based burdens must satisfy the same rigorous scrutiny as its content-based bans."[8]

---

[5] Restrictions on fraudulent speech can be justified as infringements upon the properly defined rights of others under certain circumstances. See Barnett, *Structure of Liberty*, 102–4. It is also commonly thought that defamatory speech is another exception to the claim that the content of speech does not ordinarily violate the rights of others.

[6] 529 U.S. 803, 812.

[7] As the court observed: "As this case has been litigated, [*Playboy's* programming] is not alleged to be obscene; adults have a constitutional right to view it; the Government disclaims any interest in preventing children from seeing or hearing it with the consent of their parents; and *Playboy* has concomitant rights under the First Amendment to transmit it. These points are undisputed" (ibid., 811). Notice that the government is disclaiming an improper purpose although, as with *Cleburne*, this may well have been the real purpose for the restriction on liberty. Once again, requiring a showing of necessity helps ferret out improper restrictions on liberty.

[8] 529 U.S. 803, 812.

In particular, the Court required the government to show that this restriction was truly necessary to accomplish the proper end of protecting children from viewing sexually explicit video without the consent of their parents.[9] When a statute regulates the fundamental right of freedom of speech, "based on its content," the Court explained, "it must be narrowly tailored to promote a compelling Government interest. . . . If a less restrictive alternative would serve the Government's purpose, the legislature must use that alternative. . . . To do otherwise would be to restrict speech without an adequate justification, a course the First Amendment does not permit."[10]

Notice that because the restriction infringes upon an enumerated liberty that has been held to be fundamental, the burden shifts to the government to show the way in which the restriction is necessary. A particular restriction on liberty is unnecessary if there is some other means of accomplishing the proper purpose that is less restrictive or does not restrict liberty at all. In *Playboy*, the Court found that the end could be achieved by completely blocking transmission of this channel to cable subscribers who requested the signal be blocked, and by prominently informing all cable subscribers that they could request such blocking. "Simply put, targeted blocking is less restrictive than banning, and the Government cannot ban speech if targeted blocking is a feasible and effective means of furthering its compelling interests. . . . [I]f a less restrictive means is available for the Government to achieve its goals, the Government must use it."[11]

In *Playboy*, the Court applied a limited Presumption of Liberty to protect an enumerated right. "When the Government restricts speech," wrote Justice Kennedy, citing a long line of cases, "the Government bears the burden of proving the constitutionality of its actions."[12] Because a less restrictive alternative existed, the government failed to show that its restriction on liberty was truly necessary. "When a plausible, less restrictive alternative is offered to a content-based speech restriction, it is the Government's obligation to prove that the alternative will be ineffective to achieve its goals. The Government has not met that burden here."[13]

The Court went on to justify this presumption owing to the importance of the liberty in question, not because this liberty will always be exercised wisely. "What the Constitution says is that these judgments are for the individual to make, not for the Government to decree, even with the man-

---

[9] Whether this is a "proper" end under the power of Congress to regulate commerce or trade between the states is doubtful, in which case the restriction would be considered unconstitutional without a need to reach the issue of its necessity. This possibility illustrates how limitations on powers can avoid the need to explicitly protect rights.

[10] 529 U.S. 803, 813.

[11] Ibid., 815.

[12] Ibid., 816.

[13] Ibid.

date or approval of a majority."[14] What I am calling a Presumption of Liberty is needed to protect speech because, "were we to give the Government the benefit of the doubt when it attempted to restrict speech, we would risk leaving regulations in place that sought to shape our unique personalities or to silence dissenting ideas. When First Amendment compliance is the point to be proved, the risk of non-persuasion—operative in all trials—must rest with the Government, not with the citizen."[15] In a nice summary of the Presumption of Liberty, the Court stated that, unless the government can show that the restriction was truly necessary, "the tie goes to free expression."[16]

Having established this presumption in favor of free expression, the Court then reviewed the trial court's evaluation of the evidence presented by the government that signal bleed was a problem serious enough to make its regulation necessary.

> There is little hard evidence of how widespread or how serious the problem of signal bleed is. Indeed, there is no proof as to how likely any child is to view a discernible explicit image, and no proof of the duration of the bleed or the quality of the pictures or sound. To say that millions of children are subject to a risk of viewing signal bleed is one thing; to avoid articulating the true nature and extent of the risk is quite another. . . . The First Amendment requires a more careful assessment and characterization of an evil in order to justify a regulation as sweeping as this.[17]

Justice Kennedy insisted that "the Government must present more than anecdote and supposition."[18] In this case, the district court found that " 'the Government presented no evidence on the number of households actually exposed to signal bleed and thus has not quantified the actual extent of the problem of signal bleed.' "[19]

The government also failed to offer persuasive evidence that it would be ineffective to provide notice to parents that individual blocking of sexually explicit channels was available. On this issue, as well, placing the burden on the government was crucial. When the government criticized the effectiveness of this alternative as highly speculative, Justice Kennedy responded that it "was not the District Court's obligation, however, to predict the extent to which an improved notice scheme would improve [the statute]. It was for the Government, presented with a plausible, less restrictive alter-

---

[14] Ibid., 818.
[15] Ibid.
[16] Ibid., 819.
[17] Ibid.
[18] Ibid., 822.
[19] Ibid., 821.

native, to prove the alternative to be ineffective, and [its general time blocking restriction] to be the least restrictive available means."[20]

My discussion of the *Playboy* case was not meant to endorse the Court's suggestion that the selective blocking option was a less restrictive alternative or its conclusion that the government had failed to rebut this possibility, a conclusion challenged by Justice Breyer in his dissent. Instead, my purpose was to show how the Presumption of Liberty can be rebutted by proof that there was no less restrictive alternative, and how this sort of inquiry proceeds today in cases involving the liberty of speech. If legislation is truly necessary, one would expect the government to be able to provide proof of this beyond anecdote and speculation. Such proof is the least we can expect before we accept a government restriction of liberty as legitimate.

Moreover, Justice Breyer makes the entirely warranted point that it cannot be sufficient to find a less restrictive alternative without also evaluating the relative effectiveness of this alternative. After all, there will always be less restrictive alternatives if we include those that are much less effective or entirely ineffective in achieving a purpose that is assumed, for this analysis, to be proper. Such an evaluation of effectiveness might sometimes be a difficult one for courts to make. Nevertheless, courts do make such evaluations out of necessity, for the alternative is to defer completely to legislatures and this is objectionable on grounds of constitutional legitimacy. If courts defer entirely, legislatures are likely to skip making meaningful assessments in favor of mere conclusions, assertions, speculations, and pretexts. When this happens, the likelihood that restrictions on liberty are truly necessary markedly declines.

In the final analysis, putting the burden on legislatures, as we do in the case of free speech and other enumerated rights, helps assure that legislatures will actually evaluate the necessity and propriety of their enactments, which in the absence of such a burden they are unlikely to do. If they do engage in such an inquiry before enacting statutes, we can expect that they will be able to satisfy the demands of the Presumption of Liberty and produce evidence in support of the necessity of their measures. The Presumption of Liberty simply extends the same protection now afforded to the freedom of speech to other rightful exercises of freedom.

Levels of Scrutiny

In this discussion of necessity, I have deliberately avoided mentioning what lawyers call the "level of scrutiny" to be applied to a statute. Typi-

[20] Ibid., 823.

cally, there are said to be three levels or degrees of scrutiny: strict, intermediate, and rational basis scrutiny. With strict scrutiny, which is used to protect "fundamental rights," courts require that the legislature prove that it had a *compelling interest* for a restriction that is *narrowly tailored* to address that interest. As Erwin Chemerinsky explains:

> Under strict scrutiny, a law will be upheld *if it is necessary to achieve a compelling government purpose.* In other words, the court must regard the government's purpose as vital, as "compelling." Also, the law must be shown to be "necessary" as means to accomplishing the end. This requires proof that the law is the least restrictive or least discriminatory alternative. If the law is not the least restrictive alternative, then it is not "necessary" to accomplish the end. Under strict scrutiny, the government has the burden of proof.[21]

With rational basis scrutiny, the courts accept any measure that is *reasonably related* to accomplish *any legitimate state interest.*

> [T]he government's objective only need be a goal that is legitimate for government to pursue. . . . The means chosen need only be a reasonable way to accomplish the objective. Under the rational basis test, the challenger of a law has the burden of proof.[22]

Intermediate scrutiny, unsurprisingly, lies somewhere in between. A law must be *substantially related* to an *important* governmental purpose.

> [T]he government's objective must be more than just a legitimate goal for government to pursue; the court must regard the purpose as "important." The means chosen must be more than a reasonable way of attaining the end; the court must believe that the law is substantially related to achieving the goal.[23]

Legal pundits refer to strict scrutiny—the level used in the *Playboy* case—as "strict in theory and fatal in fact."[24] In contrast, rational basis scrutiny is almost always satisfied as the courts will accept any hypothetical reason a legislature might have had to enact a statute.[25] In the 1993 case of *Federal Communications Commission v. Beach Communications, Inc.*,[26] Justice Thomas articulated the most expansive formulation of the rational basis test:

---

[21] Erwin Chemerinsky, *Constitutional Law: Principles and Policies* (New York: Aspen, 1997), 416.

[22] Ibid., 415.

[23] Ibid.

[24] Gerald Gunther, "Foreword: In Search of Evolving Doctrine on a Changing Court: A Model for a Newer Equal Protection," *Harvard Law Review* 86 (1972): 8.

[25] See *Williamson v. Lee Optical*, 348 U.S. 483 (1955).

[26] 508 U.S. 307 (1993).

[T]hose attacking the rationality of the legislative classification have the burden "to negative every conceivable basis which might support it," . . . . Moreover, because we never require a legislature to articulate its reasons for enacting a statute, it is entirely irrelevant for constitutional purposes whether the conceived reason for the challenged distinction actually motivated the legislature. . . . In other words, a legislative choice is not subject to courtroom fact-finding and may be based on *rational speculation unsupported by evidence or empirical data.*[27]

Justice Stevens took issue with this standard: "In my view, this formulation sweeps too broadly, for it is difficult to imagine a legislative classification that could *not* be supported by a 'reasonably conceivable state of facts.' "[28] And he was certainly correct when he contended that "[j]udicial review under the 'conceivable set of facts' test is tantamount to no review at all."[29] Indeed, the *Cleburne* case discussed in the previous section is famous for being one of the rare cases in which a law failed to pass rational basis scrutiny, and consequently the test it applied there is sometimes referred to as "rational basis with bite."[30]

One reason to avoid these categories is that a standard that no statute can pass is as hypocritical as a standard that every statute can pass.[31] What is required is *real* or *meaningful* scrutiny of both the necessity and propriety of restrictions on liberty.[32] Under the current approach, courts must distinguish "legitimate" from "important" from "compelling" governmental interests because they long ago abandoned the enumerated powers scheme that defined "proper," as opposed to improper, federal purposes and the Lockean conception of the police power that defined "proper" state purposes. To preserve some judicial review, it thus fell to them to distinguish from among all the myriad "legitimate" purposes of government those that were more important than others.

In contrast, with a conception of "propriety" that is limited in the ways discussed here, once a purpose is established as a proper one, then the courts need only determine if the government has shown its restrictions on liberty to be genuinely necessary. In other words, just as the Presumption of Liberty gets courts out of the business of designating some liberties

---

[27] Ibid., 315 (emphasis added).

[28] Ibid., 323, n. 3 (Justice Stevens concurring).

[29] Ibid.

[30] Two more recent examples of serious rational basis scrutiny—both by Justice Kennedy—are *Romer v. Evans*, 517 U.S. 620 (1996) and *Lawrence v. Texas*, 123 S. Ct. 2472 (2003).

[31] For an amusing critique of these categories, see Michael Stokes Paulson, "Medium Rare Scrutiny," *Constitutional Commentary* 15 (1998): 397.

[32] For a proposed unified standard of review in Equal Protection cases, see Suzanne Goldberg, "Equality without Tiers," *Southern California Law Review* 77 (2004).

or rights as "fundamental," it also gets courts out of the business of measuring the importance of government objectives. Applying meaningful scrutiny to the justifications and evidence offered by government on behalf of its laws may not always be easy, but a Presumption of Liberty has the practical advantage of eliminating two of the more difficult distinctions we currently call upon courts to make.

A glimmer of this approach can be seen in *Playboy*, when the Court noted that it "cannot be influenced . . . by the perception that the regulation in question is not a major one because the speech is not very important."[33] In other words, the court does not seek to distinguish "fundamental" speech from "nonfundamental" speech. The same can be said about other liberties that are not today deemed to be fundamental or "very important." The Ninth Amendment requires that no liberty be "denied or disparaged" just because it is unenumerated, which means that all liberties are equal in the eyes of the Constitution.

Adopting a Presumption of Liberty that places the burden on government to justify its restrictions as both necessary and proper makes possible the equal protection of liberties. As Justice Stevens argued in *Beach Communications* when considering a legislative decision to exclude some property from regulation: "Freedom is a blessing. Regulation is sometimes necessary, but it is always burdensome. A decision *not to regulate* the way in which an owner chooses to enjoy the benefits of an improvement to his own property is adequately justified by a *presumption in favor of freedom*."[34] By now it should be apparent that to have a legitimate legal system that produces laws that bind in conscience, such a "presumption in favor of freedom" should always operate.

APPLYING THE PRESUMPTION OF LIBERTY TO PARTICULAR CASES

Some readers may be suspending their judgment of the Presumption of Liberty until they see how it would decide cases about which they may care. I think this instinct, though understandable, is unfortunate. No one's judgment about how cases should be decided is infallible. For this reason, we cannot pick our methods of decision making solely by whether we like the results they achieve. To the contrary, we need sound methods of decision making to guide us to right results. If a legitimate legal system is one that produces laws that bind nonconsenting persons in conscience, and a Presumption of Liberty enhances the legitimacy of the legal system in a way that is consistent with its original meaning, then we should look to

---

[33] 529 U.S. at 826.
[34] 508 U.S. 320 (last emphasis added).

the Presumption of Liberty to tell us how to reach results in particular cases. We should not look to the results it provides to decide whether or not we approve of the presumption.

It is important, however, not to overstate this point. The Presumption of Liberty, like the Constitution itself, is a means to the end of achieving justice—which itself is a means to facilitating the pursuit of happiness by each person living in society with others.[35] As such, these ends must be used to evaluate the means. Although there is much wisdom in saying that "the ends cannot justify the means," this is meant to criticize attempts to justify evil means by apparently good ends. In fact, it is only by the ends that we are able to identify good or just means. As I was once told,[36] "if an end cannot justify a means, what can"?

Because only ends are available to justify means, we need to evaluate means to see if they are compatible with ends we are confident are good. Imagine a compass that was never tested to see if it identified north. How could we be sure that such a compass worked at other times when we were unsure of where north was located? When a method of analysis reaches the results of which we are confident, we may better trust this method in cases where we are less sure of the good result. And we may adhere to means so tested even when we are sure they lead to undesirable ends because they have proved vital to the end of justice over the run of cases.

Nevertheless, there is a fundamental obstacle to assessing in this book the Presumption of Liberty by its application to particular cases: such an analysis depends in part on an assessment of propriety and, especially, necessity that will be highly contextual. It will depend upon the particular statutory restriction in question, the justifications offered in its behalf, and the factual claims that support these justifications. We have seen it will depend on assessment of means-ends fit and whether the means chosen were the least restrictive ones available. In short, each example requires a relatively close study of the subject at hand. I do not deny that such analysis is possible. Were that the case, the Presumption of Liberty would not be a practical construction to adopt. However, this sort of extended inquiry lies outside the scope of this book.

Still, readers will demand, perhaps not unreasonably, some examples of what they are buying into by adopting a Presumption of Liberty and it will not do to leave this entirely to their imagination. Therefore, although I insist that the merits of the Presumption of Liberty are to be assessed primarily by the justifications offered in the previous chapters of this book, in this concluding section, I discuss briefly some easy cases that

---

[35] See Barnett, *Structure of Liberty* (chapter 1).
[36] I think it was by Murray Rothbard.

reinforce the merits of this presumption. I then discuss the possible results it may reach in harder or controversial cases, results we might nonetheless embrace because of the method by which they are reached.

Easy Cases

Assessing the merits of any constitutional construction by how it deals with easy cases presents an obvious problem: because a consensus about the results of cases exists so rarely, it is hard to call many cases "easy." Nevertheless, as we have already seen, the Presumption of Liberty is used when statutes restrict the exercise of the natural rights of freedom of speech, freedom of assembly, freedom of the press, or the free exercise of religion. There are few who would dispute these applications of the Presumption. When these enumerated liberties are restricted, courts and commentators do not typically urge that we trust that legislators have considered these rights fully, accurately, and in good faith before they decided to restrict their exercise. No, when these rights are restricted, courts and commentators are rightly skeptical; they require that the government prove such restrictions are necessary to accomplish a proper (or "compelling") purpose that cannot be accomplished by a less restrictive alternative. Does this not tell us something about the need for a more general Presumption of Liberty? Do legislatures become more trustworthy or reliable in their judgments simply because the liberties they are restricting are not listed in the Constitution? Hardly.

Nor do courts think them more trustworthy when certain unenumerated rights deemed "fundamental" are being restricted. As was noted in chapter 10, there are many unenumerated rights that have been recognized by courts as fundamental and therefore justifying increased scrutiny of legislation: the right to travel within the United States (which had been enumerated in the Articles of Confederation), the right to provide one's children with religious education, the right to educate one's children in one's native language, the right to associate with others, the right to choose and follow a profession, the right to marry or not to marry, the right to decide whether or not to have children and how to rear them, and the right to privacy.[37] Ask yourself whether these unenumerated liberties should be restricted just because a majority in the legislature, perhaps representing the view of a majority of the voters, think this is necessary and proper.

A Presumption of Liberty would protect all of these unenumerated rights without any inquiry into whether or not they are fundamental. Today, however, the legitimacy of judges protecting these rights is under-

---

[37] For citations see chapter 10, 253–54.

cut by the fact they are unwritten and do not fall neatly within the theory of Footnote Four. Under Footnote Four these are all hard cases because they are not "express prohibitions" on Congress and judges should not be allowed to thwart the will of the majority unless so instructed explicitly by the text. With the Presumption of Liberty, in contrast, they all become easy cases.

Hard or Controversial Cases

While these unenumerated rights are hard cases for current theory, but are recognized anyway, another liberty or right that should be an easy case under current doctrine goes unrecognized nonetheless: the right to keep and bear arms. Given that it is enumerated in the Bill of Rights, it ought to fall within the Footnote Four approach to constitutional rights and be deemed a fundamental right. To date, however, courts have not applied the criteria of Footnote Four to the Second Amendment. Although it was among the paradigms of the privileges and immunities that the framers of the Fourteenth Amendment intended to protect,[38] the right to keep and bear arms has also never been "incorporated" into the Due Process Clause and applied to state governments.

The Presumption of Liberty would have no trouble affording protection to this right and requiring that all restrictions on gun possession and use be justified as necessary. Moreover, any effort to deprive the law-abiding citizenry of their right to possess firearms by confiscating their weapons or banning all firearms would be improper and unconstitutional despite any argument from necessity that could be made on its behalf. Any such measure would be a prohibition and not a reasonable and necessary regulation. Only wrongful acts—acts that violate the rights of others—can properly be prohibited, as opposed to regulated, under either the national commerce power or the state police power.

This suggests a general implication of adopting the Presumption of Liberty that would also be controversial: government could not use its unenumerated police power to prohibit the possession or use of any object that, if properly used, does not pose an unreasonable risk of violating the rights of others. The fact that an item when used improperly might create such a risk cannot justify a prohibition on possession because any object can be improperly used to harm another and such a principle would, therefore, give the government the unjust power to prohibit possession of anything it wills.

Thus, the only items that are properly prohibited under the police power are those that, when used as they are supposed to be, create an

---

[38] See Curtis, "No State Shall Abridge."

unreasonable risk of harm to third persons. Weapons of mass destruction, whether or not considered an "arm"—for example, biological weapons— would clearly fall within this category and would properly be banned. Other inherently dangerous activities could be banned as well, provided the prohibition is the least restrictive alternative and reasonable regulation would not suffice. Thus, the manufacture and use of high explosives or what the common law referred to as "ultrahazardous" activities that do create a serious risk of violating the rights of others would be subject to regulation, or even removal from densely populated areas, but could not be entirely prohibited if regulations can reduce the risk to reasonable levels. (Zero risk is not an option.)

According to this analysis, virtually all current possessory crimes, such as laws that make illegal the possession by competent adults of ordinary firearms, intoxicating or therapeutic drugs, or pornographic images, are improper and unconstitutional, regardless of whether they are deemed necessary to achieve some worthwhile end.[39] The mere possession of such items does not violate the rights of others; and the use of these items does not invariably violate the rights of others—although under some circumstances using some of these items could create an unreasonable risk of harm to others.

Consider the example of driving a car while under the influence of alcohol. The use of neither cars nor alcohol invariably violates the rights of others, but driving a car while using alcohol in excess raises the risk substantially. Prohibition of possession of either cars or alcohol is therefore improper, but regulations against using them at the same time are proper under the state's police power because this use can create an unreasonable risk of violating the rights of others. Remember that proper regulations of liberty seek to prevent rights violations, though such regulations must also be shown to be necessary by the tests put forth in this chapter.

Moreover, setting the permissible level of alcohol in the blood is a matter of judgment that cannot be deduced logically from first principles. While individuals may vary in their capacities, a rule of law is probably preferable to placing discretion in the hands of law enforcement agents. Thus, assuming that restricting drunk driving is found to be a necessary and proper regulation of driving on government roads, some discretion to set the rule to govern this must rest in the legislature.

Before we leave this example, it is important to emphasize that, for drunk driving to create a risk to the rights of others, the possession of a car is as essential as the possession of alcohol. Yet we do not ordinarily

---

[39] As was discussed in chapter 11, mere possession is outside the powers of Congress even under the broadest original meaning of the Commerce Clause. See 312–14. At issue here is the propriety of the exercise of the police power of states to reach mere possession.

ban possession of all cars because they could possibly be misused. Neither should we ban alcohol, other intoxicants, or firearms because they could be, but need not be, misused. It is only prejudice that leads to prohibitionist movements to ban these objects while letting people drive cars subject only to reasonable regulation.

Therefore, if the use of a particular item sometimes creates an unreasonable risk of harm, then these types of potentially harmful uses, rather than mere possession or all uses of these items, can be regulated. Further, the commerce in any of these goods, such as the sale of therapeutic or intoxicating drugs—including possession for purposes of commerce or sale—can properly be regulated if necessary to protect the safety of buyers or sellers (though only interstate commerce can be regulated by Congress, leaving the regulation of intrastate commerce to the states), provided that such regulations are not pretexts for prohibition.

The Hardest Cases

The examples just discussed are controversial. Although some would think these results would be wrong, I do not agree. I think that combining a Presumption of Liberty with the original meaning of the Constitution in these instances is more consistent with the requirements of justice than is current doctrine. Despite what I said above about testing a theory against the results in easy cases, paradoxically, a constitutional construction may be suspect precisely because it seems never to produce bad or unjust results. Given the complexities of the world, no legal doctrine can perfectly capture the requirements of justice. Therefore, if a construction purports always to lead to "happy endings," then it is likely so manipulable as to provide little if any guidance in difficult cases. In short, to test whether a constitutional construction is a genuine rule of law, we must ask whether it ever leads to outcomes its proponents dislike but must live with nonetheless. What objectionable outcomes do I think would result from construing the original meaning of the Constitution through a Presumption of Liberty?

The original meaning of "commerce" applies only to the trade or exchange of goods. According to the evidence surveyed in chapter 11, manufacturing and agriculture are not "commerce." Such activities may be regulated only by state governments pursuant to their police power to prevent imposing an unreasonable risk of harm on third parties. Both manufacturing and agriculture can produce pollution of the air and water that can create an unreasonable risk of violating the rights of third parties. Such activities are well within the Lockean construction of the police power advanced in chapter 12, but air and water emissions can, and often do, cross state lines. When this occurs, state police power regulations may not be as effective in preventing these harms as federal regulations would be, yet there is no enumerated power that reaches manufacturing and agriculture. Moreover, where pollution imposes higher costs on out-of-state residents, while the industry that produces it benefits in-state businesses and residents, states have an incentive to refrain from adequately exercising their police power to prevent harmful emissions. Although interstate compacts are possible and exist today to address a variety of issues, this is a classic example of the sort of problem for which national power is the solution. Despite this, a police power to reach agriculture and manufacturing was not delegated to the national government.

We have already seen that the founders were well aware of the interconnectedness of the national economy when they chose to limit Congress to the regulation of trade between states. Nevertheless, they did not extend its regulatory power to agriculture, manufacturing or intrastate commerce. In preindustrial and sparsely settled eighteenth-century America, the founders were hardly likely to have imagined the interstate nature of emissions from these otherwise local economic activities. Given their effort to enumerate just those powers that were needed to handle genuinely national problems, it is almost certain that the founders would have granted Congress the power to handle this interstate or national aspect of manufacturing and agriculture. But lacking this foresight, this is not what they did.

Short of a constitutional amendment, can we correct by interpretation their potentially serious error while maintaining our commitment to the written Constitution? We cannot. This commitment does not permit us to alter the original meaning of the text because, sometime later, it comes to be seen, rightly or wrongly, as defective. Were we to ignore the original meaning of "commerce" to empower the regulation by Congress of harmful pollution, we would not be violating the rights retained by the people. Nevertheless, legitimating a knowing violation of the original meaning of "commerce" to reach the just or prudent outcome in this particular instance would undermine the "lock-in" feature of a written constitution. Ignoring the Constitution here where it is imperfect would create a very real danger that, in other cases, the legislature will be allowed to violate rights by means of improper laws.

Far better would it be to enact a constitutional amendment, which in this case would be easily proposed and swiftly ratified, that grants Congress the power "to regulate harmful emissions having an interstate effect." An established practice of seeking popular approval of expanded federal powers whenever such measures are popular would have the added benefit of underscoring the limitations on congressional power in other more doubtful cases. The Eighteenth Amendment, which granted Congress the power to prohibit the manufacture and sale (but not the use) of intoxicating liquors, while entirely unjust, had the virtue of confirming that Congress lacked this and any similar power in the absence of a constitutional amendment. Although an erroneous written amendment can "lock in" an injustice in a way that judicial "amendment" cannot, adhering to this process both preserves the value of the rest of the written constitution, and more precisely defines the nature of the modification that has been enacted, even when a mistake has been made.

Another implication of the original meaning of the Commerce Clause is that Congress lacks the power it now claims to regulate the legal relationship between employers and employees. Such contracts are not themselves "commerce" and their regulation is not necessary to ensure that commerce among the states remains free and unobstructed. Nevertheless, many would consider this to be a major deficiency in the constitutional scheme.

Rather than violate original meaning to get the desired results, however, it would be much safer for the enumerated powers scheme as a whole to obtain a constitutional amendment like the ones proposed in Congress—until the New Deal Supreme Court's misinterpretation of the commerce power made such amendments unnecessary.[40] For example, Senator Edward Costigan proposed granting Congress the power "to regulate hours and conditions of labor and to establish minimum wages in any employment and to regulate production, industry, business, trade, and commerce to prevent unfair methods and practices."[41] Henry Ashurst, chairman of the Senate Judiciary Committee, proposed granting Congress the power "to regulate agriculture, commerce, industry, and labor."[42]

Unlike an amendment giving Congress the power to regulate interstate pollution, I would not endorse these proposals. The "minimum wage" portion of the first proposal constitutes what I believe to be an improper infringement on the fundamental natural right of freedom of contract. The second part of the Costigan proposal, like the Ashurst proposal, while consistent with the rights retained by the people, in my view shifts too much power to the national government. The national government is far less constrained than state governments by the power of exit and, therefore, far more likely to abuse this enumerated power than are states who may regulate these activities under their police power. In my view, these latter proposals are imprudent and inexpedient—like the Seventeenth Amendment, which imprudently, but not improperly, took the selection of senators out of the hands of the state legislatures.

---

[40] See Ackerman, *We the People*, 2:337–40 (discussing various proposals to amend the Constitution pending in Congress).

[41] S.J. Res. 3, 74th Cong., 1st sess. (January 4. 1935), 104.

[42] S.J. Res 285, 74th Cong., 2d sess. (1936), 9224.

Whether or not I am right that the first of these proposals is unjust and the second imprudent, there is still great value to requiring that they be made in writing and formally ratified. Requiring a formal written amendment would engender a public debate on the scope of any proposed expansion of federal (or state) power, a debate that would serve at least three important purposes. First, it would test the true popularity of accomplishing popular ends by means of expanding government powers. All too often this popularity is merely asserted or supported only by notoriously manipulable opinion polls. Putting the public, or publicly elected representatives, to a real choice would demonstrate this preference in a more reliable manner. Second, if ratified, there would be a written provision to interpret according to its original meaning and construe according to the principles underlying the Constitution as a whole. Courts would not be the agents of this amendment, but would be the interpreters of a written change made by a process that is functionally distinct from the legislative process. The scope of this change would be known to all and reversible only by subsequent amendment.

Perhaps most importantly, by making it more difficult to change a legitimate constitution, the requirement of formal amendment helps "lock in" that legitimate meaning and preserves it over time, thereby helping to preserve that legitimacy. Moreover, by preserving original meaning until a change is made in writing, the formal amendment process also preserves the originalist method of interpretation itself. In this way, requiring written amendments is vital not only to maintain a given original meaning, but to protect the process of originalist interpretation by which "lock in" is achieved and legitimacy enhanced. Even if an unjust or imprudent power is "locked in" by a written amendment, the originalist method of constitutional interpretation that is needed to "lock in" the other legitimate written provisions of the Constitution would be preserved. Of course, if too many improper powers are granted, then the legitimacy of the entire Constitution would be called into question and all bets are off.

Restoring the Lost Constitution

> Almost all constitutional analysts, as a matter of brute fact,
> seem committed to a de facto theory of "happy endings,"
> whereby one's skills as a rhetorical manipulator . . . are de-
> voted to achieving satisfying results.[1]
>
> —SANFORD LEVINSON

THE WAY the Constitution has been interpreted over the past seventy
years has meant that, with some exceptions,[2] the Necessary and Proper
Clause has no justiciable meaning, the Privileges or Immunities Clause
has no justiciable meaning, the Ninth Amendment has no justiciable
meaning, the Tenth Amendment has no justiciable meaning, the Commerce Clause has no justiciable meaning, and the unenumerated police
power of the states has no limit. To this list could be added the Second
Amendment[3] and the Takings Clause of the Fifth Amendment[4] as well.
Can you see a pattern here? Do you not sense a systematic skewing of the
Constitution? Can we abandon what the Constitution says and still claim
credibly to follow it? How plausible is a constitutional construction like
the presumption of constitutionality or Footnote Four that requires ignoring so much of the text?

Imagine holding up a copy of the Constitution and seeing empty holes
in the parchment where these passages once appeared—or seeing ink blots
over them. Courts should not cut holes in the Constitution. Judges should

---

[1] Sanford Levinson, "Bush v. Gore and the French Revolution: A Tentative List of Some Early Lessons," *Law and Contemporary Problems* 65 (2002): 11.

[2] The Rehnquist Court has put content back into some of these provisions and been savaged for its efforts by academics. The same happened from a different direction when the Warren and Burger Courts began paying some serious attention to the Ninth Amendment, not to mention the requirements of the Fourth and Fifth Amendments in the sphere of criminal procedure.

[3] The fact that this discarded provision contains an enumerated right that falls squarely within the framework of Footnote Four suggests a powerful ideological influence at work here. But see *United States v. Emerson*, 270 F.3d 203, (5th Cir. 2001) (finding on originalist grounds that the Second Amendment protects an individual right).

[4] The Takings Clause is supposed to permit only takings of public property for public *use* and instead has been interpreted to permit takings for a public purpose, thereby gutting nearly completely a crucial limitation on this dangerous power. See Richard A. Epstein, *Takings: Private Property and the Power of Eminent Domain* (Cambridge: Harvard University Press, 1985).

not put ink blots on the provisions they do not like. A Presumption of Liberty would respect all these discarded clauses in a way that current constitutional orthodoxy does not. The construction to be preferred is the one that takes the text of the Constitution seriously. On this score, the Presumption of Liberty is clearly preferable. Adopting it would enable us to restore the lost Constitution.

Of course, one must resist the temptation to read into the Constitution everything one might want it to say. As Sanford Levinson has repeatedly observed, there is a tendency among constitutional analysts to find "happy endings" to every constitutional controversy. Some may think I have done the same in the preceding chapters—that I have made the Constitution far more "libertarian" than it truly is. To the contrary, the approach I have advanced, and taken pains to justify with historical evidence, takes seriously all these clauses that are largely ignored today. One should also resist the temptation to read *out* of the Constitution what one does *not* want it to say.

Wishful construction cannot be justified by constitutional redaction. Indeed, the process of constitutional redaction has become so ingrained in orthodox constitutional opinion that some may allege that a Presumption of Liberty is merely a product of wishful thinking. This charge might have some merit had the Constitution never included the Necessary and Proper Clause, the Commerce Clause, the Ninth Amendment, the Privileges or Immunities Clause, and the Tenth Amendment. But the Constitution does include these provisions. Only a construction based on wishful thinking can produce a redaction of the Constitution that blots them all out—thereby severely undercutting the fundamental role of courts in protecting liberty and preserving the written limits on government power. Only a Presumption of Liberty can effectuate the judicial review of these textual limits.

Even with a Presumption of Liberty, a consistently originalist interpretation of the Constitution will inevitably result in unhappy endings for those who champion liberty. The Sixteenth Amendment authorizes Congress to place a tax on incomes, and many advocates of liberty think that taxation of this sort is theft. There are other defects as well. The popular election of the Senate undermined an important check on federal power that had previously been in the hands of state legislatures. The Takings Clause permits takings of private property for public use. Congress is given power to grant authors and inventors limited monopolies on their writings and inventions, which restricts the property rights of others. The original failure to impose term limits on Congress has led to an entrenched professional class of legislative rulers who are less sensitive to the liberties of the people than citizen legislators who would know they must return to the private sector in a few years. Indeed, there are some who would reject as illegitimate any constitution with all these features.

Those who practice constitutional redaction to reach results they find congenial should ask themselves why others who find an income tax deplorable must accept it as constitutionally authorized. For that matter, why should a racist judge accept the Equal Protection Clause or even the Fifteenth Amendment? The truth is that these issues are deemed beyond dispute because professed skeptics of originalism and textualism become good originalists or textualists with respect to the provisions they like. They would consider it beyond the pale for a judge to improve upon the Constitution by redacting the Sixteenth Amendment to reach allegedly better results. After all, stopping this sort of judicial abuse is what a written constitution is for.

One thing is certain. The original meaning of the entire Constitution, as amended, is much more libertarian than the one selectively enforced by the Supreme Court. Far from wishful thinking, this conclusion is compelled by the evidence of original meaning presented here. The rights "retained by the people" was demonstrably a reference to natural liberty rights, and the "privileges or immunities" of citizens included natural rights as well as rights created by the adoption of the Bill of Rights. The term "commerce" unquestionably meant trade or exchange and did not extend to such other vital economic activities as manufacturing or agriculture. The "judicial power" included the power of to nullify unconstitutional statutes. The Ninth Amendment mandates that unenumerated rights shall not be denied or disparaged. The Fourteenth Amendment mandates that privileges or immunities shall not be abridged and places serious textual limits on the exercise of the police power of states.

That those who fervently desire to expand the power of government must expunge all these passages is an objective indicator that the original meaning of these provisions is both determinate and inconvenient to them. How can so many central passages mean so little? We are not, after all, speaking of an irrelevant antiquity, such as the authorization for Letters of Marque and Reprisal.[5] For some political agendas to advance, the heart of the Constitution must be excised and so it has been, clause by inconvenient clause, until the Constitution has been distorted and lost.

In the end, I would urge those who think the original Constitution, as amended, is too libertarian to frankly and openly oppose it like the Garrisonian abolitionists who declared the Constitution a "covenant with death and an agreement with hell" because it sanctioned chattel slavery. I would urge the same of those libertarians who conclude that the Constitution is, on balance, not good enough to provide assurances that the

[5] See U.S. Const., Art. I, § 8.

laws passed by Congress and enforced by the executive and judicial branches are binding in conscience. Candor where disagreement with the Constitution exists would help greatly to clarify the nature of the debate. Are we debating the meaning of the text, or how this meaning should be put into effect? Or are we rejecting the meaning of the text altogether? Lumping all these disagreements together under the rubric of "interpreting the Constitution" only leads all sides to talk past one another, as well as to confuse the public.

The temptation is great to try to perfect the Constitution by judicial construction that conflicts with and overrides its original meaning. "Amending" the Constitution by judicial decision, however—as has so passionately been advocated by Bruce Ackerman—not only changes its meaning for the better (or for the worse); it also weakens the power of a written constitution to impose the sorts of constitutional limits of which those doing the redaction approve. This is a serious and much neglected cost that compounds the injustice of granting to Congress an improper power. Only someone who does not believe in constitutional limits on power can safely ignore this danger. And such a person does not really believe in constitutionalism. Yet this danger is routinely ignored by those who should know better.

It is a tribute to the power of a written constitution—indeed, to the design of this particular Constitution—that all the judicial deviations from original meaning we have witnessed since the founding have not completely undercut the ability of the remaining provisions to protect our liberty. Nor have the unwritten judicial "amendments" foisted upon us completely undermined the promise of restoring the original meaning of the unrepealed text. All these lost passages may have been forgotten by the Supreme Court, but they are not gone. Had the founders not put their Constitution in writing, as did the framers of the Fourteenth Amendment, the arguments I have presented here would be impossible. For this they have my gratitude. So long as the courts profess fealty to the written Constitution under glass in Washington, the opportunity still exists to adopt a Presumption of Liberty and restore the lost Constitution.

Index of Cases

Index of Names

General Index